The Golf 100

The Golf 100

Ranking the Greatest Golfers of All Time

UPDATED

Robert McCord

CITADEL PRESS
Kensington Publishing Corp.
www.kensingtonbooks.com

For Frank Reed McCord, my first golfing buddy
and the best brother one could have

CITADEL PRESS books are published by

Kensington Publishing corp.
850 Third Avenue
New York, NY 10022

All Kensington titles, imprints, and distributed lines are available at special quantity discounts for bulk purchases for sales promotions, premiums, fund raising, educational, or instititutional use. Special book excerpts or customized printings can also be created to fit specific needs. For details, write or phone the office of the Kensington special sales manager: Kensington Publishing Corp., 850 Third Avenue, New York, NY 10022, attn: Special Sales Department; phone 1-800-221-2647.

First Printing, March 2001
First Printing (Updated Trade Paperback Edition), March 2004

10   9   8   7   6   5   4   3   2   1

Printed in the United States of America

Library of Congress Control Number: 99-39415

ISBN 0-8065-2557-6

CONTENTS

INTRODUCTION

How can one possibly determine with any objectivity which golfers are the best in history given all of the changes in the sport since WILLIE PARK SR. teed it up in the 1860 British Open, the first significant and longest-running golf championship? The number of golfers and access to equipment and golf courses has significantly grown. (There were only eight golfers, all Scottish, in that first Open.) The equipment has evolved from wooden-shafted, unmatched sets of handcrafted clubs to perfectly matched sets using Space Age materials. Instruction has progressed from primitive word-of-mouth golf tips to multimedia methodology drawing upon the disciplines of computer simulation, kinesthesiology, and sports psychology. The rules have changed from a simple thirteen first written down in the eighteenth century to a handbook of regulations with thousands of national and local golf-rules committees to administer them. The design of golf courses has evolved from natural linksland common grounds, like the Old Course at St. Andrews, to artificially contrived works of wonder featuring island greens, manmade lakes, railroad buttresses, and viewing mounds. The incentive for winning has grown from bragging rights, a championship belt, and a medal at the first British Open, to a claret jug and $1,106,140 at the 2002 British Open. Moreover, the number of tournaments has multiplied and has become more structured. Thus, there are many more avenues through which to compete, and the results are documented by the print and electronic media and disseminated throughout the global golf community.

Given all these variables and many more, I decided to use the following basic criteria to select the top one hundred:

1. Relative standing of the golfer in his era. For example, YOUNG TOM MORRIS, who retired the British Open championship belt

and won four straight Opens, was clearly the most dominant player of his day.

2. Number of significant championships won, starting with the majors, such as the U.S. Open (but taking into account that modern majors, such as the Masters, were not always major), and former majors, such as the Western Open, North and South Open, and Metropolitan Open (which are now not so major or are no longer in operation).

3. The strength of the field. For example, both the U.S. and the British Open did not have all the best players in the world competing at different times because of logistic (it took too long to get there by land and sea transportation in the old days) and economic considerations (it cost too much to get there, and events like the Great Depression depleted the field).

4. Awards won, such as Player of the Year; leading money winner; the Vardon Trophy for lowest stroke average; and honors such as selection to the Ryder Cup team.

5. Contribution to the game. A very subjective criterion that takes into account the contributions of players such as OLD TOM MORRIS, an early, multifaceted golf champion who was also a rules arbiter, equipment maker, greenskeeper, teacher, and golf-course architect; BOBBY JONES, the consummate scholar-athlete and sportsman; WALTER HAGEN, defender of golf professionals' rights and one of the Tour's first promoters; ARNOLD PALMER, the king of the modern television golf age and the economic benefactor of all professionals, especially senior golfers; and JACK NICKLAUS, the great champion, of sound mind and character, win or lose; and TIGER WOODS, who has dominated golf since he was in junior high school, winning three U.S. Junior Amateurs, three U.S. Amateurs, one NCAA individual title, and five majors, including all four tournaments in the modern Grand Slam, by age twenty-four.

Some of these factors can be quantified, but only up to a point. And the more one tries to assess the relative weight of, let's say, a British Open in the 1860s, with fewer than twenty-five regional contestants, versus the modern Open, where thousands of golfers attempt to qualify and come from the four corners of the world, the more impossible it becomes. So, inevitably, some great golfers have been left out: Alex Ross, Chandler Egan, Frank Stranahan, Johnny Goodman, Bobby Cruickshank, Dutch Harrison, Al Geiberger, Art Wall, Kel Nagle, Don January, Paul Azinger, Colin Montgomerie, and several others.

This exercise has reinforced in my own mind how few players really dominated the game, how difficult it is to win major golf tournaments with extraordinarily competitive fields, and how few golfers have been in the highest echelons of the game for a long period of time. Which brings us to Jack Nicklaus. There are sentimental or perhaps even aesthetic reasons why another golfer, such as Bobby Jones, Ben Hogan, Arnold Palmer, Harry Vardon, Tom Morris, or Tiger Woods could be named the greatest golfer of all time. But no one did it like Nicklaus did over such a long period of time, against all comers, and with such class. Tiger Woods, of course, is in close pursuit and has many years of great golf ahead of him.

So here it is, *The Golf 100,* with a shorter list of 41 great lady golfers. After considerable thought, I concluded that, at the championship level, women cannot compete with men from the same tees on the same course, and it would be unfair to make a direct comparison. As in many other sports such as basketball, hockey, and baseball, the main difference that gives men the advantage is strength, not skill. This having been said, there are indeed great lady golfers who have made outstanding contributions to the game. Among them are Mickey Wright, Babe Zaharias, Kathy Whitworth, Nancy Lopez, JoAnne Carner, Joyce Wethered, Glenna Collet Vare, and many others.

Women first had the opportunity to test their skills on a regular professional circuit when the Ladies' Professional Golf Association (LPGA) was founded in 1950. Previously, the Women's Professional Golf Association (WPGA), founded in 1944, had limited success. Until the LPGA, women were largely confined to amateur competition, limiting their opportunity to develop their considerable golfing skills. Today, the LPGA Hall of Fame is one of the few sports halls of fame with objective criteria for gaining admission (number of tournaments won and number of major tournaments won, for example), and LPGA Hall of Fame admission is considered one of the most difficult honors to achieve. As with the men's game, women's golf has become a truly international sport, with stars including Laura Davies, Annika Sorenstam, Ayako Okamoto, and Se Ri Pak advancing the game.

This pantheon of male and female of players reflects the intriguing diversity of the game and the characters who pursue the elusive goal of coaxing a little dimpled white ball into a hole under the most demanding circumstances: The wily clubmaker and greenskeeper (Old Tom Morris); the tubercular innovator with the revolutionary grip (Harry Vardon); the gamesman with the valet and several changes of clothes (Walter Hagen); the Scottish tank commander who lost his sight in one eye in World War I but lived to sit under an umbrella with a cocktail while giving golf lessons (Tommy Armour); the scholar-athlete who read Latin, lived heroically, and died tragically without complaint (Bobby Jones); the "Wee Ice Mon," who dug it out of the ground with endless practice in a search for the perfect round (Ben Hogan); Joyce Wethered, whom Bobby Jones called the best golfer he had ever seen; the Olympian Babe, who conquered every sport she tried, including golf (Mildred Didrikson Zaharias); the "King of Golf," who created an army of followers and broadened the popularity and economic base of the game (Arnold Palmer); the Golden Bear, who won his twentieth major in the 1986 Masters with a score of 30 on his final nine at the age of forty-six (Jack Nicklaus); Mickey Wright, whose flawless swing and 82 LPGA wins set a new standard in women's golf; and the Tiger, who had won three U.S. Junior Championships, three U.S. Amateur Championships, and a Masters by the time he was twenty-one (Tiger Woods). They are all here and more, the accomplished careers of these great golf champions.

Robert McCord
New York City
March 2003

ACKNOWLEDGMENTS

The development of this book was a team effort. Thanks go to my editor, Gary Goldstein, and the staff at Citadel Press who worked on this book originally, and to Walter Zacharias, Donald J. Davidson, Richard Ember, and Bruce Bender at Kensington Publishing Corp.

Many thanks to the photographers, photo archives, libraries, and others who provided assistance on this publication, most notably Marge Dewey and Saundra Sheffer at the Ralph W. Miller Golf Library and Museum in Industry City, California; Tanya Gray, Rand Jarvis, Maxine Vigliotta, Patty Moran, Rand Jarvis, and Nancy Stulack at the United States Golf Association, Far Hills, New Jersey; Khristine Januzik at the Tufts Archives, Pinehurst, North Carolina; Priscilla Jackson, St. Andrews University Library, Scotland; the LPGA, PGA, and Senior PGA Tours; and those many golfers, writers, editors, publishers, collectors, artists, archivists, and enthusiasts who have cared enough to nurture and preserve golf's rich history.

The Golf 100

1

Jack Nicklaus

1940–

Jack is playing an entirely different game—a game I'm not even familiar with.

—BOBBY JONES

As a boy in Columbus, Ohio, Jack Nicklaus, the son of a pharmacist, idolized the great Bobby Jones, winner of thirteen major tournaments in eight years. Nicklaus, a fine young athlete who especially loved football, basketball, and baseball, took up the game of golf at age ten. By the time he was nineteen, he had won his first U.S. Amateur Championship and was on the Walker Cup team. In 1960 he set a record by shooting the lowest score for an amateur, 282, in the U.S. Open, finishing second to ARNOLD PALMER at Cherry Hills. Nicklaus had been paired with the legendary BEN HOGAN for the final two rounds. After the tournament, Hogan told reporters, "I played thirty-six holes today with a kid who should have won this thing by ten strokes." The following year, Nicklaus won the NCAA Championship and his second U.S. Amateur, then turned professional.

The sheer numbers and duration of Nicklaus's career are overwhelming. He has won twenty major championships, finishing in the top three an astounding forty-five times in Grand Slam events alone. He has won four U.S. Opens (1962, 1967, 1972, 1980), three British Opens (1966, 1970, 1978), six Masters (1963, 1965, 1966, 1972, 1975, 1986), and five PGA (Professional Golf Association) Championships (1963, 1971, 1973, 1975, 1980). He has also won six Australian Opens, competed on six winning World Cup teams (1963, 1964, 1966, 1967,

1971, 1973), was a member of six Ryder Cup teams (1969, 1971, 1973, 1975, 1977, 1981), and was Ryder Cup team captain in 1983 and 1987. Nicklaus has won a total of seventy PGA Tour events, second only to SAM SNEAD (eighty-one) and ahead of Ben Hogan (sixty-three) and Arnold Palmer (sixty). He won at least one tournament for seventeen consecutive years (1962–78), a record, and was named PGA Player of the Year in 1967, 1972, 1973, 1975, and 1976. He was the leading PGA money winner seven times (1964, 1965, 1971, 1972, 1973, 1975, 1976). Nicklaus was inducted into the PGA World Golf Hall of Fame in 1974.

Among the most memorable of Nicklaus's many duels were those with Arnold Palmer, the King of Golf, beginning when Jack arrived on the scene as an amateur at the 1960 U.S. Open. By shooting a dramatic score of 30 on the final nine holes (Palmer finished with a final round of 65 and a total of 280 to win by two shots), Arnie had forever left the impression of the famous Palmer charge that would snatch victory from the jaws of defeat. Arnie's army of fans would come to view the stocky, slightly overweight, burr-headed Nicklaus as a sinister Teutonic impostor, "Ohio Fats," the interloper. But Nicklaus, who was managed by International Management (as were Palmer and GARY PLAYER), lost some weight, improved his mode of dress, and became more relaxed over the years as he gained the respect and admiration of millions of golf fans. His first important victory over Palmer occurred when he fired a final-round 69 to tie Arnie in the U.S. Open at Oakmont in 1962 and then won the play-off to gain his first U.S. Open title.

Nicklaus next took on Lee TREVINO. Their backgrounds and style couldn't have been more starkly different. Jack was a college-educated Middle American who, encouraged by his father, Charlie, also a fine athlete, learned to play golf at the Scioto Country Club, where Bobby Jones won a U.S. Open in 1926. Jack received his instruction from Jack Grout, the head professional who would become his lifelong friend and teacher. Trevino was brought up by his grandfather in a shack without electricity in Dallas, Texas. He dropped out of school at an early age and taught himself how to play golf and win wagers at the local municipal courses. Trevino defeated Jack in a memorable U.S. Open play-off at Merion in 1970, 68–71, after both finished with scores of 280 in regulation play. Nicklaus lost to Trevino again at Muirfield in the 1972 British Open when a win would have given him the third leg of the Grand Slam. Always a contender, Nicklaus finished second in the British Open seven times to TONY LEMA (1964), ROBERTO DE VICENZO (1967), Gary Player (1968), Lee Trevino (1972), JOHNNY MILLER (1976), TOM

WATSON (1977), and SEVE BALLESTEROS (1979). In total, Nicklaus finished twenty-one shots behind, or an average of three shots per tournament. For fifteen straight years, from 1966 through 1980, Nicklaus finished among the top six players in the British Open.

Nicklaus and Tom Watson, who won five British Opens, also had a great rivalry. In the British Open at Turnberry in 1977, Watson and Nicklaus were so far ahead of the field that the final day of the tournament found them in a head-to-head duel going down to the last hole. Watson was playing exceptional golf, having defeated Nicklaus by two shots to win the Masters that year. Tom took the lead on the seventeenth hole at Turnberry when he hit a beautiful 3-iron to the green, then birdied. Ahead by one stroke, Watson hit another great approach, a 7-iron to within three feet of the final hole. Nicklaus, who had pushed his drive into the rough, hit a heroic 8-iron recovery shot to within thirty-five feet and then holed his putt for a birdie. But Watson was up to the task and made his birdie to win the Open. His score of 68-70-65-65 = 268 was a new British Open record, eleven shots better than third place HUBERT GREEN. It took this kind of a superhuman effort to defeat Nicklaus. Watson did it again at Pebble Beach in 1982 when he holed a wedge shot from the rough at the edge of the seventy-first hole. He birdied that hole and the final hole to deny Nicklaus a record-fifth Open title.

When observers try to pinpoint the secret of Nicklaus's success, his tremendous powers of concentration are often cited. So is his lower-body strength and his ability to hit the ball a long way. Jack Grout, Nicklaus's instructor until his death in 1989, had a profound influence on his career, as did his father, who had the financial means to provide for Jack's early golf training and encouraged him to pursue the sport. Ken Bowden, who has authored many golf books and magazine articles with Nicklaus, gives his explanation:

> There have been prettier swings than Jack Nicklaus. There have been better ball strikers than Jack. There may have been better short game experts than Jack Nicklaus. Other putters putted as well as Jack Nicklaus. There may have been golfers as dedicated and as fiercely competitive as Jack. But no individual has been able to develop and combine and sustain all of the complex mental and emotional resources the game demands at its highest level as well as Nicklaus has for as long as he has.

Nicklaus joined the Senior Tour in 1990, playing a limited schedule but winning seven Senior "majors": the Tradition (1990, 1991, 1995), the U.S. Senior Open (1991, 1993), the PGA Seniors' Championship (1991), and the Senior Players Championship (1990). Jack has had four second-place finishes in these events but played a limited schedule until early 1999, when he had hip-replacement surgery. He has won over $8.7 million on the Senior Tour.

Just like Arnold Palmer, Nicklaus became a golf conglomerate under his nickname, "Golden Bear." In the late 1960s he became an active golf-course architect and has since designed many world-class courses, such as Muirfield Village, with Desmond Muirhead, in Ohio; Grand Cypress, in Florida; Valhalla, in Kentucky; and many others. He has also been active in various other golf businesses ranging from equipment to golf schools and publishing.

A member of the World Golf Hall of Fame, one of Jack Nicklaus's crowning achievements was his sixth Masters win at the age of forty-six in 1986. With his son Jackie caddying, he shot a final-round 65, including an awe inspiring 6-under-par 30 on the back nine, to finish by one shot over TOM KITE and GREG NORMAN. His idol, Bobby Jones, who had died in 1971, could not be there to help him on with his green jacket, but he would no doubt have been impressed by Nicklaus's performance. As Jones once graciously observed about Jack's game, "Jack is playing an entirely different game—a game I'm not even familiar with." High praise from a gentleman golfer who retired with thirteen majors championships at the age of twenty-eight.

Beginning with his first U.S. Amateur win in 1959, Jack Nicklaus was a major force in golf for over forty years, compiling the best record of all time against many of the greatest golfers ever in a game that has become increasingly competitive as the financial rewards become more attractive. That's why Jack Nicklaus is the greatest golfer who ever played.

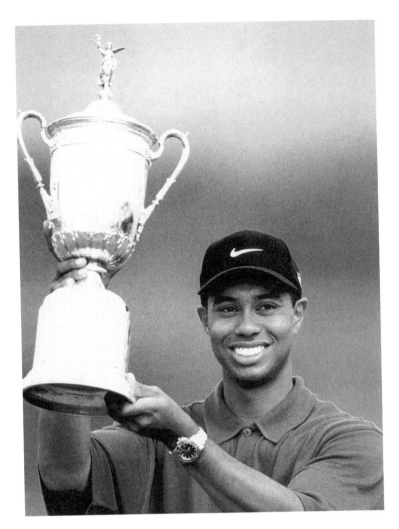

2

Tiger Woods

1976–

I don't want to be the best black golfer ever on the Tour.
I want to be the best golfer on the Tour.

—TIGER WOODS

Eldrick "Tiger" Woods is the offspring of Earl Woods, an African American who also claims Chinese and American Indian ancestry, and his wife, Kutilda, a native of Thailand, whom he met while he was serving in the U.S. Army in Southeast Asia. Tiger's mother, who is a loving but strict parent, named him Eldrick, but his father gave him the name Tiger in honor of a South Vietnamese comrade, Lt. Nguyen (Tiger) Phong. Schooled by his dad, Tiger was a golf prodigy at a very early age, even earlier than BOBBY JONES or JACK NICKLAUS. He shot 48 for nine holes at age three; was a club champion at eight; was the U.S. Junior Champion at fifteen; the youngest player to tee it up in a PGA Tour event, the Nissan L.A. Open at sixteen; the U.S. Amateur Champion at eighteen; and the Masters champion and PGA Player of the Year at twenty-one.

Including his three U.S. Amateur wins, Tiger Woods had won four majors by the age of twenty-one. He began rewriting the USGA record books when he won an unprecedented three consecutive U.S. Junior Amateur Championships, a title Nicklaus never won. A match-play event that starts with over two thousand entries in regional play, the Junior requires the champion to win six consecutive matches if he qualifies. In 1991, at the age of fifteen years six months and twenty-eight days, Tiger Woods became the youngest ever to win the Junior Amateur, defeating Brad Zwetscke on the first play-off hole (nineteenth) at ARNOLD PALMER's Bay Hill Club in Orlando. Woods was the medalist in that tournament with a score of 140. The following year, Woods was again medalist with a score of 143 at the Wollaston Golf Club in Milton, Massachusetts, and defeated Mark Wilson, 1-up, for the championship. In 1993, at the Waverley Country Club in Portland, Oregon, Woods arrived ill from mononucleosis. Almost three thousand players had tried to qualify for the tournament, and notable golfers, including Robert Floyd and Scott Miller, the sons of PGA Tour legends, had qualified. Woods reached the final against Ryan Armour and was two down with two holes remaining in the eighteen-hole championship contest. Woods put his drive 70 yards past Armour's on the seventeenth (he could even hit it 300 yards when he was a junior golfer), hit a 9-iron to seven feet, and birdied to win the hole. Armour reached the par-5 final hole in regulation, forty-five feet from the pin. Woods was in the green-side bunker, 40 yards from the pin, on his second shot. Woods hit his approach to within ten feet and birdied to even the match. He then won his third consecutive Junior Amateur with a par on the first extra hole. In four years of Junior Amateur play, Woods had compiled an incredible 22-1 match-play record. He became only the third male, and the tenth player overall, to win the same USGA event in three consecutive years.

The following year, at the age of eighteen years seven months and twenty-nine days, Tiger, a freshman at Stanford, became the youngest player to win the U.S. Amateur, an event first held in 1895 with a field of thirty-two. In 1994, 5,128 entrees played in thirty-six-hole stroke-play contests at seventy-six sites to earn the right to tee off in the match-play championship at the TPC Sawgrass Stadium course in Florida. Tiger won his first Amateur by defeating Trip Kuehne, 2-up. The following year, Woods defeated George "Buddy" Marucci Jr., 2-up, at the Newport Country Club in Rhode Island, becoming the ninth golfer to win back-to-back Amateurs. The 1996 Amateur was held at the Witch Hollow course at Pumpkin Ridge Golf Club, near Portland, Oregon. Tiger reached the finals of the Amateur and faced Steve Scott, a member of the University of Florida men's golf team. The previous year, Scott had reached the semifinals of the Amateur but lost to Buddy Marucci on the first extra hole in overtime. Scott jumped off to a five-hole lead on Woods after eleven holes, but, as if predestined, Tiger, who had won the qualifying medal with a 7-under-par 136, began to make his charge after practicing during the lunch break under the watchful eye of Butch Harmon, his instructor, and Jay Brunza, his sports psychologist.

Woods birdied the twenty-first (two-and-a-half feet), the twenty-second (two feet), then won the twenty-third with a par, reducing his deficit to two holes. Scott retained a two-hole lead with four to play, but Woods birdied the thirty-fourth from six feet to get within one. Before Tiger's putt on the thirty-fourth hole, Scott, in a gesture of sportsmanship, reminded Woods to return his ball mark to its original position after moving it out of Scott's line. Woods would not have won his third Amateur if Scott had not intervened. Woods tied the match at the thirty-fifth with a downhill 30-footer, then halved the thirty-sixth. Scott and Woods halved the first extra hole. Woods won with a par on the 194-yard, par-3 thirty-eighth when Scott could not convert his 7-foot third putt. Woods thus became the first to win three straight Amateurs. Including his three Junior Amateurs, Woods had won six USGA championships, putting him behind only Bobby Jones (nine) and Jack Nicklaus (eight) in the male category. Jones won five Amateurs and four Opens. Nicklaus has won two Amateurs, four Opens, and two Senior Opens. In 1996, Tiger also won the NCAA championship and was named Collegiate Player of the Year.

Shortly after winning his third Amateur, Woods, then a junior in college, announced that he would join the PGA Tour. Like Arnold Palmer, Jack Nicklaus, and many others before him, he signed with the International Management Group and immediately closed a number of multimillion-dollar contracts with Nike, Titleist, American Express, and a variety of others. Tiger was financially set for life without having played a golf tournament as a professional.

Tiger's debut as a professional was at the 1996 Milwaukee Open with "Fluff" Cowan, Peter Jacobsen's veteran caddie, as his guiding influence. Woods drew huge galleries, much like a rock star and Michael Jordan combined. Woods was a superstar, a multicultural global golf force who would bring new golfers to the game and generally increase interest in golf. Of course, he still had to perform.

He did. He entered eight PGA Tour events in 1996 and won two of them, the Las Vegas Invitational and the Walt Disney World/Oldsmobile Classic, and was named Tour Rookie of the Year. Then he won four tournaments in 1997, including the Masters. After each of his first two Amateur wins, Woods was invited to the Masters, as is the custom. So Tiger was familiar with the Augusta National golf course and the Masters environment when he teed it up for money for the first time. He stunned the golf world when he shot rounds of 70-66-65-69=270 to become the youngest player to win the Masters, setting a tournament scoring record and winning by twelve strokes over Tom Kite. He became the fifth-youngest winner of any major in the twentieth century after Gene Sarazen, who won two (1922 U.S. Open and 1922 PGA) before he passed Tiger's age of twenty-one years three months and five days, Johnny McDermott (1911 and 1912 U.S. Opens), Francis Ouimet (1913 U.S. Open), and Tom Creavy (1931 PGA). The youngest major winner of all was Young Tom Morris, who won his first British Open in 1868 when he was seventeen.

Woods won the PGA earnings title with $2,066,833, the Player of the Year Award, and numerous other awards. Through 1998, Tiger had won seven official PGA events and earned almost $4.7 million on the course and much more off it. His record in his first Ryder Cup, at Valderrama in Spain in 1997, was 1-3-1. His record in the 1998 President's Cup at Royal Melbourne in Australia was 2-3-0.

Tiger had a phenomenal year in 1999, winning eight PGA Tour events, setting a single season record in official PGA earnings with $6,616,585, winning the PGA Championship, and leading the Tour in stroke average (68.43) as well as total driving, greens in regulation, birdies, and all-around ranking. He contributed to the U.S. Ryder Cup win at the Country Club and was named Player of the Year. By early 2000 Tiger became, at age twenty-four and with just three and a half years on the Tour, the all-time leading money winner. He also had won six consecutive tournaments, the longest streak since Ben Hogan in 1948, which ended at the Buick Invitational in February. Only Byron Nelson, with eleven consecutive wins in 1945, has had a longer streak.

For those who thought that Tiger Woods was overrated, his record in 2000 is one of the best ever recorded by anyone in a single season. He won the U.S. Open at Pebble Beach with a record-tying 12-under-par 272, fifteen strokes better than the second-place finishers, Ernie Els and Miguel Angel Jimenez. He then set a British Open scoring record by shooting a 19-under-par 269 to win by eight over Els and Thomas Bjorn at St. Andrews. Amazingly, he did not hit a shot into a bunker during his four tournament rounds. At this point, Tiger held the record for most under par in the Masters, U.S. Open, and British Open. Woods then reaffirmed that he can rise to the occasion in any high-stakes pressure situation. He won his second straight PGA title at Valhalla in Louisville, Kentucky, a course, ironically, designed by Jack Nicklaus. Tiger and Jack played the first two rounds together in a symbollic passing of the "golf's greatest" mantle. Nicklaus, after missing the cut, used the same words that Bobby Jones had use to describe him when he noted, "He's playing a game with which I am not familiar."

Woods tied journeyman professional Bob May with an eighteen-under-par score of 270, a PGA record, at the end of regulation. In a new format requiring three playoff holes to decide the championship, Tiger won the championship by one shot. Having shot three consecutive rounds of 66 prior to the playoff, Bob May still could not win the tournament. By the end of November 2000, Woods was rated 28.64 in the World Rankings, almost three times higher than Ernie Els (11.80), the second-ranked player. He had won $20,503,450 in PGA Tour money in his short career, over $5.5 million more than Davis Love III, ranked number two. He had won three majors in 2000 and the Canadian Open as well as four other PGA Tour events. He dominated other events such as the World Cup in Malaysia, where he teamed with Mark O'Meara to win the team title. He shot a 25-under-par 263 to win the individual title by nine shots. Woods won the PGA Player of the Year Award and the Vardon Trophy for lowest scoring average. And he led the Tour in season earnings as well as other statistics, including all-around, average score, eagles, greens in regulation, birdies, and total driving. He was second in putting (average strokes per hole) and driving distance (298.0).

Woods has adjusted to the grueling professional circuit and the demands of fame. The well-conditioned, 6-foot-2-inch, 175-pound Woods could conceivably play competitively almost forty more years, including senior events. After all, Jack Nicklaus finished tied for sixth in the 1998 Masters at age fifty-eight. In the meantime, he's hoping that more young people are attracted to golf: "Young people who have played more so-called core sports now think golf is cool. They'll identify with my age, and they'll start playing." But if Tiger Woods retired today, with three U.S. Junior Amateur titles, three U.S. Amateur championships, and eight major professional victories, it would have been a career most golfers would envy.

Through 2002, Tiger Woods had won thirty-four PGA Tour events, placing him twelfth on the all-time list. His $33,103,852 in career earnings places him first, over $11 million more than PHIL MICKELSON, who is second on the list. Woods won the Masters in 2001 to become the first player to hold all four professional majors championships at once. He also won the Player of the Year and the earnings title for a third consecutive year. In 2002, he won the Masters again and the U.S. Open at Bethpage Black on Long Island. He again won Player of the Year award—his fourth straight—and led the Tour in earnings. He also won his third consecutive Vardon Trophy for lowest scoring average. He now has won eight professional majors: three Masters (1997, 2001, 2002), two U.S. Opens (2001, 2002), the British Open (2000), and the PGA Championship (1999, 2000). In fact, Woods has won seven of the last eleven majors.

3

Ben Hogan

1912–1997

A golfer loses a lot more tournaments than he wins.

—BEN HOGAN

There have been many golfers but few golf legends: JACK NICKLAUS, ARNOLD PALMER, HARRY VARDON, WALTER HAGEN, BOBBY JONES and a few others. Ben Hogan is one of those legends. A determined loner who came out the hardscrabble area of Depression-era Texas and, despite family tragedy and a near-fatal automobile accident, through hard work and endless perfectionism rose to the top of his profession, is the stuff of legends with a Hollywood ending. In 1951 a film was made of Hogan's life, *Follow the Sun,* with Glenn Ford.

Hogan was born in Stephenville, Texas, on August 13, 1912. His father, a blacksmith, committed suicide when Ben was nine years old. Hogan began to caddie at age eleven and struggled mightily against a tendency to hook. Both Ben and BYRON NELSON caddied at the Glen Garden Country Club in Fort Worth during those days, but by 1937, Byron had won the Masters and was playing on the Ryder Cup team, while Ben had resigned his job at a club in Fort Worth in order to join the Tour. In 1931, Hogan tried to compete on the professional golf circuit with the backing of a wealthy Fort Worth businessman, Marvin Leonard, but he came back to Fort Worth unsuccessful. He again tried to break in while making ends meet with stopgap jobs as an oil-field worker, mechanic, and bank clerk.

Hogan was stubborn, a perfectionist, and a legendary and methodical regular on the practice range. At 5 feet 9 and 135–150 pounds in his prime, "Bantam Ben" made constant adjustments in his game and gradually overcame his tendency to hook. In 1940, at the age of twenty-eight, Hogan established himself on the PGA Tour by winning the North and South, Greensboro, and Asheville Opens in succession. He led the PGA in earnings in 1940, 1941, and 1942. He also led the Tour in wins, with six, in 1942. But just as Hogan was reaching the peak of his game, he was inducted into the Army Air Force in 1942. Earlier that year he had lost in a play-off to Byron Nelson in the Masters, 69–70. After the war, corporations, chambers of commerce, departments of tourism, and other organizations were more than happy to support PGA tournaments. Golf, which had taken a double hit from the Great Depression and World War II, was gradually regaining popularity. Hogan resumed his rivalry with Byron Nelson, SAM SNEAD, and the rest of the Tour players and won the PGA Championship in 1946, defeating Ed "Porky" Oliver in the final at the Portland Golf Club in Oregon. Hogan won thirteen tournaments that year and twenty-nine in the first three years after the war. He almost won his first Masters in 1946, but he three-putted from twelve feet on the seventy-second hole, enabling Herman Keiser to win by one shot.

Then Hogan was dealt a cruel blow. Traveling with his wife, Valerie, he was almost killed when a bus hit his car head-on along a Texas road on February 2, 1949. Hogan, who slid across the front seat to protect his wife, suffered a double fracture of his pelvis, a broken collarbone, a broken left ankle, and a broken right rib. He spent a month in the hospital, and it was assumed he would never play again. But he miraculously recovered and rejoined the Tour early the following year, even though he had to severely curtail his schedule for the rest of his career. Never again would he play in the PGA Championship, a grueling match-play event. After trying nine times in thirteen years to win the Masters, he finally broke through in 1951 when he shot a final-round 68 to win by two shots over Skee Riegel. Hogan won the Masters again in 1953; at age forty, he shot rounds of 70-69-66-69=274, a tournament record, to win by five shots over Ed Oliver.

Hogan won the U.S. Open four times, beginning with a two-stroke win over his friend JIMMY DEMARET at the Riviera Country Club in Los Angeles in 1948. For his size, Hogan was extremely long off the tee. Riviera proved ideal for his combination of distance and accuracy; he recorded a score of 67-72-68-69=276. Hogan's win in the 1950 Open at Merion added to his reputation as someone who had the nerve and determination to reach a goal through flawless execution and steel willpower. The Open was played in June, just six months after Hogan, his legs encased in elastic bandages, played his first round of golf since his accident. Merion, a 6,696-yard, par-70 layout, was noted for its twisting fairways and its difficult, slippery greens. Ben was one shot behind after fifty-four holes. On the final day he reached the sixteenth tee needing two pars and a bogey to tie LLOYD MANGRUM and George Fazio, who finished at 287. Hogan then parred the 445-yard, par-4 Quarry hole but bogeyed the par-3 seventeenth after he bunkered his tee shot. He needed a par on the difficult 458-yard, par-4 finishing hole. Hogan hit a long drive, then a classic 1-iron to within forty feet of the pin. He two-putted to tie. In the playoff, Hogan was one stroke ahead of Mangrum and three ahead of Fazio on the sixteenth hole when Mangrum inadvertently lifted his ball to remove an insect from it while on the green. This gained him a two-stroke penalty; when Hogan holed a 50-foot birdie putt on the seventeenth, he clinched the championship. Hogan had shot a 69 to win by four over Mangrum and six over Fazio.

Hogan won his third Open at Oakland Hills, a difficult 6,927-yard Donald Ross–designed layout that had been toughened up by Robert Trent Jones Sr. prior to the Open. Jones lengthened the course and added bunkers in strategic positions in fairway landing areas. The par was reduced from 72 to 70 by converting two par-5s to par-4s for the tournament. Hogan opened with a 76 ("The stupidest round of golf I ever played," he claimed) to put himself in forty-first place. But by the final round he played himself back to a two-shot deficit, behind leaders BOBBY LOCKE and Jimmy Demaret. Using a brassie (2-wood) for control off the tee, Hogan parred the front nine, then hit a critical 3-iron to within five feet and birdied the tenth. Hogan shot a flawless round of 67 to win by two shots over Clayton Haefner. Locke slipped to 291 (to Hogan's 287), and Demaret faded from contention. At the trophy ceremony Hogan intoned, "I'm glad I brought this course, this monster, to its knees." He later said, "If I had to play this course every week, I'd go into some other business."

Hogan won his final Open at the Oakmont Country Club in 1953. For some reason the USGA (United States Golf Association) decided that everyone had to qualify for the Open that year, forcing Hogan to play an additional thirty-six holes. His qualifying score was 77-73=150, and he opened the tournament with eight birdies in twenty-two holes. At the end of fifty-four holes he led Sam Snead by one shot. Hogan shot an indifferent 38 on the front nine the final day but rallied for a 33 on the back to total 283 and win by six shots over Snead. Hogan birdied the last two holes to clinch his victory. His birdie on the 462-yard, par-4 finishing hole featured a 300-yard drive and a 5-iron to within seven feet.

Hogan played the best golf of his career in 1953. When he arrived at Carnoustie for the British Open, he had entered five 72-hole tournaments and won four: the Masters, the Pan American, the Colonial, and the U.S. Open. He could not try for a Grand Slam because the final match of the PGA Championship was scheduled for July 7, the same day as the second day of qualifying for the British Open, and everyone had to qualify. Hogan, who had never played in the British Isles before, qualified with rounds of 70 and 75. He went over early and learned to play the smaller British ball from firm ground and tight lies. But it was difficult to get used to the slow greens and the deceptive flagsticks which varied in height and made depth perception difficult. Hogan shot 73-71-70-68=282 to win by four strokes over Frank Stranahan, an American amateur, and PETER THOMSON, from Australia, who would later win five Opens. Hogan, whom the Scots dubbed the "Wee Ice Mon" for his disciplined style of play, returned to the United States a national hero and was given a ticker-tape parade in New York, just as Bobby Jones had before him in 1930.

The 1953 British Open would be the last major that Hogan, then age forty-one, would win. He came close on several occasions, finishing second in the U.S. Open in 1955, a heartbreaking overtime loss to Jack Fleck at Olympic, and joint second in the 1956 Open, one shot behind

CARY MIDDLECOFF at Oak Hill. Hogan finished second in the Masters in 1954, losing a play-off to Sam Snead, and in 1955 he finished second to Cary Middlecoff. In the 1960 Open at Cherry Hills, Hogan, who was tied for the lead with Arnold Palmer at the time, missed a pitch shot approach by six inches on the seventy-first hole. The ball hit the bank and spun back into the water fronting the green. Hogan, paired with amateur Jack Nicklaus, staggered in with a 73 to finish four shots behind the victorious Palmer. Hogan's last PGA Tour victory was at Colonial in 1959, the fifth time he won that event. His last best round in a major was at the Masters in 1967; he shot 66 in the third round and, at age fifty-nine, finished tenth.

Hogan had played a limited schedule after his accident but managed to win eleven tournaments, including six majors. He won a total of sixty-three Tour events and the British Open, putting him third all-time behind Nicklaus (seventy) and Snead (eighty-one). He had forty-six second-place finishes and out of 292 career tournaments finished in the top three 139 times and the top ten 241 times. He won the Vardon Trophy in 1940, 1941, and 1948, and the PGA money title in 1940, 1941, 1942, 1946, and 1948. He was named Associated Press Athlete of the Year in 1953 and received the Hickock Belt as athlete of the year. He was named PGA Player of the Year four times, in 1948, the first year it was awarded, and in 1950, 1951, and 1953. He was undefeated as a Ryder Cup player (1941, 1947, 1951) or captain (1947, 1949, 1967).

Ben Hogan began an equipment business while active as a professional and continued after he retired from the Tour. He collaborated with Herbert Warren Wind to write the instructional classic *Five Lessons: The Modern Fundamentals of Golf,* first published in 1957 and still in print.

Hogan was a member of the World Golf Hall of Fame. He died on July 25, 1997, in Fort Worth, Texas. Curt Sampson concludes in his biography *Hogan*: "He (Hogan) became an idea quite apart from golf. His name alone defined concentration, determination, even perfection. The Little Man had no yardage book, no golf glove, no self-congratulation, no bullshit and no pretense. Everything he accomplished he dug out of the ground."

4

Bobby Jones

1902–1971

I maintain that golf and tournament golf are two different things (and it may be that I can speak with a little show of authority from personal experience); so maybe that is the answer—the solid and negative and altogether unromantic attribute of patience. After all, it's Old Man Par and you, match or medal.

—BOBBY JONES

Robert Tyre Jones is one of those legendary gentleman athletes who, like a shooting star that splashes the sky with light, comes along rarely, leaving an indelible impression on both the record book and the imagination. Born in Atlanta in 1902, Jones was a sickly boy and did not eat his first solid food until he was five. The son of an Atlanta lawyer, he preferred to play baseball as a child, but lacking enough neighborhood friends to get up a ball game, he took up golf at age six. He learned by observing Stewart Maiden, a Scot from Carnoustie who was the professional at the East Lake Country Club, where his father played. Jones started with a few cut-down clubs. He was a quick study and soon became a golf prodigy, winning the Atlanta Athletic Club Junior Golf Championship at age nine, the East Lake Country Club Championship at age thirteen, the Georgia State Amateur at fourteen, and several other events. He entered his first U.S. Amateur in 1916, qualified, then lost in the quarterfinals to Bob Gardner, the defending champion. At this point, Jones and others expected him to win national championships, but it took him seven years to learn how to control his legendary temper and learn how to win.

During his formative years, Jones (who was later "iconized" as a scholar-athlete), threw clubs and tantrums and screamed epithets when the golf ball wouldn't do what he wanted. At the 1921 British Open at St. Andrews he walked off the course during the third round after shooting 46 on the front nine and playing poorly at the outset of the home nine. Up until 1923, Jones had played in ten national championships, but the closest he came to winning was placing second in the 1919 U.S. Amateur and runner-up in the 1922 U.S. Open. Jones's breakthrough came at the Inwood Country Club on Long Island in the 1923 U.S. Open. He was tied by Bobby Cruickshank, a native Scot, when the latter parred the final hole after Jones had scored a double bogey. Jones gathered himself and won the eighteen-hole play-off when he hit a heroic 2-iron on his approach shot on the final hole to score par and win by two shots. Up until then Jones had always had trouble in head-to-head match play. He finally realized that if he played against par, rather than the opponent, he would likely have more success.

At the age of twenty-one, Jones had his first national title. He was 5 feet 8 inches and a stocky 165 pounds and could generate power off the tee with his long swing. He had somewhat modified the Carnoustie swing he learned from Maiden. Jones had a B.S. in mechanical engineering from Georgia Tech and fully understood the mechanics of the swing. He had a narrow stance, a full hip turn, and a cocking of the chin to the right as he kept his head still and behind the ball. He had excellent hand-eye coordination and used various techniques to reduce his natural nervousness and tension, including minimal grip pressure at address to help relax his arms and shoulders for a slow, smooth start to his backswing. The advent of steel-shafted and other types of clubs that replaced the hickory shaft enabled golfers to use a shorter swing than the flowing, rhythmic swing employed by Jones in his prime. The strongest parts of Jones's game were his driving and putting, but there were no weak aspects to it. He favored a right-to-left draw, but he could fade the ball when required.

Jones won the U.S. Amateur in 1924, 1925, 1927, 1928, and 1930. He finished second in 1926 and was eliminated only once during the first round of any match play competition he ever entered—by Johnny Goodman, in 1929, on the last hole of the first round of the U.S. Amateur at Pebble Beach. He was named to the first Walker Cup team in 1922 and also played in 1924, 1926, 1928, and 1930. The United States won all of those contests. Jones captained the team in 1928 and 1930. The United States did not lose a Walker Cup contest until 1938. By then it was evident that the best golfers in the world were being developed in the United States.

Jones earned a B.S. degree in English literature at Harvard and, having attended Emory University Law School in Atlanta, passed the Georgia state bar examination and began to practice law in his father's firm in Atlanta in 1927. An excellent writer, Jones found time to write *Down the Fairway*, his autobiography, with O. B. Keeler, at the age of twenty-five. He later authored *Golf Is My Game* and *Bobby Jones on Golf*.

Jones won his first British Open in 1926 after scoring his famous 66 in the qualifier at Sunningdale. By then, Jones, with the assistance of WALTER TRAVIS, who had won the 1904 British Amateur and three U.S. Amateurs on the strength of his short game, had become an expert putter. Travis advised that Jones have his wrists work more in conjunction with each other and concentrate on taking the club back with his left hand. Jones changed his putting grip to an overlapping grip, adopted a breath-control technique to alleviate his nervousness, and improved his diet by eating breakfasts of sliced oranges, cornflakes, and coffee before tournaments. He also managed his diet in between rounds on those days, such as the U.S. Open, when thirty-six holes of championship golf were played per day. In the British Open qualifier Jones shot 444-334-434=33 on the par 36 front nine whose holes were: 554-334-434. He then shot 434-343-444=33 coming in against par: 554-344-434=36 for his 66. He had putted for birdies on thirteen holes and eagles on four others. Jones was clearly ready for the Open, which he won with a score of 72-72-73-74=291 at Royal Lytham and St. Anne's. Jones won two more British Opens, by six shots at St. Andrews in 1927 and by two shots at Hoylake in 1930.

Bobby Jones became the first golfer to hold both the U.S. Open and British Open titles in one year when he returned to the United States and, after a parade in his honor in New York City, won the 1926 U.S. Open at Scioto in Columbus, Ohio. Jones shot rounds of 70-79-71-73 to win by one shot over Joe Turnesa. One of Jones's most famous Open victories occurred at Winged Foot in Mamaroneck, New York, in 1929. He led the tournament after fifty-four holes with a four-shot margin over Al Espinosa, a Spanish American from Monterey, California. Espinosa took twenty-two shots on the final six holes, while Jones lost four stokes to par on the sixty-ninth and seventieth holes, parred the seventy-first, and then made a nasty 12-foot putt on the final hole to finish tied at 294. Jones shot 72-79=151 the following day to defeat a struggling Espinosa by twenty-three strokes.

The year 1930 was Bobby's famous Grand Slam year. He sailed to Britain to play in the Walker Cup matches, then won the British Amateur at St. Andrews for the first time in four tries. Jones next won the British Open at Hoylake with a total of 70-72-74-75=291 to win by two shots over LEO DIEGEL and MACDONALD SMITH. Jones returned to the United States, was given another Broadway parade, and then departed for Minneapolis, where he won the U.S. Open at Interlachen by two shots, with a score of 71-73-68-75=287, the only below-par total, to edge Macdonald Smith by two strokes. Jones was the medalist at the U.S. Amateur qualifier at Merion with a score of 69-73=142. He defeated Jess Sweetster in the semifinals, nine and eight, and then won the final, eight and seven, over Eugene Homans.

At the age of twenty-eight Jones retired from competitive golf. He had been a national champion for eight years before he retired to practice law in Atlanta. He had won thirteen major tournaments in eight years, a total that only JACK NICKLAUS has exceeded. In retirement, Jones wrote about golf and developed a series of golf instructional films, *How I Play Golf,* which are still relevant and available on video. He codesigned the Augusta National golf course with Alister Mackenzie, the architect of Cypress Point, Royal Melbourne, and other great golf courses. With Cliff Roberts and others, Jones founded the Masters Invitational, which has evolved into one of the modern majors.

Bobby Jones played his last round of golf in 1948. He had developed syringomyelia, a rare, disabling, and painful spinal disease, which was formally diagnosed in 1950. This crippling illness confined Jones to a wheelchair, but he continued to practice law and attend the Masters. When noted golf writer Charles Price became emotional about Jones's condition when they were working on a book project one day, Jones gently admonished him: "Now Charles, we will have none of that; we all must play the ball as it lies." In 1958, Bobby Jones was honored by the city of St. Andrews, which granted him the Freedom of the City of St. Andrews, the first American so honored since Benjamin Franklin in 1757. In his moving acceptance speech, Jones said, "I could take out of my life everything except my experiences of St. Andrews and I'd still have a rich, full life."

In 1974, Robert Tyre Jones was elected to the World Golf Hall of Fame, along with other inaugural members: Patty Berg, Walter Hagen, Byron Nelson, Jack Nicklaus, Francis Ouimet, Arnold Palmer, Gary Player, Gene Sarazen, Sam Snead, Harry Vardon, and Babe Zaharias. He died in 1971 at the age of sixty-nine.

5

Sam Snead

1912–2002

*Laddie, you've just won yourself a
championship worth more than a seat
on the stock exchange.*

—TOMMY ARMOUR, prematurely
congratulating Sam Snead
on his win at the 1937 U.S. Open

Samuel Jackson Snead was born in 1912, the same year as the other
members of the "Big Three" of his era, BEN HOGAN and BYRON
NELSON. Raised in the mountains of western Virginia, Snead possessed
a natural golf swing that produced prodigiously long drives. His first
club was a homemade implement with a swamp-maple limb that he
carved with a penknife, leaving some bark for a grip. He imitated his
older brother, Homer, a natural athlete. Sam, playing barefoot, would
hit acorns with his swamp stick, adjusting the grip and stance until he
obtained the length and accuracy he sought. He became a caddie at the
Homestead resort in Hot Springs, Virginia, and improved his game. An
all-round athlete at Valley High School, he swam and played basketball,
football, tennis, track, and baseball and even participated in some
regional golf tournaments.

After high school, Snead became more serious about golf when
he was hired as an assistant in Homestead's pro shop. He won his first
golf purse in 1936 at the Cascades Open, finishing third and collecting

$358.66. Up until that time he made a few dollars giving golf lessons to hotel guests and had become adept at repairing clubs. Sam used an unmatched collection of ten clubs that cost him $12.50 to win his first tournament. But he was worried that his time was running out. "You've seen these small-town star athletes who run out of eligibility and don't marry a rich girl or land a job selling stocks and bonds and hang around the hometown pool hall and cigar store, wondering where the cheers went. That's the way I seemed to be headed."

Luckily, Mr. Fred Martin, manager of the Greenbrier Hotel in nearby White Sulphur Springs, West Virginia, caught a glimpse of Sam's fluid swing while visiting the Homestead resort in 1936. Martin offered Sam the job of professional at the Greenbrier for forty-five dollars a month plus room, board, and any cash he could earn by giving lessons. Sam gladly took the job and first ventured out of the region to play in his first professional tour event, the Hershey Open, held in Pennsylvania in late summer of that year. There he met some of the cast of characters from the tour, including JIMMY DEMARET, WALTER HAGEN, CRAIG WOOD, HENRY PICARD, and others. Snead finished fifth, and Craig Wood, representing Dunlop, offered him five hundred dollars in cash, two dozen golf balls a month, and a set of new golf clubs to sign with Dunlop and endorse their products. Thus began a Tour odyssey that would net Snead a record eighty-one PGA tournament wins. His first was in the 1937 Oakland Open and his last the 1965 Greensboro Open, the eighth time he won that tournament, when he was fifty-two years old.

Among Sam's many notable accomplishments were three PGA money titles (1938, 1949, 1959), four Vardon Trophies for lowest scoring average (1938, 1949, 1950, 1955), and selection to the Ryder Cup team seven times (1937, 1947, 1949, 1951, 1953, 1955, 1959), for which he was captain in 1951 and 1959, and nonplaying captain in 1969. His overall Ryder Cup record in singles and foursomes is 10-2-1. Snead won seven majors, including three Masters (1949, 1952, 1954), three PGA Championships (1942, 1949, 1951), and the 1946 British Open. His most exciting Masters win was in 1954 when he finished in a tie with Ben Hogan, with a seventy-two-hole score of 289. Snead took a one-shot lead into the final hole of the eighteen-hole play-off by virtue of a birdie on the par-5 thirteenth. He was able to match pars with Hogan on the final hole to win, 70–71. During his career Snead never lost to Hogan in a play-off. His other playoff win over Hogan was in the 1950 Los Angeles Open.

In 1938, Snead suffered a humiliating eight and seven loss to 128-pound short-hitting PAUL RUNYAN in the PGA Championship final.

Snead gradually realized that he never would be a complete player unless he improved his game from 150 yards in. BOBBY JONES advised him, "Distance is fine, accuracy is better. Be sure to take an inventory of your whole game, Sam. Do that after every round, with particular attention to how your close shots come off." Snead worked on his short irons and grew to consider the 8-iron as his money club. As a result of this improvement, Snead's first PGA Championship victory came in 1942, just before he was inducted into the navy. He delayed signing his induction papers in order to compete at the Seaview Country Club, near Atlantic City, New Jersey. Snead defeated Jimmy Demaret, three and two, to reach the finals against Jim Turnesa, who had eliminated Byron Nelson, 1-up, on the first extra hole of his thirty-six-hole semifinal match. Snead made a decisive 60-foot chip shot on the thirty-fifth hole to clinch his first major championship.

Snead entered the U.S. Navy the Monday after he won the 1942 PGA Championship. He would not return to the tour until 1944, when he entered four tournaments, winning the Portland Open and the Richmond Open. He entered the British Open at St. Andrews in 1946, and when he reached Britain, he was appalled by the effects of the war. Although Snead did not enjoy traveling outside the United States, he had played on Ryder Cup teams and had finished eleventh at Carnoustie in 1937 in the only other British Open in which he had competed. Snead was chagrined at the low prize money that the British Open had to offer, $600 for first place (compared to $3,500 for the PGA, $2,500 for the Masters, and $1,500 for the U.S. Open), realizing, as many American golfers did up until that time, that playing in the Open was a money-losing proposition unless you won and could benefit financially from the prestige the title conferred. When Snead saw St. Andrews for the first time, he mistook it for "an old, abandoned golf course," but its large greens would benefit him because his length would get him on in regulation and he was very skilled on longer putts. Snead won the Open with a score of 290, four strokes better than Johnny Bulla and BOBBY LOCKE. Snead never played another British Open. He would later say, "As far as I'm concerned, any time you leave the U.S.A., you're just camping out."

Although Snead became the leading Tour tournament winner of all time, he was found lacking by some pundits because he never won a U.S. Open. And it was the way that Snead lost at least one Open that caused critics to claim that he lacked the intelligence and finesse to adjust to the rigors of Open competition. His first Open disappointment was in 1937 at Oakland Hills. Snead was the Open favorite despite the fact that he had yet to win a major event and was relatively new to the Tour. The "hillbilly" from Virginia was one of the most colorful players on the Tour and a big gate attraction. He eagled the final hole, a 537-yard par-5, to complete solid rounds of 69-73-70-71=283 and was congratulated on his apparent win by Tommy Armour, who said, "Laddie, you've just won yourself a championship worth more than a seat on the stock exchange." But RALPH GULDAHL, who had been tied with Snead after the end of fifty-four holes, was still out on the course. Guldahl shot a 33 on the front nine and finished with a final round of 69 to win by two shots. This would be the first of four second-place Open finishes for Snead.

At the 1939 Open at the Spring Mill course of the Philadelphia Country Club, Snead needed a bogey and a par to win the tournament. He bogeyed the par-4 seventy-first, leaving a 6-foot putt a full foot short. He then proceeded to record an eight on the 558-yard, par-5 final hole by hooking his drive into the rough, pushing a brassie into a bunker 100 yards short of the green, fluffing the bunker shot, then hooking his escape wide of the green, chipping on and then three-putting—much like watching a train wreck in slow motion. Snead finished in fifth place, two strokes behind Byron Nelson (who won the play-off), Craig Wood, and DENNY SHUTE. Snead would later say, "If I'd murdered someone, I'd have lived it down sooner than the '39 Open." Snead's next chance came in the 1947 Open when he birdied the seventy-second hole at the St. Louis Country Club to tie Lew Worsham, forcing an eighteen-hole playoff. Both golfers were tied going into the last hole, a par-4. Each player hit perfect tee shots and excellent approaches to within twenty-five feet of the pin. Worsham, who was just off the green, rimmed the right edge of the cup and left his ball a few feet away from the hole. Snead's putt stopped a few feet short. Thinking he was away, Snead addressed his putt, but before he could swing, Worsham asked for a measurement. Snead proved to be away after his distance was measured at 30½ inches. Distracted by the interruption, Snead missed his putt by two inches. Worsham holed his for the win, and Snead was forever labeled as having a U.S. Open jinx.

Fred Corcoran, tournament manager of the PGA from 1936 to 1947 and promotional director from 1952 to 1954, helped create the Snead mystique when the PGA was trying to establish itself during the difficult Depression and World War II years. Corcoran promoted Sam as a hillbilly golf prodigy who preferred to play barefoot. Snead provided memorable copy and got national press coverage when he won the 1937 Oakland Open. When shown a picture of himself in a New

York paper, he commented: "How in the world did they ever get that? I have never been to New York in my life." Snead was also an expert woodsman who liked to fish and track game, was a nonsmoker, seldom drank, and prided himself on physical fitness. Sam's suppleness and conditioning contributed to his golf longevity. He was third in the PGA Championship at age sixty-two and won his sixth PGA Senior title in 1973 by fifteen strokes at age sixty, with scores of 66-66-67-69=268.

In addition to his numerous tournament victories and his colorful personality, Sam Snead will be remembered for his graceful, flowing, powerful swing that he learned by trial and error, largely by feel. He said, "Thinking instead of acting is the number-one golf disease." Snead is a member of the World Golf Hall of Fame.

6

Byron Nelson

1911–

My game had gotten so good and so dependable that there were times when I actually would get bored playing. I'd hit on the fairway, on the green, make a birdie or par, and go on to the next hole.

> —BYRON NELSON, remembering his golf game in 1945,
> when he won eleven consecutive tournaments
> and a record total of eighteen

John Byron Nelson Jr. became one of the dominant golfers of his era because of his one-piece, upright, left-side dominant, flex-kneed swing. This method keeps the moving clubhead at ball height for a longer period of time in the hitting area, improving the golfer's chances of consistent, solid contact. During this process Nelson used his legs to generate more power. His swing became an important blueprint for modern golfers, but he picked up some of his early techniques watching his boyhood idol, WALTER HAGEN, at the 1927 PGA Championship in Dallas, Texas. Hagen started the club down, with his hips sliding to the left, bringing his club down to the ball on a flatter plane than that of his contemporaries. Nelson began to perfect his swing in the 1930s while an assistant to George Jacobus at the Ridgewood Country Club in New Jersey. It was there that he moved from a hand-type swing to one that would minimize the moving parts in his play. As a confirmation of his transition to a consistent player, his swing mechanics were incorporated into a mechanical device called "Iron Byron," long used by the USGA to test golf balls.

Byron's love of golf began in his native Fort Worth, Texas, where he came up through the caddie ranks at the Glen Garden Country Club, just as his contemporary BEN HOGAN did. As a teenager, Nelson shot 118 his first round, but by the time he was fifteen years old, he was good enough to defeat fellow caddie Ben Hogan by one shot in the Glen Garden caddie championship. Nelson joined the pro Tour in 1932, winning seventy-five dollars for placing third in the Texarkana Open. In the early years, wins didn't come easy. Sometimes he would have to sell a silver cup, plate, or other prizes that he had won to raise money to get to the next tournament.

Nelson won his first major title, the 1937 Masters, when he opened with a record score of 66 and finished with a 283 to win by two shots over RALPH GULDAHL. During his phenomenal first round he hit every par-3 green in one shot and all the others in two. He one-putted only two greens, both from less than three feet. Nelson won his first and only U.S. Open in 1939 when he defeated CRAIG WOOD and DENNY SHUTE in a playoff at the 6,706-yard Spring Mill course at the Philadelphia Country Club. This is the Open where Sam Snead recorded an eight on the seventy-second hole. A par would have won him the Open, a title he never gained. Craig Wood and Nelson tied after eighteen play-off holes with scores of 68 to Shute's 76. USGA officials then gave Wood and Nelson the option to play a sudden-death play-off, but they elected to play another eighteen. Nelson, one of the best long-iron players ever, sent a message to Wood when he holed a 210-yard 1-iron for an eagle on the fourth play-off hole. Wood later said that the 1-iron shot "sure was a heartbreaker for me. It was one of the best shots I ever saw in a championship." Nelson won the play-off with a score of 70 to Wood's 73. The closest Byron would again come to winning an Open was in 1946 when, involved in a three-way play-off, he finished tied for second with Vic Ghezzi, one shot behind LLOYD MAN-GRUM. The three had been tied with scores of 72 after the regulation eighteen-hole play-off and had to play another eighteen to determine the champion.

Nelson won the Masters again in 1942 in a thrilling play-off against his old caddie competitor, Ben Hogan. World War II had begun to deplete the Tour as forty-two players of the eighty-eight invited accepted invitations. Top golfers JIMMY DEMARET, SAM SNEAD, and others joined the field, the smallest in the nine-year history of the event. Nelson recorded rounds of 68-67-72=207 to hold a three shot lead over Hogan going into the final round. Hogan, playing ahead of Nelson, was down two shots as he approached the tee at number seventeen. He parred that hole, and Nelson bogeyed, cutting Byron's lead to one. Then Hogan birdied the last hole, forcing a play-off when Nelson parred. Nelson started the eighteen-hole play-off with a shaky six, and at the end of four, he was down three strokes. He gained back two strokes on the sixth hole with a birdie 2 to Hogan's bogey. Nelson picked up another two strokes on the 510-yard, par-5 uphill eighth when he hit his wood approach to within six feet and eagled. Nelson had a three-shot lead after thirteen but lost a stroke to Hogan's birdie at number fourteen and another at number fifteen when he three-putted for par. Hogan lost a stroke when he bogeyed the sixteenth, putting him two down with two to play. Nelson hung on to win, 69–70.

Nelson excelled in PGA Championship play, winning in 1940, a 1-up victory over Snead, and in 1945. He finished second in 1939, 1941, and 1944. Byron was elected to the Ryder Cup in 1937, 1939 (the event was not played), and 1947 and was nonplaying captain in 1965. Before World War II, Nelson had won twenty-six tournaments. He tried to enlist but was rejected for military service because of a blood condition. Nelson's tour buddy, Harold "Jug" McSpaden, was also rejected, for severe allergies and sinusitis. They became "the Gold Dust Twins," playing 110 exhibitions for the Red Cross and USO for the war effort from 1942 through early 1944. Nelson won three tournaments in 1941, three in 1942, and none in 1943, when he was doing exhibitions on a full-time basis. President Roosevelt had encouraged major sports to continue during World War II, but the pressures of war, gasoline rationing, and other factors depleted the Tour until 1944, when twenty-three events were scheduled. Nelson, then head professional at Inverness, entered twenty-one of these tournaments and won eight of them. He was second five times, third five times, fourth once, and sixth twice. He led the Tour in earnings with $37,967.69, which were paid in war bonds. Nelson was named Athlete of the Year by the Associated Press and again in 1945, when he won an incredible eleven consecutive tournaments and a total of eighteen. He also played nineteen consecutive rounds under 70 during his streak. Nelson averaged 68.33 strokes in 1945 and led the tour in earnings with $63,335.66 in war bonds. Byron also managed to shoot a seventy-two-hole record 62-68-63-66=259 in the Seattle Open, bettering Hogan's record 261 in the Portland Open in 1945.

Ben Hogan and Byron Nelson dominated the tour in 1946 when Hogan won thirteen tournaments and Nelson six. During the 1940s, Nelson played in 113 consecutive events without missing a cut, still the all-time record. His fifty-two total official Tour wins place him fifth behind Snead (eighty-one), JACK NICKLAUS (seventy), Hogan (sixty-three), and ARNOLD PALMER (sixty). But Nelson essentially retired after 1946, at the age of thirty-four, to live on a ranch that he had bought for himself and his wife, Louise, in Texas. Nelson was burned out from playing exhibitions and from the hectic Tour schedule. Moreover, there was not that much money to be made playing professional golf at the time. "I was a short time on the Tour, I will admit, and a lot of people say I didn't play long enough. That's their opinion, not mine. But at any rate, I only made $182,000 on tournaments, endorsements, and exhibitions in fourteen years. That is less than $14,000 a year. I lived on that, and I still had enough money to pay for that ranch. That is what the Depression taught me."

Nelson played sporadically after 1946, competing in the 1947 Ryder Cup and winning the 1951 Bing Crosby Pro-Am and the French Open in 1955. He became a swing doctor and mentor to KEN VENTURI and Tom Watson, and a golf commentator. In 1995 the Byron Nelson Award was presented on the PGA Tour for the first time to honor the PGA Tour's scoring leader. Nelson is a charter inductee into the World Golf Hall of Fame (1974). On his decision to retire, he said, "Smartest thing I ever did. I had accomplished what I wanted to accomplish in golf. There were other things I wanted to do with my life."

7

Arnold Palmer

1929–

I may shoot sixty-five. What would that do?
—ARNOLD PALMER, before his final-round 65
at the 1960 U.S. Open

Like Elvis, he is called "the King," someone larger than life who transcends his field of endeavor. In Arnold Palmer's case, he was always a man of the people, someone they could identify with.

Arnold Palmer's character and career were influenced greatly by Milfred "Deacon" Palmer, his father, a greenskeeper and club professional at the Latrobe Country Club in Pennsylvania, who taught him to remember some basic rules, like not to throw clubs and not to play on the private Latrobe course unless under special circumstances, how to properly grip a club, and to swing hard at the ball.

Arnold Daniel Palmer, the oldest of five children, was born on September 10, 1929, and grew up in a modest house near the fifth tee of the Latrobe Country Club, which he now owns. He began playing golf when he was three, using a set of junior clubs, and by the time he was five, accompanied by his father and using his mother's clubs, he was playing full eighteen-hole rounds. By age seven, he was breaking 100, and when he began to caddie at the club, he won the caddie championship four times. (His dad, out of some sense of propriety, wouldn't allow him to keep the prize.) He practiced for hours at Latrobe when he wasn't caddying or helping out around the club. He swung hard from the beginning, sometimes losing his footing, as he would later when he hitched up his pants and mounted his famous charges.

Palmer won three Western Pennsylvania Championships and five Western Pennsylvania Amateurs. He wanted to become a golf professional, even though his high school coach told him he could never make a living playing golf. Arnold did not intend to go to college, but his friend Buddy Worsham, the younger brother of touring pro Lew Worsham, was offered a golf scholarship to Wake Forest and persuaded the coach to take Arnold, too. Palmer became the school's leading player and won the Atlantic Coast Conference title three times and in 1950 won the Southern Intercollegiate Championship. Later, many fine young golfers, including CURTIS STRANGE and LANNY WADKINS, earned Arnold Palmer golf scholarships from Wake Forest.

In Palmer's senior year, Buddy Worsham was killed in an automobile accident. Shaken, Palmer dropped out of school and enlisted in the Coast Guard. He came out in 1954, found a job representing a paint-manufacturing company, took up golf again, and won the U.S. Amateur. Over Labor Day weekend, he met Winifred Walzer at a tournament in Shawnee-on-Delaware. After they were married, in December 1954, they set out on the professional tour in a secondhand trailer. Arnie won his first tournament, the Canadian Open, and finished thirty-second on the 1955 money list with $7,958. He steadily improved, winning two tournaments in 1956, four in 1957, and his first major, the Masters, in 1958, by one shot over DOUG FORD and Fred Hawkins, who both missed birdie putts on the last hole. Palmer won $11,250, the first five-figure prize for a major, and won the PGA money title with $42,608. Arnie won the Masters again in 1960, by one shot over KEN VENTURI; in 1962 in a play-off with his friends DOW FINSTERWALD and GARY PLAYER; and in 1964 by six shots over JACK NICKLAUS and Dave Marr. Only

Nicklaus, with six, would win more Masters than Palmer. Palmer won the PGA money title again in 1960, 1962, and 1963. Today the money title is called the Arnold Palmer Award, in his honor.

By 1968, Arnold became the first man to win over $1 million on the PGA Tour. He also became the first golfer to buy his own jet airplane and to win aviation awards while navigating the expanding world of international golf and meeting the demands of his various golf ventures, which included golf-course design, equipment, communications ventures, and golf schools. Arnie would later say, "You know, I was the first golfer to buy my own airplane. But when I bought my first one, I had won the Masters twice. Now these guys win anywhere and they buy a plane."

Palmer and his lawyer-agent, Mark McCormack, who once played against Arnie's Wake Forest team while Mark was at William & Mary, redefined the golf business and expanded its opportunities for everyone. Palmer became McCormack's first major client and built the International Management Group (IMG) from the Palmer franchise. Palmer signed with McCormack in 1958, initially for booking exhibitions. As demands began to increase after Arnie's Masters wins and money titles, however, McCormack and IMG managed all his golf-related business dealings, as he would do for Jack Nicklaus, Gary Player, Nancy Lopez, Tiger Woods, and many others. Arnie's agreement with McCormack was sealed with a handshake.

Palmer, in the rising age of television and global communications, became golf's first superstar. He was named Sports Illustrated Sportsman of the Year in 1960; he won the Vardon Trophy in 1961 (69.85), 1962 (70.27), 1964 (70.01), and 1967 (70.18). He was named PGA Player of the Year in 1960 and 1962. Palmer sought new competitive horizons when he entered the British Open for the first time in 1960. He finished second to Kel Nagle by one stroke, with rounds of 70-71-70-68=279 at St. Andrews. Palmer's charisma and prestige gradually attracted more American competitors, which improved the British Open field, rescuing the world's oldest championship from its doldrums, caused by the Great Depression and World War II. Arnie won his first British Open in 1961, by one stroke at Royal Birkdale, with a score of 70-73-69-72=284. The following year, he won by six shots at Troon, with a score of 71-69-67-69=276. Arnie played his last Open at St. Andrews in a farewell gesture commemorating his thirty-fifth Open appearance in 1995.

Palmer's most famous and defining victory was in the 1960 U.S. Open at Cherry Hills, a 7,004-yard layout near Denver, Colorado.

Palmer, who badly wanted to win an Open, shot 72-71-72 through three rounds to put him in fifteenth place, seven shots behind the leader, Mike Souchak. In a locker-room conversation before his final round, Ken Venturi, Bob Rosburg, and Bob Drum, a reporter, were speculating as to whether Souchak could hold on to his lead. When Palmer wondered out loud whether a 65 and a total of 280 would be enough to win, Drum told him he was too far back. Annoyed, Arnie replied, "The hell I am. A sixty-five would give me two-eighty, and two-eighty wins Opens." Palmer went out and hit a 350-yard drive (aided by the thin air at an elevation of five thousand feet) off the first tee and reached the green on the short par-4. He two-putted for a birdie, played the front nine in 30, then shot a 5-under-par-65 for his predicted total of 280. He did win the Open by two shots over a burly young amateur by the name of Jack Nicklaus. At this stage, Palmer had won the Masters and the U.S. Open, but in his quest for a Grand Slam, he lost the British Open by one shot and the PGA Championship, a major he would never win, by five.

Palmer became noted for his charges and, with the body of a football running back and a rugged handsomeness, brought star quality and athleticism to the game of golf in the age of television. Palmer, Player, and Nicklaus were deemed the "Big Three" of golf when Arnie ran up against BILLY CASPER, one of the best players on the tour, at the Olympic Club in the 1966 U.S. Open. Leading Casper by seven strokes going into the final nine holes, Palmer decided to go for the Open record of 276 set by BEN HOGAN at Riviera in 1948. Arnie ran into trouble on the final holes, shooting 39 for a round of 71, while Casper methodically recorded a 68 to tie Palmer at 278. Casper defeated Palmer 69–73 in the eighteen-hole play-off; at thirty-six years of age, Arnie would never win another major. He finished second to Jack Nicklaus in the 1967 Open at Baltusrol, where, ironically, his 279 was not enough to overcome Jack's record-breaking 278. Arnie finished second to DAVE STOCKTON, by two strokes, in the 1970 PGA at Southern Hills.

Nicklaus, LEE TREVINO, Player, and a new generation of golfers began winning the majors and other tournaments. Arnie won his last regular Tour event, the Bob Hope Classic, for the fifth time, in 1973. He gave the Tour and himself a second life when he became the focal point of the Senior Tour, which he put on the map beginning with his win in the 1980 PGA Seniors Championship. Thanks to Arnie, players like Tom Wargo, Walter Zembriski, and Larry Laoretti, as well as PGA Tour graduates Lee Trevino, Dave Stockton, Jim Colbert, HALE IRWIN, and others, were earning more money than ever. Trevino, for example, earned almost $3.5 million on the regular Tour but has earned over $13 million on the Senior Tour.

Palmer won ten Senior PGA Tour events, including its majors, the U.S. Senior Open (1981), the PGA Seniors' Championship (1980), and the Senior Players Championship (1984, 1985). His sixty PGA Tour wins place him fourth on the all-time list behind SAM SNEAD (eighty-one), Nicklaus (seventy), and Hogan (sixty-three). Palmer is second to Jack Nicklaus (seventeen) in most consecutive years in the top-ten money list, fifteen, from 1957 through 1971. Arnie played on six Ryder Cup teams (1961, 1963, 1965, 1967, 1971, 1973) and compiled an overall record of 22-8-2. He was the captain of the Ryder Cup team in 1963 and 1975 and captained the President's Cup team in 1996.

Even though Nicklaus and a few others were better golfers than Arnie, no one has done more for the game and no one has done more to contribute to the financial success of the PGA Tour and Senior Tour golfers than Arnold Palmer. John Feinstein, in his book *A Good Walk Spoiled,* observed that Palmer, though the king, still has not lost the common touch. "To this day, Palmer approaches everyone he meets the way a club pro would. The club pro is the guy who has time to listen to the members go through their rounds shot by shot and smiles and somehow looks interested even if he's been at work for twelve hours that day. He is patient, always courteous, always manages to give everyone the impression that their life is very, very important to him. Walk the golf course with Palmer and you can see the club pro's son at work." Palmer is a member of the World Golf Hall of Fame.

8

Gary Player

1936–

One thing I can say: I've got the best world record, which was my ambition.

—GARY PLAYER

Gary Daniel Player was never one to hide his light under a bushel, but then he has many things to be proud of. He has won more than 160 tournaments worldwide, including 13 South African Opens, 7 Australian Opens, and a career Grand Slam (3 Masters, 2 PGAs, a U.S. Open, and 3 British Opens). He was the first foreign-born winner of the Masters and the first non-American to lead the PGA Tour in earnings (1961). He won twenty-one times on the PGA Tour before joining the Senior PGA Tour, where he has won over $7 million since 1985.

Noted for his deadly short game, which compensated for his lack of distance off the tee, Player, 5 feet 7 and 150 pounds, got the most out of his ability through hard work, practice, and an intensive physical-fitness program that emphasizes proper diet and rigorous workouts. A miner's son, he played his first round of golf at age fourteen, earning his way onto the golf course by giving golf lessons in his native Johannesburg, South Africa. He hung around the Virginia Park Golf Course and later married Vivienne Verway, the daughter of the club professional. He turned professional in 1953 at age eighteen, after completing high school, where he lettered in rugby and cricket, ran high and low hurdles in track, and was an excellent diver. After succeeding on the South African Tour, he entered his first British Open at the age of twenty in 1956 and finished fourth. At a time when it took forty-five hours to travel by commercial airlines from South Africa to the United States, Gary Player become the first true international golfer.

Player's first major victory came in the 1959 British Open at Muirfield. He spent ten days practicing on the course before the event. Player shot 75-71-70 in the first three rounds, then finished with a strong 68 despite a six on the last hole, for a total of 284, two strokes better than Flory Von Donck and Fred Bullock. He won the British Open again in two other decades, in 1968 at Carnoustie, defeating JACK NICKLAUS and BOB CHARLES by two shots, and in 1974 at Royal Lytham, when he won by four shots over Peter Oosterhuis.

Gary played in his first Masters in 1957 but did not finish in the top ten in that event until 1960, when he shot 289 to finish tied for sixth behind the winner, ARNOLD PALMER. Player then determined that he needed to be long enough on the par-5 holes in order to reach them in two shots if he was ever to score enough birdies to win the tournament. He consulted a bodybuilder on ways to gain strength, added one-half inch to the length of his clubs, and changed his swing to generate more distance. In the 1961 Masters he reached all the par-5s in two and shot 69-68-69-74=280 to win the Masters by one stroke over Arnold Palmer and Charlie Coe, an amateur. Player shot a 74 on the final round after he came in with a 40 on the back nine. Palmer, playing behind Player, needed a par on the final hole to win the tournament. Palmer hit his approach into the bunker to the right of the green on the par-4 finishing hole, then skimmed his ball out of the trap, across the green, and down the steep bank on the left side of the green. He then putted up the slope and well past the hole. He missed the putt coming back and scored a fatal double bogey. Player won his second Masters in 1974 when he fired 71-71-66-70=278 to edge DAVE STOCKTON and TOM WEISKOPF by two strokes.

At age twenty-two, Player competed in his first U.S. Open at the Southern Hills Country Club in Tulsa in 1958 and finished second, four shots behind TOMMY BOLT. Player shot a tournament-low 68 in the second round, but Bolt finished with a strong 69–72 to win. In 1965, at the Bellerive Country Club in St. Louis, Player became the first foreigner to win the U.S. Open since TED RAY, an Englishman, won at Inverness in 1920. Player's rounds of 70-70-71-71 tied Australian Kel Nagle at 282. It seemed that Player had the Open won with a three shot lead with three holes to go, but he hit his tee shot into the bunker on the 218-yard, par-3 sixteenth, then triple-bogeyed the hole. Nagle birdied the 606-yard, par-5 seventeenth to square the match.

In the eighteen-hole play-off, the forty-four-year-old Nagle ran into trouble on the fifth hole. He pulled his drive into the gallery along the fairway and wounded an elderly lady, who had blood streaming from her forehead. A shaken Nagle then hooked another ball into the crowd, hitting a woman on the ankle. Nagle double-bogeyed the hole and at that point was three strokes down. By the fifteenth hole, when television picked up the match, Nagle was down five. Player coasted in to win, 71–74. Player, who had won the PGA Championship in 1962, now had his Grand Slam and joined the select company of GENE SARAZEN, BOBBY JONES, Jack Nicklaus, and BEN HOGAN (who won each of the four majors at least once in his career).

Player's 1962 PGA championship was won at the 7,045-yard, par-70 Aronimink Golf Club in Newton Square, just outside Philadelphia. Player shot a 72-67-69-70=278 to hold off Bob Goalby, who shot a final-round 67 to lose by one shot. Player won again in 1972 despite anti-apartheid demonstrations that easily could have unnerved him. Playing at the 7,054-yard par-70 Oakland Hills Country Club in Birmingham, Michigan, Player launched a "miracle," blind 9-iron shot on the sixty-ninth hole, where he hit his ball over a willow to within four feet of the hole. He holed his birdie putt and went on to win the tournament by two strokes.

Player continued to prove his international mettle by winning a come-from-behind victory over TONY LEMA in the Piccadilly Matchplay Championship in 1965, one of his five victories in that event. He also teamed with Harold Henning in 1965 to win the Canada Cup in Madrid. Since joining the PGA Senior Tour he has won over $5.4 million, three PGA Seniors' Championships (1986, 1988, 1990), Senior Players Championship (1987) and two U.S. Senior Opens (1987, 1988). Player is a member of the World Golf Hall of Fame.

9

Walter Hagen

1892–1969

*One thing a tournament golfer has to learn is that it is not
the game he played last year or last week or probably will
play the week after next that he commands in any one
event. He has only his game at the time; and it may be far
from his best—but it's all he has, and he'd just as well
harden his heart and make the most of it.*

—Walter Hagen

Walter Charles Hagen, one of the great competitors and one of the
most colorful raconteurs in golf, was born in Rochester, New York, in
1892. The son of a blacksmith, Hagen learned to play golf while a
caddie at the Country Club of Rochester. At 5 feet 10 inches and 175
pounds in his prime, Hagen was also an excellent baseball pitcher who
could hurl with either arm and was once offered a tryout by the
Philadelphia Phillies. He chose golf instead, becoming an impeccably
dressed scrambler who somehow could overcome the bad breaks of the

game and snatch victory from the jaws of defeat. As he expressed it, "I've never played a perfect eighteen holes. There is no such thing. I expect to make at least seven mistakes a round. Therefore, when I make a bad shot, I don't worry about it. It's just one of the seven."

Hagen was especially deadly at match play, and in one stretch between 1916 and 1927, he won thirty-two out of thirty-four PGA Championship matches at a time when each match was thirty-six holes. His average margin of victory exceeded five holes, and he lost only to JOCK HUTCHISON on the final hole in 1916 and GENE SARAZEN at the thirty-eighth hole in 1923. During this period he won the PGA Championship five of the seven times he entered it.

Hagen played numerous exhibitions to supplement the then-meager income a professional could make from tournament purses. In one famous seventy-two-hole contest against BOBBY JONES in Florida in 1926, Hagen, who hit several fine recovery shots, won eleven and ten. Jones commented on what it was like to play against the scrambling Hagen: "I would rather play a man who is straight down the fairway with his drive, on the green with his second, and downs two putts for his par. I can play a man like that at his own game, which I call par golf. If one of us can get close to the pin with his approach or hole a good putt—all right. He earned something that I can understand. But when a man misses his drive and then misses his second shot and then wins the hole with a birdie, it gets my goat!"

Hagen was known to practice recovery shots and delighted in coming from behind. He had tremendous self-confidence and a competitive flair, but perhaps more importantly, he could accept bad shots and luck, both good and bad, as an inherent aspect of the game. He seldom let bad luck divert his concentration from the game, and he accepted both defeat and victory with the same élan. Jones claimed that this made him a first-rate golfing companion: "I love to play with Walter. He goes along, chin up, smiling away; never grousing about his luck, playing the ball as he finds it. He can come nearer beating luck itself than anybody I know."

Hagen, however, made some of his own luck through skill with a deadly short game that enabled him to recover from wayward drives and approach shots. He made the same swing with different short clubs, his chipping stroke crisp, his weight on his left foot. His putting stance was wide and somewhat open, his left foot pulled three to four inches farther back than his right from the main target. He said, "Gripping the putter too tightly is one of the surest ways to miss. Probably the single thing is to feel that you are going to hole the putt, then stroke the ball right away." Hagen had a wide, baseball-style stance, his head well back of the ball, much like Bobby Jones and JACK NICKLAUS. He held his head position until after impact, when he allowed the weight of the moving clubhead to pull his arms, shoulders, and head forward and upward. He had difficulty with the longer clubs because there was an incompatibility between his swing style and the whippy, wood-shafted clubs of his day. His lower body tended to be a bit ahead of his hands on the downswing, putting a bit too much stress on the club shaft. To remedy this problem, he put a slight bend in the shafts of his wood clubs at the bottom of the grip so that the clubhead would more likely be square at impact.

Hagen played his first U.S. Open in 1913, at the Country Club in Brookline. A year earlier, he had watched JOHNNY MCDERMOTT win his second consecutive U.S. Open at the Country Club of Buffalo. The twenty-year-old Hagen assured McDermott before the first round at the Country Club that he'd "come down to help you fellows stop Vardon and Ray." However, it was local amateur FRANCIS OUIMET, also a twenty-year-old ex-caddie, who would defend America's honor by scoring an upset victory over the British champions, HARRY VARDON and TED RAY, in a play-off. Hagen acquitted himself well, though, shooting 73-78-76-80=307 to finish in a four-way tie for fourth.

Hagen won his first U.S. Open in 1914 at the Midlothian Country Club near Chicago. He shot a course-record 68 the first round, then followed with 74-75-73 to finish at 290, tying George Sargent's record-low score to win by a stroke over amateur CHICK EVANS. At this stage of the game, the Europeans were still the best golfers, but Hagen would soon lead professionals to celebrity status and American golfers to the top ranks in the world. Walter won his second U.S. Open in 1919 at the Brae-Burn Country club in West Newton, Massachusetts. He tied Mike Brady at the end of regulation with a score of 301. Hagen had finished 1-under-par in the final six holes of regulation to catch Brady, who soared to an 80 on the final round. Noted for his gamesmanship and smelling blood, Hagen mentioned to Brady on the second tee of the play-off, "Mike, if I were you, I'd roll down my shirtsleeves." "Why?" Brady asked. Hagen replied, "Everyone in the gallery will see your muscles quivering." Hagen went on to win, 77–78, and at age twenty-six, he had his second Open championship. But it was his last, although he competed in this event until 1937.

Then the professional at Oakland Hills, Hagen decided in 1919 to become a full-time tournament professional, the first American golfer ever to do so. Hagen played his best golf in the 1920s and in the process put himself on the international golf map by winning the British Open (1922, 1924, 1928, 1929), the French Open (1920), and the Belgian Open (1924). He became the first American to win both the U.S. Open and the British Open when he won the 1922 British Open by one stroke over George Duncan and JIM BARNES at Sandwich in England. Perhaps his most gratifying British Open win was in 1928 when, having lost a challenge match to Archie Compston, eighteen and seventeen, earlier in the year, Hagen won the Open, again at Sandwich, by two strokes over Gene Sarazen. Compston finished third.

Hagen was the captain of the first Ryder Cup team in 1927 and played in all the Ryder Cup matches until 1937. His overall record is 7-1-1. He set the precedent for the international professional golf traveler because he was the first who, unaffiliated with a club, could generate enough income through exhibitions, tournament earnings, endorsement deals, and other golf-related enterprises. He traveled in North America, South America, Europe, Asia, and Africa, as did Gene Sarazen, his contemporary. Always the showman, he was accompanied by Joe Kirkwood, the famous trick-shot artist. By this time Hagen was wearing fashionable pinstripes, cashmere sweaters, paisley ascots, and two-tone custom-made shoes. He traveled with an entourage, usually in a large chauffeur-driven car such as a Pierce-Arrow or a Stephen-Duryea. His sports psychology seemed to be wine, women, and song. And one of his favorite phrases was "Never Hurry. Never Worry."

Hagen died of cancer at age seventy-six. He lived out his later years in Traverse City, Michigan. Gene Sarazen acknowledged the debt all professional golfers have to Hagen: "Golf never had a showman like him. All the professionals who have a chance to go after the big money today should say a silent thanks to Walter every time they stretch a check between their fingers. It was Walter who made professional golf what it is." Hagen had raised the status of the golf professional at a time when he was not allowed into the locker rooms of private clubs to change during tournaments. In later life Hagen observed, "[It's] amusing how deadly serious the businessmen pro of the new day were." Hagen was the individualist-entrepreneur who knew that golf was part entertainment. The game would later become a corporate enterprise.

Hagen was the greatest money player of his time. He is credited with forty Tour wins during an era when there were a limited number of events. This places him tied for seventh with CARY MIDDLECOFF on the all-time list. Hagen is in the World Golf Hall of Fame.

10

Gene Sarazen

1902–1999

I've got mine. Let them get theirs.
—GENE SARAZEN, after finishing with
a score of 288 in the 1922 U.S. Open

Gene Sarazen, along with WALTER HAGEN and BOBBY JONES, put American golf on the map in the 1920s and 1930s, replacing Great Britain as the standard for international golf excellence. The son of a carpenter and born Eugene Sarceni in 1902 in Harrison, New York, Gene went against his father's wishes and decided to become a professional golfer. He had caddied at the Apawamis Golf Club in Rye, New York, and later became a clubmaker and an assistant professional. He won his first Tour event, the New Orleans Open, in 1920, and the next year defeated "superstar" JOCK HUTCHISON in an early-round PGA Championship match at the Inwood Country Club. In 1922 he defeated Walter Hagen in a challenge match over seventy-two holes, thirty-six at the Oakmont Country Club and thirty-six at the newly opened Westchester Country Club.

Sarazen played on instinct. His swing was short and compact, befitting his short, sturdy physique. He was innovative, developing playing techniques that suited him alone. He liked thick handles on his clubs but had small, pudgy hands, requiring him to hold the club in a "baseball" grip and interlock the little finger of his right hand with the index finger of his left. A poor bunker player at first, Sarazen designed the first modern sand wedge. His improvement on earlier versions of the wedge revolutionized his game and that of others. A skillful self-promoter and creative thinker, Sarazen once insured himself for $400,000 against injury to his hands, suggested a Tour fund to which every golfer in America (4 million at the time) would contribute ten cents for a professional prize pool, and advocated that the width of the golf hole be expanded to eight inches in diameter rather than four and a quarter.

Sarazen backed up his bravado on the golf course. He won his first U.S. Open in 1922 at Skokie Country Club in Glencoe, Illinois. This was the first Open in which spectators were charged admission. Sarazen, then twenty, had already competed in Opens but was still an unknown. He began the final round four strokes behind the leaders, Bobby Jones and "Wild" Bill Mehlhorn. Deciding it was first place or nothing, Sarazen began to make long putts and execute daring approach shots to card a final-round total of 68 and a 72-hole score of 288. While waiting for the favorites to finish, Sarazen commented, "I've got mine. Let them get theirs," when asked how he felt. As it turned out, no one could match him. Bobby Jones and John Black finished second at 289. Gene won the PGA Championship at Oakmont in August of that year, becoming the first player to win the U.S. Open and the PGA Championship in the same year. He won a total of three PGA Championships (1922, 1923, 1933), his second coming against Walter Hagen, whom he defeated, 1-up, in a classic final at the Pelham Country Club in Pelham Manor, New York. Tied at the end of their regulation thirty-six-hole match, the contest went into sudden-death overtime. On the second extra hole, Sarazen hit a magnificent recovery shot to within inches of the pin. Hagen almost holed his wedge after his approach found a green-side bunker, but it was not enough. Sarazen closed him out with his birdie.

Sarazen won one more U.S. Open in 1932 at Fresh Meadows on Long Island. Earlier in the year, Sarazen developed his new sand wedge and was using it for the first time. After playing two conservative rounds that left him five shots behind the leaders, Sarazen adopted a more aggressive approach. He shot a 70 his third round for a total of 221, one shot off the pace. He then finished with a record score of 66 to win the championship by three strokes. With the help of his sand wedge, he had totaled only a hundred strokes on the last twenty-eight holes.

Shortly before winning his second U.S. Open, Sarazen ventured to Sandwich, England, to compete in the British Open at Royal St. George's. Up until this time, his highest finish in the Open was second place, behind Walter Hagen, in 1928, also at Sandwich. Traveling to the British Open was an expensive proposition, especially during the Great Depression. But Sarazen wanted to win badly and confided to Hagen in 1928, "I've invested thousands of dollars coming over, and I'll probably go right on doing it until I win that title or get too old to play." Sarazen, at Hagen's suggestion, used his old caddie, Skip Daniels, who knew Sandwich quite well. Hagen believed that one of the keys to winning a British Open was having a good caddie. Sarazen led after every round to win the 1932 British Open with a score of 70-69-70-74=283, five shots better than MACDONALD SMITH. Sarazen joined JIM BARNES, TOMMY ARMOUR, and Walter Hagen as the only golfers to win the three majors in professional golf.

The original sports "shot heard round the world" was not Bobby Thomson's home run against the Dodgers in the 1951 National League play-off game but Gene Sarazen's double eagle at the 1935 Masters. The Masters began as an informal invitation-only event in 1934, shortly after Bobby Jones and Alister Mackenzie designed Augusta National. It was only later that the Masters was considered a major, and Sarazen's dramatic victory in 1935 helped to increase interest in it. Seventy-two golfers competed in the first Masters, then called the "First Annual Invitation Tournament at Augusta." Sixty-three golfers teed it up at the Masters in 1935. Sarazen started with rounds of 68-71-73 and was three shots behind Bobby Cruickshank going into the final day of play. The course was rain-soaked and the weather near freezing as Sarazen began the fifteenth hole, a 485-yard par 5. Sarazen's tee shot was hit approximately 265 yards, leaving him 220 yards to the green. Sarazen, who was playing with Walter Hagen, knew that Craig Wood had birdied the eighteenth to finish with a 73 and a total of 282 to take the lead. Sarazen would need three birdies on the last holes to tie. Golf journalist Tom Flaherty, in *The Masters: Profile of a Tournament* by Dawson Taylor, describes what happened:

> Sarazen turned away from his ball in the wet fairway grass and peered down the long slope to the 15th green, 220 yards away. A freezing wind disturbed the flag and ripped through his protective sweater. . . . Before the green lay a pond. Not much of a pond, really, perhaps forty feet across at its broadest. It protected the green as well as a moat protects a castle. Yet it was no obstacle to an easy birdie for the player who could put together two excellent shots and was willing to gamble. Gene Sarazen was that gambler. He reached for his favored 4-wood, took another quick glimpse ahead through the mist, and swung away. He watched his ball as best he could as it sailed up into the haze and over the moat to the 15th green. It dropped on the apron, popped up twice on the turf, and rolled steadily toward the cup as though homing on a magnet. A thousand voices in the gallery screamed as the ball disappeared into the cup for a double-eagle 2.

In fact, there were not many observers on that nasty day. Sarazen then parred in to force a play-off with the stunned Wood, who had already been prematurely congratulated as the winner.

Sarazen won the thirty-six-hole play-off, 144–149, the next day. His miracle shot and his subsequent win put the Masters on the map as a major event. From that time forward it received extensive press coverage and eventually became one of golf's modern Grand Slam tournaments. Gene Sarazen was the first golfer to win all four: the Masters, U.S. Open, British Open, and PGA Championship. Only Ben Hogan, Jack Nicklaus, Gary Player, and Tiger Woods have done it since. (Only Bobby Jones has done it in the same year, with a different mix of tournaments: the British Amateur, British Open, U.S. Open, and U.S. Amateur, all in 1930.)

Although Sarazen was only thirty-two years of age, his Masters victory was his last major-tournament win. He did finish third in the 1936 Masters and second in the 1940 U.S. Open. He is credited with winning thirty-eight PGA events, placing him ninth on the all-time list, just

behind Walter Hagen and CARY MIDDLECOFF, who won forty. Sarazen
has been active in a variety of golf business ventures over the years,
including Shell's pioneering television show *The Wonderful World of
Golf*. His book *Thirty Years of Championship Golf* (1950), written with
Herbert Warren Wind, is a classic and still in print. Known as "the
Country Squire" because of farmland he once owned in the Northeast,
Sarazen remained fit and active in his later years. He continued to play
in the British Open until 1973. That year, at Troon, the seventy-one-
year-old Sarazen holed his tee shot on the 126-yard, par-3 "Postage
Stamp" hole. He also found time to hit the honorary first ball at the
Masters on several occasions. Gene Sarazen will always be remembered
as one of America's great golfers during the Golden Age of Sports in
the 1920s. He is a member of the World Golf Hall of Fame.

11

Harry Vardon

1870–1937

Henry, my boy, never give up your golf, it may be useful to you one day.

—Advice to Harry Vardon at age twenty
by an employer, MAJOR SPOFFORD

Harry Vardon is one of those rare golfers who raised the level of the game and had a lasting influence on the sport. The son of a gardener, Henry "Harry" Vardon was born in Grouville, Jersey, a channel island in England in 1870. He attended the Gory village school, whose headmaster was Aubrey Boomer, the father of golf champion Aubrey Boomer and golf teacher Percy Boomer. As a child, Vardon amused himself by constructing and playing a rudimentary four-hole short course. He made his own golf balls and clubs, becoming quite adept as a clubmaker. He didn't have real clubs until he was seventeen years of age. He worked as a caddie but played only sporadically because of the various jobs that he held in order to contribute to his large family, which included seven brothers and sisters. He was working as an apprentice gardener at age twenty when his brother Tom, a club professional (and then considered a better golfer than Harry), urged him to take a job as a professional at the Studley Royal Golf Club at Ripon in Yorkshire.

Harry soon moved to the Bury Club in Lancashire, where he was able to play in more competitive match-play events and develop his game. Vardon, 5 feet 9 inches and lean, was long off the tee, using an upright stance rather than the then-conventional, slashing St. Andrews swing. He used an open stance and at the beginning employed the conventional palm grip of his era. He eventually adopted the overlapping grip, pioneered by such golfers as J. E. Laidlay, because he felt the right hand tended to overpower the left at impact with the palm grip. In his book *My Golfing Life* (1933), Vardon explained how he concluded that the overlapping grip helped to coordinate both hands with the rest of the body while swinging the golf club:

> It is absolutely incorrect to assume that the arm, or the wrists, or the hands have to be especially applied when hitting a golf ball. The one important thing that really matters is the club head, and the hands, wrists and arms should be considered as part of the club, all working together as one piece of machinery. This being the case, I set to work to try out different ways of gripping the club. After trials with many methods, I arrived at the conclusion that the overlapping grip answered the purpose better than any other.

This grip, which later become popularly known as the Vardon grip, enabled the ball to carry farther and would later serve Vardon well in his famous match-play showdown with WILLIE PARK JR. in 1899.

As Vardon's game improved and as he was tested in more matches, he grew to appreciate the value of practice as he explained in his book *My Golfing Life*: "There is not the slightest shadow of doubt that the continued success of American golfers year after year in the British Open Championship is the result of time which they put regularly practising their strokes. I came to the conclusion at Bury that if I was to achieve any success in the golfing world, I must give some serious thought to my game. . . ." Evidently Vardon's practice paid off when he won his first of a record six British Opens at Muirfield in 1896. Earlier in the year, he became professional at Ganton in Yorkshire and defeated J. H. TAYLOR, the defending British Open champion, eight and six, in a thirty-six-hole challenge match. Vardon's Open victory was gained in a thirty-six-hole play-off with Taylor, 157–161, after they had tied at 316 after seventy-two holes.

Vardon later recalled his feelings after he won his first major title: "It was an occasion that I will never forget as long as I live. To achieve the greatest ambition a golfer can aspire to prevents anyone from having clear, distinct thoughts. This is how it seemed to me. With the cheering all around me and with everyone talking at the same time, I was too stunned to have any more feelings than those." Vardon had now become a member of "the Great Triumvirate," which included Taylor, who would win five Opens, and JAMES BRAID, who would do the same. Four of Vardon's six Open wins (1896, 1898, 1899, 1903) were won with nine golf clubs: two woods, six irons, and a putter. This was before the era of matched sets of clubs, which became prevalent in the 1930s. Vardon's first three Opens were won with the gutta-percha ball, handmade from Asian rubber, which replaced the featherie ball in the late 1840s. When the new Haskell rubber-cored ball was introduced at the turn of the century, Vardon and most other golfers had to adjust their games. Vardon saw the advent of the rubber-cored ball as the beginning of the end of domination by British golfers: "I am firmly convinced that with its passing much of the real skill of golf was gone forever. . . . The advent of the rubber ball was instrumental in creating an entirely different method of striking the object. The solid ball required to be hit for carry, whereas it was quickly apparent that the Haskell lent itself to an enormous run." Vardon felt that hitting for distance would overshadow shotmaking, putting the British golfer at a disadvantage.

Vardon won his second British Open championship at Prestwick in 1898, defeating Willie Park Jr., the pride of Scotland, by one stroke. Park, noted for his putting and overall short game, then challenged Vardon to a thirty-six-hole match-play face-off, held at North Berwick, one of Park's home courses, and Ganton, Vardon's club, in the spring of 1899. Before a crowd estimated at seven thousand, Park held his own at North Berwick, making many brilliant recovery shots, but when the final eighteen holes were played at Ganton, Vardon pulled away to a decisive

11-up victory. Vardon believed that Park lost because his game didn't fit the course: "My prediction regarding the first three holes turned out to be correct. I won all three. Park failed, as I had thought to be the case, to carry hazards from the tee with his drives." Vardon noted that Park's old-style Scottish technique, hitting a low, running hook off the tee, was not suited to situations like the first three holes at Ganton, where a long carry is required.

Besides Vardon's British Open victories, he advanced the game of golf by conducting a series of exhibitions on a tour of North America in 1900 sponsored by A. G. Spalding, the sporting-goods impresario who was seeking to popularize golf in North America. This tour served to promote golf, then nascent in the United States. Some of Vardon's observations about Americans were amusing as well as insightful:

> The Americans seemed to appreciate the way I hit my tee shots for carry. When they saw the ball driven high in this manner, it appealed to them as resembling a home run in their national sport, baseball. Their interest in how the different strokes were executed was quickly aroused, and it was almost laughable to hear the many heated arguments about how I achieved my results. The Americans quickly grasped any particular point which they thought was an important part of the swing, and no technical detail, however small, appeared to escape them. This kind of interest in the mechanics of the swing was new to me.

Vardon returned to Britain in mid-tour, finished second to J. H. Taylor in the British Open at St. Andrews, then returned to the United States to win the U.S. Open with a score of 313 at the Chicago Golf Club.

The British, led by the Great Triumvirate, were clearly masters of the golf universe. But a young American amateur by the name of FRANCIS OUIMET later slew the Goliaths by defeating Vardon and countryman TED RAY in a playoff at the Country Club in the 1913 U.S. Open. Ironically, Vardon did more to popularize golf in the United States than his grand tour and U.S. Open win did in 1900. In one last brave attempt in 1920, Vardon, then fifty years of age, was the victim of a driving rainstorm on the final day of the Open at Inverness and lost a six shot lead with seven to play, struggling home to finish one stroke behind Ted Ray. Vardon made these observations about how far American golf had come since his 1913 visit:

During my previous visit I found that it was the tendency of players in the U.S. to indulge in an excess of wild swiping. They were to a great extent a nation of hookers. Their courses required considerable alteration. The design did not emphasize that basic element of tournament golf: the skill to keep the ball on the fairway. Now, seven years later, I found all this changed. The courses had been vastly improved, and it was now necessary to drive both accurately and long if good scores were to be had. Golf, in short, was not only booming, but the level of skill in which it was being played had risen dramatically.

Vardon gradually adjusted to the new golf ball, which he started to use in tournament play after Sandy Herd won the 1902 British Open with the rubber-core ball. Vardon managed to win the 1903 Open at Prestwick by shooting 73-77-72-78=300 with the rubber-cored ball to win by six shots over his brother Tom. He was newly appointed professional at South Herts, north of London, but he was having health problems due to recurring tuberculosis, which weakened him in the Open.

In 1903, shortly after the Open, Vardon hemorrhaged from the lungs and was taken to Mundesley-on-Sea in Norfolk, where he recuperated for many months. He recovered and came back to win the Open in 1911 and 1914, his record sixth win at age forty-four. Vardon was head professional at South Herts until his death in 1937. Along the way, he authored many golf books, including *The Complete Golfer* (1905), *How to Play Golf* (1912), *Progressive Golf* (1920), and *My Golfing Life* (1933). When Ryder Cup championships are held in Britain, it is traditional for the U.S. team to make a pilgrimage to Vardon's grave in Totteridge, near the South Herts club. He is a member of the World Golf Hall of Fame.

12

Tom Watson

1949–

This is what it's all about, isn't it, Jack?

—TOM WATSON to Jack Nicklaus at the
fourteenth tee of the final round of
the 1977 British Open at Turnberry

Tom Watson was born in Kansas City, Missouri, in 1949. His father, Raymond, was an insurance broker and a scratch golfer who inspired Tom to play. Young Watson began hitting golf balls when he was six, using a cut-down mashie, similar to a 7-iron. Stan Thirsk, a former Tour player and professional at the Kansas City Country Club, began to work with Tom when he was ten, helping to develop Tom's upright swing, which he took back high and in a U-shape, then quickly brought his club down with strong left-hand action and considerable leg drive. Watson learned early to work the ball on a golf course, showing his intelligence and his interest in learning to play different kinds of shots. At age thirteen he shot a 67 and at fourteen he won the Kansas City Match Play Championship. At age eighteen he played an exhibition match against JACK NICKLAUS and lost by two strokes. While in high school, he won the state high school golf championship and also played quarterback on the football team and guard on the basketball team. He won the Missouri Amateur four times. Watson attended Stanford, as did his father and both brothers. After graduating with a degree in psychology in 1971, he joined the PGA Tour.

After a slow start on the Tour, Watson began to take lessons from BYRON NELSON in 1974. That year, he tied for fifth in the U.S. Open at Winged Foot after leading the tournament after fifty-four holes. He won his first major when he captured the British Open title in a play-off at Carnoustie in 1975, the first of his five Open wins, tying him with J. H. TAYLOR, JAMES BRAID, and PETER THOMSON for second in all-time Open wins, just behind HARRY VARDON's six. Watson scored 71-67-69-72 to tie Jack Newton at 279 in the Open. Going into the final round, more than ten players had a chance to win, and on the final few holes it came down to five players: Watson, Newton, Bobby Cole, JOHNNY MILLER, and Jack Nicklaus. Watson's birdie at the 448-yard, par-4 finishing hole enabled him to tie Newton; Nicklaus, Cole, and Miller finished one shot back at 280. The eighteen-hole play-off was also decided at the final hole. The match all even, Watson parred and Newton bogeyed after bunkering his approach to finish with a score of 72, one behind Watson. Watson thus became one of three Americans to win the British Open the first time they entered. The others were BEN HOGAN, in 1953 at Carnoustie, and TONY LEMA, in 1964 at St. Andrews.

Watson's other Open wins were in 1977 (Turnberry), 1980 (Muirfield), 1982 (Troon), and 1983 (Royal Birkdale). The most memorable of these is the Watson-Nicklaus duel in the sun at Turnberry in 1977.

Watson had won the 1977 Masters by two shots over Nicklaus, and they renewed their battle for supremacy at Turnberry. At the end of three rounds, Watson and Nicklaus had outdistanced the field with identical scores of 68-70-65= 203, making it a two-man showdown for the championship. Like heavyweight fighters exchanging blows, each player traded shots without yielding ground. On the fourteenth tee, Watson, whose gap-toothed Huckleberry Finn smile sometimes concealed a killer instinct, had said to Nicklaus, "This is what it's all about Jack, isn't it?" Nicklaus agreed. At the end of seventy holes, the match was all even. They both hit good drives at the par-5 seventeenth; then Watson put his 3-iron approach about twenty-five feet above the hole. Nicklaus hit a 4-iron to the right edge and chipped to within six feet. Tom two-putted for his birdie, but Jack lost a stroke when he missed his putt. On the 430-yard, par-4 finishing hole, Watson hit a crisp 1-iron into perfect position, but Nicklaus pushed his drive into the thick rough. Watson then hit a brilliant 7-iron approach to within three feet of the pin, and Nicklaus slashed a heroic 8-iron to within thirty-five feet. Jack then drained his putt to put some pressure on Watson, but Tom's putt was too easy, and he holed it to win the championship. Watson's final-round 65 gave him a total score of 268, lowering the British Open record by eight shots. HUBERT GREEN, the U.S. Open champion, was third, eleven shots back.

Watson became the fifth player to win the Masters and the British Open the same year. The others were Hogan, ARNOLD PALMER, and Nicklaus (twice) up to this point. Later, NICK FALDO (1990) and MARK O'MEARA (1998) would duplicate the feat. Tom won the Masters again in 1981, leaving Nicklaus and Johnny Miller in second place, two shots behind. Nicklaus was four shots ahead of Watson with opening rounds of 70-65, but his last two rounds of 75-72=282 did him in. Miller finished with a strong round of 68, for a total of 282, but it was too little too late. At this stage of his career, Watson was considered one of the best players in the world and one of the best golfers ever. He won the money title four consecutive years (1977–80) and another in 1984. He led the Tour in wins five consecutive years (1977–81). He won the Vardon Trophy for lowest scoring average in 1977 (70.32), 1978 (70.16), and 1979 (70.27). And he was named PGA Player of the Year six times (1977–80, 1982, 1984).

But his showdowns with Jack Nicklaus in major championship play were not over. Their rivalry compared with the great pairings of American golf, including Nicklaus and Palmer, Nicklaus and LEE TREVINO, SAM SNEAD and Hogan, Hogan and Nelson, WALTER HAGEN and GENE SARAZEN, and Hagen and BOBBY JONES. The 1982 U.S. Open was played at Pebble Beach, a course Watson had played frequently during his college days at Stanford, in nearby Palo Alto. Watson had never won an Open, and it didn't look as if he would win in 1982 when he recorded a thirty-six-hole score of 144, leaving him five strokes off the lead. Nicklaus was also at 144 at the halfway point but shot 71 to pull within three shots of the lead, held by Bill Rogers and Tom Watson, who had a third-round score of 68. Nicklaus, playing four twosomes ahead of Watson the final round, ran off five consecutive birdies on holes number three through seven to tie for the lead. Nicklaus played the front nine in 33 and finished with a 36-69=284 and waited in the clubhouse for Watson. Rogers and other contenders dropped out of contention. After Watson bogeyed the sixteenth, he was tied with Nicklaus. The par-3 seventeenth hole at Pebble Beach was set up to play 209 yards that day. Watson elected to hit a 2-iron but was a little quick with his swing, and the right-to-left shot caught the weedy rough to the left of the green, two feet from the edge and approximately twenty feet from the pin. It looked as if Watson would have a par at best and more likely a bogey because of the thick rough and the downslope of the green flowing away from him. Watson, a deadly putter (until he ran into problems later in his career) and a skilled wedge player, saw that he had a fluffy lie rather than a buried one. When his caddie said, "Get it close," Watson replied, "I'm not going to get it close; I'm going to make it." Watson played a quick, slicing wedge through the deep grass and lobbed the ball just on the green; it hopped twice and curled in the hole for an improbable birdie 2. He then birdied the famous oceanside par-5 finishing hole to win by two strokes with a score of 282. Watson would later say, "I've been dreaming about this moment since I was ten years old. It is the championship I most wanted to win, on one of my favorite golf courses." Nicklaus, always a gentleman in defeat, greeted the 5-foot-9-inch, 160-pound Watson at the eighteenth green: "You little son of a bitch, you're something else. I'm proud of you." Watson had denied Jack a record-fifth Open.

Watson's last best year was 1984 when he was named Player of the Year for a record-sixth time. He had won three times on the PGA Tour and finished second in the British Open and the Masters. The last of his thirty-three PGA victories was the 1996 Memorial, placing him eleventh in all-time Tour wins, behind LLOYD MANGRUM. Watson was a member of the 1977, 1981, 1983, and 1989 Ryder Cup teams. His Ryder Cup record is 10-4-1. He was captain of the 1993 Ryder Cup team that defeated the European side, fifteen and thirteen, at the Belfry in England. Watson was inducted into the World Golf Hall of Fame in 1988. He joined the Senior Tour in 1999 and has won $3.8 million through the 2002 season. He has also won the Senior Tour championship (2000, 2002) and the Senior PGA championship (2001).

13

Lee Trevino

1939–

I'm just trying to build up as big a lead as I can so I don't choke.

—LEE TREVINO, on his way to winning the 1968 U.S. Open

Lee Buck Trevino was born in 1939 in Dallas, Texas, and molded his swing on a local public course, sometimes improvising clubs from a large, taped Dr. Pepper bottle. He was born into extreme poverty and, raised by his grandfather, lived in a sharecropper's house with no electricity and no plumbing. There was, though, a golf course nearby. Lee learned to play golf and hustle bets on munis, and when he joined the marines at age seventeen, he was good enough to be selected for marine golf competitions. Initially a machine gunner for the Third Marine Division, Trevino spent the second half of his four-year tour in Special Services as a golfer. When he returned from the marines, he worked at a driving range and par-3 course, and with the encouragement of the owner, Hardy Greenwood, he honed his golf skills. Lee then went to El Paso to serve as professional and handyman at the Horizon Hills Country Club, where, in 1965, he defeated RAYMOND FLOYD in two of three head-to-head money matches. Trevino entered his first Tour event, the 1965 Texas State Open in Houston, and three years later he became the first man in history to shoot four subpar rounds in the U.S. Open, a 69-68-69-69=275, to win by four shots over JACK NICKLAUS at Oak Hill.

Many experts thought that Lee Trevino, with his self-made game, was a shooting star, a Jack Fleck who would never win another major. But he proved them wrong while competing against Hall of Fame golfers, including Nicklaus, ARNOLD PALMER, TOM WATSON, and BILLY CASPER. Trevino won his second U.S. Open at Merion in 1971, and again Nicklaus was the victim. Going into the final round of that tournament, the leader was Jim Simons, a twenty-one-year-old Walker Cupper. Nicklaus was two shots off the pace; Trevino, four behind. Paired with Simons in the third round when the amateur shot 65, Trevino usually lagged behind Simons as they approached the green, allowing him the applause and his day in the sun. On the final day, Simons held a one-stroke lead over Nicklaus and a two-shot lead over Trevino going into the back nine. By the fifteenth hole, Simons fell off the pace, and it seemed to be a contest between Nicklaus and Trevino. Trevino was one shot up on Nicklaus going into the par-4 finishing hole, but after his drive, he pushed a 3-wood into the crowd gathered around the green. He failed to get up and down, missing an 8-foot putt, and finished with a 69 and a total of 280. Nicklaus needed a par on the eighteenth to tie, and Simons, returning to the fray, needed a birdie 3. Simons faded to a 6 and finished third at 283. Nicklaus hit a drive and a 4-iron to within fourteen feet but could not sink his putt, which slid off the right edge.

On the following day, at the first tee of the eighteen-hole play-off, Trevino found a rubber snake in his bag while rummaging around for some tees and threw the snake toward Jack in jest. Jack laughed good-naturedly but found too many bunkers on the front nine, going out in 37, one stroke behind Trevino. At the fifteenth, Nicklaus was down two shots, with Trevino twenty-five feet away from the hole and his ball eight feet away for a birdie. Trevino made his putt, and Jack matched his birdie, gaining no ground. Jack hit into another bunker with his tee shot on the seventeenth and lost another stroke to Trevino, who shot a fine score of 68 to win his second Open by three shots.

Just how good a year did Trevino have in 1971? He was selected the *Sporting News* Man of the Year, the *Sports Illustrated* Sportsman of the Year, and the Associated Press Male Athlete of the Year. He won three national championships in less than a month. After his U.S. victory in the Open, he won the Canadian Open and in July, the British Open at Royal Birkdale. Trevino shot rounds of 69-70-69-70=278 to defeat Lu Liang Huan of Taiwan by a single shot in the British Open. Lee joined BOBBY JONES (1930), GENE SARAZEN (1932), and BEN HOGAN (1953) as the only Americans to win both the British and American Opens in the same year. He returned to Muirfield in 1972 to defend his title and again fought a classic battle against Jack Nicklaus. Trevino opened with rounds of 71-70-66=207 to lead Nicklaus by six going into the final round. Nicklaus, who had already won the 1972 Masters and U.S. Open, was bidding for a Grand Slam, but he was running out of holes. He dropped his conservative playing strategy, which did him little good the first three rounds, and pulled even with Trevino on the fifteenth.

With Trevino playing behind him, Nicklaus bogeyed the 188-yard, par-3 sixteenth, then parred out for a 66 and a total of 279. Trevino, playing the sixteenth, needed to par out to better Nicklaus's score, as did his playing partner, TONY JACKLIN, a British Open winner in 1969. Both Jacklin and Trevino parred the sixteenth; then, on the 542-yard, par-5 seventeenth, Trevino bunkered his tee shot, and Jacklin hit his up the middle. Trevino played out of the bunker and, still away, hit his third shot into the left rough, short of the green. Jacklin's 3-wood came up slightly short of the putting surface. Trevino's pitch came out hot and skidded across the green into the rough. It looked as if he had ruined his chances to win his second Open. Jacklin then hit a poor pitch, leaving himself a 15-foot putt. Trevino, disgusted with his predicament, quickly hit his wedge from the fringe before Jacklin even marked his ball. However, his shot was like a dagger to the heart, because it rolled into the cup. A stunned Jacklin missed his birdie putt by three feet and missed his par putt coming back. Jacklin was now down two strokes to Trevino, who briskly walked to the next tee, parred the final hole, and won by one shot over Nicklaus. Nicklaus missed his Grand Slam by a total of seven strokes, one at the British Open and six at the PGA Championship.

Trevino won twenty-seven PGA Tour events in his career (eighteenth all-time) and six majors, including two PGA Championships, two U.S. Opens, and two British Opens. He never could quite get used to Augusta National, both on and off the course. He felt the golf course was a high hitter's golf course, and he tended to be a low-ball Texas golfer, one of the best wind players of all time. His best finish in the Masters was a tie for tenth in 1975. Trevino won the Vardon Trophy for lowest PGA scoring average in 1970, 1971, 1972, 1974, and 1980. He was named PGA Player of the Year in 1971 and was the leading money winner in 1970 with $157,037.63. He was selected to the Ryder Cup team in 1969, 1971, 1973, 1975, 1979, and 1981, compiling a record of 17-7-6. He was captain of the 1985 Ryder Cup squad that was defeated by Europe, $16\frac{1}{2}$–$11\frac{1}{2}$, at the Belfry. Trevino won almost $3.5 million on the PGA Tour but has thrived on the PGA Senior Tour, which he joined in 1989. Trevino was the Senior Tour scoring leader in 1990, 1991, and 1992. He had twenty-nine victories through 2002, including the U.S. Senior Open (1990), PGA Seniors' Championship (1992, 1994), and the Tradition (1992), and has won over $10 million. Lee had no regrets leaving the Tour, explaining, "No way I'm going to play with flatbellies when I can play with roundbellies."

Elected to the World Golf Hall of Fame in 1981, Trevino was known as the "Merry Mex" on the tour. His humor was a way for him to relax, but it also goes back to his days at Horizon Hills, when he was a club pro. He commented,

> I believe my sense of humor comes out because I'm the last of the club pros who turned touring professional. I'm the last guy out there who sold someone a pair of shoes and gave lessons. You have to be a salesman in that pro shop. Tell your members a few jokes, laugh with them, even if it's just for five minutes. You're not there only to promote the game, but also to make the guy forget his work at the office, forget a bad marriage, forget illness. For that little moment you give him in the pro shop, when you're laughing and giggling and raising hell, you're something special to the member.

14

Billy Casper

1931–

Just get comfortable. Then stroke the putt the best way you know how. Don't try to copy anyone else, unless of course you're doing something drastically wrong, like aiming a foot off line or something.

—BILLY CASPER, on how to putt

William Earl Casper Jr. was born in San Diego, the same city that has produced GENE LITTLER, Mickey Wright, CRAIG STADLER, and other great golfers. Casper had an early reputation as a bit of a pool shark, which perhaps helped him develop into one of the finest putters the game has produced. He had a solid amateur career, attended the University of Notre Dame for a semester, then spent four years in the U.S. Navy before turning professional in 1954. In the early days, Billy was 5 feet 11 inches tall and weighed a portly 210 pounds. But he later followed a strict, if bizarre, diet due to allergies. Some of his meals included buffalo meat, elephant, whale, and other delicacies, which somehow enabled him to lose weight.

Casper, who patterned his game after his idol, BEN HOGAN, won his first golf tournament in 1956, the Labatt Open, and gradually rose to the level of golf's elite players, including ARNOLD PALMER, JACK NICKLAUS, and GARY PLAYER. Billy won his first major in 1959, the U.S. Open at Winged Foot, taking only 114 putts on those tricky Tillinghast greens. He used a Golfcraft Glasshaft mallet-headed putter as his magic wand in that event, although he later switched to Wilson equipment when he was made a member of their staff. Casper won his 1959 Open by one shot with a score of 71-68-69-74=282 to edge Bob Rosburg. Due to a rain-shortened Saturday, the Open had a final Sunday round of eighteen holes for the first time in fifty-nine years. Casper opened his round with five 1-putt greens, having concluded his fourth round with four consecutive 1 putts. On thirty-one of seventy-two holes, Casper had put his first putt in the cup.

Casper, unlike Hogan, didn't like to practice, preferring to go fishing as a way to relieve himself of golf cares. However, he practiced enough to win five Vardon Trophies (1960, 1963, 1965, 1966, 1968). He made his reputation with his second U.S. Open win against Arnold Palmer in 1966 at Olympic in San Francisco. By this time, Casper was on his new diet and had trimmed down to 185 pounds. Some commentators called him "Buffalo Billy" because of his dietary habits.

Palmer opened with rounds of 71-66-70=207 to take a three-shot lead over Casper. The two were paired the final day, and Palmer came out firing with a front-nine score of 32 to take a seven-shot lead over Casper and nine strokes over Nicklaus. Confident that he had the tournament won, Palmer turned his attention to breaking the U.S. Open record of 276 set by Ben Hogan at Riviera in 1948. Palmer needed a back-nine score of 36 and a total of 268 to set the record. Instead, Casper shot a 68, making up seven strokes on Palmer, who staggered in with a 39.

Casper has never been given enough credit for his performance on the final nine. He hit every fairway, shot a 32, and made up seven strokes in eight holes. He parred ten, to Arnie's bogey; they both birdied eleven; then Casper parred the 191-yard, par-3 twelfth, and Palmer bogeyed; both men parred fourteen; then Palmer bogeyed the short par-3 fifteenth; Casper birdied the 604-yard, par-5 sixteenth, Palmer bogeyed; then Palmer bogeyed the 435-yard, par-4 seventeenth to Casper's par, and the match was all even. Palmer then showed his heart and the charisma that made him "the King." Casper hit his drive on the eighteenth down the fairway, but Palmer hooked his drive into heavy rough on the left. He then hacked the ball out with a wedge and somehow reached the green. Palmer putted from thirty feet downhill and missed six feet to the right. But he holed his putt to match Casper's par, and the Open went into an eighteen-hole overtime. Palmer led at the turn, 33–35, in the play-off, but the back nine thwarted him. Casper tied Palmer at the eleventh when he birdied and Arnie bogeyed. Casper then holed a 55-foot birdie putt on the par-3 thirteenth to go ahead by a stroke. Casper finished 4-3-6 to Palmer's 5-5-7 and a 69–73 win. In regulation, Casper had used 117 putts and had no three-putt greens.

Billy Casper was named to seven consecutive Ryder Cup teams (1961–73) and compiled a record of 20-10-7. Casper was the nonplaying captain of the victorious 1979 Ryder Cup team that defeated the Europeans, 17–11, at Greenbrier. Casper won his last major, the 1970 Masters, again in a play-off, against Gene Littler. The previous year, Casper had tied for second with a score of 282, one stroke behind George Archer. In the 1970 Masters both Casper and Littler had makable birdie putts on the last two holes but had to settle for pars. Gary Player just missed the play-off by one stroke when he bogeyed the eighteenth on the final day. In the play-off, Casper one-putted six greens on the first seven holes and defeated Littler, 69–74.

Casper made his only serious run at the British Open in 1968 at Carnoustie when he led after three rounds but shot 78 on the final day to finish fourth, three shots behind the winner, Gary Player. Casper played in Britain many times and was a member of the British PGA but never had much success there. During his PGA career he won the money title in 1966 ($121,944.92) and 1968 ($205,168.67). He won the PGA Player of the Year Award in 1966 and 1970. Casper won fifty-one PGA tournaments, placing him sixth on the all-time list, one behind BYRON NELSON. Casper joined the Senior Tour in 1981 and has won nine times. He was elected to the World Golf Hall of Fame in 1978.

15

Nick Faldo

1957–

Big Jack. I just remember watching him hit the ball and thinking, I'd like a go at this.

—NICK FALDO, recalling watching Jack Nicklaus play on a televised broadcast of the 1971 Masters

Nicholas Alexander Faldo was born in Welwyn Garden City, England, also the birthplace of seed merchant Samuel Ryder, sponsor of the first official Ryder Cup matches. Faldo played in his first Ryder Cup match in 1977, at the age of twenty-one, and has played on more Ryder Cup teams (eleven) and won more points (twenty-five) than any other golfer in history. One of Faldo's most notable wins came on the final hole of the last day in his singles match against CURTIS STRANGE in the 1995 Ryder Cup at Oak Hill in Rochester, New York. Faldo, the ultimate grinder, dug out pars, while Strange recorded bogeys down the stretch, and the European team prevailed. This has been a recurring pattern in Faldo's career—other golfers faltering under tournament pressure while he somehow keeps himself together, especially in the majors.

Faldo became singularly obsessed with golf after watching JACK NICKLAUS win the 1971 Masters on television when Nick was thirteen. At 6 feet 3 inches and 195 pounds, Faldo was an excellent athlete, having been a swimmer, cyclist, and cricket player. An only child, he gravitated toward the solitary regime of a golfer, taking lessons at a nearby club and spending hours practicing. His father, in finance at a plastics company, and his mother, a cutter and pattern designer in a clothing business, encouraged him. Faldo remembers, "I was an only child. I believe that was the single most important factor in that part of my character that has led me to become a champion golfer. I was the apple of my parents' eye and received total encouragement in the pursuit of whatever interest—usually sporting—that grabbed me during my formative years."

After success as an amateur, he decided he was going to become a professional. He dropped out of school at age sixteen, and by age eighteen he had won eleven amateur championships. He briefly attended the University of Houston but, deciding he would better learn from experience on the European Tour, returned to England and at age nineteen turned professional.

In 1977, Faldo was named Rookie of the Year on the European Tour, finished eighth in the Order of Merit (tournament earnings), and in his first Ryder Cup, won two team matches and defeated TOM WATSON, then the Masters and British Open champion, in singles. Faldo began playing in the United States in 1981, and his first impressions of the American golf scene, as opposed to the then-limited opportunities in Europe, were: "America was a real eye-opener. To play week after week in glorious weather on courses that were in better condition than I believed possible and to experience the range of facilities provided for players—you felt if you couldn't play well there, you were never going to. It was on the first days of the American Tour that I learned what hard practice really meant."

Faldo won the Order of Merit in 1983 and the Sea Pine Heritage Classic on the American PGA Tour in 1984, but he could not seem to win a major tournament. He decided that his game and his swing needed an overhaul, so he went to David Leadbetter and, beginning in

1985, began to rework his technique. Leadbetter had estimated that it would take two years for Faldo to develop a reliable swing that would withstand tournament pressure. By 1987, Faldo's game started to come around. He posted four consecutive rounds of 67 and finished second in the Deposit Guaranty Classic in Mississippi. Faldo then won his first major, the 1987 British Open at Muirfield, with rounds of 68-69-71-71=279 to edge Paul Azinger and Roger Davis by one shot. Azinger had a three-shot lead after 63 holes and a one-shot lead going into the seventy-first, a par-5. Trying to reach the green in two, Azinger teed off with a driver, against the advice of his caddie, found a bunker, and then bogeyed the hole. Tied with Faldo, Azinger hit his approach into a bunker on the eighteenth and could not get up and down, costing him the tournament. Twelve Opens had been played at Muirfield since it began in 1860, and Americans had won the last three: Jack Nicklaus (1966), LEE TREVINO (1972), and Tom Watson (1980). Faldo became a national hero by becoming the first Englishman to win the Open since TONY JACKLIN in 1969. He was awarded an M.B.E. (Member of the British Empire) for his efforts.

Faldo almost won the 1988 U.S. Open at Brookline, losing in a play-off, 71–75, to Curtis Strange. He won his first of three Masters the following year when he shot rounds of 68-73-77-65=283 to tie Scott Hoch in regulation. Before starting the final round, he switched to a mallet-headed putter and promptly sank a 50-foot putt on the first hole for a birdie. Faldo played the front nine in 32 and then finished with four birdies on the six finishing holes to record a 65. Hoch parred the final hole to force a play-off but missed a downhill, left-to-right 2-foot putt on the first play-off hole, allowing Faldo, who had also bogeyed the hole, a reprieve. Nick took advantage of the opportunity and closed Hoch out on the second play-off hole, the 455-yard par-4 eleventh, by hitting a 3-iron approach to within twenty-five feet and sinking the birdie putt. During regulation play, Faldo had scored four consecutive fives on this hole. ,

In 1990, accompanied by his new caddie, Fanny Sunneson (one of the few female caddies in men's golf), Faldo found himself in another play-off after tying RAYMOND FLOYD with a score of 278 after seventy-two holes. Eleven was again a decisive hole for Faldo when Floyd pulled his 7-iron approach into the water. Faldo won the play-off with a par and became the first person to win consecutive Masters since Jack Nicklaus in 1971 and 1972. Faldo's last Masters win will be remembered more for GREG NORMAN's agonizing collapse than for Faldo's fine final round of 67. Norman, who had a history of coming in second in major tournaments, had a six-shot lead over Faldo after fifty-four holes, and it seemed that this provided enough of a cushion to win. But Norman's game came apart on the back nine, and he finished with a 78 to finish second, five shots behind Faldo. This was Norman's eighth second-place finish in a major. Faldo had made up ten shots over the last twelve holes to become the fifth person to win three Masters, along with Nicklaus (six), ARNOLD PALMER (four), JIMMY DEMARET (three), and SAM SNEAD (three).

Nick Faldo won his second British Open, at St. Andrews, in 1990, shooting the lowest total for any major win since Tom Watson's all-time low of 268 at Turnberry in 1977. Faldo shot rounds of 67-65-67-71= 270, five shots better than PAYNE STEWART and Mark McNulty. Faldo won his third Open at Muirfield in 1992. Leading by four shots after three rounds, Faldo came to the fifteenth tee on the final day two shots behind John Cook. He then birdied both the fifteenth and the seventeenth to overtake Cook, who bogeyed the final hole. Faldo finished with 66-64-69-73=272 to win by one stroke.

In 1992, at age thirty-five, Faldo had established himself as one of the best golfers of all-time. He had won six tournaments in 1992 and placed first in the European Order of Merit. At this writing he has won thirty-seven tournaments on the PGA and European tours. With his controlled swing, he is considered one of the best midiron players in the game. He is noted for his straight hitting off the tee and his mental toughness and determination. Elected to the World Golf Hall of Fame in 1997, Nick Faldo is the best English golfer since HARRY VARDON.

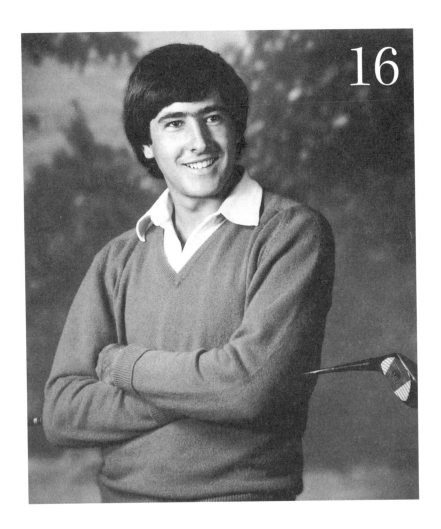

Seve Ballesteros

1957–

Seve Ballesteros can do things with a golf club that no one thought about before, let alone tried.

—LEE TREVINO

Severiano Ballesteros, a farmer's son, grew up in Pedrena, a small farming and fishing village in Spain. He began to play golf at the age of seven, starting out by experimenting with a rusty 3-iron head fitted to a shaft whittled from a stick. Golf balls were rare and expensive, so he developed his technique by hitting stones on the nearby beach. At age eight, Seve followed in the footsteps of his three elder brothers and became a caddie at the nearby Real Club Golf de Pedrena, one of the best golf courses in northern Spain. At age nine he advanced to a steel-shafted 3-iron and continued to experiment, improvise, and develop the magic golfing touch that would make him famous. Almost at once Seve could hit a real golf ball with it from near his family's house over a stand of pine trees onto the second green of the golf course 150 yards away. As his skills developed and his passion for the game increased, he would sneak onto the golf course, often at night, to play as many holes as he could. He measured his ball-striking progress by how close he could get to the 198-yard, par-3 second hole with his iron from the tee. He would later recall, "My ambition to reach that green with an iron was every bit as intense as my ambition to win a major championship."

He won his first caddie tournament at age twelve when he shot a 79 playing with a real set of golf clubs. At age thirteen, he was a scratch golfer, and on January 1, 1974, the sixteen-year-old Ballesteros became a professional golfer. This was six months after a friend of his brother, an American serviceman, gave him a brand-new set of clubs and a bag. In his first year on the professional circuit, Ballesteros's highest finish in seven European and five South African tournaments was second place in the Italian Open. In 1975 he competed fourteen times in European Tour events and once in Japan, with a third-place finish in the Lancome Trophy event in Paris his best performance. He advanced to the world stage when, at age nineteen, he led the 1976 British Open at Royal Birkdale after thirty-six holes, then tied for second with JACK NICKLAUS, six shots behind JOHNNY MILLER. Later that year, he helped Spain win the World Cup. A year later, he won the European Order of Merit.

Though a bit wild off the tee, Ballesteros was gaining a reputation for his brilliant iron play and his dramatic ability to recover. He soon led the advance of European golfers determined to end America's dominance in international golf. Ballesteros won his first major, the 1979 British Open, at Royal Lytham and St. Anne's. In the 1977 Open, Seve had finished fifteenth, behind winner TOM WATSON, after a weak 74-73 finish. The following year, he finished seventeenth, behind Jack Nicklaus. At the beginning of the final round of the 1979 Open, Seve trailed HALE IRWIN by two shots, with seven golfers in a position to win the tournament. Spraying the ball off the tee but hitting brilliant recoveries and putting well, Ballesteros took the lead by birdieing the thirteenth after nearly driving the green on that 339-yard par 4. Even though he played the next two holes in 1 over par, Seve moved two strokes ahead.

On the 356-yard, par-4 sixteenth, a strong left-to-right wind pushed Ballesteros's drive into the right rough in what was a makeshift parking lot. Allowed a free drop, he lofted a 9-iron to within twenty feet, then holed his putt for a birdie. Seve then scrambled for pars on the final two holes to finish with a round of 70, a tournament total of 283, and a three-shot win over Jack Nicklaus and BEN CRENSHAW, who finished tied for second.

In 1980, Ballesteros made a strong impression in the United States when, with a more disciplined game but with the same charismatic intensity, he won the Masters, becoming the youngest player to do so. He led the tournament by ten shots going into the final nine holes but, after a few wild shots, finished with a wire-to-wire win and a seventy-two-hole score of 275, four shots fewer than runners-up Gibby Gilbert and Jack Newton. He won the Masters again in 1983 with rounds of 68-70-73-69=280 to win by four shots over TOM KITE and Ben Crenshaw. RAYMOND FLOYD and CRAIG STADLER were tied for the lead going into the final round but faded to a 75 and 76, respectively. Seve's win signaled the European advance on American golf. BERNHARD LANGER from Germany won the Masters in 1985 and 1993; SANDY LYLE, a Scot, won it in 1988; NICK FALDO, an Englishman, won it in 1989, 1990, and 1996; IAN WOOSNAM, from Wales, won it in 1991; Spaniard JOSE-MARIA OLAZABAL won it in 1994 and 1999; and Vijay Singh, from Fiji, won it in 2000.

Ballesteros won his second British Open in 1984 at the Royal and Ancient Golf Club's venerable Old Course at St. Andrews. The issue was decided on the final hole when Seve, tied with Tom Watson, who was seeking a record-tying sixth Open, hit a solid recovery shot out of the rough to reach the green in regulation for the first time during the tournament. He picked up two strokes on his playing partner, Watson, who flew the green on his approach, was stymied against a stone wall, and finally dug his way to a bogey. Seve finished with a total of 69-68-70-69=276 to win by two over Watson and Bernhard Langer.

In a return to Royal Lytham, the scene of his first Open win, Ballesteros won his fifth major and third Open in 1988. Seve scored a final-round 65 for a seventy-two-hole total of 273 to edge NICK PRICE, his final-round playing partner. Rain washed out the third day of play, requiring Monday Open play for the first time in 128 years. Price and Nick Faldo had led at the end of three rounds with a total of 208, but then Seve parred the final hole with a brilliant wedge shot and a putt, after hitting his approach into the rough beyond the green, Price had to settle for second even though he had a final-round 69. Faldo finished third after a final-round 71. Seve graciously said of Price's performance, "It's a pity that there is only one champion."

Before Ballesteros was thirty years old, he had won over fifty tournaments worldwide. He further established his reputation as a money player and a leader through his Ryder Cup performances. The Ryder Cup expanded from a contest between American and British professionals to include European golfers in 1979. Ballesteros played on that first European team and in every Ryder Cup thereafter until 1997, when he was the nonplaying captain of the team at the Valderrama Golf Club in Soto Grande, Spain, the first time the Ryder Cup was contested on continental European soil. Seve's overall Ryder Cup record is 19-10-5, making him one of the best Ryder Cup competitors. He was a key player in 1985 when the Europeans reached international golf parity by defeating the United States, 16½–11½, at Sutton Coldfield in England. Seve scored 3½ points and his countryman, Manuel Pinero, 4½, in that victory. Ballesteros was also a big contributor (4 points) in Europe's 15–13 win at Muirfield Village in 1987, and in the 1989 14–14 tie at the Belfry (3½ points) that allowed Europe to retain the cup. Ballesteros and his foursomes and four-ball playing partner, José María Olazabal, have formed a successful partnership and are known as the Spanish Armada of Ryder Cup play.

The ultimate satisfaction for Ballesteros, the son of a poor fisherman, was to bring the Ryder Cup competition to Spain and to captain the victorious European team, which won, 14½–13½, and brought Europe's overall record to 4-5-1 since the Ryder Cup team was expanded to include Europe in 1979. Ballesteros had reaffirmed his position as a national hero and an inspirational golf leader, although he had never had the benefit of professional instructors or the ideal practice conditions of many of his more affluent contemporaries. In a way, Ballesteros is a throwback to the caddie-yard days when other former caddies, such as WALTER HAGEN, BEN HOGAN, BYRON NELSON, SAM SNEAD, and ARNOLD PALMER, found their own games. In his search to find his own golf game, Ballesteros felt he became a better player than if he had been more privileged. Seve was elected to the World Golf Hall of Fame in 1997. He has won seventy-two tournaments worldwide, including forty-eight on the European tour.

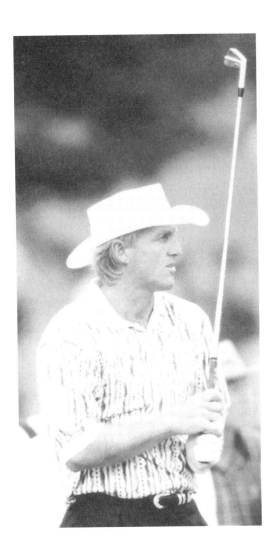

17

Greg Norman

1955–

Greg can only play one way—aggressively. When he tries to play conservatively, his brain short-circuits, his wires get crossed, and sparks start flying. He could change, but it would take months of programming help from a sports psychologist.

—JOHNNY MILLER, commenting on Greg Norman after the 1996 Masters

Greg Norman, "the Great White Shark," is the modern international golf conglomerate, taking to a new level what WALTER HAGEN, ARNOLD PALMER, and JACK NICKLAUS refined. Norman is a world-class golf champion who has competed internationally since he won his first professional tournament, the West Lakes Classic, in his native Australia in 1976. Millions in prize money and golf-business ventures later, he is a brand-name player, developer of instructional materials, golf-course architect, designer of golf equipment, golf-clothing purveyor, and more. Norman is among the leading all-time leading money winners on the golf course, having earned over $21 million worldwide; he has leveraged that into many millions more in revenue off the course. He has won over seventy-five golf tournaments worldwide, including two majors, the 1986 and 1993 British Opens.

But the flamboyant Norman, who exudes confidence and charisma as he moves about the golf course, his golden locks flowing from underneath a shark-logoed straw hat, is as noted for his heartbreaking losses, especially in the majors, as he is for his jet airplane, his $6-million yacht, or his multimillion-dollar business deals. Norman's most famous collapse in a major came in the 1996 Masters when, having shot rounds of 63-69-71, he had a seemingly insurmountable six-shot lead over NICK FALDO. But Norman then appeared to have lost control of his swing and his golf-course management skills as he dropped ten shots to Faldo on the last twelve holes, shot a final round of 78, and finished second by five shots. On the eighteenth green on the final day, Faldo walked over to Norman and said, "I don't know what to say. I just want to give you a hug." Norman later explained his collapse to George Peper, editor of *Golf* magazine: "Yeah, and I didn't know what to do. I knew that the problem was my swing, but I didn't know how to correct it. My swing had gone to a place I didn't know, and I couldn't retrieve it. Normally I can make things work. I can manufacture the shots, even on a bad day. But not that day."

On another occasion, Norman was snakebit at the Masters, but in an entirely different and less cruel way. In the 1987 Masters, Norman, SEVE BALLESTEROS, and Larry Mize were tied at 285 after seventy-two holes of play. On the first extra hole, a 485-yard par 4, Seve played himself out of it, but Norman was on the green in regulation, while Mize, who had pushed his approach shot to the right of the green, had to attempt a 40-yard chip shot. Mize, who was born in Augusta, Georgia, and had won only one PGA Tour event since joining the circuit in 1981, chipped in for a birdie, leaving a stunned Norman with a long putt to tie. Norman missed his effort, and Mize was the new Masters champion. The previous year, in 1986, Norman bogeyed the final hole to miss a chance to tie Jack Nicklaus and force a play-off.

Norman also had his problems in the PGA Championship, losing in dramatic fashion in 1984 at the Inverness Club in Toledo, Ohio. Norman led Bob Tway by four strokes after three rounds but lost when Tway holed a bunker shot on the seventy-second hole. Tway became the first PGA Champion to win with a birdie on the final hole. Norman's 76 on the last day enabled Tway to get within a position to win. In 1993, Norman tied Paul Azinger with rounds of 68-68-67-69=272 at the PGA, again at Inverness. Azinger had birdied four of the last seven holes to set a back-nine record score of 30 and catch Norman. Norman's birdie putt attempt on the seventy-second hole just grazed the hole, denying him an outright victory. On the first playoff hole, Norman missed another opportunity to win when his putt literally spun out of the cup. On the next hole, a 365-yard par 4, Norman three-putted from twenty feet, and Azinger was the winner. At this point in his career, Norman was the only man to lose all four major championships in play-off.

In 1984, Norman made a brilliant recovery to save par on the final hole of the U.S. Open at Winged Foot. He posted a score of 70-68-69-69=276 by birdieing the seventeenth and then sinking a 45-foot putt on the finishing hole. FUZZY ZOELLER tied Norman, however, and then easily won the eighteen-hole play-off with a score of 67 to Norman's 75. Norman finished second in the 1995 U.S. Open at Shinnecock Hills on Long Island when, after being tied with Tom Lehman after fifty-four holes, he shot a final-round 73 to lose to COREY PAVIN, who finished with a round of 68, by two shots. Norman had started out with rounds of 68 and 67 but then inched up to 74 and closed with a 73, eliminating his chances.

The British Open seems a bit more to Greg's liking. He won his first Open in 1986 at Turnberry with rounds of 74-63-74-69=280 to win by five over Gordon Brand. The rough was extremely high and the fairways very narrow at Turnberry, but Norman showed his determination and strength when he slashed a 7-iron out of the high grass on the 440-yard, par-4 fourteenth on the final round, hit the flagstick, and made his birdie putt. There would be no Norman collapse in this major. Norman had one of his best years in 1986. He won seven tournaments and the PGA money title ($653,296) even though he played only nineteen Tour events. He was ahead going into the final round of all four majors, and his total stroke margin in his three major losses was eleven shots.

Many critics were not so sanguine about Norman's judgment in the 1989 British Open when he shot a magnificent final-round 64 to tie Mark Calcavecchia and Wayne Grady for first place at Royal Troon with a score of 275. It looked as if Norman were in control in the early stages of the four-hole stroke-play play-off. He birdied the first two holes, then bogeyed the third, making him even with Calcavecchia and two up on Grady. After Calcavecchia hit a 3-wood up the right side, placing him well short of a fairway bunker, Norman then unaccountably hit a driver, bringing the bunker into play. His friend Jack Nicklaus, reporting on the tournament from a TV broadcast booth, was prompted to say, "I can't imagine what Greg is thinking taking a driver out here. The only thing he can do by hitting a driver is bring the bunker into play, which is the one place out there he wants to avoid." As fate would have it, Norman landed his ball in the bunker, played out safely with a wedge, and then hit his third shot into a bunker in front of the green. Calcavecchia safely landed his 5-iron approach onto the green. Norman, now desperate, hit his bunker shot out-of-bounds and never finished the hole. Calcavecchia won his first and only major to date. Norman redeemed himself in 1993 at Royal St. George's, shooting a British Open record score, 66-68-69-64=267, to win the Open by two shots over Nick Faldo. Greg's score of 267 eclipsed TOM WATSON's British Open record score of 268 at Royal Turnberry in 1977.

Two majors and more than seventy-five tournament victories is not a bad record for someone who took up golf at the age of sixteen in his native Australia. Norman's interest in golf began when he caddied for his mother, a three-handicapper, and he grew to like the game. His mother gave him two Jack Nicklaus instructional books, *Golf My Way* and *My 55 Ways to Lower Your Golf Score*. Greg turned professional in 1976 when he was twenty-one years old. He has won numerous honors, including three Arnold Palmer Awards as PGA leading money winner (1986, 1990, 1995), three Vardon Trophies for low scoring average (1988, 1989, 1994), and PGA Tour Player of the Year in 1995. He has won over $13.8 million on the PGA Tour, twelfth all-time, and has earned twenty victories, tying him for thirty-first. He also was selected to the first three President's Cup teams (1994, 1996, 1998, 2000). In 2001, Norman was elected to the World Golf Hall of Fame.

At 6 feet and 180 pounds, Norman is one of the most superbly conditioned athletes on the Tour. He claims he will play his best golf in his forties even though shoulder surgery in 1998 slowed him up. But the issue is not his physical skills; it is his ability to adapt his game and manage his play under major tournament pressure. In assessing Norman, his friend NICK PRICE indicates that this will not be an easy adjustment: "I don't want to stereotype, but Australians, generally, are very outgoing and friendly, very opinionated, and usually convinced they are a hundred percent right in every opinion they have. If you think about it, that's Greg."

18

Cary Middlecoff

1921–1998

*I was always so highly strung that I always tried to accept
the most negative outcome I could think of. I figured that
no matter how badly I missed the shot, I wasn't going to
die and probably wasn't even going to have a heart attack.*

—CARY MIDDLECOFF

Cary Middlecoff was born in Halls, Tennessee, into a family of dentists and surgeons. He became a dentist and a fine amateur golfer before serving in the Army Medical Corps in World War II. Middlecoff, a dentist in the army, relates: "I pulled seven thousand teeth before

I found out the army had another dentist." While still in the service, he won the North and South Open in 1945. He reached the quarterfinals of the U.S. Open in 1946 and was named to the Walker Cup team. Rather than play in the Walker Cup, he opted instead to turn professional in 1947 and won his first tournament as a pro, the Charlotte Open, that same year.

Middlecoff was a perfectionist who spent considerable time preparing for his shot. In addition to a variety of rituals addressing the ball, he might take as many as twenty looks at the target while standing over the ball. Middlecoff viewed it thusly: "The most important part of golf is getting ready for the shot. It takes a world of self-development and self-control. There is nothing unusual about learning and technique, but conquering the mental side is something else." Middlecoff was meticulous, indecisive, and nervous. He was known to pick up and drop out of a tournament if his play wasn't up to his standards, but most of the time he continued to grind away. He was tall and long off the tee but had a relatively short backswing and a somewhat small shoulder turn. He had excellent timing, and his ability to pause at the top of his swing gave his legs and hips time to clear and lead his forward swing. Middlecoff was also an excellent putter. One of his most famous was an 82-foot eagle putt that he holed on the par-5 thirteenth in the 1955 Masters.

Cary Middlecoff is often overlooked among golf's all-time greats. He won a total of twenty-five PGA Tour events, placing him twenty-fifth, along with JOHNNY MILLER. Middlecoff was one of the biggest money winners in American golf in the fifteen years following World War II. His first big year was 1949 when he won the U.S. Open and five other tournaments. The Open was played at Medinah, and while struggling to a first-round 75, Middlecoff almost quit after being 5-over-par after fourteen holes. But he rallied to shoot 67 and 69 on his next two rounds and was the leader going into the final eighteen. Clayton Haefner tied Middlecoff on the front nine of the last round, but Middlecoff was able to pick up a stroke on the home nine to win with a final-round score of 75 and a total of 286. SAM SNEAD tied for second.

Middlecoff led the Tour in wins in 1949 with seven, in 1951 with six, and in 1955 with six. Cary won his second major, the 1955 Masters, with the help of a 65 on the second round. He covered the front nine in 31, a new course record; then, highlighted by his eagle 3 at thirteen, he finished the back nine in 34. Middlecoff shot 72 on the next round to lead by four over BEN HOGAN. He finished with a score of 70, for a seventy-two-hole total of 279, to win by seven strokes over Hogan and eight over Snead.

At the height of his career, Middlecoff was considered the longest straight driver in the game. He was also a solid iron player and putter. All of these skills served him well at the 1956 U.S. Open at Oak Hill in Rochester. Sometimes called "the Rhubarb Open," the 1956 event was the scene of many arguments. A major issue was the professionals' threat to boycott the tournament because they viewed the total prize money as too small—$25,480 in total and $6,000 for first place—less than several PGA events. The pros agreed to play only after the equipment companies, which sponsored many of them, advised them to tee it up. Another dispute involved Middlecoff. He and his playing partner, JIMMY DEMARET, thought HENRY COTTON, the British champion, had nicked his ball while addressing it with a putter on the seventeenth. Cotton denied it, and the officials ruled that he did not have to take a penalty stroke.

Hogan and Middlecoff were 3–1 favorites to win the Open, but at the end of the first round, Bob Rosburg led with a 68. At the halfway point, PETER THOMSON, the twenty-six-year-old winner of two British Opens, took the lead with a score of 139. On the final day, fifty golfers made the cut and qualified to play the last thirty-six holes. Middlecoff took the lead at the end of the morning eighteen; then, coming into the final three holes with a three-shot lead, Middlecoff took two bogeys and was in trouble on the finishing hole when he hooked his drive into the rough and then hit his second shot short of the green and was still in the rough. Playing behind Middlecoff were Ben Hogan and JULIUS BOROS, one stroke from the lead. Middlecoff hit his wedge approach to within four and one-half feet. The ball trickled into a swale from which Cary had missed several putts during his practice rounds. Middlecoff made the necessary adjustments and dropped his tricky putt for a seventy-two-hole total of 281. Later, a relieved Middlecoff would say, "It was like a rattlesnake to me. It was absolutely the greatest shot I ever made." Hogan could not get his birdie to tie, and neither could Boros. They finished tied for second, one shot back. Ted Kroll, who was up one stroke with four to play, lost a stroke to par on the 441-yard, par-4 sixteenth, then triple-bogeyed the 463-yard, par-4 seventeenth to shoot himself out of contention. As BOBBY JONES once said, "No one ever wins the U.S. Open. Everyone loses it."

Middlecoff almost won the U.S. Open again at Inverness in 1957. He fell behind by eight shots at the halfway point but then fired a 68 in the third round. He worked his way into contention in the final round, needing birdies on the last three holes to tie. He hit an excellent drive on the 412-yard, par-4 sixteenth, pitched to within twenty feet, then made his putt. After parring the next hole, he reached the eighteenth in regulation, leaving himself a 9-foot putt. He deliberated over it for a seemingly endless amount of time but finally stroked in the hole for a round of 68 and a tie at 282 with Dick Mayer. Middlecoff, who had a history of hay fever and vulnerability to sunstroke, color blindness, back problems, and other maladies, was not able to cope with the stress and 100-degree heat and heavy humidity during that Ohio summer. He lost 72–79 in his eighteen-hole play-off with Mayer.

Middlecoff was selected to three Ryder Cup teams (1953, 1955, 1959) and had a 2-3-1 record. He won the Vardon Trophy in 1956 with a 70.41-stroke average. Cary Middlecoff won his last Tour event in 1961. A back ailment, which gave him chronic back pain from 1956 on, led him to undergo an operation in 1963 to remove a disc, effectively ending his golfing career. He is a member of the World Golf Hall of Fame.

19

Jimmy Demaret

1910–1983

Hey, I won it three times, and I never even got an outhouse.

—JIMMY DEMARET, wondering why a bridge wasn't
named for him at Augusta National

James Newton Demaret was born in Houston, Texas, in 1910, another great golfer to come out of the Lone Star State. His father was a carpenter-painter. Demaret was the fifth of nine children. At the age of nine he started to caddie at a local course with sand greens for fifteen cents a round. He ran barefoot until he was fifteen. By that time he had won the Houston scholastic golf tournament with a score of 74. At sixteen he was taken on by Jack Burke Sr. as an assistant at River Oaks Country Club. One of his jobs was to baby-sit JACK BURKE JR. who would later become his business partner.

After a short-circuited attempt to play on the California pro circuit, Demaret came back to Texas after losing his money, car, and clubs in a pool game in Mexico. He took a club job in Galveston, Texas, and mastered the fine art of playing shots in the wind. Demaret was a happy warrior who had a brief career as a nightclub singer and frequented clubs and other late-night establishments. During his early days, bandleader Ben Bernie and Sam Maceo, a Galveston nightclub owner, helped sponsor Demaret on the Tour. He was one of the most colorful golfers to come out of the Great Depression, one who realized that golf was a form of entertainment.

Demaret, considered one of the best low-ball wind players of his era, had a unique style. He addressed the ball with his feet close together, lined up to the left of the target. He would then push the club away from him until the hosel was near the ball, take his club back inside the line, and hit a controlled fade by cutting across the ball. A man with strong hands, Demaret had very little body movement on his swing but a great deal of hand action. Unlike BEN HOGAN, his ofttimes playing partner, Demaret did not spend much time on the practice range. Like most of his contemporaries, he preferred to work on his game by playing. A colorful dresser, he was a kaleidoscopic contrast to Hogan, who preferred basic white, gray, or black. Demaret wore plaid and other rakish hats at interesting angles, donned luminescent shirts and pants, and on occasion would wear knickers or shorts to brighten up his day.

But like another seemingly happy-go-lucky Texan, LEE TREVINO, Demaret liked to win and was a great competitor. During the 1930s he won five consecutive Texas PGA titles (1934–38), then returned to the Tour in 1940 and won six tournaments, including the Masters and the Western Open, which, at the time, had a more competitive field than the Masters. Demaret opened the 1940 Masters with a sensational score of 67 but found himself three shots behind LLOYD MANGRUM, who shot a 64. Demaret's 30 on the back nine tied the USGA record set by WILLIE MACFARLANE in the 1925 U.S. Open. Demaret then shot rounds of 72 and 70 to enter the final round one shot ahead of Mangrum. Demaret finished with a score of 280 to win by four shots over Mangrum and five over BYRON NELSON. On the last five holes, Demaret had putts for birdies or eagles, all within fifteen feet.

He was inducted into the navy in 1942 and was discharged from the military in 1945. Demaret held jobs as a club professional and would play fifteen to twenty PGA tournaments a year prior to the war. After winning three events in 1946, Demaret won six more in 1947, including his second Masters. He set the tone for his Masters victory in the first round when he made a spectacular recovery shot from the pond in front of the noted 520-yard, par-5 fifteenth, the same hole where GENE SARAZEN scored his double eagle in the 1935 Masters. Going for the green on his second shot, Demaret carried the pond fronting his target, but the ball hit the bank and slid back into the shallow water below. After surveying the situation, Jimmy removed his right shoe and sock, rolled up his trousers, then, after testing the water, took off his other shoe and sock and addressed the submerged ball, which was precariously resting on the steep slope just below the water. Under the rules, Demaret could not ground his club, nor could he test the water's depth. He somehow was able to slash his wedge through the water, lofting the ball to within four feet of the pin. He holed his birdie putt, shot a round of 69, then finished 71-70-71 to win the Masters by two shots over Byron Nelson and Frank Shanahan.

Jimmy Demaret led the Tour in earnings in 1947 with $27,936.83 out of a total pool of $352,500. He won the Vardon Trophy with a stroke average of 69.9. His six tournament wins, out of a total of thirty-one Tour events, was second only to Ben Hogan's seven. Demaret won three tournaments in 1948 and came close to winning the U.S. Open, finishing second to Ben Hogan at the Riviera Country Club. After opening rounds of 71-70 in that event, Demaret putted for a birdie on sixteen of eighteen greens in the third round and scored a 68. But Hogan also scored a 68 to hold a two-stroke lead. He then shot a final-round 69 to win by two shots over Demaret with a 276, a new U.S. Open record. Demaret's last best effort to win the Open was in 1957 at Inverness when he missed a play-off with coleaders Dick Mayer and CARY MIDDLECOFF by one stroke.

Demaret became the first player to win three Masters when he shot 70-72-72-69=283 to win in 1950. After his first two rounds, Demaret trailed Jim Ferrier by five shots, but Ferrier ballooned to 73-75 on the last two rounds to finish two shots off the pace. Ferrier, who was at the twelfth hole when Demaret finished his final round, needed to finish the final seven holes in 2-over-par to win the tournament. Instead, he could record only two pars on the final seven holes. Byron Nelson later recalled that after the members of Augusta National named three bridges after Gene Sarazen, Ben Hogan, and Nelson, Demaret jokingly said, "Hey, I won it three times, and I never even got an outhouse!"

Jimmy Demaret won a total of thirty-one official Tour events, six of them as a four-ball partner of Ben Hogan, placing him tied for thir-

teenth on the all-time list with HARRY COOPER, yet another Texan. He
was selected to the Ryder Cup team in 1947, 1949, and 1951. Demaret
played a total of six Ryder Cup matches and never lost. He won his last
PGA tournament, the Arlington Hotel Open, in 1957. Late in his career,
Demaret joined Jack Burke Jr. to own and operate the Champions Golf
Club in Houston. Demaret is a member of the PGA Hall of Fame.

Demaret is remembered for his sunny disposition, his sartorial
splendor, and his love of the game as much as for his considerable
accomplishments. He often knew when to fold them. When a struggling golfer asked Demaret for advice, Jimmy suggested, "Take two
weeks off—then quit the game." Ben Hogan once said, "He was the
most underrated golfer in history. This man played shots I hadn't even
dreamed of. I learned them. But it was Jimmy who showed them to me
first." Demaret is a member of the World Golf Hall of Fame.

20

Willie Anderson

1878–1910

Na, na. We're na goin' t'eat in the kitchen.

> —WILLIE ANDERSON, when told that the professional golfers entered in the 1901 U.S. Open at the Myopia Hunt Club could not eat in the dining room

Willie Anderson was the first dominant champion of the U.S. Open at a time when British-born professionals usually won that event. This was during golf's infancy in the United States, when the Open and the U.S. Amateur were the country's major golf events, along with other tournaments, such as the Western Open (established in 1901), Western Amateur (1899), Metropolitan Open (1905), Metropolitan Amateur (1899), North and South Amateur (1901), and the North and South Open (1903).

Anderson was born in Scotland in 1878. His father, Tom Anderson Sr., was greenskeeper at North Berwick, learned to play golf on that course, then moved the family to the United States in the mid-1890s at the urging of Frank Slazenger, of the sporting-goods family. Anderson was a dour figure with muscular shoulders, brawny forearms, and large hands. He was an excellent mashie (an approach club similar to a 5-iron) player. He had a smooth, deliberate swing with a full pivot. GENE SARAZEN, practicing bunker shots prior to an exhibition after World War II, commented to old pro Bill Robinson, who played against Anderson, "Say, Bill! Could Willie Anderson get out of traps this good?" Robinson replied, "Get out of them? Hell, he was never in them!"

The U.S. Open was first held in 1895, the year after the USGA was formed. The USGA was established by founding-member clubs— St. Andrews, Shinnecock, the Country Club, Chicago, and Newport—in order to ensure that golf rules were consistent and properly administered and to sponsor national championships. Eleven golfers entered the first U.S. Open at the Newport Country Club in Rhode Island. Four rounds were played on that nine-hole course, and Horace Rawlins, the head professional at Newport, won with a score of 45-46-41-41=173. His first prize was a $50 medal and $150. That year, the course measured 2,755 yards, was a par-35, and had six par-4 holes, two par-3s, and a 485-yard par-5. It also had blind holes and hazards, including a stone quarry, an open ditch, swampy ground, and high earth bunkers. Total prize money was $355.

Willie Anderson entered his first Open in 1897, at the Chicago Golf Club in Wheaton, Illinois. Anderson finished second, by one stroke behind Joe Lloyd, with a score of 79-84=163. The Open was expanded to four rounds of eighteen holes conducted over two days at the Myopia Hunt Club in South Hamilton, Massachusetts, the following year. Anderson shot rounds of 81-82-87-86=336, eight shots behind the winner, Fred Herd. Thirty-five golfers entered the contest. The following year, in a field of eighty-one golfers vying for a total of $650 in prize money, Anderson shot 77-81-85-84=327 to finish fifth at the Baltimore Country Club, twelve strokes behind Willie Smith of the Midlothian Club.

Anderson, then a professional at the Pittsfield Country Club in Massachusetts, won his first Open in 1901 at the Myopia Hunt Club. He shot 82-82-87-80=331 to finish in a tie with ALEX SMITH of the Washington Park Golf Club in Chicago, necessitating the first U.S. Open play-off. Anderson won the eighteen-hole play-off by one stroke with a score of 85. The 72-hole score of 331 is still the highest in U.S. Open history. The sixty golfers in this Open played with gutta-percha balls. The following year, the rubber-cored Haskell ball was introduced to championship play, changing the game because it added distance (at least 20 or more yards) to the average drive. The ball was made by winding strips of rubber thread around a solid core and holding it together with gutta-percha.

After finishing tied for fifth in the 1902 Open at the Garden City Golf Club on Long Island, Anderson found himself in another play-off in the 1903 Open at Baltusrol, this time against David Brown, the 1886 British Open champion from Musselburgh, Scotland, who was then playing out of the Wollaston Club in Massachusetts. Both players finished the regulation seventy-two holes with scores of 307. Anderson shot an 82 in the play-off and managed to win by two strokes. At this stage of his career, Anderson was considered the best player in the United States. Willie had won the 1902 Western Open, then the nation's second-most-important professional tournament, shooting a record 299 at the Euclid Club in Cleveland. Anderson won the Western again in 1904, 1908, and 1909. He had been professional at several clubs, including Watch Hill, Baltusrol, New York, Pittsfield, and Apawamis.

Golf courses were just getting started in the United States. In 1895, when the first Open and the first U.S. Amateur were held, there were approximately seventy-five golf courses. Five years later there were over a thousand in the United States. Golf was quickly gaining popularity, and skilled professionals, like Anderson, were in great demand. Commenting on the state of the game in the United States, Anderson lamented that there was not more interest in money matches among professionals:

> I am an optimist on golf. It has not reached its climax and will not for many years. There is not a golf club of any consequence in the U.S. that has not a waiting list. New clubs are springing up almost weekly. Municipalities are seeing the handwriting on the wall and are making appropriations for public links. Golf really is in its infancy here, comparatively speaking. My only complaint is that in the United States there is not the same desire to see the best exponents of the sport play the finished game for money purses as exists in the old country.

Anderson became the first golfer to win three consecutive U.S. Opens when he won his third Open at the Glen View Golf Club in Illinois in 1904. Willie shot rounds of 75-78-78-72=303 to win by five strokes over Gilbert Nichols. Then he won a record-third-straight Open, a feat that has never been equaled, when he shot 81-80-76-77=314 at Myopia to win in 1905. Willie had been down one shot going into the final round but caught Smith at the tenth hole and went on to win by two strokes. At twenty-five years of age, Anderson had won four U.S. Opens, an achievement matched only by BOBBY JONES, BEN HOGAN, and JACK NICKLAUS. (The 1905 Open had eighty-three entries and $970 in total prize money. The 2000 U.S. Open, by comparison, had $4.5 million in total prize money and over seven thousand golfers who attempted to qualify for the 156 starting positions.)

It seemed that Willie Anderson would add many more titles to his outstanding record. In the 1906 Open at Onwenstia in Lake Forest, Illinois, Willie shot a final-round 84 to finish fifth. He finished fourth in the Open in 1908 and again in 1909. Unbeknownst to him, though seemingly in robust health, Anderson was suffering from arteriosclerosis, although others speculated that he might have suffered the ravages of alcohol. He played in his last exhibition match at the Allegheny Country Club in October 1910. Anderson teamed with fellow professional Gil Nicholls against William C. Fownes, the U.S. Amateur champion, and Eben Byers, the 1906 Amateur champion. Down 69–72 after the morning round, Anderson and Nicholls rallied to tie on the thirty-fifth hole. Byers then holed a chip from the edge of the green on the last hole to win the match. Two days later, Willie Anderson, then the head professional at the Philadelphia Cricket Club, died at his home near Philadelphia at the age of thirty-two.

Golfer Fred McLeod, another product of North Berwick, would later recall of Anderson: "When you played golf with him, you played golf. He would even tell you on the first tee: 'We're the best friends, but friendship ceases right here.' When you played him, if he was one-up he wanted to be two-up, and if he was two-up he wanted three. If he beat you he was the nicest person in the world." Willie Anderson is a member of the World Golf Hall of Fame.

Raymond Floyd

1942–

*I could name many highly talented players who should
have made more of their ability but lacked good attitude;
I cannot think of one enduring champion who has a poor one.*

—RAYMOND FLOYD, who changed his attitude and won
PGA tournaments in four different decades

Raymond Loran Floyd was born in Fort Bragg, North Carolina. He learned to play golf from his father, L.B., a career soldier and a golf professional who ran a driving range in Fort Bragg and later owned his own golf course. At the age of thirteen, Raymond was scoring in the low seventies, and at the age of seventeen he won the International Jaycee Junior Championship. He accepted the first golf scholarship ever offered by the University of North Carolina, then dropped out of school after three months and served an eighteen-month hitch in the U.S. Army. He joined the PGA Tour in 1963 and, in his eleventh start, won the St. Petersburg Open. At just over twenty years old he was the youngest golfer to win a Tour event since the 1920s.

Floyd became known on the tour as a money player. His hitting style is to take the club low on the takeaway and, with his hands back high, lift the club almost straight up while cocking his hands. At the top, he lifts his left heel rather high. He then makes a short turn of his left side, countered with a strong kick targetward of his right knee, as he extends his hands and club through the ball and toward the target. An excellent fairway wood player, Floyd is most noted for his short game, his ability to play in the wind, and his tendency to close out a win when he gets a lead.

After his first Tour win, Raymond's game was somewhat erratic until 1969, when he won the Greater Jacksonville Open, the American Golf Classic, and the PGA Championship, tying him for most Tour wins with JACK NICKLAUS, Dave Hill, and BILLY CASPER. Floyd had developed a style that combined power and touch, which served him well at the 6,915-yard, par-71 NCR Country Club South course during the 1969 PGA Championship. He shot opening rounds of 69, 66, and 67 to build a five-shot lead over GARY PLAYER. Raymond, paired with Player, was seemingly more distracted by a group of antiapartheid demonstrators heckling Player, a South African, than Player himself was. Floyd bogeyed number eleven, and Player birdied number fifteen, but Raymond then rallied to sink a 35-foot birdie putt on number sixteen to enable him to win the tournament by one stroke despite a final-round 74.

A major turning point in Floyd's career came in 1973 when he married Maria Fraietta, a businesswoman and the owner of a fashion and design school. Raymond had heretofore been known as a playboy on the Tour. Maria, sensing that Raymond had no goals and was not playing up to his potential, set him straight: "If you don't want to play golf, get into something else that would interest you." Raymond changed his attitude and started winning more tournaments. He would later say, "My attitude improved dramatically when I realized, after nearly a decade of underachieving as a professional and being beaten down by the game's disappointments, that if I truly wanted to be as good as I could be, a good attitude would be as essential as a good swing or a putting stroke."

Raymond won his next major, the 1976 Masters, by shooting rounds of 65-66-70-70 to tie Jack Nicklaus's Masters record of 271 recorded in 1965. BEN CRENSHAW finished second, eight shots behind, on the strength of a final-round 67. TIGER WOODS shot a record 270 in

1997 to break Floyd's mark. Raymond's last best chance to win another Masters came in 1990 when he led after fifty-four holes with a total of 206, but NICK FALDO shot a 69 to Floyd's 72 on the final day and tied him at 278. Raymond managed to salvage the tie when Faldo, playing ahead of him, parred the final hole. Floyd had hit his tee shot on the par-4 eighteenth into a fairway bunker, then hit his approach into a green-side bunker. He managed to get up and down after leaving his sand shot six feet from the hole. The play-off began on the 485-yard, par-4 tenth, the "Camilia" hole. Both players drove into the fairway; then Faldo hit his approach into a green-side bunker. Raymond's approach was fifteen feet from the hole. Faldo, who bogeyed this hole from the same bunker in his 1989 play-off with Scott Hoch, managed to get up and down. Raymond could not convert his putt, however, so they advanced to the 455-yard, par-4 "Dogwood" hole. Raymond spun out on his left foot a bit too much on his 7-iron approach shot from a hanging lie, pulled it into the water, and ended his chance to become, at age forty-seven, the oldest player to win the Masters.

One of Floyd's crowning achievements was winning the 1986 U.S. Open at Shinnecock Hills, a tough, windswept, links-style course woven through the dunes of Long Island. By doing so at age forty-three, he became the oldest player to win the Open since TED RAY in 1920. Raymond shot rounds of 75-68-70-66=279 to win by two shots over Chip Beck and LANNY WADKINS. Floyd felt that he won his championship in the first round when he fought to a 75 in severe winds that caused forty-five players to shoot 80 or more. Raymond, by virtue of his victory, became the twelfth player to win three different majors.

Raymond won his last regular PGA Tour event, the Doral-Ryder Open in 1992 to become the first player to win on both the Senior and regular Tour in the same year. He is tied for twenty-fifth in all-time PGA victories and has won over $8.4 million on the Senior Tour. Among his victories are the Tradition (1991), the Senior PGA Championship (1995), the Senior Players (1996, 2000), and the Champions Tour Championship (1992, 1994). Raymond won the Vardon Trophy in 1984, was selected to eight Ryder Cup teams (1969, 1975, 1977, 1981, 1983, 1985, 1991, 1993), and was nonplaying captain in 1989. Given Raymond's reputation as a money player, it is interesting that he is 4-11 in PGA Tour play-offs and 12-16-2 in Ryder Cup play. Yet in 1993, at the age of fifty-one, Raymond was chosen to play in his eighth Ryder Cup, becoming the oldest competitor in the event's history. He scored the clinching points for the winning American side when he defeated JOSE-MARIA OLAZABAL, 2-up, in the final day's singles matches. His twenty-two career PGA victories tie him with JOHNNY FARRELL for twenty-fifth place all-time.

22

Hale Irwin

1945–

That was years of emotion pouring out of me. I remember looking up after the putt dropped at some people in the gallery. They were so happy. I realized they were happy for me . . . for me. All I could think to do was go thank them. . . . I guess that startled some people, coming from a dull old guy.

> —HALE IRWIN, commenting on how he reacted after sinking a 50-foot putt for a birdie on the seventy-second hole to gain a play-off in the 1990 U.S. Open

Hale Irwin was born in Joplin, Missouri, in 1945 and earned his reputation as an intense competitor at the University of Colorado, where he served as an all-conference free safety on the football team and won the 1967 NCAA golf championship. Irwin, who was also an excellent baseball shortstop and played semipro ball, never took a golf lesson but taught himself how to play. He joined the Tour in 1968 and won his first tournament, the Heritage Classic, in 1971. Through sheer hard work and determination, he built up his golf resumé in a quiet way, ranking among the top-sixty money winners in every year from 1970 through 1985. He has won twenty PGA Tour events, placing him tied for twenty-ninth on the all-time list with JIM BARNES, Bill Mehlhorn, and Doug Sanders. During one stage in his career, Irwin made eighty-six straight cuts from the 1975 Tucson Open until the 1979 Bing Crosby. Only BYRON NELSON (113 events) and JACK NICKLAUS (105) have had longer streaks of finishing in the money.

Irwin has won three U.S. Opens. He won his first at Winged Foot in 1974 in a field that included ARNOLD PALMER, TOM WATSON, GARY PLAYER, Jack Nicklaus, RAYMOND FLOYD, and other Hall of Fame golfers. With his long hair and wire-rimmed glasses, Irwin was hardly noticeable. He seemed the nondescript journeyman professional. But Irwin likes to play tough courses, and he opened with solid rounds of 73-70-71 to put himself one shot behind the twenty-four-year-old Tom Watson. Paired with Watson on the final round, Hale shot a 73 for a winning score of 287 as Watson ballooned to a 79 and a total of 292 for a tie for fifth. Irwin, an excellent iron player, clinched the tournament on the final hole when he drilled a 2-iron to the heart of the green to ensure his par.

Irwin captured the 1979 Open held at Inverness in Toledo, Ohio, with a two-shot win over Jerry Pate and Gary Player. Hale started off with a mediocre 74 but rallied for rounds of 68 and 67 to lead TOM WEISKOPF by three going into the final round. He built his lead to five shots after the seventieth hole, then stumbled home with a double bogey and bogey for a back-nine total of 40 and a final-round score of 75, the highest finishing-round total for an Open champion since CARY MIDDLECOFF won by one shot at Medinah in 1949. Hale became the fourteenth player to win the Open more than once.

Irwin, at age forty-five, became the oldest player to win a U.S. Open, at Medinah in 1990. He was up against a new wave of challengers, including GREG NORMAN, JOSE-MARIA OLAZABAL, and amateur PHIL MICKELSON as well as some of the old guard, including Jack Nicklaus, LARRY NELSON, and a few others. Twenty-five golfers were within four shots of the lead going into the final round. Irwin had rounds of 69-70-74, placing him four shots back. Paired with Greg Norman the final day, Hale was still four shots behind after nine holes on the grueling 7,195-yard layout. Mike Donald, a ten-year Tour veteran from Virginia, held the lead. Irwin started to score on the final nine, dropping to 7 under par to reduce Donald's lead to two. He birdied the eighteenth, sinking a spectacular 50-foot putt, ran a lap around the green and high-fived the gallery, and then waited for Donald and the other contenders to finish. Hale had shot a 31 on the back nine and carded a total of 280. Billy Ray Brown missed a birdie putt on the eighteenth to finish at 281, but Donald made his par for a total of 280 and a play-off with Hale Irwin.

As opposed to the other majors, the U.S. Open operates under the eighteen-hole play-off system that was in effect at Medinah in 1990. The Masters goes to sudden death, the PGA Championship to a three-hole medal play, and the British Open has a four-hole, medal-play format. At different times in its history, the U.S. Open has had a thirty-six or eighteen-hole play-off setup. Regular Tour events went to a sudden-death play-off venue in 1972 to accommodate television and tournament schedules. Both Irwin and Donald started out shakily, with Donald having a 37–38 edge on the front nine. With three holes to play, Irwin was two shots down, but then Irwin hit a 2-iron stiff to the flag and made an 8-foot putt to cut the lead to one. Donald made his first major mistake of the tournament on the next hole when he snap-hooked his drive and bogeyed, allowing Irwin to tie him with a par. Now, iron-ically, the Open was to be decided in sudden death, the first in U.S. Open history. Irwin holed an 8-foot birdie putt on the ninety-first hole to win his third Open, placing him one behind WILLIE ANDERSON, BOBBY JONES, BEN HOGAN, and Jack Nicklaus. An exhausted Irwin somehow won the Buick Classic the following week.

Hale's last PGA Tour win was the 1994 MCI Classic. He joined the Senior Tour in 1995 and has had phenomenal success, winning thirty-six tournaments and over $16 million, both all-time Senior Tour records. Among his victories are the Senior PGA championship (1996, 1997, 1918), the U.S. Senior Open, the Senior Players (1999) and the Tour Championship (1998). Hale was inducted into the World Golf Hall of Fame in 1992.

During his PGA Tour career, Hale Irwin won over $5.9 million. He was a member of the Ryder Cup team in 1975, 1977, 1979, 1981, and 1991. His Ryder Cup record is 13-5-2. He was also on two World Cup teams, winning the individual title in 1979. And he was the playing captain of the 1994 President's Cup team.

23

Tommy Armour

1895–1968

The first thing that determines how well you're going to be able to play is how you grip the club.

—Tommy Armour

Thomas Dickson Armour, the legendary "Silver Scot," was born in Edinburgh in 1895. He was originally known as the "Black Scot," but when his hair turned silver, so did his nickname. Like most of his countrymen, he took up golf at an early age. While in high school, he teamed with Bobby Cruickshank to win seventeen of eighteen match-play contests. Armour got more interested in the game after he saw "the Great Triumverate"—Harry Vardon, J. H. Taylor, and James Braid—play exhibition matches. He later traveled to England and took lessons from Vardon and George Duncan, starting his lifelong study of the golf swing.

Armour was enrolled at Edinburgh University when World War I broke out. He served as an officer in the British army as a machine gunner in the Tank Corps and rose to the rank of major. Wounded, he lost the use of one eye in the war and carried eight pieces of shrapnel in his left shoulder, but when he returned to Scotland, he resumed playing golf. Armour took a job with a golf-ball manufacturer, the North British Rubber Company, which enabled him to come to the United States to play. He won the French Amateur in 1920 and, as an amateur, was a member of a British team that met the American team in 1921 in a competition that led to the founding of the Walker Cup matches in 1922. Armour emigrated to the United States in the early 1920s and took more lessons from J. Douglas Edgar, who had defeated Armour in a Canadian Open play-off in 1920. After turning professional in 1924, he played for a team of professionals that met a group of British professionals in an informal match that foreshadowed the first Ryder Cup contest in 1927.

Armour first made his impact in the United States by winning the U.S. Open at Oakmont and five other tournaments, including the Canadian Open, in 1927. Oakmont was over 6,900 yards from the championship tees and, with more than two hundred bunkers and treacherous greens, was one of the most punishing golf courses in the world. In the first round of the tournament, more than half the scores were eighty, and no one broke par. On the next eighteen, Armour was 1 under par with a 71, the only golfer other than Al Espinosa to do so. At the halfway point, Armour was one shot behind GENE SARAZEN, who had a pair of 74s for a 148. Sarazen shot an 80 on the third round, putting him out of contention, but on the last round, several players, led by HARRY COOPER, had a chance to win.

Cooper was among the top-ten professionals in the United States in the 1920s and 1930s but somehow could never win a major tournament. Born in England but raised in Texas, Cooper was nicknamed "Light Horse" Harry because of the speed with which he played, sometimes seemingly chasing after his shots. On the seventy-first green at Oakmont, Cooper stroked too aggressively on a 12-foot downhill putt and then missed a 4-footer coming back to take a bogey 5. He finished with a 77 and a total of 301, opening the door for Armour, who was playing behind him. Armour, however, took a 7 at the twelfth hole, and it looked as if he were finished. He then gathered himself and played the next five holes in 1 under par and needed a birdie on the final hole, a 456-yard par-4, to tie Cooper. He rose to the occasion, hitting a 3-iron to within ten feet and then holing his putt to force an eighteen-hole play-off. After fourteen play-off holes, Cooper was ahead by one, but Armour sank a 50-foot putt for a birdie on the fifteenth and picked up another stroke on the next hole. Cooper hit his approach to within eighteen inches on the short par-4 seventeenth, but Armour hit his to within one foot and then halved the hole. Armour went on to win, 76–79.

Tommy Armour became an accomplished golf instructor, working out of Winged Foot in Westchester County, New York, and the Boca Raton Country Club in Florida. Known for his tremendous hand strength, Armour is said to have been able to lift a pool cue horizontally while holding its thin end between his index finger and thumb. Grantland Rice said of Armour: "Well equipped mentally, he also had the finest pair of hands I've seen in sport. They are long and exceptionally powerful. This asset was a big help in his long iron play, in which he has been acknowledged to be one of the masters." Armour also was superb off the tee and was noted for standing over his putts for a long time, no doubt because he only had one eye to work with. As an instructor, he had a thorough knowledge of the golf swing and an exceptional ability to analyze a pupil's problems and suggest easily comprehensible solutions. PGA Tour players, talented women players, and the rich and famous were among his clients. Armour often dispensed his advice with a cocktail in one hand while he sat in the shade of an umbrella on the practice tee at the Boca Raton Club. He wrote, with Herb Graffis, the bestselling instructional book *How to Play Your Best Golf All the Time* (1953), which sold over 400,000 copies when it was first issued and is still in print.

Armour won the Western Open in 1929 with a record score of 273. Tommy won his next major tournament in 1930 when he outdueled Gene Sarazen at Fresh Meadows Country Club in the PGA Championship. Sarazen was then the professional at Fresh Meadows, but his local knowledge did not help him in the thirty-six-hole play-off against Armour. During their championship match, neither golfer had more than a two-hole lead. After the morning round, Armour had a 1-up lead after shooting 71 to Sarazen's 72. After twenty-seven holes the match was all square, and they went to the final tee all even. Each player bunkered his shot on the par-4 finishing hole. Armour hit his sand shot to within twelve feet; Sarazen, to within ten. Armour, after stepping away from his putt to collect himself after a photographer disturbed him, made his birdie, but Sarazen missed to lose, 1-up.

The following year, Armour returned to Scotland to play in the British Open at Carnoustie, fifty miles from his place of birth. After opening with scores of 73-75, he closed with strong rounds of 71-71 to defeat José Jurado of Argentina and Peter Alliss by one shot. Armour had now won golf's triple crown: the U.S. Open, PGA, and British

Open. The Masters, first held in 1934, came a bit too late for Tommy. As time went on, Armour became a legendary figure and a colorful statesman for golf and its most sought after and expensive instructor. In his essay "Golf's Greater Teacher—Who?" Herb Graffis asked Tommy Armour what a great golf teacher is. Armour replied, "The best the golf instructor can do, and it's astonishing how well some can do it, is to use extensive knowledge of the game and inherent ability to impart some of that knowledge in vivid one- or two-syllable words. And at that I believe that the highest achievement of the golf instructor may not be in teaching but in getting the pupil to learn. It takes great learners to make great reputations for teachers."

Armour was also very important, along with WALTER HAGEN, JIM BARNES, Gene Sarazen, and other champions of his era, in getting the early PGA Tour on its feet as a member of its first tournament committee in 1929 and bringing American golf to the forefront of international golf competition.

Armour won three majors, three Canadian Opens, and a total of twenty-five PGA events, placing him twenty-first on the all-time list, tied with JOHNNY MILLER. He played golf exhibitions to raise money for the World War II effort and visited soldiers in hospitals, although he dreaded it, saying, "Why should that kid be there instead of me?" He had long been on the MacGregor sporting goods company staff, designing clubs that were commercially successful. Armour spent his final years in Florida at the Delray Beach Country Club and Boca Raton and, in summer, at Winged Foot. He passed away in 1968. Tommy Armour is in the World Golf Hall of Fame.

24

Julius Boros

1920–1994

*Concentration is not an element that should be applied
all the way around a golf course. It is not the least bit
important until you are ready to shoot. There's plenty
of time to concentrate when you step up to the ball.*

—JULIUS BOROS, who liked to play fast
and relax between shots

Julius Boros was born in Fairfield, Connecticut and turned professional at the advanced age of twenty-nine but quickly made his impact on the world of golf by winning the 1952 U.S. Open. Boros was noted for his relaxed, languid swing, which TONY LEMA described in the following manner: "It's all hands and wrists, like a man dusting furniture."

Boros, a large man of Hungarian descent, never spent much time worrying about a shot. Perhaps his habit came from the days of his youth when, with a handful of old clubs, he would scale the fence at the nearby Fairfield Golf Course before the greenskeeper or nightfall closed in on him.

In his first U.S. Open at Merion in 1950, Boros had a fairway wood to the green. A par would have given him a first-round score of 67. He topped his shot but calmly strolled after the ball and recovered for a bogey and a 68. Boros finished ninth at Merion and would finish in the top ten nine times in his U.S. Open career. Boros's first major tournament victory was at the 1952 U.S. Open, played at the Northwood Country Club in Dallas. Boros shot rounds of 71-71 in the blistering heat on the first day. The following day, he shot a 68 in the morning round to lead the tournament with a fifty-four-hole score of 210. Boros then closed with a 71 in the afternoon to register a 281 and win by four shots over Ed "Porky" Oliver, who holed a fifty-foot putt on the last green to nose out BEN HOGAN for second.

Julius Boros won $4,000 for his first-place finish in the 1952 U.S. Open and made $25,000 for his win in George May's World Championship of Golf held at the Tam O'Shanter Country Club, near Chicago. The World Championship of Golf, which May sponsored for seventeen years, from 1941 through 1957, was golf's first big-money event, dwarfing the regular Tour events in prize money. Boros's win enabled him to capture the money title in 1952, although SAM SNEAD and JACK BURKE JR. won three more tournaments than he did. Boros was also named PGA Player of the Year in 1952, and he won another money title in 1955.

George May was one of the early pioneers of televised golf, becoming the first tournament impresario to nationally televise a Tour event. His timing couldn't have been better, because in the 1953 World Championship, Lew Worsham holed a long wedge shot on the final hole to score an eagle and win the tournament and $25,000 by a one-shot margin. Much like baseball promoter Bill Veeck, May was colorful and outrageous. In 1954 he raised the first prize money to $50,000, but the professionals objected to the many promotional practices, including the useful suggestion that players utilize numbers so that the viewers could easily identify them. May had a bitter falling out with the pros, and the Tour lost a tournament whose total prize money, $101,200, was almost triple the next-largest PGA event. May set a precedent, however, and the big-money tournaments and made-for-television events, such as the Skins Game, were soon to come.

Julius Boros, at age forty-three, became the second-oldest golfer to win the U.S. Open when he captured his second Open at The Country Club in Brookline, Massachusetts, in 1963, fifty years after local son FRANCIS OUIMET's play-off victory over HARRY VARDON and TED RAY. In 1952, Ben Hogan was favored to win the Open, while Boros was an obscure professional without a win on the Tour. In 1963, Boros was old by conventional standards, making JACK NICKLAUS and ARNOLD PALMER the favorites. Nicklaus missed the cut at the Open, and Boros found himself in a battle with Arnold Palmer and Jackie Cupit, a young Tour player from Texas. All three players tied with totals of 293, nine strokes over par. (This was the highest seventy-two-hole Open total since Sam Parks won at Oakmont with a total of 299 in 1935.)

High winds made the course play extremely difficult on the final day of regulation play, and none of the fifty-one finalists shot par. In the play-off, Boros played the first five holes in 1 under par to give him a three-shot lead. He went on to shoot 70 to Cupit's 73 and Palmer's 76. Boros always played well against Palmer and called him his "pigeon." He would later recall: "I always felt that I could beat Palmer. The thing you had to remember about playing Arnie was that his best shot was hitting balls into all those people. They'd be all over the place, right up to the fringes, and he'd hit one among them, and next thing you know, it'd come rolling back onto the green."

Boros became the oldest player to win the PGA Championship when, at the age of forty-eight, he won by a single stroke over Arnold Palmer at the Pecan Valley Country Club in San Antonio in 1968. Palmer, who never won a PGA Championship in his illustrious career, missed several birdie opportunities in the final round, including a 9-footer at the seventy-second hole, which would have tied Boros. Julius continued to play on Tour despite arthritis and other afflictions. His eighteenth and final PGA Tour victory came at the 1968 Westchester Classic. At age fifty-three he finished seventh in the U.S. Open, and at fifty-nine, Boros teamed with ROBERTO DE VICENZO to win the Legends of Golf Tournament. Julius birdied the last hole in regulation to force a play-off against Art Wall and TOMMY BOLT. This nationally televised play-off, won at the sixth hole by the Boros team, added marketability to the PGA Senior Tour, which started the following year. Prior to his Legends win in 1979, Boros won the 1971 and 1979 PGA Seniors' Championship.

Julius Boros was selected four times to the Ryder Cup team (1959, 1963, 1965, 1967). His overall record was 9-3-4. Boros's career Tour earnings totaled just over $1 million, reflecting the growth of golf in the 1950s and 1960s. In contrast, Sam Snead won $620,125 for his eighty-four Tour victories. Boros's eighteen Tour wins tie him for fortieth place on the all-time list with Nick Price, Jim Ferrier, "Dutch" Harrison, and Johnny Revolta. He is a member of the World Golf Hall of Fame. Julius Boros died in 1994, but the Boros golf legacy continues with his son, Guy Boros, a member of the PGA Tour, and three other sons who are golf professionals.

Lloyd Mangrum

1914–1973

*I don't know the traffic regulations of every city I get
to, either, but I manage to drive through without being
arrested.*

> —LLOYD MANGRUM, after being penalized two strokes
> in the 1956 U.S. Open play-off when he
> picked up his ball to remove a fly

Lloyd Eugene Mangrum was a smooth-swinging Texan who learned
to play golf while caddying in the Dallas area and turned professional in
1929 at the age of fourteen. He played in his first PGA-sponsored event
when he was nineteen and won his first PGA tournament at the

Thomasville Open in 1940. Mangrum had won the Pennsylvania Open in 1938 and was picked for the Ryder Cup team in 1939, but the match was never played because of World War II. Mangrum narrowly missed winning the 1940 Masters after he opened with a record round of 64, which would stand until 1965, when JACK NICKLAUS tied it on the way to his Masters win. Mangrum was one shot behind JIMMY DEMARET going into the final round but shot a 74 to finish second, four shots behind Demaret's 280.

Like his contemporaries BEN HOGAN, SAM SNEAD, Jim Turnesa, Vic Ghezzi, and many others, Mangrum's golf career was interrupted by World War II. He had been the seventh-leading money winner in 1941 and fourth in 1942 before entering the army, where he attained the rank of staff sergeant. A Purple Heart winner, he was wounded twice in the Battle of the Bulge and spent part of his convalescent period in St. Andrews, where he won a GI golf tournament in 1945. When the war ended, Mangrum and one other enlisted man were the only survivors from his original outfit. Mangrum rejoined the PGA circuit in 1946, and in the next nine years he was always among the top-ten money winners, capturing thirty-five tournaments.

Mangrum was known as a cool, tough competitor with an excellent short game. Somewhat short off the tee, Lloyd was a brilliant recovery player around the greens and a nerveless putter. One of his most memorable victories came in the 1946 U.S. Open at Canterbury in Cleveland. BYRON NELSON and Ben Hogan were favored to win the event, and a large crowd came out to watch them, Sam Snead, and the other pro stars in the first post–World War II Open. After regulation play, Mangrum, Nelson, and Vic Ghezzi were tied at 285. Nelson had bogeyed the last two holes to miss his chance for an outright win. Hogan had missed a 2-foot putt on the last hole and failed to gain a play-off spot.

In the first play-off round, all three players shot 72, requiring another eighteen-hole round. Mangrum saved himself from totally falling out of the race when he saved a bogey on the par-5 ninth. He hit his tee shot out-of-bounds. Then he hit his third shot into the right rough. His approach was short, and his chip left him at least a 40-foot putt for a bogey. He somehow managed to hole that putt and later explained, "I was just trying to put it up there for a seven." Mangrum was three strokes behind Ghezzi and two behind Nelson with six holes to play. But despite playing in a thunderstorm at the end of the match, Mangrum scored three birdies on the last six holes to finish with a 72, one shot better than Nelson and Ghezzi.

Mangrum's best money year was 1948, when he won seven Tour events. In one week he earned $22,000 out of his total of $48,000 by winning the All-American tournament and the Tam O'Shanter. Unusual penalty situations became part of the Mangrum legend. Leading the field in the second round of the 1948 Masters, Lloyd imposed a penalty on himself because his ball moved in the rough as he addressed it. He finished tied for fourth, nine shots behind winner Claude Harmon. A penalty in the 1950 U.S. Open was more costly. Ben Hogan, making a comeback from his near-fatal automobile accident in 1949, miraculously tied Mangrum and George Fazio by hitting his famous 1-iron approach to within forty feet and then two-putting for par on the seventy-second hole. In the play-off, Mangrum was behind Hogan by one shot at the sixteenth hole as he prepared to address his ball to putt. As he was about to stroke the ball, he noticed an insect crawling on it. He placed his putter near his ball to mark it, blew the bug away after picking up the ball, replaced the ball, holed the putt, then walked to the seventeenth tee thinking he had a par. A USGA official then advised him that it was a two-stroke penalty for cleaning his ball on the green. Hogan went on to win by four shots after sinking a 50-foot birdie putt on seventeen to clinch his victory. Hogan had shot 69 to win by four over Mangrum and six over Fazio.

Mangrum was selected to four Ryder Cup teams (1947, 1949, 1951, 1953) and had a 6-2 record in Ryder Cup matches. He was playing captain in 1953 when the United States edged Great Britain, 6½–5½, at the Wentworth Golf Club in England. Mangrum won the Vardon Trophy for lowest PGA Tour stroke average in 1951 (70.05) and 1953 (70.22). From 1947 through 1956, Mangrum finished among the top eight in the Masters. His thirty-six career Tour victories places him tenth on the all-time list, two behind GENE SARAZEN. His last PGA tournament win was the 1956 Los Angeles Open.

Byron Nelson recently said of Mangrum, "Lloyd's the best player who's been forgotten since I've been playing golf." Mangrum was elected a member of the World Golf Hall of Fame in 1998.

26

Young Tom Morris

1851–1875

In another respect his victories did a great deal of good to golf. By winning the Belt for the third consecutive year at the age of nineteen, he made it his own property, and the whole scheme of the running of the Open Championship had to be brought under review.

—ROBERT BROWNING, assessing Young Tom Morris's impact on the game in *A History of Golf*

Tom Morris Jr., the son of TOM MORRIS, the venerable professional, equipment maker, and golf-course architect from St. Andrews, Scotland, was born in 1851 and soon followed in the footsteps of his father, a four-time British Open champion and deadly challenge-match player. At age thirteen, Young Tom, as he came to be called, won five pounds in a match-play championship at Perth. At the age of sixteen he defeated WILLIE PARK SR., then a three-time British Open winner, and Bob Andrews in a play-off of a match at Carnoustie. In the same year, he finished fourth to his father, who won the 1867 British Open at Prestwick.

Young Tom's growing dominance of the game became evident in 1868 when he shot a 157 to win the British Open, succeeding his father as champion. In 1869 he shot a 154 for thirty-six holes (3 twelve-hole rounds) to win the British Open by three strokes over his father. This score would stand for thirty years as a British Open record, eclipsed only when the rubber-core ball was introduced to the game. The following year, he won by twelve strokes, shooting 149, an astonishing score on windswept, unmanicured terrain during the gutta-percha era. With his three consecutive victories, Young Tom, at age nineteen, earned the right to retire the championship belt, forcing the Open tournament procedures to come under review. The Open was suspended for a year, and the Royal and Ancient Golf Club of St. Andrews and the Honourable Company of Edinburgh golfers joined the Prestwick Club in subscribing for a silver cup, which became the permanent trophy, a claret jug then valued at thirty pounds sterling, for that event. Thus, the British Open rotation began with three clubs taking over the management of the championship that would henceforth be played at Prestwick, Musselburgh, and St. Andrews.

At the Open in Prestwick in 1872 eight contestants played for the championship, as had been the case in the inaugural event in 1860. Young Tom won his fourth consecutive Open at the age of twenty-one, shooting 166 to defeat Davie Strath of St. Andrews by three shots. By adding courses to the tournament rotation, the field gradually expanded, beginning with twenty-six golfers in 1873, when the event was held at St. Andrews for the first time.

Young Tom was a big hitter with broad shoulders and an ability to play full shots from bad lies. He was considered by his contemporaries to have no weaknesses in his game. He had great skill with approach shots and an excellent putting game. He is credited with improving upon the refinements of Allan Robertson (the acknowledged leading professional golfer before the Open was set up to determine an annual champion) in approach play by developing skill with a niblick (later known as a mashie and similar to an 8-iron) coming into the green.

Tom finished third in the 1873 Open held at St. Andrews. He tied Bob Kirk with a score of 183, four shots behind Tom Kidd, who won eleven pounds sterling for his efforts. The following year, Tom shot 83-78=161 at Musselburgh to finish second, two shots behind Mungo Park. Given the limited number of organized professional tournaments, a major source of Tom's income was from challenge-match contests with other leading professionals of his era. Notable among these rivalries were contests against Willie and Mungo Park from the famous Park golfing family in Musselburgh.

In 1875, after he and his father avenged an earlier loss to the Parks at North Berwick, Young Tom received notice that his wife was gravely ill. There being no better available form of transportation, Tom borrowed a boat and sped across North Berwick Harbor, but en route Old Tom received notice that his son's wife and newborn son had died. Old Tom broke the news to his son when they reached the Harbor at St. Andrews. Young Tom had been married only a year.

Brokenhearted, Young Tom played one last match, defeating a Mr. Molesworth of Westward Ho!, nine and seven, despite giving him three strokes a side over a match of thirty-six holes per day over three days. Perhaps this match, played in snow, contributed to Tom's premature death at the age of twenty-four on Christmas Day, 1875.

Six golfing societies contributed to Young Tom's memorial at St. Andrews cathedral, which reads: "Deeply regretted by numerous friends and all golfers, he thrice in succession won the Championship Belt and held it without rivalry and yet without envy, his many amateur qualities being no less acknowledged than his golfing achievement."

Young Tom Morris will be remembered for the competitive spirit and the flair he brought to the game. His average winning medal score of 156.5 in four Opens was fully ten strokes less than the average scores of other great early Open winners, Willie Park and Old Tom Morris who combined for eight Open wins. Old Tom and Young Tom hold the most father and son Open victories with eight, two more than Willie Park and his son, Willie, Jr. Young Tom was a golf prodigy who raised the game to a new level, much the way others such as HARRY VARDON, BOBBY JONES, JACK NICKLAUS, and TIGER WOODS would do later. Young Tom is in the World Golf Hall of Fame.

27

Ernie Els

1969–

Three years ago, when I won the U.S. Open, it was like a war out there.

—ERNIE ELS, after winning his second Open
at Congressional in 1997

Ernie Els, a 6-foot-3 inch, 210-pound strapping lad with a graceful swing, is a product of Johannesburg, South Africa, joining GARY PLAYER and BOBBY LOCKE as the greatest players to come out of that country. An excellent athlete and a champion junior tennis player as a youth, Els took up golf at the age of nine, then began concentrating on the sport at the age of fourteen. At age eighteen he came to the United States and won the Junior World Championship in San Diego. Els turned professional in 1989 and became a fan favorite in 1992, then won six tournaments in Africa, including the South African Open, the South African PGA, and the South African Masters, at the age of twenty-two. Els joined the European Tour in 1992 and recorded his first victory in the Dubai Desert tournament. In 1994, Els joined the PGA Tour and won his first U.S. Open at Oakmont that same year. Since then, he has won five more Tour events, including a second U.S. Open, four European Tour events, and seventeen other professional tournaments. Els has already won $10 million on the PGA Tour even though he has played an annual schedule of twenty events or less. He has won over $18 million in total tournament winnings, placing him, at age thirty-one, among the top-twenty money winners in golf history.

Els earned his spot in the 1994 U.S. Open because he finished seventh in the Open the previous year at Baltusrol, shooting final rounds of 68 and 67 to finish seven shots behind the winner, LEE JANZEN. At Oakmont, one of the most difficult golf courses in the world, Els opened with a 69, to trail TOM WATSON, the leader, by one shot. Colin Montgomerie took the lead at the halfway point with a 71-65=136, four shots better than Ernie. After fifty-four holes, Els led the field with 69-71-66=206 on the strength of a third-round 66, highlighted by a record score of 30 on the front nine. Ernie was able to record this superb score despite missing five fairways. Frank Nobilo was in second place, two shots behind Els, and Loren Roberts, who shot 64 on Saturday, was tied for third with HALE IRWIN, Watson, and Montgomerie with a score of 209.

On the final day, Watson, who shot 74, Nobilo (76), and Irwin (78) fell off the pace, leaving the tournament to be decided among Els, Montgomerie, and Roberts. Montgomerie, who finished his final round first, played 3 under par through the first ten holes, but bogeys on the final two holes dropped him to 1 under for the round and a total of 279, 5 under par. Roberts was 6 under and tied with Els going into the seventy-second hole, but hit his approach over the back of the green into deep rough and bogeyed to finish in a tie with Montgomerie. Els, in the last pairing, hooked his drive behind a grandstand and was given a drop. He wisely pitched safely out to the fairway, then bogeyed for a three-way tie and an eighteen-hole play-off the following day. Els, as it turned out, didn't know the tournament situation when he approached the tee of the 456-yard, par-4 finishing hole. He thought that Roberts had parred the last hole and that he needed a birdie to tie. He used a driver off the tee rather than a 3-wood that might have landed in the fairway.

The play-off was a war of attrition, not pretty but interesting. Montgomerie parred the first hole, double-bogeyed the next two, went out in 42, and finished with a 78. After Els bogeyed the first hole and triple-bogeyed the 342-yard, par-4 second, he asked his caddie, "Why did I make that putt on the eighteenth and get into this thing?" Els then settled down and caught Roberts after five holes, and they finished tied at 74 after regulation play. Montgomerie had been eliminated, and now it was a sudden-death play-off. Els won the Open with a par on the second extra hole. He became the second South African player, after Gary Player, winner of the 1965 Open, to win the U.S. National Championship. This was the thirty-first time since the first Open in 1895 that the outcome was determined in a play-off.

Ernie Els found himself in another wild U.S. Open finish at Congressional in 1997. The Open was last played at Congressional in 1964, when KEN VENTURI staggered through thirty-six hot and muggy holes like a great heavyweight champion, going the distance to win his only major. That was the last year the final round of the Open was a thirty-six-hole marathon. In 1964 the course measured 7,053 yards, and in 1997 it was lengthened to 7,213, the longest in Open history. As an added twist, what had been the 211-yard, par-3 sixteenth in 1964 was made the finishing hole for the 1997 Open. This was the first par-3 final hole at a U.S. Open since 1909 at the Englewood Golf Club in New Jersey. Els opened with rounds of 71-67-69=207 and was two shots behind the leader, Tom Lehman. Ernie birdied three of the last four holes of his third round, which he had to complete on Sunday because of a storm delay on Saturday. Also tied with Els in second position was Jeff Maggert. Colin Montgomerie was one shot back with a score of 208.

Maggert, in the last pairing with Lehman, tied for the lead with seven holes to play but took himself out of contention early when his putter went bad on the back nine. He came in with a 40 to finish with a 74 and a 1-over-par total of 281. Lehman, who led the Open going into the final round for the third consecutive year, began to slip when he hit his 7-iron approach into the lake on number seventeen. He later said, "I wish I could have had a mulligan." Montgomerie, paired with Els, tied with him at even par going into the seventeenth, a 480-yard par-4, which had been the finishing hole in the 1964 Open. After his drive, Els hit a 5-iron approach to fifteen feet behind the pin. Monty then pushed a 6-iron to the right rough and pitched his third shot to within five feet. Els left his birdie attempt 2$\frac{1}{2}$ feet past the hole. Bothered by the gallery noise around the nearby eighteenth, less than 100 yards away, Montgomerie waited for five minutes for a lull in the noise. But it didn't help him. He missed his short putt for his fourth consecutive bogey on the seventeenth hole in the tournament. The unflappable Els made his putt and held a one-shot lead on Monty. Unlike 1994 at

Oakmont, Els looked at the scoreboard before he hit his tee shot on the last hole. He knew he needed a par to win after Lehman put his ball in the lake. Both Monty and Ernie parred out. Ernie had won by one stroke with a 4-under-par score of 276.

Els later observed, "I'm sure the crowd was bothering him, but I felt that we could have played the hole without waiting so long. You're not going to get twenty thousand people quiet when a couple of international boys are leading the U.S. Open." Lehman finished third at 278, and Maggert was fourth with a score of 281. Els became the third player to win two Opens in his first five tries. WALTER HAGEN did it in 1914 and 1919, and so did JOHNNY MCDERMOTT, within four tries, in 1911 and 1912.

Els has reinforced his credentials as an international competitor. He posted a 3-1-1 record in the 1996 President's Cup at the Robert Trent Jones course in Lake Manassas, Virginia, and a 3-1-1 mark in 1998 at the Royal Melbourne's composite course. After Ernie dropped several long putts on the way to the International team's first victory in 1998, the press dubbed him "the Big Easy." However, in the 2000 President's Cup, Els was shut out, 0-4, at the Robert Trent Jones Golf Course in Virginia.

Ernie Els solidified his golf reputation by winning the 2002 British Open at Muirfield in Scotland. He shot rounds of 70-66-72-70 = 278, which tied him with Stuart Appleby, Steve Elkington, and Thomas Levet. He and Levet were tied after the four-hole playoff and Els then won on the first sudden-death playoff hole. By the end of 2002, Els had won ten times on the PGA Tour and twenty-nine international victories. He was ranked number three in the world behind TIGER WOODS and PHIL MICKELSON. His $15 million plus PGA Tour earnings put him seventh on the all-time list even though he has never played a full PGA schedule.

28

Ralph Guldahl

1911-1987

If I can't do it, I'm a bum and I don't deserve to win the Open.

—RALPH GULDAHL, who needed a 37 on the last nine holes to win the 1937 Open

Ralph Guldahl is one of the more obscure great golfers who packed most of his major achievements into a brief period between the ages of twenty-five and twenty-nine when he won two consecutive U.S. Opens, three straight Western Opens, a Masters, and a number of Tour events.

Guldahl began as an instinctual golfer who learned the game on municipal courses in his native Texas. A slow and meticulous player, he made a full pivot of the shoulders but moved the lower half of his body very little. He generated clubhead speed and power with strong right-hand action. He turned professional in 1929 at the age of eighteen and won his first Tour event, the Santa Monica Open, in 1931 and his last, the Inverness Invitation Four-Ball, in 1940.

One of Guldahl's defining moments came in the 1933 U.S. Open at the North Shore Golf Club in Glen View, Illinois. Guldahl, then twenty-two years old, opened with rounds of 76-71-70 to put himself in contention, six strokes behind the leader, Johnny Goodman. Guldahl made up the deficit and came to the final tee needing a par-4 to tie Goodman, who had finished with a total of 287. Ralph hit a long drive down the middle but put his approach shot into the bunker to the right of the green. He then hit a fine niblick (an old club equivalent to an 8-iron) to within four feet but pulled the putt to the left and lost the championship by an excruciating single stroke. After this disappointment, Guldahl began to lose confidence in his game. He gamely finished eighth in the Open in 1934, and then, after finishing fortieth in the Open in 1935, he lost his job as a club professional in St. Louis. He went home to Dallas, gave up the tour, and tried to sell cars for a living. An acquaintance asked him to lay out a nine-hole course in Kilgore, Texas, and his short retirement from competitive golf ended.

Guldahl moved to the Los Angeles area in order to find an ideal climate for his young son, Buddy, who suffered from a lingering illness. Ralph worked as an assistant carpenter at several movie studios, taught at the Lakeside Club in Hollywood, and played occasional tournaments. He did not break back into the Tour until two backers sent him to the True Temper Open in Detroit in the spring of 1936. Guldahl finished sixth and won $245 in that tournament, finished eighth in the U.S. Open at Baltusrol, won $360 in another event, then won the Western Open, shooting a final-round 64. Guldahl won the Radix Trophy (the predecessor of the Vardon Trophy) for lowest average strokes per round (71.65).

Guldahl continued to regain his competitive touch. He won his first U.S. Open at Oakland Hills Country Club in Birmingham, Michigan. After three rounds, he was tied with SAM SNEAD, one shot behind the leader, Ed Dudley. Snead, then twenty-five years of age, was the rising star on the Tour. His flawless swing and 300-yard drives added to his allure. Snead, playing his first U.S. Open, had won the Oakland Open and the Crosby Open earlier in the year, making him one of the favorites in the Open. Snead shot a 71 for a total of 283, one shot more than Tony Manero's U.S. Open record, set at Baltusrol in 1936. When Snead entered the locker room, Dudley was already in with a total of 287. TOMMY ARMOUR congratulated Snead on being the Open winner.

But Guldahl was still out on the course and had a chance. He shot a 33 on the front nine and needed a 37 on the back nine to win the Open. His front nine was highlighted by an eagle on the 491-yard, par-5 eighth, which resulted when Ralph holed a 65-yard chip shot. Before teeing off on the home nine, Guldahl reasoned, "If I can't do it, I'm a bum and I don't deserve to win the Open," when he realized he needed a 37 on the back nine to win. After bogeying the next two holes, Guldahl birdied the following two, then parred three in a row. Guldahl repeatedly stepped away from his ball as he tried to compose himself on the last hole. He turned to his playing partner, HARRY COOPER, a fellow Texan, and asked, "What should I do on this one?" Cooper suggested, "Just don't drop dead." Guldahl parred the hole and finished with a final-round total of 69 to better Manero's seventy-two-hole U.S. Open record by one shot. He won the $1,000 first prize. Snead would win a record eighty-one Tour events but not a U.S. Open.

Guldahl had managed to fight his way back into economic solvency in the middle of the Great Depression. By 1938 he had paid off all his debts and was hired as a celebrity pro at the Miami-Biltmore in Florida and at the Braidburn Country Club in New Jersey. Now that he was a winner, other professionals knew that "the Dumb Swede" (Guldahl was actually of Norwegian extraction) was a force to be reckoned with on the golf course. Experience and Guldahl's phlegmatic single-mindedness in tournament play added to his reputation as a competitor. His basic golf philosophy was "All that matters in golf is the next shot."

The 1938 U.S. Open was held at the Cherry Hills Country Club in Denver, the first time the event was held west of Minneapolis. Dick Metz of Chicago took the lead after three rounds, three strokes up on Guldahl, who had rounds of 74-70-71. Metz, who played just ahead of Guldahl in the final round, lost his lead at the sixth, a 164-yard par-3, after he bogeyed and Guldahl birdied. Guldahl finished with a strong 69 and a total of 284 to gain ten strokes on the faltering Metz, who finished second at 290. Guldahl had become the fourth man to win two consecutive U.S. Opens, along with WILLIE ANDERSON (1903–05), JOHNNY MCDERMOTT (1911–12), and BOBBY JONES (1929–30). BEN HOGAN (1950–51) and CURTIS STRANGE (1988–89) are the only others to do it. Guldahl won his third consecutive Western Open in 1938 and collected a total of $8,600 in prize money for the year. Sam Snead led the Tour in earnings with a record $19,534.49 out of a total of $158,000 in purses available in thirty-eight official events.

Ralph Guldahl almost won the Masters in 1937, but after landing his ball in Rae's Creek on number thirteen and hitting into the pond on the following hole, he saw his four-shot final lead disappear. BYRON

NELSON fired a birdie 2 on the twelfth hole and an eagle 3 on the thir-teenth to pick up six strokes on Guldahl in two holes. Guldahl's final-round 76 cost him dearly, causing him to lose to Nelson by two strokes. Ralph finished tied for second in the 1938 Masters, won by HENRY PICARD, but his day finally came in 1939.

Guldahl fired an opening round of 72-68-70 to put himself two shots ahead of Sam Snead, Billy Burke, and Byron Nelson going into the final round of the 1939 Masters. Snead shot a final-round 68 and was in the clubhouse with a score of 280. Guldahl, still out on the golf course, hit a brilliant 230-yard fairway wood to within six inches of the hole on the par-5 thirteenth and holed out for an eagle-3. He parred the next hole, birdied the sixteenth, then finished bogey, par to win the tournament by one stroke. Burke and LAWSON LITTLE tied for third, two shots back at 282.

Guldahl's best year was 1939, when he finished third in earnings and won three tournaments in addition to the Masters. In 1940, teamed with Sam Snead, he won his last tournament, the Inverness Four-Ball. Al Barkow, in his book *Golf's Golden Grind*, theorizes that Guldahl's final decline, beginning at the age of twenty-nine, might have been due to Ralph's work on a golf-instruction book, which could have caused him to overanalyze his own swing: "He holed himself up in a room with paper, pencil and a mirror, and wrote his own book. For the first time in his life he had to figure out what he was doing. He agonized, he introspected, he watched himself in the mirror, and after he completed the book he couldn't break glass, as the saying goes. He never played championship golf again." Sam Snead observed, "When Ralph was win-ning, he had some peculiar habits, like all of us. His left elbow used to be stuck out a bit. He used to toe his irons. He drew the ball a little. But those small things didn't amount to anything. When Ralph was at his peak, his clubhead went back on the line and went through on the line as near perfect as anyone I've seen. I don't know what happened to Ralph."

Guldahl was selected to the Ryder Cup team in 1937 and 1939. He won his singles and foursomes matches in 1937, but the team did not play in 1939 due to World War II. Guldahl won sixteen Tour events in his career, tying him with NICK PRICE and MARK O'MEARA. He left the Tour in 1942, returned briefly in 1949, then left and never played the circuit again. He was elected to the World Golf Hall of Fame in 1981.

29

Gene Littler

1930–

I would have quit, but my wife wouldn't let me.

—GENE LITTLER, commenting on his
two-year slump from 1957 to 1959

After Gene Littler won the U.S. Amateur in 1953, he was hailed as the likely successor to BEN HOGAN, then reaching the end of his peak years. A quiet, modest person with huge hands and a rhythmic swing, Littler made striking a golf ball seem fluid and effortless. Nicknamed "the Machine" because of his ball-striking skills, Littler felt that he learned his stroke by osmosis, watching other golfers. But he recalls that SAM SNEAD might have been his model: "Sam was in the navy in San Diego when I was first getting into golf, and I sort of gravitated to watching him more than anyone else."

The 5-feet-9-inch, 160-pound Littler had a slow, grooved swing and an unhurried putting stroke. A native of San Diego, he attended San Diego State University for two years and played in one NCAA championship. He left school in January 1951, at the height of the Korean War, to enlist in the U.S. Navy. For three years, he was assigned to Special Services, did all his time in the San Diego area, and was able to refine his golf game in the process. In 1953, Littler won the California State Amateur at Pebble Beach and then played on the Walker Cup team. In the fall of 1953 he won the U.S. Amateur, one year before ARNOLD PALMER won it. In the early stages of their professional careers, Palmer and Littler were seen as being the next PGA Tour stars, with Littler generally given the edge because of his classic form. Palmer lost in the sixth round of the 1953 Amateur and thus did not confront Littler head-on in that event.

At first, Littler did not think he would turn professional even though he won the San Diego Open in 1954 as an amateur, the first to win a Tour event since Fred Haas in 1945. Littler later recalled: "Back in the mid-50s the prospects in professional tournament golf weren't all that good. The purse money wasn't much. At the time, a friend of mine from Seattle offered to bring me into his clothing business. I went up there and tried it but discovered pretty quickly that it wasn't for me."

Littler joined the Tour in 1954 and almost won the U.S. Open at Baltusrol. He shot rounds of 70-69-76 and needed to hole an 8-foot birdie putt on the final hole to tie Ed Furgol for the lead. Littler missed the putt for a score of 70 and a total of 285. After this near miss, Littler won four Tour events in 1955, three in 1956, and one in 1957. He had a severe slump until he won five tournaments in 1959 and two more in 1960. He had considered leaving the Tour during his slump, but as he later explained, "I would have quit, but my wife wouldn't let me."

Littler won the U.S. Open in 1961 at Oakland Hills, the fourth time the Open had been played at that site. In 1951, when Hogan won the Open at Oakland Hills, the course had been remodeled and toughened up by Robert Trent Jones. Only Ben Hogan and Clayton Haefner managed to break par on any round. In 1961, Jones made minor modifications. Seven of the 120 bunkers were removed, and the rough was lower and not so thick. But the large, undulating greens remained treacherous. As a result, several players broke par, but after three rounds, the golf course prevailed, and only Doug Sanders was under par.

After three rounds, Littler had a 73-68-72=213, 3 over par and three strokes behind Sanders. Prior to the tournament, Littler had improved his short game, taking lessons from PAUL RUNYAN, but he injured a rib in early 1961 and was coming back from that injury. On the final round, playing a few groups ahead of Sanders, Littler's strategy was to keep his ball on the fairway and try to win the tournament with his short game. This seemed to work. He holed a 15-foot putt for birdie on the seventh hole, birdied the eleventh with a six-footer, then gained the lead with a 15-foot birdie putt. After Littler finished with four pars and a bogey for a final-round 68 and a total of 281, Sander's only chance for a tie was to birdie one of the last two holes. Doug just missed a 16-foot birdie putt at seventeen and barely missed a birdie chip on the last hole. Sanders and Bob Goalby tied for second.

Littler almost won two more majors. He lost a play-off to BILLY CASPER in the 1970 Masters and another in the 1977 PGA Championship to LANNY WADKINS, the first sudden-death play-off in the history of that championship. Littler was selected to the Ryder Cup team six consecutive times (1961–71) and again in 1975. He posted a 14-5-8 record, and never played on a losing team. He underwent surgery for cancer of the lymph system in the spring of 1972 and miraculously returned to the Tour that fall. In 1973 he was awarded the BOBBY JONES and the Ben Hogan Awards for his courageous comeback. He won five more Tour events to bring his total to twenty-nine, tied for sixteenth on the all-time list with his instructor, Paul Runyon. Littler won his last Tour event in 1977, twenty-three years after his first victory. He joined the Senior Tour in 1981 and won eight tournaments and over $2.2 million. Gene Littler is in the World Golf Hall of Fame.

30

Jim Barnes

1887–1966

I always do better after lunch.

—JIM BARNES, just before he won his
first PGA Championship, after
lunch, on October 14, 1916

Born in Lelant, Cornwall, England, in 1887, Jim Barnes was a caddie and apprentice clubmaker before coming to the United States in 1906. At 6 feet 3 inches, he was graceful, straight, and long off the tee. A quiet and taciturn gentleman, "Long Jim" was well respected by the golf community. He became one of the early pioneers of the PGA Tour, along with WALTER HAGEN, TOMMY ARMOUR, GENE SARAZEN, and other great players of his era.

Barnes's first important victory came in 1914; he won the Western Open, then a major golf championship, in Minneapolis. In 1916 he won the first PGA Championship, held at the Siwanoy Country Club in Bronxville, north of New York City. The PGA Championship got its start when department-store magnate Rodman Wannamaker saw the merchandising opportunities of the Professional Golfers Association. On January 16, 1916, in New York City, seventy-five individuals, including Walter Hagen, convened for an exploratory meeting which resulted in the formation of the PGA of America. The PGA agreed to hold a championship of professional golfers who would play thirty-six-hole match-play contests to decide a winner after sectional qualifiers were held throughout the country.

Three British-born golfers, WILLIE MACFARLANE, Jim Barnes, and JOCK HUTCHISON, reached the semifinals along with Walter Hagen. Hutchison defeated Hagen, 2-up, when Walter hit his approach shot into the water in front of the green on the final hole of their match. Barnes easily defeated Willie MacFarlane, who later won the 1925 U.S. Open, six and five. In the final, Hutchison, a native of St. Andrews, Scotland, went 3-up after the first nine holes, but Barnes reduced the lead to one hole after both golfers scored 77 and took a lunch break. Barnes told the gallery, "I always do better after lunch," before he teed it up for the afternoon round. Long Jim squared the match at the twenty-first hole; then, after having Hutchison down one, the Scot evened the match at the thirty-first hole and took a 1-up lead at the thirty-third. Barnes squared the match when Hutchison missed a 5-footer on the thirty-fifth. On the final hole, both players had 5-foot putts for par, and after a measurement, it was determined that Hutchison was away. He again missed his short putt, and when Barnes holed his, he was the first PGA champion. Barnes won $500 and a diamond-studded medal. Hutchison received a gold medal and $250. The total purse of the event was $2,580 (compared to the $3 million purse in 1998 and the $540,000 first prize awarded Vijay Singh).

Under Mr. Wannamaker's sponsorship, the tournament was a success, and after a two-year break for World War I, the second PGA Championship was held in 1919 at the Engineers Club in Roslyn, Long Island, New York. The tallest man, Barnes, and the shortest man, 5-foot-3 inch Fred McLeod, a Scotsman from North Berwick who had won the 1908 U.S. Open in a play-off with Willie Smith, reached the final. This time the match was decided early after McLeod went down five after eighteen and lost six and five when Barnes holed a forty-foot birdie putt on the thirty-first hole.

Barnes won his next major tournament by capturing the 1921 U.S. Open at the Columbia Country Club in Chevy Chase, Maryland. Barnes started out strongly with a 69, and his score of 144 after thirty-six holes put him in the lead, three strokes ahead of Fred McLeod. Barnes closed with a seventy-two-hole total of 289, a nine-stroke margin over Walter Hagen and McLeod, who finished tied for second at 298. BOBBY JONES, then nineteen years old, finished fifth with a 303. President Warren G. Harding motored out to suburban Chevy Chase from Washington to present the trophy.

By 1925, Barnes had won two PGAs, one U.S. Open, three Western Opens, two North and South championships, and several others. He had been joint runner-up in the 1922 British Open, finishing one stroke behind Walter Hagen at Sandwich. Barnes had also made a good showing in the 1920 British Open at Deal, finishing sixth, six shots behind George Duncan, a Scotsman and member of the Ryder Cup team. Barnes added the 1925 British Open to his golf-championship resumé, winning by one stroke over Archie Compston and TED RAY at Prestwick.

Jim Barnes's last PGA tournament win was the Long Island Open in 1937. He is credited with winning twenty official PGA tournaments, tied for thirty-first all-time with HALE IRWIN, Bill Mehlhorn, GREG NORMAN, and Doug Sanders. Barnes wrote *Picture Analysis of Golf,* a bestselling golf instructional manual. He is a member of the World Golf Hall of Fame.

31

Horton Smith

1908–1963

Of these new young golfers, Horton Smith impressed me the most.

> —WALTER HAGEN, commenting on the new
> big hitters coming on Tour in 1928

Horton Smith was born in Springfield, Missouri, in 1908 and took up golf at the age of twelve. He won the Class B (for assistant professionals) Championship of the Midwest PGA in 1926 while attending Missouri State Teachers College in Springfield. In 1927, convinced that he needed to play golf full-time to be competitive, he left school to play

professionally. While working at the Jefferson City Country Club, Smith qualified for the U.S. Open at Oakmont, his first national competition. He finished out of the money in that event but made his impact on the professional golf scene in the winter of 1929–30 when he won seven out of nineteen of the tournaments he entered and was second in four others. He earned $20,000 in prize money, a huge amount for the time and significantly more than the first official PGA money winner, PAUL RUNYAN, who won $6,767 in 1934.

Smith, a nonsmoking, nondrinking straight arrow, caught the attention of Walter Hagen, who came in second to Smith in the Catalina Island Open in 1928. Hagen observed: "Of these new young golfers, Horton Smith impressed me the most." Hagen noted that the young golfers coming up tended to be "home-run hitters," like Babe Ruth, rather than finesse players or shotmakers. Smith, however, had an excellent short game. GENE SARAZEN ranked him among the best wedge players and putters he had seen during his competitive years. Smith, with his eerie, taciturn presence, was nicknamed the "Joplin Ghost." He was the last man to defeat BOBBY JONES in formal competition, the 1930 Savannah Open, which Jones used as a tune-up for his Grand Slam events. By the age of twenty-two, Smith had won thirteen official professional Tour events. One of the few college-educated players on the circuit at the time, Smith became heavily involved in PGA-tournament-committee activities in 1932 and later became PGA president and president of the Seniors.

Many observers thought Smith's administrative activities in the fledgling PGA Tour reduced his effectiveness on the golf course. The closest he came to winning the U.S. Open was in 1940 at the Canterbury Golf Club, near Cleveland. Smith had a first-round 69 to lead the field, then finished the first day with a 72, tying him for the lead with LAWSON LITTLE. A third-round 78 was costly because he closed with a 69 to finish one shot back of Gene Sarazen and Little, who won the play-off. Smith reached the semifinals of the 1928 PGA Championship at Five Farms Country Club but lost, six and five, to Al Espinosa. It was the best showing Smith made in the tournament. His highest British Open finish was a fourth-place tie in the 1930 Open, won by Bobby Jones, at Hoylake.

Smith was invited by Jones to the first Augusta National Invitational Tournament in 1934. The Augusta National golf course had been designed by Jones and Alister Mackenzie, architect of Cypress Point and other great courses. It was situated within a former nursery, called Fruitlands, owned by the Berckman family since the mid-nineteenth century. When Jones first surveyed the land from the crest of the hill where the clubhouse now stands, he said:

> I stood at the top of the hill before that fine old (manor) house and looked at the wide stretch of land rolling down the slope before me. It was cleared land for the most part, and you could take in the whole vista all the way to Rae's Creek. I knew instantly it was the kind of terrain I had always hoped to find. I had been told, of course, about the marvelous trees and plants, but I was unprepared for the great bonus of beauty Fruitlands offered. Frankly, I was overwhelmed by the exciting possibilities of a golf course set in the midst of such a nursery.

Jones and Mackenzie designed the course strategically, allowing a variety of routes or methods of attack on par. The golfer is rewarded in proportion to the type of shot required of him and how well that shot is played. The fairways are open, with no rough and few bunkers, but the greens are large, subtly undulating, firm, fast, and at tournament time, bedeviled by tricky pin placements.

Jones was the center of national press attention at the inaugural "Masters," then a good event but not yet considered a major tournament. Bobby Jones teed it up in a tournament for the first time in four years. He shot rounds of 76-74-72-72=294 and tied for thirteenth with Walter Hagen. Horton Smith led the field after three rounds with a score of 212 and birdied the seventeenth hole (now the 520-yard, par-5 eighth because the nines were reversed after the first tournament) on the final round, parred the eighteenth, and scored a 284 to win by one shot over CRAIG WOOD. Ralph Stonehouse, a club professional from Florida who participated in the event, described the first Masters as informal: "While I was very serious, dedicated to making a good showing, I still remember the atmosphere as very informal. Some of the fellows made a big party out of it. There was nothing like the pressure there is today."

Gene Sarazen's famous double eagle on the par-5 fifteenth in the final round in 1935 added to his reputation. On the strength of that miracle, he rallied from three shots behind to tie Craig Wood and win the Masters in the play-off. That shot also added to the aura of the Masters and, along with the goodwill everyone had for Bobby Jones, increased its importance. Smith collected $1,500 for his first Masters win, compared with the $828,000 Vijay Singh collected in 2000. Smith won his second Masters in 1936 with rounds of 74-71-68-72=285 to win by one shot over HARRY COOPER, who had led each of the first three rounds but shot a 76 on the final day.

Horton Smith is credited with thirty-two official PGA Tour wins, placing him twelfth on the all-time list, one behind TOM WATSON and one ahead of JIMMY DEMARET and Harry Cooper. Smith was named to the Ryder Cup team five times (1929, 1931, 1933, 1935, 1937) and had a 3-0-1 record in competition. Smith played his last PGA tournament in 1941 before going into the Special Services of the U.S. Army, where he used golf to entertain the troops. Before joining the war effort, Smith was a professional at the Oak Park Country Club in suburban Chicago and was active in sectional PGA work. After the war he became a professional at the Detroit Golf Club.

Smith was stricken with Hodgkin's disease in 1957 and underwent several operations in the next few years. In 1961 he received the BEN HOGAN Award for his courageous fight against his physical handicap. Smith was president of the PGA (1952–54) and the PGA Seniors (1962–63). He was elected to the World Golf Hall of Fame in 1990.

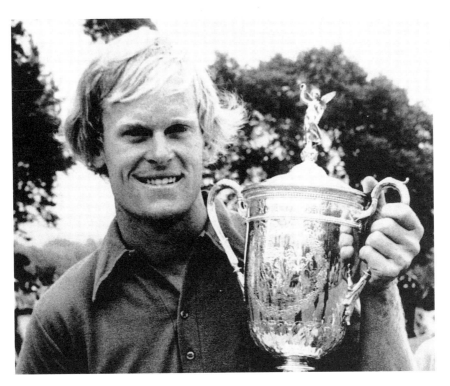

32

Johnny Miller

1947–

An out-of-body experience, almost like it was meant to be.
—JOHNNY MILLER, on his 1973 U.S. Open win at Oakmont

John Laurence Miller was born in San Francisco. His father, Larry, who began taking him to the golf course at a young age, always told Johnny, "You're going to be a champion." Miller won the 1964 U.S. Junior Amateur, taking the final, two and one, at the Eugene Country Club in Oregon. He also won the medal with a score of 139. At the age of nineteen he was the low amateur, finishing in a tie for eighth, in the 1966 U.S. Open at the Olympic Club. He was a member of the club at the time and signed up to be in the caddie pool for the Open, but after he succeeded in the Open qualifying rounds, he decided to compete. Johnny played varsity golf at Brigham Young University and turned professional after he graduated in 1969.

As a young man, Miller was an excellent putter with a natural feel. He can remember when he was a twelve-year-old playing at Golden Gate Park in San Francisco: "Adults say I couldn't make this putt one out of ten times even if I tried. But kids don't have 'adult' eyes. Kids can get magical. At Golden Gate, I one-putted the first five greens. It got so ridiculous I was putting everybody's ball in. I walked up and hit it, and it went in. Didn't even have to line them up. It was magic." One of Miller's early mentors was BILLY CASPER, also a devout Mormon, winner of the 1966 Open, and one of the best putters on the Tour. As Miller's game developed, he refined his compact swing and became an extremely accurate iron player.

Miller won his first Tour event in 1971, the Southern Open Invitational, and won the 1972 Sea Pines Heritage Classic. He came close to winning the 1971 Masters, a tournament he later said was overrated, tying for second with JACK NICKLAUS, two shots behind Charles Coody. Miller's most memorable achievement came at the 1973 U.S. Open at Oakmont, where he shot the best round in U.S. Open history to make up six strokes on the final day and win his first major.

Beginning the final round, the twenty-six-year-old Miller was behind twelve other competitors, including Jack Nicklaus, ARNOLD PALMER, LEE TREVINO, and TOM WEISKOPF. Miller told his wife to pack their bags for a late-afternoon flight out of Pittsburgh that Sunday. He felt he had no chance. But he did. Johnny hit all but one fairway at Oakmont, which had been softened a bit by weekend rains. He reached every green in regulation. Miller collected nine birdies and a single bogey on one of the most difficult golf courses in the world. If Miller had not taken twenty-nine putts, the same number he had taken on Friday, when he shot a 69, his record score might have been lower. Miller recalled that after birdieing the first four holes and being only two shots behind, he went into a gagging period:

> I did some simple math and knew I would be only two behind with fourteen holes to play. So I immediately went through a four-hole choking period that cost me at least two strokes. I left my birdie putt eight feet short on number five, then on number eight, the long, two-hundred-forty-four-yard par-three, I hit a beautiful four-wood thirty feet below the hole. Then I gagged my first putt and left it about three feet short. Then I missed that little one for my only bogey of the day. I didn't have any problem off the tee, but I was choking with my putting. . . . Then I started making birdies and birdied nine, eleven, twelve, and thirteen.

Miller also birdied number fourteen to go eight under and almost had a 62, but his birdie putt spun out on the final hole.

Miller finished with a total of 71-69-76-63=279. His final-round 63 was the lowest score in any major tournament up until that time. His third-round 76 was partly caused by his forgetting to bring his yardage notebook to the course. In the early seventies, competitors were not allowed to bring their own caddies to the U.S. Open. Johnny, who could hit laserlike iron shots on his approaches, had taken detailed notes of the yardages from various landmarks on the course during his practice rounds. He didn't want to have to be totally dependent on the caddie provided by the host club. Not having his yardage book threw him off: "I went into shock Saturday without my yardage book. . . . It's just that I was used to dialing in the exact yardage, to the yard, from the fairway when I hit an iron onto a green. I didn't want to hear that it was somewhere between 155 yards and 162 yards. I wanted to know in my own mind exactly how far it was to the pin. Without my yardage notes, I felt lost. My brain was going crazy. My confidence wasn't there, and it showed." Miller was 5 over par on the front nine, before his wife, Linda, could retrieve his book for him from their hotel. He had a par-35 on the back nine to salvage a 76.

After the tournament, Johnny recalled the pressure he felt after he shot himself back into contention in the last round. "There is a lot of pressure on the back nine. I was watching what was happening behind me, and I knew the guys behind me were watching what I was doing. I knew I needed at least one more birdie on the last four holes. When I hit a 4-iron in there about ten feet on number fifteen and made birdie, I really felt like I was going to win the Open. . . . You could feel the pressure on them (the other players) coming down the stretch. It was U.S. Open pressure—there's nothing else like it." Upon reflection, Miller also thought there might have been an element of predestination in his win: "I don't know if any round of golf was inspired from above— except the final round at Oakmont. Clear as a bell, He told me what to do. Twice the voice said, 'Open your stance up.' I opened it up and hit every green with an average putt of eight or ten feet." Miller won the U.S. Open by one shot over John Schlee. His final round was among the best U.S. Open finishes in history, ranking up there with BEN HOGAN's 67 at Oakland Hills in 1951 and Palmer's 65 at Cherry Hills in 1960.

Miller finished second to Tom Weiskopf in the British Open at Troon in 1973. He teamed with Jack Nicklaus to win the 1973 World Cup team play and won the individual title. Johnny had his best money year in 1974 when he won his first three tournaments, beginning with

the Crosby, and finished the year with eight PGA Tour wins, a total that
has not been equaled since. He set the one-year PGA earnings record
with $353,021.59 and was named PGA Player of the Year. He continued
his streak in 1975, winning the Phoenix Open with a 24-under-par score
of 67-61-68-64=260, giving him a fourteen-shot margin. Miller then won
the Tucson Open by nine shots, with a total of 263, and won the Bob
Hope Classic. He was becoming known as the best golfer in the desert.
Over half his twenty-four Tour victories were won on desert courses.

Miller won four tournaments in 1975, narrowly missing a Masters
win by one stroke, with a 66-66 finish. He won two Tour events in 1976
and the British Open at Royal Birkdale. Miller's final-round 66 in the
Open gave him a total of 279, easily distancing himself from nineteen-
year-old SEVE BALLESTEROS and Jack Nicklaus, who tied for second at
285. Miller then went into a prolonged slump that lasted until 1980,
when he won the Inverrary Classic. Miller won two tournaments in
1981, one in 1982 and again in 1983, cutting back his schedule due to
knee problems, which required a series of operations. Then, after establishing himself as an excellent golf analyst on NBC-TV, he won the 1987
AT&T Pebble Beach National Pro-Am, his last Tour win.

Miller had put limits on his commitment to golf at an early stage
in his career. By 1977, Johnny was the father of four children and
wanted to do other things, having concentrated on the game since he
was eight years old. "Golf to me was cool, but I wanted to do other
things. Go fishing. Do family things. Go fast in my cars. I couldn't just
play golf." By 1978, Miller had twenty-two endorsement contracts worth
$1 million and was financially secure. "After I was twenty-eight, I bet I
didn't hit a bucket of balls a week," Miller recalls.

Johnny Miller was selected to the 1975 and 1981 Ryder Cup teams
and posted a 2-2-2 record. His twenty-four Tour victories places him
twenty-first on the all-time list, tied with TOMMY ARMOUR. Johnny
joined the Senior Tour in 1997 but has played only a few events due to
knee problems, his broadcasting schedule, and other interests, including
his six children and growing number of grandchildren. Miller considers
his number-one accomplishment being a good father. He was elected to
the World Golf Hall of Fame in 1996.

33

J. H. Taylor

1871–1963

Flat-footed golf, sir, flat-footed golf.
—J. H. TAYLOR, describing
his stance

John Henry Taylor, a member of golf's first "Big Three," along with HARRY VARDON and JAMES BRAID, won five British Opens with a flat-footed stance that provided him with a solid base from which to execute well-positioned tee shots and accurate full-approach shots. Bernard Darwin, the noted English golf journalist, observed in his classic *The Darwin Sketchbook*, that Taylor's swing "was a marvel of compactness with his elbows close to his body throughout. It needed a strong man to play in his style and he was and is a very strong man. . . . (he) was a master of the low flying shot with backspin when the art of backspin was not perhaps so generally understood as it is now." He had a short follow-through, more like a punch shot than the elongated, lazy grace of a Vardon or a BOBBY JONES. Taylor executed his pitch shots well with a cleek, a shallow-faced, hickory-shafted iron similar to a 4-wood, but he was not known for being an excellent putter, although he was consid-

ered good. He introduced the mashie to the game, using it to cut
through linksland winds with uncommon accuracy.

Born in 1871 in Northam, Devon, England, a short distance from
Westward Ho!, the first seaside course in England, Taylor was the first
outstanding English professional. He left school at the age of eleven
and toiled as a caddie at Westward Ho! until he was fifteen. At age fifteen, caddies had to seek a permanent livelihood, so J.H. became a gardener's boy for three years and was a mason's laborer. At the age of
seventeen he became a member of the greenskeeping staff at Westward
Ho! Taylor was turned down by the army six times, once because he
was underage and at other times because of flat feet and poor eyesight.
He then decided to take a position at Burnham, in Somerset, where he
became the professional and greenskeeper. He later served as club professional at Winchester, at the recommendation of Andrew Kirkaldy,
then Wimbledon, before moving to Royal Mid-Surrey, where he served
as professional for the last forty years of his life.

Taylor was a high-strung man and took the game of golf very seriously. He once wrote: "To try to play golf really well is far from being a
joke, and lightheartedness of endeavor is a sure sign of eventual fail-
ure." Taylor won his first British Open in 1894 at Sandwich, the first
Open held outside Scotland and the first of sixteen Opens won by
Braid, Taylor, and Vardon during a span of twenty-one years. Up until
this time, the Scots, represented by such notables as OLD TOM MORRIS,
YOUNG TOM MORRIS, WILLIE PARK SR., WILLIE PARK JR., and JAMIE
ANDERSON, tended to dominate the Open. In 1895, Taylor won again at
St. Andrews with scores of 86-78-80-78=322. He went into the final
round three shots behind Sandy Herd but, despite headwinds and rain,
prevailed by four shots. In a flowery description in the June 21, 1895,
issue of England's *Golf* magazine, one H. S. C. Everard notes: "The
heroes of antiquity, who managed to win the spolia optima, were a small
band, to be counted on five fingers; those who have won consecutive
championships are also few, but very fit; and Taylor now joins the band,
and if there does not happen to be a temple of Jupiter Feretrius at Winchester (Taylor's home club), it is plain that one will have to be con-
structed for the champion's special benefit, and the accommodation of
his well-envied trophies." Taylor was becoming a national hero, and the
English were coming into their own in international golf competition.
However, at this time, the British Open was largely a contest among
Scottish and English golfers representing major clubs, such as St.
Andrews, Prestwick, Troon, Carnoustie, Musselburgh, and Hoylake. In
the field of seventy-six in the 1895 Open, there were twenty-one golfers
from St. Andrews alone.

Taylor, representing Mid-Surrey, won the 1900 Open at St. Andrews, defeating runner-up Harry Vardon by eight shots. Taylor considered his final round of 75 one of the best he ever played. Both Vardon and Taylor had been on tour in North America promoting golf and their own golf equipment under the aegis of A. G. Spalding, the Chicago sports and sporting-goods entrepreneur. Vardon promoted his new Vardon Flyer golf ball. Vardon, usually playing the better ball of his opponents, won over fifty matches, halved two, and lost thirteen. Taylor, who had married Clara Fulford and then formed a clubmaking partnership with his friend George Cann in 1895, came to the United States to promote his product line. He also was hired by Harper & Brothers to write articles for its magazine *Golf*, the first golf magazine published in the United States. At this stage, organized golf was just developing in the States. The USGA had been formed in 1894, and the first national championships, the U.S. Open and U.S. Amateurs, were held in 1895. British professionals were imported to staff the growing number of clubs, and British golfers won many of the early tournaments. An American-born golfer did not win the U.S. Open until 1911, when JOHNNY MCDERMOTT broke through.

Vardon and Taylor returned to the United States to resume their golf promotional tour, stopping at the Chicago Golf Club, one of the five founding clubs of the USGA, to play in the U.S. Open in October. Vardon won the Open with a score of 313, and Taylor finished second with a score of 315, demonstrating that the Americans had a long way to go before they could compete successfully with the British. Robert Sommers observes in his classic book *The U.S. Open: Golf's Ultimate Challenge*:

> Vardon and Taylor were an interesting contrast in styles. Vardon played high, soaring, slightly faded shots that were occasionally tossed about by the wind. Taylor hit low, running right-to-left shots, which weren't as effective in America as on his native links because the entrances to so many American greens were protected by cop bunkers (those with a high bank on the greenward face). Except for the strong southerly wind that would blow most of the championship, Vardon's style seemed more suited for the golf course.

Although Vardon won the U.S. Open with a gutta-percha ball, Taylor, who normally drove the ball around 175 yards with a guttie, found that he could add 50 or more yards to his drives with the new Haskell rubber-cored ball. He soon adopted the new ball, as did everyone else. He finished second in four consecutive Opens (1904–1907) and won the 1909 Open at Deal by four shots over James Braid. Taylor shot rounds of 74-73-74-74=295. J. H. Taylor won his fifth British Open in 1913 at Hoylake, where he fired 73-75-77-79=304 to win by eight strokes over TED RAY. The last two rounds were played in gale conditions, which Taylor described as follows: "I know something of what a gale wind is like, but this visitation was much worse than I ever experienced." His third-round 77 was considered an amazing accomplishment under the conditions. Only one other player, the two-time U.S. Open winner, Johnny McDermott, equaled Taylor's 77. This was the last Open held until 1920 because of World War I. Taylor also won the British Professional Matchplay Championship in 1904 and 1908, the French Open (1908, 1909), and the German Open (1912). His last best finish was fifth place in 1924 at Hoylake, at the age of fifty-three, six shots behind WALTER HAGEN, who won with a score of 301. Taylor never returned to the United States to play competitive golf. As nonplaying captain, he led the British team to a win in the 1933 Ryder Cup at Southport and Ainsdale.

A natural leader and a self-educated man, J. H. Taylor, a gentleman and a competitor, raised the standards for professional golfers, then an uneducated and unruly lot. He was founding member of the British PGA in 1900 and author of the book *Golf, My Life's Work* (1943). He retired to his home on a hill above Westward Ho! He called the view "the finest in Christendom." In 1950 he was chosen as an honorary member of the Royal and Ancient Golf Club of St. Andrews, as was James Braid and Willie Auchterlonie. In 1957, Taylor was elected president of the Royal Devon Club.

In addition to his activities as a professional, golf spokesperson, author, and clubmaker, Taylor designed, with F. G. Hawtree, several golf courses, including the Heliopolis Sporting Club in Egypt, the Royal Mid-Surrey Golf Club's Ladies Course in England, and the Nivelle Golf Club in France. Taylor used his considerable influence to promote the development of public golf courses in England. He is a member of the World Golf Hall of Fame.

34

Bobby Locke

1917–1987

Very early in my career I realized that putting was half
the game of golf; no matter how well I might play the
long shots, if I couldn't putt, I would never win.

—BOBBY LOCKE

Robert D'Arcy Locke is one of those skilled and colorful figures who
is remembered for his individualistic style as well as his golf ability. Born
in Germiston, Transvaal, South Africa, in 1917, Locke took up golf at an

early age and became a champion in his teens. His swing was a slow, loopy, inside-out stroke which generated a wide hook with seemingly little effort. He also hooked his putts, using a wristy stroke with an old, rusted, hickory-shafted blade putter. Locke's unorthodox playing style was complemented by his attire. He dressed in knickers and often wore a long-sleeved white shirt with a four-in-hand tie and a white linen cap. A big, roundish man, Locke had heavy cheeks and jowls, earning him the nicknames "Muffin" or "the White Rabbit."

Prior to World War II, Locke won a number of local events, including the South African Amateur (1935 and 1937) and three South African Opens. He won four more Opens after the war. He also won the Irish Open (1938) and the New Zealand Open (1938). He flew more than one hundred missions during World War II, then resumed his golf career, winning the Canadian Open (1947) and four British Opens (1949, 1950, 1952, 1957). He finished second in the British Open in 1946 and 1954.

The difficulties and cost of travel had limited the quality of the field in the British Open during the Depression, and World War II caused the suspension of play altogether from 1940 to 1945. Although most of the best American golfers stayed home during the 1946 Open, SAM SNEAD played and won with a score of 290 at St. Andrews, four strokes better than Locke and Johnny Bulla. Locke persuaded Snead to come to South Africa for some exhibition matches. When Locke won twelve of sixteen of those contests, Bobby was convinced that he could compete on the American Tour. Locke played in the 1947 Masters, paired with BOBBY JONES, and finished fourteenth, eight shots behind the winner, JIMMY DEMARET. Jones had a tremendous influence on Locke's golfing career: "When I was thirteen, my dear old dad gave me Bobby Jones's book on golf, and he said to me, 'Son, here is the finest golfer in the world, and I want you to learn how to play from his book. A lot of people are going to try to help you, but just let it go in one ear and out the other. You just model your game on Bobby Jones and you will be a fine player.' So that's what I did when I started and what I have done all my life."

In 1947 the twenty-nine-year-old Locke then won the Carolinas Open and the Houston Open, then won again in Philadelphia, making up ten shots on BEN HOGAN in the final two rounds. Next he took the Goodall Round-Robin when he birdied three of the last four holes.

Locke made his presence felt in the 1947 U.S. Open at the St. Louis Country Club, opening with a 68. Locke had become the first serious foreign threat in the Open since HARRY VARDON and TED RAY played at Inverness in 1920. Locke shot a 68-74-70-73 to tie for third, three shots behind Sam Snead and Lew Worsham, who defeated Snead, 69–70, in their play-off. Locke won seven times on the U.S. Tour and earned more than $24,000, placing him second in earnings to Demaret, who won $27,936.83 playing a full schedule. Bobby played on the American pro circuit for two and one-half years, competing in fifty-nine tournaments, of which he won thirteen, was second in ten, third in seven, and fourth in five others.

Before the war, Locke was a trim young man, intense and totally absorbed by golf. After his stint in the South African Air Force as a Liberator pilot, he was a bit rotund and mellow. He liked to tip a few and was known to play the ukulele at parties on the American Tour. But the money pressure of the PGA Tour and the resentment some Americans felt toward a successful young foreign golfer on their turf, caused him to become more hard-edged. One American pro commented on Locke in the 1950s: "The guy gets to me before we ever hit a shot. I look at that nutty outfit and I'm one down. I listen to that accent and I'm two down trying to figure out what he said. I watch that crazy swing and go three down trying to work out why he doesn't flat whiff it. Then he starts hooking those fifty-foot putts into the cup, and I'm done, cooked to a turn." In 1949, Locke left the American Tour to play in the British Open, which he won by twelve shots (135–147) in a thirty-six-hole play-off against Harry Bradshaw at Sandwich. Because he missed some PGA Tour events by staying in Britain, Locke was temporarily barred from the Tour by the PGA. The ban was lifted in 1951, but Locke rarely played in the United States after that.

Locke was never out of the top ten in the British Open from 1938 through 1957. During his five attempts to win the U.S. Open, he was in the top five each time. The closest he came to winning the U.S. Open was at Oakland Hills, in 1951, when he led by two strokes over Ben Hogan after fifty-four holes. Hogan finished with his stellar 67, and Locke closed with a 73 to finish third. Playing the tenth hole, when he heard of Hogan's great final round, Locke reportedly asked, "I say, did he play them all?"

In 1959, Bobby Locke was in an automobile that was struck by a train at a railway crossing in South Africa. Unconscious for days, he was lucky to have survived. But what bothered him most was the thought that he had lost his treasured old putter that had been in the car at the time of the accident. Days later, after Locke's concern was publicized, the putter was returned by someone who found it by the side of the road. Locke never won another significant tournament.

Locke was known for his methodical play on the course and his ability to score when not playing well. He believed that most putts were missed because they were misread, not because they were mishit. He was not a believer in excessive practice, but he had a passion for playing the game every day. Very early in life, Locke learned that physical relaxation, or at least lack of muscular tension, is essential to playing good golf shots; the game can be played one shot at a time, and there will always be an element of luck in golf.

Bobby Locke is a member of the World Golf Hall of Fame and an honorary member of the Royal and Ancient in St. Andrews.

35

Paul Runyan

1908–2002

I recognized early that I had to be very good at the short game or I wasn't going to go anywhere. All my playing career I was made fun of for my small size and being a short hitter. . . . I lived with being an unorthodox player. . . . I swayed way back behind the ball intentionally and lunged past it to get more leverage. I never learned to hit it far.

—PAUL RUNYAN

Paul Runyan was born in Hot Springs, Arkansas, in 1908. As a boy he began to sneak away from his father's dairy farm to caddie at the Hot Springs Golf and Country Club. His father considered golf a "frivolity" and never accepted it as a vocation. But Paul would bring home forty-five to ninety dollars a week hauling golf bags and shagging balls for pro lessons.

Runyan advanced to apprentice pro and won the Arkansas State Open four times before joining the professional Tour in 1930. He was quickly recognized for his excellent short game and controlled swing, which later enabled him to sustain his competitive game well into his senior years. (Runyan, now in his nineties, is still giving tips.)

Runyan won his first professional Tour event in 1930—the North and South Tournament—then one of the most prestigious events on the circuit. Among the notable golfers who have won this event are Donald Ross (1903, 1905, 1906), Alex Ross (1904, 1906, 1907, 1908), Fred McLeod (1909, 1920), Tom McNamara (1912, 1913), JIM BARNES (1916, 1919), Mike Brady (1917), WALTER HAGEN (1918, 1923, 1924), JOCK HUTCHISON (1921), MACDONALD SMITH (1925), Bobby Cruickshank (1926, 1927, 1943), HORTON SMITH (1929, 1937), BYRON NELSON (1939), BEN HOGAN (1940, 1942, 1946), and SAM SNEAD (1941, 1949, 1950), among others. The tournament, held in Pinehurst, North Carolina, where Donald Ross pioneered the design of fine golf courses in that region, was discontinued in 1952.

Runyan was selected to the Ryder Cup team in 1933 and again in 1935. In the 1933 Ryder Cup matches at the Southport and Ainsdale Golf Club in England, Runyan, paired with CRAIG WOOD, lost his foursomes match to William Davis and Syd Easterbrook, 1-up; then he lost a tight singles match, two and one, to Percy Alliss. The U.S. team lost to the British that year, 6½–5½. Runyan and the American team had better luck in 1935 at the Ridgewood Country Club in New Jersey. Runyan and Horton Smith easily defeated Bill Cox and Edward Jarman, nine and eight, in the foursomes; then Paul won his singles match, five and three, against Richard Burton. The American team won the contest, 9–3.

Paul Runyan's best tournament year was 1934, when he won his first PGA Championship and five other Tour events. He won the first official PGA earnings title that year with $6,767 in Tour prize money. The 1934 PGA Championship was held at the Park Club of Buffalo, in Williamsville, New York. Thirty-two golfers competed after a thirty-six-hole qualifying match. Runyan defeated JOHNNY FARRELL, eight and six; Vic Ghezzi, two and one; Dick Metz, 1-up; and Gene Kunes, four and two, to reach the final against Craig Wood, who had once been Runyan's golf instructor. It was a classic contrast in styles: Runyan, the diminutive 5-foot-7-inch, 125-pound, short-game artist against Wood, the big power hitter.

After the first eighteen holes, Wood held a 1-up lead but lost it on the front side of the afternoon round. Wood eagled the twenty-ninth, a par-5, to go 1-up, but Runyan squared the match with a birdie on the thirty-second. Runyan won the next, but Wood took the thirty-fifth hole to even the match. Both players made 12-foot putts on the final hole, necessitating a sudden-death play-off. Runyan hit a crucial chip-shot stiff to score a birdie on the first play-off hole; then Wood missed his 8-foot eagle putt to halve the hole. Both players scrambled on the thirty-eighth. Wood hooked his drive under a tree and sent his second shot into the gallery to the left of the green. Runyan pushed his approach shot to the right of the green but chipped to within eight feet. Wood's chip was twelve feet short of the pin, and he missed his putt. Runyan made his par putt to win his first major.

Runyan won the 1938 PGA held at the Shawnee Country Club, a Tillinghast-designed course, in Shawnee-on-Delaware in Pennsylvania. Beginning in 1931, the PGA had given an exemption to the defending champion, in this case DENNY SHUTE. But the other sixty-three players in the event had to qualify in a thirty-six-hole medal-play competition held on Sunday and Monday, before the tournament. In 1935, the format of the PGA Championship had been changed from 36-hole match-play contests to eighteen-hole matches in the first three rounds and thirty-six-hole matches in the quarterfinal, semifinal, and final rounds. The all-thirty-six-hole matches were revived during the PGA Championships held during World War II (1942, 1944, 1945), then reverted back to a mix of eighteen-hole and thirty-six-hole match-play contests until the PGA became a stroke-play event in 1958.

Runyan defeated Levi Lynch, five and four; Tony Manero, three and two; Ray Mangrum, 1-up in thirty-seven holes; Horton Smith, four and three; and HENRY PICARD, four and three, before he met Sam Snead in the final. Up until this point, both golfers had played approximately 160 holes of tournament golf, including the qualifier, in less than a week. The tournament was played in sweltering 100-degree heat and 90 percent humidity. Runyan would soak in a tub of cold water before play. Seemingly overmatched by the long-hitting Snead, Runyan outwitted the course and his opponent with his short game, firing a 67 and building a five-hole lead on the first eighteen. He shot 35 on the next nine to go up seven and closed out the match, eight and seven, at the twenty-ninth. Runyan's margin of victory was the greatest in the history of the PGA Championship final and is still the record for a match-play final in the PGA.

While successful in the PGA Championship, Runyan never made a serious run at the U.S. Open Championship. His best finish was a seventh-place tie in the 1938 Open, won by RALPH GULDAHL at Cherry Hills in Denver. And he was never a contender in the British Open. Runyan did win twenty-nine PGA Tour events, tied for seventeenth with GENE LITTLER. He led the Tour in wins with nine in 1933 and seven in 1934. His last Tour win was the 1941 Goodall Round Robin.

In 1961, Runyan won the PGA Seniors' Championship at PGA National, having tied for second the previous two years. His seventy-two-hole score of 278 earned him $1,500 from a total purse of $15,000. Runyan won again in 1962, also with a score of 278, to win $2,000. Paul Runyan is a member of the World Golf Hall of Fame.

Macdonald Smith

1892–1949

*If we all played golf like Mac, the National Open
Championship could be played on one course every day
in the year and never a divot mark would scar a beautiful
fairway. He has the cleanest twenty-one-jewel stroke in
golf. He treats the grass of a golf course as though it were
an altar cloth.*

—TOMMY ARMOUR, on Macdonald Smith's swing

Macdonald Smith, the younger brother of ALEX SMITH and Willie Smith, was born in 1892 in Carnoustie, Scotland. He won his first professional tournament, the Claremont Open, in 1910, after emigrating to the United States. That same year, Smith entered the U.S. Open at the Philadelphia Cricket Club and shot rounds of 74-78-75-71=298 to tie his older brother, Alex, then the professional at Wykagyl, and JOHNNY MCDERMOTT. Alex missed a 3-foot putt on the seventy-second hole that would have won him the championship. However, Alex prevailed in the eighteen-hole playoff, shooting a round of 71 to McDermott's 75 and Macdonald Smith's 77. This would prove the closest that Macdonald Smith, considered a better golfer than his brother, would get to winning a victory in a modern major championship. He won the Western Open (1925, 1933), the North and South (1925), and the Metropolitan Open (1926, 1931), considered major events in his day, and nineteen other PGA events.

Smith worked in a shipyard in World War I and returned to tournament golf in 1923. He had the chance to win the British Open at Prestwick in 1925, a year when neither WALTER HAGEN nor BOBBY JONES entered the tournament. Smith started off with a 76, then fired a 69 and a 76 to go into the final round five shots ahead of JIM BARNES. Barnes finished his final round with a score of 74 before Mac Smith teed off, making Smith aware that he needed a 78 to win the tournament. Herbert Warren Wind, in his book *The Story of American Golf,* describes what happened:

> That afternoon one of the most tragic chapters in the history of championship golf was written. Too intent on not being careless, Smith began to overstudy his shots and fussed away one stroke after another until he had used up 42 of them on the first nine. His enormous, all-too-devoted gallery, swarming over a course that was not made for galleries, pressed in closer on their hero, reassuring him that they knew he could play back in even 4s, completely forgetting their usually instinctive regard for a player's feelings because they wanted so much for Mac to win. They killed old Mac with their ardor. Whatever chance he might have had for coming home in 36 was smashed in the unruly rush of the unmanageable thousands, strangling the pace he wanted to play at, forcing him to wait ten minutes and more before playing a shot until they had filed across the narrow foot

bridges and pounded through the bunkers ahead and grudg-
ingly opened an avenue to the greens. Despairing but impo-
tent, Macdonald Smith played out his nightmare of a round,
posted his 82, and then, all to late, was finally left alone.

Smith finished third with a score of 303.

The British Open and U.S. Open brought added frustration to
Smith, for he had the dubious distinction of finishing second to Bobby
Jones on two legs of his Grand Slam in 1930. The British Open, played
at Hoylake, was a battle among Jones, Compston, Smith, and LEO
DIEGEL. Compston's final-round 82 cost him the championship, as did
Diegel's 75. Smith's final-round 71 left him two shots shy of Jones and
tied for second with Diegel at 293. The U.S. Open was played in blistering heat at the Interlachen Country Club in Minneapolis. Smith
opened with rounds of 70-75-74 to fall nine strokes behind Jones, who
shot a third-round 68 and led with a score of 212. Smith gamely closed
with a round of 70 for a total of 289, two shots behind Jones, who holed
a 40-foot birdie putt on the final hole to ensure his victory.

Smith's last close run at a major came in 1932; he finished second
in the British Open at Prince's. A 76 on the second round cost Smith
dearly as GENE SARAZEN put together scores of 70-69-70-74 to win by
five strokes over Smith, who had rounds of 71-76-71-70=288. Sarazen
rated Smith among the best 5-iron and spoon (similar to a 3-wood) players of his day. But with all his shotmaking skills, Smith would come
within a frustrating three shots of the winner of the U.S. Open or
British Open ten times—the U.S. Opens in 1910, 1913, 1930, and 1934
and the British Opens in 1923, 1924, 1925, 1930, 1931, and 1932.

Despite his problems with the majors, Smith won over fifty tournaments, twenty-four of them officially counted as PGA events. He
ranks tied for twenty-third with GARY PLAYER on the all-time PGA Tour
victory list. His best tournament year was 1926: He won five tournaments, including the Texas Open and the Canadian Open. Smith's last
PGA Tour win was the 1936 Seattle Open. Macdonald Smith, one of the
greatest players never to win a major, died in 1949.

37

Craig Wood

1902–1968

*A long hitter, Craig Wood was like the little girl who had
a curl right in the middle of her forehead. He was very
handsome.*

—HERBERT WARREN WIND, in *The Story of American Golf*

Craig Wood was the GREG NORMAN of his day, runner-up in all four majors, until he won the Masters and the U.S Open in 1941, when he was thirty-nine. Known as the blond bomber, the native of Lake Placid, New York, was noted for his style, good looks, and power game. He drove a Pierce-Arrow roadster around the tournament circuit and was one of the most popular competitors on the Tour.

Wood started his career as a pro at a nine-hole course in Manchester, Kentucky, and was an assistant bookkeeper for a tobacco warehouse during the off-season. His first significant professional tournament victory was in the 1925 Kentucky Open. He won sixteen more tournaments over the course of the next fifteen years, but he never could quite win the elusive majors. After losing a play-off to DENNY SHUTE in the 1933 British Open at St. Andrews, Wood was again in contention in the 1934 PGA Championship at the Park Club of Buffalo. Wood defeated Denny Shute, two and one, in the thirty-six-hole semifinals after defeating Al Watrous, two and one, in the thirty-six-hole quarterfinals. He then faced PAUL RUNYAN, a pupil of Wood's and an excellent putter. Wood had a chance to close Runyan out with an 8-foot putt on the thirty-sixth hole but missed, allowing Runyan to win on the next hole when Wood missed a 12-footer for a bogey five. In the 1935 Masters, Wood was in the clubhouse with what appeared to be a certain win. He had finished with a total of 282 after playing the final eight holes in 4 under par. GENE SARAZEN, the only contender left on the course, needed to make up three strokes on the last four holes to tie. Sarazen stunned the world when he picked up all those strokes in one swing when he holed a 225-yard 4-wood to double-eagle the fifteenth. He then parred in to tie the tournament. Wood, who had been runner-up in the first Masters, by one shot to HORTON SMITH the previous year, lost the play-off by five shots.

The fates continued to plague Wood in the 1939 U.S. Open, which was held at the Philadelphia Country Club's Spring Mill course. He tied with Denny Shute and BYRON NELSON, prompting the first three-way Open play-off since FRANCIS OUIMET defeated HARRY VARDON and TED RAY at the Country Club in 1913. The three finalists were beneficiaries of a collapse by SAM SNEAD on the seventy-second hole when he scored a triple-bogey 8 to finish with 286, two shots behind the leaders. Wood and Nelson each shot 68s in the play-off. Shute was eliminated when he shot a 76. Wood needed a par on the eighteenth hole to win the Open outright, but after hitting a spectator on the head with his hooked tee shot, he was barely able to get home with a bogey 5. Wood and Nelson played another eighteen-hole play-off round. Byron shook Wood's confidence with an eagle 2 on the fourth hole when he holed a 1-iron. Nelson won the play-off by a score of 70–73 for his second Open play-off win.

At this stage, Wood was a sympathetic figure in the golf world. In order to be more competitive, he decided to refine his game, opting for accuracy rather than length. The man who once hit a drive over 350 yards in the British Open reminded himself that golf is a target game: "Too many players—I was one of them—seek only to gain distance off the tee. They think that as long as they belt one out from two hundred and twenty-five to two hundred and seventy-five yards . . . the tee shot has been a success. This is not true. The tee shot is not a perfect shot unless it is so placed as to open up the hole for the second shot." With this in mind, Wood started to use a brassie rather than a driver off the tee. He concluded that the sacrifice in distance was a good trade-off for accuracy. The standardized steel-shafted sets of clubs that came onto the market in the 1930s provided more margin for error, enabling Wood to make these adjustments.

In the 1941 Masters, Wood started out with a 66 and, after rounds of 71-71, had a three-shot lead going into the final round. On the last day, he started with a shaky 38 on the front nine but rallied for a 2-under-par 34 and a score of 280, edging Byron Nelson by three shots. Nelson, who shot 33 on the front side, went to his watery grave when his approach shot on the par-5 thirteenth went into Rae's Creek.

Wood almost retired from the 1941 U.S. Open because of severe back pains. He had suffered a back injury in a 1932 automobile accident which continued to give him problems. Nonetheless, wearing a corset for back support, he teed it up at the five-year-old Colonial Country Club in Fort Worth, Texas, a very young course by U.S. Open standards. Wood's opening drive on the 569-yard, par-5 first hole reached a fairway bunker. He topped two shots, reached the green in five, and scored a 7. He was tempted to quit, but he composed himself and shot a respectable 73. Despite heavy rains during the afternoon round, Wood was tied for the lead with Denny Shute after thirty-six holes. The final thirty-six holes were played on Saturday. Local hero BEN HOGAN was five shots behind but finished tied for fifth with a score of 289. Wood shot two rounds of 70 to win the tournament with a score of 284, three shots ahead of runner-up Denny Shute.

This was the first time the Open had been held south of Maryland. Colonial's owner, department-store magnate Marvin Leonard, who first sponsored Ben Hogan on the Tour, attracted the Open by guaranteeing the USGA $25,000 in gate receipts. Leonard had golf-course architects John Brademus and Perry Maxwell submit five plans each for the golf course and supposedly chose the best eighteen holes out of the possibilities presented. The narrow 7,000-yard par-70, with its Bermuda grass greens and difficult weather conditions, made Wood's victory all the more commendable.

Craig Wood won the Canadian Open in 1942 and the Durham Open in 1944, his last Tour victory. Wood played on the 1931, 1933, and 1935 Ryder Cup teams and had a 1-3-0 record. He had a total of 21 Tour victories, twenty-seventh on the all-time list, along with PHIL MICKELSON, WILLIE MACFARLANE, and LANNY WADKINS. He was head professional at Winged Foot from 1939 to 1945 and, later, at the Lucayana Beach Club on Grand Bahama Island before he passed away in 1968.

James Braid

1870–1950

James Braid's championship career was the briefest of the
three (vs. Vardon and Taylor) but the most brilliant.

—ROBERT BROWNING, in *A History of Golf*

Bernard Darwin, in *Darwin Sketchbook*, describes James Braid as
follows:

> He was a superb iron player, famous especially with the
> now departed cleek, a master of every kind of running shot,
> and though not naturally a good putter, he made himself for
> one period of his career almost a great one. A better player
> out of difficulties I am sure was never seen, for not only
> could he by pure strength remove tons of sand and acres of
> heather, but he was as skillful and resourceful as he was
> strong. In fact at his best, he was almost impregnably armed

at all points, but it was his driving that delighted people when he first appeared, and it is still his driving, more especially against the wind, that they remember him best. It was at once so appalling in its ferocity, so rhythmical in its majesty.

Braid, a noted member of golf's Great Triumverate, along with the Englishmen HARRY VARDON and J. H. TAYLOR, made his mark on the professional golf world by winning five British Opens during a ten-year span (1901–10) and winning four British Professional Matchplay Tournaments (1903, 1905, 1907, 1911) and one French Open (1910). Born in 1870 in Earlsferry, Fife, Scotland, fifteen miles from St. Andrews, Braid was the son of a ploughman. After quitting school at the age of thirteen, he went to work as a joiner. He had first taken up golf at the age of four, won his first tournament at age eight, and played his early golf with Jack and Archie Simpson, noted Scottish professionals, and his cousin Douglas Rolland, runner-up in two British Opens. Braid was a scratch player by the time he was sixteen.

Vardon and Taylor were established young professionals when Braid, a very good amateur golfer, at the urging of his clubmaker-friend, C. R. Smith, joined the trade and became a golf professional in 1893. He moved to London to start his new career and played in his first professional match at Limpsfield in 1893. He showed that he could play with the best when he halved a thirty-six-hole match against J. H. Taylor, the reigning British Open champion, at West Drayton in December 1895. Taylor, in a postmatch speech, said that he could honestly assert that he had never played a better game in his life than he had against Braid. Although he knew that Braid was a good player, he acknowledged that the form shown by his opponent that day was a revelation to him.

In an article in *Golf* magazine on March 5, 1897, a commentator noted that Braid was equally good in match or medal play but match play brought out his strengths:

> . . . the stress of a hard match is the best psychological medium in which to note the temperament of a player. It is during the ups and downs of a match that we can see Braid at his best. . . . It (Braid's even temperament) is one of Braid's main strengths as a player. But along with this essential attribute which all our great players have in a more or less degree, there go two other qualities in the case of Braid—a judicious compounding of caution and brilliant dash. . . . Braid is cautious in all the shots he has to play. . . . But when

the adversary begins to rivet the chains of bondage on him, then there is an awakening and the game is forced for all it is worth.

As a result of his strong showing against Taylor, Braid was hired as a professional at Romford, Essex, in 1896. But it was not until he was past thirty that he would win his first British Open.

Braid won most of his money in challenge matches, high-stakes contests in which the opposing players would have backers and might even bet their own money. He also was in demand for golf exhibitions. A large man at 6 feet 1½ inches tall and 175 pounds, Braid was long off the tee, which pleased the galleries at his demonstration matches. Many of these exhibitions were with Harry Vardon and J. H. Taylor, and Braid often teamed with fellow Scot Sandy Herd, who, in 1902, became the first golfer to win the British Open using the rubber-core ball. Braid, along with J. H. Taylor, became active in the founding of the British Professional Golfers Association. In 1902 the London and Counties Professional Golfers Association was founded with Taylor as chairman and Braid as captain. This organization later added other chapters and became the Professional Golfers Association of Great Britain.

Braid was the first winner in the News of the World (1901) match-play championship, which was later called the British Professional Matchplay Championships. Braid became the first player to win five British Opens, beginning with his 1901 win at Muirfield. This record was later broken by Harry Vardon, who won six Opens, and equaled by J. H. Taylor, PETER THOMSON, and TOM WATSON. Braid was considered a formidable opponent in the gutta-percha era but, because of his putting, came into his own in the rubber-core era, which began at the turn of the twentieth century. He changed from a cleek, with the equivalent loft of a 2-iron, to an aluminum putter, reduced his hand action, and developed a smooth, pendulum movement with a slow takeaway of the club. But he still had enough trouble with his putting to miss a short one for a tie in the 1904 Open at Sandwich.

The following year, in 1905, Braid shot a 318 at St. Andrews to win the Open over J. H. Taylor and Rowland Jones by five strokes. He won the following year at Muirfield, firing a 300 to win over Taylor by four shots. In 1908 he won by eight, shooting 70-72-77-72=291 at Prestwick, then won his record fifth and final Open at St. Andrews in 1910, edging Sandy Herd by four with a score of 299. Braid was arguably the best player in the world from 1901 through 1911, when he won five British Opens, a French Open, and four British Matchplay Championships.

Even though his failing eyesight began to bother him in 1910, Braid reached the finals of the News of the World Professional Match-play Tournament when he was well into his fifties. His eyes had begun to bother him when he was in his teens, after lime was accidentally thrown into his eyes when he was a joiner. This possibly was the cause of some of his putting problems later on. He became a golf-course architect after his first Open win but designed courses (mostly with John R. Stutt) only in England because he feared the ocean and seldom traveled abroad.

Braid became the club professional at newly opened Walton Heath in 1904 and stayed there until his death in 1950. Braid was one of the earliest professionals to be granted membership in the Royal and Ancient Golf Club of St. Andrews. He is a member of the World Golf Hall of Fame.

39

Henry Picard

1907–1997

"The Chocolate Soldier"
—PICARD's nickname

Henry Picard was born in Plymouth, Massachusetts, in 1907 and at age seventeen moved to Charleston, South Carolina, where he won the Carolina Open (Charleston Open) in 1925, 1926, 1932, and 1933. Before he turned professional in 1935, he had already won two Tour-sanctioned events, the 1932 Mid-South Open and the 1934 North and South Open, which were included in twenty-six official Tour wins. In 1935 he was appointed professional at the Hershey Country Club in Pennsylvania, earning him the nickname "the Chocolate Soldier." He won five Tour events in 1935, three in 1936, and two in 1938, including the Masters.

Rain caused cancellation of the first round of the Masters in 1938. The tournament was rescheduled for eighteen holes on Saturday, thirty-six on Sunday, and eighteen for Monday. Picard had an opening-round

71, putting him three shots behind HARRY COOPER. He then shot two rounds of 72 to take a one shot lead over Cooper, RALPH GULDAHL, and Ed Dudley. Picard, who had changed his grip from an interlocking to an overlapping one shortly before the tournament, fired a 70 on the final day for a total of 285 and a two-shot win over Cooper and Guldahl.

Picard was the leading money winner on the PGA Tour in 1939, with $10,303 and six tournament wins, including his second Metropolitan Open and the PGA Championship. The Metropolitan Open, one of the best tournaments in the country, had past champions, including ALEX SMITH (1905, 1909, 1910, 1913), WALTER HAGEN (1916, 1919, 1920), GENE SARAZEN (1925), MACDONALD SMITH (1914, 1926, 1931), TOMMY ARMOUR (1928), and BYRON NELSON. The PGA Championship was played at the Pomonk Country Club in Flushing, New York. Picard defeated Earl Martin, six and four; Joseph Zarhardt, 2-up; Al Watrous, eight and seven; Rod Munday, two and one; and Dick Metz, 1-up, before meeting Byron Nelson in the final.

Picard led the thirty-six-hole match play final most of the way until Nelson birdied the twenty-ninth hole to square the match. When Nelson birdied the thirty-second hole, it was the first time in the match that he had the lead. Nelson and Picard halved the next hole; then Picard tied the match by sinking a 25-foot birdie putt on the thirty-fourth hole. They halved the next hole, and Picard went to the final tee 1-down. Both players hit their shots within pitching distance on the short, par-4 finishing hole. Nelson chipped to within three feet, and Picard hit his twelve inches from the pin (laying Nelson a dead stymie). The stymie was a legitimate strategy until 1951, when it was outlawed, taking an interesting gambit out of golf competition. Nelson tried to hop his ball over Picard's and into the hole with a lofted club but missed. Picard made his birdie to square the match. On the first extra hole, Nelson hit a perfect drive down the middle, but Picard hit his under a radio truck. (This was the first golf tournament broadcast on radio in the United States.) Nelson hit his approach to within five feet of the pin; then, after getting relief, Picard hit his second shot to within twenty feet. Picard made his clutch putt, but Nelson, never known to be a good putter, missed his. Picard was the new PGA champion.

Henry Picard was selected to the Ryder Cup team in 1935, 1937, and 1939. In 1935, paired with Johnny Revolta, he won his foursomes match, six and five, against Percy Alliss and Alf Padgham. He then defeated Ernest Whitcombe, three and two, in singles as the United States won easily, nine and three, at the Ridgewood Country Club in New Jersey. In 1937, the American team won, eight and four, at the

Southport and Ainesdale Golf Club in England. Picard and Revolta lost their foursomes match, two and one, to Percy Alliss and Richard Burton. Picard then won his singles match, four and one, over Arthur Lacey. It was the first time a visiting team had won the Ryder Cup. The 1939 Ryder Cup teams did not compete due to World War II. The competition would not be played again until 1947, and the British team would not win again until 1957.

Henry Picard had one of the great golf swings of his day and was an excellent long-iron player. Walter Hagen rated Picard, along with BOBBY JONES and CRAIG WOOD, the best 2-iron players of the era. He is credited with twenty-six PGA Tour wins, placing him twentieth all-time, one victory less than LEE TREVINO. Picard's last victory was the 1945 Miami Open. His last serious run at a major was when he reached the semifinals of the 1950 PGA Championship at Scioto before losing, 1-up, to Henry Williams Jr. at the thirty-eighth hole. Williams was down six with eight holes to play but came back to tie the match. Picard lost the match at the second extra hole when he missed a 20-inch putt.

40

Lawson Little

1911–1968

It's all mental. The man who doesn't plan out every shot to the very top of his capacity for thought can't attain championship form. I say this without any reservations whatsoever. It is impossible to outplay an opponent you can't outthink.

—LAWSON LITTLE, one of golf's greatest match play champions

William Lawson Little Jr., born in Newport, Rhode Island, was an outstanding amateur who turned professional, then won the U.S. Open and several important professional tournaments. The son of a U.S. Army officer, Little spent his childhood on the road with his family. He learned golf in San Antonio and then lived in the Philippines, where he played a nine-hole course, and spent some time in Tientsin, China, which had an eighteen-hole course maintained by expatriates in the

Russian concession. When the family returned to the States, Little received instruction from club professionals and, at age seventeen, was good enough to play in the 1927 U.S. Open at Oakmont. There he spent a considerable amount of time watching TOMMY ARMOUR, the winner of that championship, work his way around the golf course.

He was a powerful hitter who played the ball back in his stance with his club shut-faced. In the beginning of his career he had a strong right-hand hooker's grip but modified it over the years. He then took lessons from Tommy Armour, which helped him with his iron play and enabled him to better control his tee shots. Little had a deft touch around the greens. And he had a tough, almost pugilistic competitiveness on the golf course. He planned out every golf move like a battle strategy, the ideal mind-set for match play.

Little attended Stanford and was selected to the Walker Cup team in 1934, joining Johnny Goodman, FRANCIS OUIMET, Chandler Egan, and other fine American amateurs. He and Johnny Goodman won their foursomes match, eight and six; and Little easily defeated Cyril Tolley, six and five. At that time, Tolley was considered a long hitter, but the burly Little, 6 feet tall, was outdriving him by ten to twenty yards. The U.S. team easily won, nine and two. Based on Little's performance in the Walker Cup, some bookmakers had him at fourteen to one to win the British Amateur at Prestwick. In his seven eighteen-hole matches on his way to the final in that championship, Little was in danger only once. In the semifinals Leslie Garnett stayed with Little all the way, going into the eighteenth hole 1-down. Garnett holed a long putt to square the match, but Little came back on the first extra hole to win the contest. Little faced Scotsman Jock McLean, who had eliminated five Walker Cup players to advance. Little started out with a blaze of glory to bury his opponent, 12-down on the first round, by shooting a 33-33=66. He closed out the match, fourteen and thirteen, the largest margin of victory in a British Amateur final.

The golf world was called to attention as news of Little's achievement spread. He returned to the United States for the U.S. Amateur at the Country Club in Brookline, Massachusetts. The USGA set up the tournament so that 188 golfers who qualified in the twenty-four districts from New England to Hawaii would automatically enter the tournament match play. This meant that six rounds of eighteen-hole matches plus two rounds of thirty-six hole matches would determine the champion. Under this grueling format, many big names, including Francis Ouimet, Johnny Goodman, and defending champion George Dunlap, were eliminated in the first three rounds. Little's strength and stamina helped him survive. He reached the final against Spec Goodman, who lost seven and six to Little. Lawson shot 69 on the morning round in that match.

Little returned to Great Britain in 1935 to defend his British Amateur title at Royal Lytham and St. Anne's. He shot 80 in his first match and barely won, 1-up. Lawson reached the final and defeated Dr. William Tweddell, the 1927 Amateur champion, 1-up. Little had led after the morning round, 3-up, but Tweddell fought back, squaring the match at the thirtieth hole. Little won the thirty-second and thirty-third, but after a halve, Tweddell won the thirty-fifth with a great bunker shot and a long putt to cut Little's lead to one. Tweddell just missed squaring the match at the finishing hole when he missed an 18-foot putt.

Lawson completed his unprecedented amateur-title run by retaining his U.S. Amateur crown at the Cleveland Country Club that September. There were 201 sectional qualifiers for the 1935 Amateur, the largest field in the championship's history. Lawson eked out a 2-up win in the first round against nineteen-year-old Rufus King, a former trap-shooting champion who birdied the first four holes. Little reached the semifinal against Johnny Goodman, his former Walker Cup teammate, who made himself famous by eliminating BOBBY JONES in the first round of the U.S. Open at Pebble Beach in 1929. Both Little and Goodman were fearless competitors, and both were on their game. The match was all square after the twenty-eighth; then Little made his move. He scored four birdies in the next six holes to win the match, four and three. The final was played against Walter Emery, a law student from Oklahoma, who also proved a tough competitor. Emery, 3-down after twenty-eight holes of play, won the next two holes, but Lawson closed him out by shooting 4, 3, and 3 to win back two holes; then he eagled the 520-yard, par-5 thirty-fourth to win the tournament, four and two.

No one has matched Little's double double, winning both the U.S. and British Amateurs in successive years. Little won a phenomenal thirty-one consecutive matches under the most difficult conditions. Lawson turned professional in 1936 and won the Canadian Open. He won the U.S. Open at Canterbury, near Cleveland, in 1940. Little shot rounds of 72-69-73-73 to tie GENE SARAZEN with a 72-hole score of 287. Then he edged Sarazen in the play-off, 70–73. Sarazen thought the turning point of his play-off against Little came at the fourteenth, a medium-long par-4 where Sarazen, down two strokes, birdied the hole with a shot from off the green. Little had a difficult putt for par, a nasty downhill putt with a sidehill break, but he made it to preserve a one shot lead. Sarazen later said, "That stroke restored his confidence, completely and immediately. . . . He was going to be tough to overhaul now, I felt, and I was right. Little played the last holes in 3-4-4-4, hitting every shot with breathtaking conviction, and I couldn't break through that."

It was the first time Little had played well in a major tournament since 1935. It had become evident that he was a more formidable match-play competitor than a stroke-play golfer. Little's last PGA Tour win was the St. Petersburg Open in 1948. He won a total of seven official PGA tournaments. Little was elected to the World Golf Hall of Fame in 1980.

41

Peter Thomson

1929–

If golf schools were really effective in making champions, the United States would have one hundred players now better than anyone else in the world. . . . The best players are still the self-made ones.

—PETER THOMSON

Peter Thomson was born in Melbourne, Australia, in 1929, the son of a sign painter and club cricket player. Thomson learned golf during the World War II years at a nine-hole course called Royal Park, not far from the Melbourne Zoo. His goal, originally, was to be a chemist; he won three scholarships to technical schools in Melbourne, studied applied chemistry, then worked as a rubber technologist for a major sporting-goods company. But after success as an amateur golfer, he turned professional in 1949.

Thomson established his international reputation when he won the British Open Championship five times. He had a game suitable to seaside linksland courses and was a master at finesse shots that required improvisation. He hit low off the tee and was exceedingly accurate with the wood, long and midirons. He tended to be more successful on the international circuit than on the American Tour, where he spent a limited amount of time.

At the age of twenty-four, Thomson won his first British Open title at Royal Birkdale. Peter recorded scores of 72-71-69-71=283 to win by a stroke over three golfers, including BOBBY LOCKE. He won again in 1955 at St. Andrews with a 71-68-70-72=281 total and again in 1956 at Hoylake with rounds of 70-70-72-74=286. He finished second to Bobby Locke in 1957 at St. Andrews but regained his title in 1958 by defeating D. C. Thomas in a play-off at Royal Lytham, 139–143.

Strong international players such as Locke, GARY PLAYER, Dai Rees, ROBERTO DE VICENZO, and Christie O'Connor, among others, competed in the first four Opens that Thomson won. Then ARNOLD PALMER made his pilgrimage to the Open in 1960, forever endearing him to the British. JACK NICKLAUS, TONY LEMA, and the best Americans soon followed, and the Open was fully revived to its past splendor as one of the leading championships in the world. Thomson proved his mettle in the 1965 Open at Royal Birkdale when he bested a field that included Palmer, Nicklaus, Lema, Player, de Vicenzo, and other greats. The Royal Birkdale course measured over 7,000 yards but played downwind on the back nine, where four of its five par-5 holes are located. As a result, the short-hitting Thomson could reach those greens in two, enabling him to compete with such big hitters as Nicklaus, who in practice rounds had reached the 510-yard seventeenth with a drive and a sand wedge.

The 1965 British Open was the last occasion on which the final two rounds were played on one day. Paired with Lema, Thomson shot 72 in the morning round and 71 in the afternoon to finish with a seventy-two-hole total of 285, two shots better than Christie O'Connor and Brian Hagget. Lema, who was the defending Open champion, was the top American finisher with 289. On the final eighteen, Thomson went out in 34 but missed four short putts of less than ten feet on holes eleven through fourteen and closed with a 37 on the back nine. Lema ruined his chances with a five and a six on the final two holes. Thomson and TOM WATSON, JAMES BRAID, and J. H. TAYLOR are the only golfers to win five Opens, one behind HARRY VARDON.

Thomson traveled to the United States in 1953, and from 1953 to 1959 he finished in the top ten in twenty-two events but only won one tournament, the Texas International Open in 1956, where he beat CARY MIDDLECOFF and GENE LITTLER in a play-off. Thomson later played on the PGA Senior Tour, winning the money title in 1985, with $386,724, and nine tournaments.

In his own country, Peter Thomson is acknowledged as the man who put Australian golf on the international map, paving the way for DAVID GRAHAM, GREG NORMAN, Steve Elkington, and other outstanding golfers. In addition to his fine British Open record, Thomson won the New Zealand Open eight times, the Australian Open three times, and the British Professional Matchplay Tournament four times. Thomson and Kel Nagle won the Canada Cup for Australia in 1954 and 1959.

Thomson has made a variety of contributions to golf. He has written regular golf columns and has served as a golf announcer in the broadcast media. He has been very active in the Australian PGA and is responsible for developing the Far East Tour. He is a golf-course architect who designed a variety of courses in the United States, Australia, the Caribbean, and Asia, mostly with Michael Wolveridge. Thomson is coauthor of *The World Atlas of Golf*, a respected, basic golf reference first published in 1976. His personal test of good golf design is "If my grandmother can't play it, it's a lousy course."

As a self-made man, Thomson does not believe in the modern trend toward golf academies, saying the best golfers are those who rely on their own wits and skill. Among the best modern self-made players are ERNIE ELS, TIGER WOODS, NICK FALDO, SEVE BALLESTEROS, and Greg Norman, according to Thomson. One of his most recent achievements was to captain the International team to a decisive 20½–11½ win over the U.S. team at the Royal Melbourne Golf Club in the President's Cup in December 1998. Two of his self-made men, Greg Norman and Ernie Els, played on that team. Jack Nicklaus, America's team captain, commented at the awards ceremony: "We used to think golf was only played in the United States. We didn't even invent it. I'm not even sure how we will play it anymore." In 1949, Thomson had to leave his native Australia to play against world-class competition. By 1998 golf was truly an international game. Peter Thomson was elected to the World Golf Hall of Fame in 1988.

42

Larry Nelson

1947–

I learned something valuable about myself there (in PGA Qualifying School). I learned that I like playing with guys who were better than me because I could learn from them. Eventually I learned I could beat them.

—LARRY NELSON

Like WALTER TRAVIS, Larry Nelson is one of the few great golfers who did not take up the game until he was an adult. Born in Fort Payne, Alabama, in 1947, Larry was a good high school athlete. He lettered in baseball and basketball, then attended Southern Tech for a year before he was drafted into the military and served in the Vietnam War. After his discharge from the military, he attended Kennesaw Junior College in Georgia and graduated with an engineering degree. While studying for his degree, Nelson did some work as a draftsman in an aircraft plant and during his free time went to a local driving range and discovered he liked hitting golf balls. In 1969 he went to work at Bert Seagrave's shop at the Pine Tree Club in Kennesaw. Seagrave gave him BEN HOGAN's book, *The Modern Fundamentals of Golf*, whose principles he applied to his golf game. In 1972, Nelson was good enough to venture onto the mini-Tour. He finished bogey-bogey to lose by one shot in the Florida State Open. This was the first seventy-two-hole event he had ever played in. By fall of that year he had earned his PGA Tour playing card.

Nelson gradually worked his way up the PGA Tour money list. His game began to come together in 1979 when he won his first Tour event at Inverrary, captured the Western Open, finished fourth in the U.S. Open, and tied for second in the World Series of Golf. He had nine top-ten finishes and was the second-leading money winner. In his first Ryder Cup at the Greenbrier in 1979, Nelson teamed with LANNY WADKINS to win his four-ball match, two and one, over Antonio Garrido and SEVE BALLESTEROS the first day, then beat them again the next day, five and four. In the foursomes, Nelson and Wadkins defeated Brian Barnes and Bernard Gallacher, two and one, then defeated Ballesteros and Garrido the second day. In the singles, Nelson defeated Ballesteros, three and two, to ring up a total of five points in the 17–11 U.S. team triumph.

Nelson won his first major in 1981, winning the PGA Championship at the Atlanta Country Club, less than a half hour from his home in Georgia. He shot 70-66-66-71=273 to win by four strokes over FUZZY ZOELLER. Larry again excelled in Ryder Cup play, teaming with LEE TREVINO in foursomes to win, 1-up, over BERNHARD LANGER and Manuel Panero. He then was paired with TOM KITE, and they defeated SANDY LYLE and Mark James in four-balls, 1-up. Nelson won two more matches, one with Kite, three and two, over Des Smyth and Bernard Gallacher in foursomes, and a 2-up singles victory over Mark James. The American team easily won the match, 18½–9½, at the Walton Heath Golf Club in Surrey, England, and again Larry Nelson had contributed four points to the cause.

Despite playing poorly before the 1983 U.S. Open at Oakmont (missing the cut in nine of his sixteen previous tournaments and withdrawing from another), Nelson somehow recovered his game. After a slow start with rounds of 75 and 73, which put him seven shots off the pace, Nelson shot a 65 to bring him to even par for the tournament and one shot behind the leaders, Seve Ballesteros and TOM WATSON. Nelson was paired with Calvin Peete in the final round and teed off just ahead of the leaders. Nelson, still applying Ben Hogan's techniques, used his sound, uncomplicated, compact, repeating swing to go to 3 under par through seven holes. He bogeyed the eighth, then birdied the ninth for a score of 33 on the front side. However, he had lost ground to Watson, who had six birdies on the first nine for a total of 31 and a three-shot lead. Ballesteros had a 36 to fall off the pace, and Peete dropped back with a 37. Watson then began to falter, and Nelson caught him on the fourteenth hole, where he hit a wedge stiff and birdied to pull even for the lead. Rain then caused play to be suspended until the next day.

Play resumed on Monday with Watson facing a thirty-five-foot putt on the fourteenth and Nelson about to tee off with a 4-wood on the 230-yard, par-3 sixteenth. Watson made par, but Nelson's tee shot landed well to the left of the pin, approximately sixty feet away. Nelson examined his putt for a long time, stepped up and stroked it firmly, then ran around the green pumping air with his fists when the ball some-how found the hole for a clutch birdie. Nelson, one stroke ahead of Watson, just missed a birdie putt on the seventeenth, then bogeyed the final hole for a round of 67 and a 4-under-par total of 280. Watson then bogeyed the seventeenth and parred the final hole to lose by one shot. Nelson had played the final two rounds in 65-67=132, breaking GENE SARAZEN's Open record for the final thirty-six holes, set in 1931 at Fresh Meadows, by four strokes.

Larry Nelson had his best earnings year in 1987, winning $501,292, placing him fourteenth on the money list. He won his second PGA Championship at PGA National that year. Nelson shot rounds of 70-72-73-72 for a 1-under-par total of 287 to tie with Lanny Wadkins, the only other player to break par. Nelson won on the first extra hole to become the fifteenth player to win more than one PGA Championship. He holed his putt from six feet, and Wadkins missed his from four. Nelson has a career record of 3-2 in play-offs.

In 1987, Nelson played on his third Ryder Cup team and lost three tough matches as the European team upset the U.S. squad at Muirfield Village in Ohio, 15–13. Nelson and PAYNE STEWART lost to Seve Ballesteros and JOSE MARIA OLAZABAL, 1-up, in the foursomes the first day; Nelson and Wadkins lost to Lyle and Langer, two and one, in the morning foursomes on day two; then they lost, 1-up, to Lyle and Langer in four-balls that afternoon. Nelson halved his singles match with Langer to bring his Ryder Cup playing record to 9-3-1, one of the best winning percentages in the history of the event.

Many thought that Larry Nelson should have been the Ryder Cup captain in 1997 rather than Tom Kite. The argument was that Nelson would be forty-nine years old in 1997, Kite forty-nine in 1999, BEN CRENSHAW forty-nine in 2001, and CURTIS STRANGE forty-eight in 2003, providing a strong continuum in American leadership as players reached the end of their Tour playing days. But many people have underestimated Larry Nelson and have not given him his due. John Gerring, a club professional who has followed Nelson's career, recalls: "When Larry started out, there were guys all over Georgia who said they could beat him. . . . In fact none of them ever beat Larry. He never let up when he got a lead and just quietly got better and better. His ball striking reminded me of Ben Hogan, and like Hogan, he let his game do the talking. I like to think of Larry, in fact, as Hogan with a smile."

Nelson's last win on the PGA Tour was the Georgia-Pacific Atlanta Classic in 1988. Nelson won ten PGA Tour events and over $3.8 million in his career. He joined the Senior Tour in 1997 and has now won a total of sixteen tournaments and more than $6 million.

43

Payne Stewart

1957–1999

I began to wonder whether I was ever going to win again.
— PAYNE STEWART, after winning the Shell Houston Open
in 1995, ending a four-year tournament drought

Payne Stewart learned the game of golf from his father, who twice won the Missouri State Amateur Championship. Payne played golf at Southern Methodist University and graduated with a business degree in 1979. In the family tradition, he won the Missouri State Amateur in 1979 before turning professional. After failing to qualify for the Tour, he played on the Asian and European circuits. He won the Indonesian Open and the Indian Open in 1981, then won the Quad City Open for the first of his ten PGA Tour wins in 1982. He also had seven international wins to his credit.

Stewart's best money year was 1999, when he was seventh in tour earnings with $2,077,950. Prior to that, his best year was 1989, when he won the MCI Heritage Classic and the PGA Championship. Payne's PGA Championship win at Kemper Lakes near Chicago had a classic finish. Stewart started out with a score of 74 but then shot solid rounds of 66 and 69 to position himself six strokes behind the leader, Mike Reid. Payne started his final round with a 36 on the front nine, making his chances look slim to none. But then, beginning at the thirteenth hole, a seven-shot swing between Reid and Stewart took place. Payne birdied four of the last five holes to shoot a 67, for a total of 276. Reid bogeyed sixteen, double-bogeyed seventeen, and missed an 8-foot birdie putt on the final hole to lose by one shot. Reid tied for second with Andy Bean and Curtis Strange.

Stewart was a fine shotmaker, long off the tee, a superb chipper, and an adequate putter. He differentiated himself on the Tour with his attire as well as with his play. He landed a marketing deal with the National Football League (NFL) and for a time wore golf attire that included knickers color-coordinated with NFL team colors. This was a modern marketing version of Jimmy Demaret or Doug Sanders wearing outfits that would make them identifiable without a scorecard. Writer Dan Jenkins once remarked that Stewart looked like "a parking valet." No matter. Stewart established his own line of golf clothes (including knickers for the uninhibited).

Stewart was not unfamiliar with disappointments on the Tour. After winning his second major, the 1991 U.S. Open, in a play-off with Scott Simpson at Hazeltine, Stewart went through a winless drought spanning 1991 to 1995, when he won the Shell Houston Open. This win helped catapult him from 123rd on the money list in 1994 to 12th in 1995. Another dry spell set in through 1998, but Payne won his tenth Tour event in a rain-shortened fifty-four-hole outing at the AT&T Pro-Am in 1999. That brought his Tour earnings to over $11 million, placing him in the top five all-time on the PGA Tour. With over $13 million, he was in the top twenty in all-time worldwide tournament earnings.

Stewart experienced two tough losses in the U.S. Open, both to Lee Janzen. In the 1993 Open at Baltusrol, Stewart shot 70-66-68=204, placing him one shot behind the leader, Janzen, going into the final round. Payne and Lee were paired the final day, and after nine holes, Lee was still ahead by one. Stewart evened the match at the twelfth but then fell one shot behind when Lee birdied the fourteenth. Then Lee broke Payne's heart with a chip-in birdie on the sixteenth and carried a two-stroke cushion into the final hole. Both players parred the eighteenth, and Lee Janzen was the winner by two shots, with a score of 272, tying JACK NICKLAUS's U.S. Open record, also at Baltusrol, in 1972. The five lowest scores in U.S. Open history have been made at Baltusrol, including Payne Stewart's 274 in the 1993 Open.

In the 1998 Open at Olympic, Stewart had rounds of 66-71-70=207 to lead the field after fifty-four holes, but he couldn't hold the lead. He shot a final-round 74 on a golf course that is much tighter and tougher than Baltusrol, with greens that are not easily read. Janzen shot a fine final round of 68 to finish with an even-par 280, one better than Stewart, who just missed a birdie putt to tie on the final hole. The difference between the first- and second-place finish was $220,000.

Stewart had a few disappointments in the British Open. For example, in 1985 he almost won the tournament when he shot a final-round 68 at Royal St. George's and came up one shot short of SANDY LYLE, who won with a score of 282. Payne Stewart was selected to five Ryder Cup teams (1987, 1989, 1991, 1993, 1999) and held his own against tough European competition with an 8-9-1½ record.

Stewart had his best year as a golfer in 1999 when he won his second U.S. Open at Pinehurst by holing a clutch putt on the final hole to win by one shot over PHIL MICKELSON. He was selected to the victorious U.S. Ryder Cup Team and was at the top of his game. But on October 25, 1999, Stewart tragically died in a private plane crash. The PGA Tour announced that, beginning in 2000, it would present the annual Payne Stewart Award to the PGA Tour member who best represents the professionalism and commitment to charity, golf tradition, and personal presentation. Not since 1966, when Tony Lema and his wife died in the crash of a private airplane one day after the PGA Championship in Akron, Ohio, had a PGA Tour golfer in his prime been so tragically lost. Payne was elected to the World Golf Hall of Fame in 2001.

44

Harry Cooper

1904–2000

*Drove ninety all the way and got only one ticket. The cop
was the village blacksmith, the justice, the town barber, who
sat up in his chair and took twelve dollars and costs. In Van
Horn, Texas. Ever hear of it?*

> —HARRY COOPER, describing travel on the
> professional golf tour in 1939

"Lighthorse" Harry Cooper was born in Leatherhead, Surrey, England, in 1904 but moved with his parents to Texas at a young age. His father, Syd, who had worked as an assistant under Old Tom Morris in St. Andrews, was a golf professional at the Tenison Park municipal course in Dallas. Harry learned to play golf under his father's watchful eye and turned professional in 1923. He won his first Tour victory, the Galveston Open, that same year. He won the Texas Open in 1923 and again in 1924, the Los Angeles Open and the Monterey Peninsula Open in 1926, and the Pebble Beach Open in 1927. By this time he was dubbed "Lighthorse" by the writer Damon Runyan because of the speed with which he played shots and chased after them. A fine shot-maker from tee to green, he sometimes had trouble putting, and despite his thirty-one official PGA victories, he never won a modern major, although he did win the Canadian Open (1932, 1937) and the Western Open (1934).

Cooper almost won the U.S. Open at Oakmont in 1927. He opened with quality rounds of 74-76-74 on that difficult 6,900-yard, heavily bunkered layout. On the first day, no one scored par, and half the scores were above 80. Going into the final round, Cooper was one stroke ahead of TOMMY ARMOUR, one of seven players in contention. Harry reached the seventy-first green the leader and seeming winner. He had a delicate downhill putt of twelve feet for a birdie. Leader boards were not in use at the time, and the front runners were often randomly given tee times rather than being placed in the last groups to play each round. Cooper, lacking accurate information about where he stood in the tournament, thought he needed a birdie to preserve his lead. He hit his putt a bit too boldly, missed, then missed again and made a bogey 5. Cooper finished with a 77 and a total of 301, which was later matched by Tommy Armour, who birdied the final hole by hitting a 3-iron stiff. The eighteen-hole play-off between the twenty-three-year-old Cooper and Armour, a wounded war hero from World War I, was even after the front nine. Cooper had gained a one-shot lead as they went to the fifteenth, but Armour drained a 50-foot putt for a birdie to even the match. Armour picked up two more strokes at the 226-yard, par-3 sixteenth after Cooper bunkered his approach shot and went on to win the play-off, 76–79.

Cooper was rated one of the best golfers in America from 1927 to 1937, but by the time the 1936 U.S. Open was played at Baltusrol, Harry had yet to win a major tournament. He led for the first three rounds of the 1936 Masters but shot a 76 on the final round and lost by one shot to HORTON SMITH. At Baltusrol, three players broke 70 the first day, an unusual achievement during an era of nonstandard, hickory-shafted clubs and golf balls that were not consistent in quality, even those from the same manufacturer. Cooper shot rounds of 71-70-70=211 to set a new U.S. Open record for fifty-four holes. He was two shots ahead of Vic Ghezzi going into the final round. Harry scrambled on the front nine to record a solid 35 at the turn. After bogeying the fourteenth, fifteenth, and eighteenth holes, Harry came in with a 38 for a final-round total of 73 and a seventy-two-hole score of 284, two shots better than CHICK EVANS's U.S. Open record of 286, set in 1916. Vic Ghezzi shot a final-round score of 81 to take him out of the running.

Fans were congratulating Harry on his victory, but he had been disappointed before. He cautiously replied, "I haven't won this thing yet." And he was right. Tony Manero, a young professional from the Sedgefield Club in Greensboro, North Carolina, was still out on the golf course. He had started the final round four strokes behind Cooper but had shot 33 on his front nine. By the time he completed the sixty-eighth hole, he needed to finish at 1 over par to win. Realizing the situation, the gallery swarmed all over the course to position themselves for the finish. There were no marshals of any significance in those days. As a result, the lack of crowd control sometimes delayed Manero's shots several minutes. But his playing partner, GENE SARAZEN, a veteran competitor and U.S. Open champion, calmed him down and "talked him in." Manero finished with a 34 and a total of 67 to win by two strokes. Manero's 67 was a new course record, and his score of 282 set a new Open record. Ironically, Cooper would have to calm down a nervous RALPH GULDAHL, who won the Open at Oakland Hills the following year.

One of Cooper's best years was 1937: He won seven tournaments and was the leading money winner with $14,138.69 in prize money from Tour events. This was a sizable amount of money considering that 20 million people were unemployed in the Depression and it cost approximately ten dollars a day to travel the Tour circuit. He won the Vardon Trophy (then called the Radix Award) for low stroke average. Cooper's thirty-one triumphs on the Tour are the most by any player who did not win a major tournament. He is fourteenth on the all-time PGA Tour win list, tied with JIMMY DEMARET. As a foreign-born golfer, Cooper was not eligible for the U.S. Ryder Cup team. Harry won his last PGA Tour event at the 1939 Goodall Palm Beach Round Robin.

PAUL RUNYAN, one of Cooper's longtime friends and a Hall of Fame golfer in his own right, in a 1997 interview with Dave Anderson of the *New York Times*, remembered Cooper as one of the best fairway wood players in the world, along with BOBBY JONES and BYRON NELSON. He also believed that Cooper needed a more positive, patient attitude to win majors: "He was the most pessimistic, negative thinker I have ever known. He made things too hard for himself. It kept him from being a superstar." Yet Cooper is in both the PGA and the World Golf Halls of Fame, elected in 1992.

Cooper continued to teach golf while in his early nineties as a professional at the Westchester Country Club. He emphasized two swing thoughts: (1) Keep your head still as you turn your belly button (not your shoulders) and (2) align your stance to the left of the target. When asked to comment about the modern PGA Tour, Cooper, one of the most colorful players of his day replied: "They fine guys on the Tour these days for having a personality."

45

Harold Hilton

1869–1942

*I could fight pretty well myself when I could see
the humor in it.*

—HAROLD HILTON, describing his competitive style

Harold Hilton is the only Englishman ever to win the U.S. Amateur
Championship. He also won four British Amateurs and two British
Opens. Hilton was born in West Kirby, Cheshire, in 1869, the same year
the Royal Liverpool Club was formed. Royal Liverpool was one of the
most important golf clubs in the world; it hosted the first British Amateur in 1885. Situated midway between the golfing centers of London
and Scotland, Royal Liverpool arranged for the first amateur invitational
match between Scotland and England in 1902, and it hosted the first

amateur international competition between Great Britain and the
United States in 1921. This international amateur match presaged the
Walker Cup matches, first held in 1922 at the National Golf Links on
Long Island. One of Harold Hilton's leading rivals, JOHN BALL, was a
member of Royal Liverpool, as was Hilton.

Powerfully built but relatively short at 5 feet 6 inches, Hilton had
an explosively fast swing, jumping onto his toes just before he started his
stroke. But he had great control and was a very good putter, using top-
spin to approach the hole. Hilton was also a knowledgeable player who
understood technique and brought a lively intelligence to the game. He
spent long hours practicing a variety of shots, which enabled him to
confidently improvise in tournament situations. He was a master of
backspin, enabling him to develop a solid short game. Hilton was also
considered the best wood player of his day.

Herbert Warren Wind gave this assessment of Hilton's style in *The
Story of American Golf*:

> He was medium-sized, suave, contained and worldly—
> the kind of chap you would expect to take plenty of time
> choosing the colors in his hose and who would have H.H.H.
> neatly engraved on his cigarette case. He smoked fifty ciga-
> rettes a day on the days that he played golf. . . . He appreci-
> ated the nuances of the English language and expressed
> himself in practiced delicacy. He was sensible about his golf.
> He knew precisely how well he could play, and experience
> told him that few amateurs could keep up with him, so he
> played his own game and let nature take its course.

Hilton had a reputation as a better stroke player than a match-play
golfer. Nevertheless, he won at the top levels of competition in both
formats. He won his first major competition, the 1892 British Open at
Muirfield, then a relatively new course. It was the first year that the
Open was a four-round seventy-two-hole event. Hilton shot a 78-81-72-
74=305 to edge John Ball, Hugh Kirkaldy, and Alexander "Sandy" Herd
by three shots. He won his second Open at Hoylake in 1897, winning
over JAMES BRAID by a single shot, with a score of 80-75-84-75=314.
Braid had shot a 74 in the second round, the lowest eighteen-hole total
during the event, but had a 6 on the sixteenth and a 5 at the seventeenth on the final day, which cost him the tournament. It was believed
that a rare mistake in club selection cost Hilton a third Open title at
Prestwick the following year. He selected an iron rather than a spoon,

pulled his shot badly, and scored an 8 on a par-3 hole. Hilton finished third, two strokes behind HARRY VARDON.

Hilton's great amateur-match-play rival was Lt. F. W. "Freddie" Tait, a professional soldier, who played for the Highland Brigade of the Black Watch. Tait was the pride of Scotland at a time when the Scottish dominance of international championship golf was on the wane. A great head-to-head competitor, Tait soundly defeated Hilton, eight and seven, in the final of the 1896 British Amateur at Sandwich. That same year, Tait was the low amateur in the British Open, finishing behind J. H. TAYLOR and Harry Vardon, who won in a play-off. Hilton won his first amateur at Royal St. George's in 1900, defeating James Robb, eight and seven, in the thirty-six-hole final. At St. Andrews the following year, Hilton beat Horace Hutchinson, two and one, in the semifinal, then edged John Low by one hole in the championship match. Hilton won his third Amateur in 1911 at Prestwick, four and three, over E. A. Larsen.

Hilton ventured to the United States in 1911 after finishing tied for third in the Open at Royal St. George's with Sandy Herd, one shot behind Arnaud Massy and Vardon, who won the championship play-off. A 5 on the par-3 sixteenth in the final round cost Hilton that tournament. Harold entered the U.S. Amateur at the Apawamis Country Club in Westchester County and won the qualifying medal with a score of 76-74=150. He steadily advanced through the early rounds, closed out JERRY TRAVERS, three and two, in the third round, won the semifinal round early, then faced the big-hitting Fred Herreshoff in the final.

Hilton built a six-hole lead in the morning round, but Herreshoff pulled himself together and cut Hilton's lead to one hole with four to go. Hilton was by then playing a defensive game, allowing Herreshoff to square the match by getting up and down on the thirty-fourth hole. Herreshoff barely missed two putts that would have given him the win on each of the last two holes, but he could not convert them, so the match went to sudden-death overtime. On the 377-yard, par-4 extra hole, Hilton hit a spoon on his approach shot and got a favorable bounce onto the green. Herreshoff was short after mishitting his second. After a poor chip, Herreshoff lost the hole and the championship.

Hilton's win sent a message to Americans that they weren't quite ready for big-time international golf, even though JOHNNY MCDERMOTT had won the U.S. Open earlier that summer, the first home-bred American to do so. Hilton unsuccessfully defended his U.S. Amateur title in 1912. He won his fourth British Amateur at St. Andrews in 1913, defeating Robert Harris, six and five. Hilton was runner-up in the British Amateur three times (1890, 1891, 1896). He won the Irish Open four times (1897, 1900, 1901, 1902).

Hilton authored books on golf, including *My Golfing Reminiscences* (1907) and *The Royal and Ancient Game of Golf* with Gordon Smith (1912). He also was the editor of *Golf Illustrated,* an authoritative British golf magazine. Hilton was one of the few amateurs, along with John Ball, CHICK EVANS, FRANCIS OUIMET, Jerry Travers, WALTER TRAVIS, BOBBY JONES, LAWSON LITTLE, and a few others, who could hold his own against professionals and amateurs. His success in match-play competition was only tainted by his lack of success against F. W. Tait, who usually beat him. Tait's life was cut short prematurely at age thirty in the Boer War. Harold Hilton was elected to the World Golf Hall of Fame in 1978. He died in 1942.

46

John Ball

1861–1940

One of the finest golfers never to turn professional.

—HARRY VARDON,
    commenting on John Ball

Born in Hoylake, Cheshire, England, in 1861, John Ball is one of the finest amateur golfers of all time. Ball won an unequaled eight British Amateurs (1888, 1890, 1892, 1894, 1899, 1907, 1910, 1912). During this fifteen-year run of championships, he served in the Boer War and was not available to play in three Amateurs (1900, 1901, 1902). In 1890 he became the first Englishman and the first amateur to win the British Open. Ball also won the Irish Open Amateur (1893, 1894, 1899), the Royal St. George's Cup (1888, 1889, 1890, 1891), and the Nice Challenge Cup (1905). He captained England against Scotland in international matches every year from 1902 through 1911.

Ball seemed destined to play golf. His father, a fine amateur golfer himself, owned the Royal Hotel when there was a small racecourse on the land that soon became the Royal Liverpool golf course. John Ball learned to play golf on that early course and became so proficient that he entered the British Open at the age of fifteen, finishing sixth. He not only led the English golf revolution against the Scots, soon to be followed by HAROLD HILTON, J. H. TAYLOR, and HARRY VARDON, he also pioneered the open stance with an upright swing that enabled him to hit high shots right to the hole. This technique would later be refined by Vardon. He had a somewhat unorthodox style, using the old-fashioned palm grip with both hands well under the shaft. He had a smooth and easy swing, and his determined temperament was ideal for the game. An unsigned article in the January 30, 1891, issue of *Golf* magazine describes Ball's style:

> His style of play is extremely taking; a very powerful driver, he stands with the ball nearer his right foot than the left, and grips so far around with the right hand that a wild draw would appear now and then inevitable, but since he adopted the 'bulger' (a wooden club, similar to a driver, with a slightly convex face) his long game has become markedly straight. . . . Perhaps of all his clubs his cleek is the strongest; his weakest point used to be his putting and holing out. . . . In his 1890 championship victories, in the course of which he used his wooded putter, his short game was, one may say, extraordinarily good. His iron play is marvelously strong. . . .

Ball participated in many challenge matches, including a match in 1899 in which he and Harry Vardon defeated Freddie Tait of Scotland, also an amateur, and WILLIE PARK JR. over thirty-six holes at Ganton, five and four. This "international" foursomes match was foreshadowed by an earlier match between Harry Vardon and Willie Park at North Berwick in Scotland in 1899.

Approximately ten thousand spectators showed up for that match, reflecting the strong appetite that the public had for competitive golf. At that time, Vardon was the world's best professional; Ball, the best amateur.

Ball attained one of his most satisfying British Amateur wins in 1899, meeting F. W. Tait, who had won the Amateur in 1896 and 1898 in the final at Prestwick. Tait jumped off to a five-hole lead after fourteen holes of the morning round because Ball missed several short putts. Ball went to lunch three down, and after a few putting tips from his friend Harold Hilton, also a member of Royal Liverpool and an amateur champion, Ball squared the match after six holes. Ball took a 1-up lead with two holes to play. At the "Alps" hole, a blind par-4, both golfers hit into a bunker on their tee shots. Tait had a lie in water in the bunker, was allowed no relief, but hit his recovery shot onto the green. Ball also hit a great recovery shot, and the hole was halved. Tait squared the match with a birdie 3 on the final hole, but Ball closed him out on the thirty-seventh hole to win the Amateur.

Ball won five of his Amateurs and one Open playing the gutta-percha ball. He won his other three Amateurs playing the rubber-core ball. He was at Hoylake for the British Open in 1902 and persuaded Sandy Herd to use the new rubber-cored Haskell, which had just come on the market. Herd won his one and only Open with that ball. Bernard Darwin, in *Darwin's Sketchbook,* noted that Ball

> . . . was a supreme match player . . . he did it by playing, as we now say, "against par." It was his business to go faultlessly down the middle and let the other man make the mistakes. . . . He was, I think, a lazy starter, inclined not to bother himself overmuch, but there was never a fierier finisher, and there seemed something about that relentless concentration that used to paralyze the enemy. . . . Mr. Ball had a splendid nerve, and he also had a swing traveling in so smooth and well-oiled a groove, that nothing, apparently, could disturb it.

Ball's swing and nerve stood the test of time. He won his last British Amateur, in 1911, at the age of fifty. He played in his last Amateur at the age of sixty-five.

Ball was of the old school. A modest man, he once got out of a train before it reached his hometown of Hoylake and walked home because he knew a crowd of well-wishers was awaiting him after he returned from winning a championship at Royal Liverpool. He retired to a farm in Wales to enjoy the farming, hunting, riding, and other activities that he loved. Robert Harris, a British Walker Cupper and a fine amateur player, once asked Ball to lend him some of his championship medals for an exhibit in London. Ball regretfully declined, writing: "I'm sorry, but I don't know where they are. I think I've given most of them away to my friends." John Ball was elected to the World Golf Hall of Fame in 1977. He died in Wales in 1940.

47

Nick Price

1957–

I had about five different swing planes. I knew it was bad, but I never dreamed it was that bad.

> —NICK PRICE after looking at a video of his swing
> in the early 1980s

Nicholas Raymond Lerge Price was born in Durban, South Africa, in 1957. His parents, British citizens, were world travelers who volunteered for the Indian army in World War II. His father was a major in the infantry, his mother a lieutenant in the nursing corps, when they met in India. They had a son, Kit, in 1946; then they moved to South Africa when the India-Pakistani war broke out. Another son, Tim, was born in 1950; then Nick, in 1957. In 1961 the Prices moved to Rhodesia (now Zimbabwe) and opened a clothing factory. Tim Price introduced his brother Nick to golf when he was eight years old. Nick started as a left-hander, then moved to a right-handed cross-hand grip when his mother bought the boys one set of clubs to share. His father, Raymond, died when Nick was ten. Nick refined his game and at sixteen decided he wanted to become a professional. His career as an amateur was interrupted when he was drafted into the Rhodesian air force in 1975. Price later felt that the major benefit of military service was discipline: "Being in the military changes you forever, though. It gives you discipline like nothing else can. When you have to be up at four o'clock every morning, backpack ready for inspection, floor area all around your bed shined and cleaned, you learn about self-discipline."

Price was discharged from the military when he was twenty-one, turned professional, and played on the European Tour beginning in 1978. After a slow start, Nick placed eleventh on the Order of Merit in 1980 but, after a slump, consulted David Leadbetter, also from Rhodesia. After six weeks of work with Leadbetter, Price almost won the 1982 British Open, shooting rounds of 69-69-74-73=286 to finish second, tied with Peter Oosterhuis, one shot behind Tom Watson at Royal Troon. Price could not hold a three-shot lead after birdieing the tenth, eleventh, and twelfth holes in the final round.

In 1983, Price qualified for the American PGA Tour and won the World Series of Golf, gaining himself a ten-year exemption on the Tour. The next eight years he could not put together four good rounds in big tournaments: "I always threw in one bad round. I hadn't learned yet how to shoot seventy or seventy-one on the day I was going badly. It was always seventy-five, and that would be the difference between first, fifth, or eighth." He led the 1988 British Open by two shots going into the final round at Royal Lytham and St. Anne's, but Seve Ballesteros shot a 65 to his 69 and won by two. At that tournament, Price realized that his swing was good enough to win under pressure but that he had to work on his putting.

Price began to come into his own in 1991 when he won the Byron Nelson Classic and Canadian Open, earning $714,389 on the Tour and finishing seventh on the money list. His first major victory was the 1992 PGA Championship at the Bellerive Country Club in St. Louis when Price made birdies on the 222-yard, par-3 sixteenth and the 536-yard, par-5 seventeenth on the final day and finished with a 70-70-68-70=278 to record a three-shot win over John Cook, NICK FALDO, Jim Gallagher Jr., and George Sauers. Price moved up to fourth in PGA earnings with $1,135,773 in 1992. The following year, he won four Tour events and the money title with earnings of $1,478,557. He also won two other tournaments on the international circuit. Price won the 1993 Vardon Trophy with a stroke average of 69.11 and was named PGA Player of the Year.

Price's best year was 1994: He won the money title again ($1,499,927), the PGA Player of the Year Award, and two majors. At this point Price was living in Florida in Hobe Sound, near his friend GREG NORMAN. He had purchased Norman's plane (the Shark had traded up) and had left International Management, his agent, just as Norman and JACK NICKLAUS had, to get more control of his schedule and business activities.

Nick's first major tournament win in 1994 came in the British Open at Turnberry in Scotland. Price had shot 69-66-67=202 his first three rounds, one shot behind FUZZY ZOELLER and Brad Faxon. He started slow on his final round, bogeying three of the first five holes. His game then began to improve, but Jesper Parnevik, the young Swedish professional, who was playing ahead of Price, had moved into the lead with a birdie at number seventeen. At this stage, Parnevik was 12 under par and three shots ahead of Price, who was playing the par-4 sixteenth. Price hit his approach shot to within twelve feet and made his birdie to cut Parnevik's lead to two. Jesper, approaching the eighteenth tee, had unaccountably decided not to monitor his position on the leader board. He thought he was behind and needed a birdie on the final hole to win the tournament. He hit his drive to the middle of the fairway but then risked going for the pin and pulled his 5-iron approach into the gorse, flopped a good wedge shot to within ten feet, but missed the putt for bogey and finished with a 67 and a seventy-two-hole total of 269, 11 under par. Parnevik's lead was down to one stroke. Meanwhile, Price had reached the 515-yard, par-5 seventeenth in two, leaving himself a 55-foot putt for eagle. The putt had only a small break, about eight inches, and Price read it perfectly, dropping it in the edge of the cup to take a one-shot lead. He and his caddie, Squeeky Medlin, jumped up in the air. For the first time all week, Price had the lead. The par-4 eighteenth plays 430 yards. Price hit a 3-iron off the tee and a 7-iron to the center of the green in comfortable two-putt range. As Price began his walk up to the green, there was thunderous applause from the huge gallery, and he insisted that Squeeky, who deliberately stayed back, join him for the victory march. He advised his caddie, "Enjoy this together. Who knows when we'll ever get to do it again." Nick finished with a 69-66-67-66=268 to win by one shot. Price was right. A few years later, despite considerable support from Nick, Squeeky Medlin passed away from chronic myelogenous leukemia.

Price won his second PGA Championship at Southern Hills with rounds of 67-65-70-67=269 to win by six shots over COREY PAVIN. He was in the zone and was rated the best golfer in the world. John Cook, who played well in the 1994 PGA, said, "We should have stuck an extra club in his bag. Then we might have had a chance. No, come to think of it, that wouldn't have helped, either. The most it could cost him is four (penalty) shots." Nick Price had come into his own at the highest echelons of golf at a time when it was the most competitive in the game's history. His next goal was to win the four majors, the Masters, and a U.S. Open. In 1994 no American had won a major. JOSE-MARIA OLAZABAL of Spain won the Masters, ERNIE ELS of South Africa the U.S. Open, and Price the other two.

Nick Price has twenty-three international victories and eighteen PGA Tour wins, placing him tied for fortieth with JULIUS BOROS, Jim Ferrier, E. J. Harrison, and Johnny Revolta on the all-time Tour winners list. Price was the leading PGA Tour money winner in 1993 and 1994. He has earned over $16 million on the PGA Tour, fifth all-time. His career President's Cup record is 6-9-9.

48

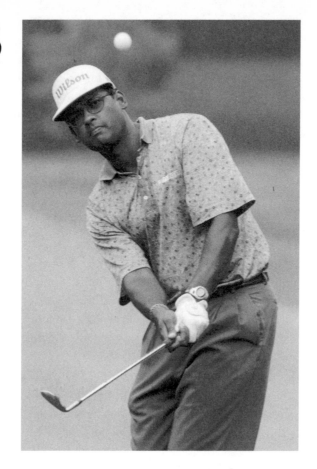

Vijay Singh

1963–

"I was out there in the jungle hitting balls and practicing in hundred-degree heat and trying to think about what to do next. I had to earn some money so I could go on tour again. That was the lowest point. I don't even like to think about it."

—VIJAY SINGH, recalling his days
as a club professional in Borneo

Vijay Singh was born in Lantoka, Fiji, and learned the game of golf from his father, an airplane technician who also was a golf instructor. In 1977 he saw an article in a magazine that modeled Tom Weiskopf's swing, which became the basis for his own swing. Vijay, after serving as a club professional in Borneo, played on the international circuit, winning his first tournament, the Malaysian PGA Championship, in 1984. And since he began to play regularly on the circuit in 1993, he has won a total of nine events on the U.S. PGA Tour. He has won more than $9 million in official PGA earnings, placing him in the top fifteen on the all-time list. A four-time member of the President's Cup team (1994, 1996, 1998, 2000), Singh is a noted grinder who constantly works on his game. According to NICK PRICE, who has won three major championships, "I've never seen anyone work as hard as that man does. You talk to his caddies . . . the guy's torn up more practice tees. I wonder how much earth he's moved over the years."

Singh moved into the elite level of international competitors when he won his first major, the 1998 PGA Championship, at the Sahalee Country Club, a tight, 6,906-yard, par-70 tree-lined layout in Redmond, Washington. Vijay shot a final round 68 to record a 9-under-par score of 271 to edge Steve Stricker by two shots. Singh scrambled down the stretch on the final day to earn his $540,000 first-prize money and the Wannamaker Trophy. On the eleventh hole, where the green is guarded by two huge trees that serve as goal posts, Vijay pushed his 3-wood approach shot to the right, but the ball rattled around in the tree and kicked out in front of the green, twenty feet away from the cup. Singh then took two putts to record his birdie. He saved par from the bunker at the thirteenth hole, and played a hard hook out of the trees on fourteen onto the green for a two-putt par. He saved par from the bunker on seventeen from about 18 feet. Vijay went to the final tee with a two-shot lead over Stricker. With his wife and eight-year-old son, Qass, waiting for him behind the eighteenth green, Vijay parred the 475-yard par-4 to preserve his victory. He said, "I've practiced so hard for this. It's a dream come true. What I did was unbelievable." Singh had come a long way since he started off as a caddie at the Nadi Airport Golf Club in Fiji, a country with only ten golf courses and approximately two thousand registered golfers.

Vijay proved that his PGA Championship was no fluke when he again successfully scrambled on the final nine holes at Augusta National to win the 2000 Masters Championship. In preparation for that event, the fairways were narrowed and the rough was cut higher than usual, placing a premium on distance and accuracy. Vijay, who played with DAVID DUVAL on the final day, had to finish his weather-delayed third round on Sunday morning. He holed a curling downhill putt on the seventeenth hole; then Duval missed a par putt, enabling Singh to carry a three-shot lead into the final round that afternoon. Singh was nearly done in by Augusta's notorious Amen Corner during the closing nine. He pulled his approach shot into the pond fronting the left side of the eleventh green and it seemed like he was going to have a difficult shot from a deep area behind the pond. But, after getting his line from marshals, Singh was able to drop from the right of the pond where he had a much easier pitch. Vijay knocked it within two feet and made it for a bogey five. Singh then almost made a critical mistake on the dangerous par-3 twelfth. His tee shot went over the green into some bushes, but slid out and into the back bunker. Singh managed to get up and down to preserve a one-shot lead over Duval.

Duval succumbed to pressure on the next hole, a par 5 fronted by Rae's Creek, after Singh had hit his second shot onto the green within eagle range. Duval blocked his approach into the water, taking himself out of the running. Ernie Els, playing ahead of Singh, had three birdies down the stretch to come within two shots of Vijay, but he missed a fifteen-foot birdie putt on the final hole to take the pressure off Singh. Vijay's 10-under-par score of 72–67–70–69 = 278 edged Els by three shots and earned Singh $828,000. Vijay had come a long way since he earned less than $200 a month as a club professional in the 1980s. He recalled his equatorial experience: "I was out there in the jungle, hitting balls and practicing in hundred-degree heat and trying to think about what to do next. I had to earn some money so I could go on tour again. That was the lowest point. I don't even like to think about it. I never thought about coming to America, let alone winning a golf tournament here." Singh earned his Masters with accuracy. Ranked twelfth on the Tour in distance off the tee and fourteenth in accuracy, he led the Masters field in reaching greens in regulation at 80.6 percent. Singh's game proved a perfect fit for the reconfigured Augusta layout in 2000.

Singh's two best years have been 1998, when he won the PGA Championship and finished second in PGA Tour earnings with $2,238,998, and 2000, when he made twenty-five cuts in twenty-seven PGA events that he entered and won over $2.6 million with eight top-ten finishes. Vijay's international odyssey and hard work were finally paying off. Vijay Singh now ranks fourth in all-time PGA Tour earnings, with over $18 million in prize money. He won his second major victory in the 2001 Masters, further solidifying his position as a great golfer.

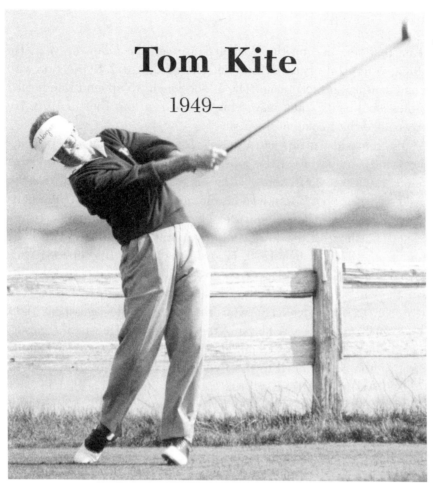

Tom Kite

1949–

49

Certainly the most spectacular of those shots was the chip-in on seven—and I've got the flag to prove it. After the tournament I got the superintendent to go out on the course and get me the flag from that hole.

—TOM KITE, after collecting a souvenir from his first major, the 1992 U.S. Open

T om Kite was born in McKinney, Texas, in 1949 and first started playing golf when he was six years old. His family moved to Austin, and Tom met BEN CRENSHAW, his lifelong friend and rival ever since, on the tenth tee of the Austin Country Club, where Harvey Penick would become their golf guru. Tom went to a different high school than Ben and competed against him in secondary-school golf tournaments and other amateur events. In 1970, Kite was medalist at the Western Amateur, runner-up at the Southern Amateur, and second to LANNY WADKINS in the U.S. Amateur. He played on the winning World Amateur team that year and on the Walker Cup team the following year. He attended the University of Texas and shared the 1972 NCAA title with Ben Crenshaw, his teammate. The 5-foot-8 inch, 155-pound Kite turned professional in 1972 and played his first year on the Tour in 1973. He was named the Rookie of the Year.

A constant worrier and grinder, Tom Kite is known to practice incessantly, trying to get the most out of his ability and improve his game. DAVIS LOVE III notes: "Tom's a grinder in every way, even to building up his body." Tom won his first major victory in 1976, the IVB-Bicentennial Golf Classic, and steadily improved his earnings performance, finishing in the top-twenty-five money winners on the PGA Tour from 1974 through 1990. He won the money title in 1981 with $375,699, finishing in the top ten in twenty-one tournaments. Kite also won the Vardon Trophy (69.80 strokes per round) and repeated in 1982 with a 70.21 average. He won the money title again in 1989 ($1,395,278) and the PGA Player of the Year Award. He won the Nestlē Invitational, the Players Championship, and the Nabisco Championships. Tom was named to the Ryder Cup team seven times (1979, 1981, 1983, 1985, 1987, 1989, 1993) and has compiled a solid 15-10-3 record in Ryder Cup competition. He was captain of the 1997 Ryder Cup team that lost by a point to the Europeans in Spain.

By the late 1980s, Kite had become one of golf's all-time leading money winners. Yet he was constantly reminded that he was the best player not to have won a major tournament. It seemed that he had solved that problem in 1989 at Oak Hill in Rochester when he opened with rounds of 67-69-69 to lead the tournament, three shots ahead of defending U.S. Open champion CURTIS STRANGE. This was the Open where four players—Doug Weaver, Mark Wiebe, Jerry Pate, and NICK PRICE—all scored a hole in one on the same hole, the 167-yard sixth, within a few hours of each other during the second round. Kite's atypical collapse began when he triple-bogeyed the 406-yard, par-4 fifth hole. He hit a high, arcing drive into a creek to the right. After he dropped, he laid up in front of a pond in front of the green and pitched to within ten feet. Inexplicably, Kite three-putted for a 7. Tom seemed drained even though he was 3 under par and even with Scott Simpson and one stroke up on Strange and Jumbo Ozaki. Kite bogeyed the eighth and then the tenth and faded to a 78, finishing in a tie for fifth, five shots behind the winner, Curtis Strange.

After this devastating loss, Kite slipped from first place to fifteenth on the money list in 1990, winning the Federal Express St. Jude Classic. He slid to thirty-ninth on the list in 1991 but won the Infiniti Tournament of Champions. He started to recover his game and his confidence in 1992 when he ended a sixteen-month victory drought by winning the Bell South Classic. At this stage in his career, Tom was the all-time leading money winner. At this writing he is still in the top ten worldwide. But Kite still hungered for a major, and at age forty-two, he knew that time was running out. His wife, Christy, recalled the pressure: "We never admitted it publicly, but I'd see Tom's anxiety the week of a major. It wasn't a good time to ask him which wallpaper he liked for the kitchen."

Tom Kite finally got his major at the 1992 U.S. Open at Pebble Beach. In the previous two Opens at Pebble, JACK NICKLAUS won by three in 1972, making it the fifth time in his career that he started the year winning the Masters and the Open; then TOM WATSON stole one from Nicklaus in 1982, winning by two shots after his amazing chip-in on the seventy-first hole. Kite shot rounds of 71-72-70-72=285 to edge Jeff Sluman by two shots in 1992. Kite, Sluman, and Colin Montgomerie, who finished third, were the only players to finish under par for the tournament. Gil Morgan held the lead each of the first three rounds, but an 81 on the final wild and windy day dropped him to a tie for thirteenth place. Kite, who held the course record of 62 at Pebble Beach, liked the layout and played accordingly on the critical last day.

Kite has always maintained that he became a good player when he began to carry three wedges in his bag beginning in 1980. He was the first Tour player to consistently do this. Tom's solid short game, including some amazing recovery shots with the wedge, enabled him to win his major. His most memorable shot was a 60-foot chip to birdie number seven, the short, scenic par-3 that juts out into the Pacific Ocean. He made a series of critical putts and clutch up-and-down chip shots on the fifth, eighth, tenth, and fourteenth. The U.S. Open trophy was delivered to Harvey Penick by Tom's wife. Three years later, Harvey passed away just before the Masters. His loyal pupils, Tom Kite and Ben Crenshaw, were among the pallbearers. Then Ben went out and won the Masters.

Kite loves the game of golf and enjoys what other people call the grind of practice. He developed a disciplined game which features driving accuracy to compensate for lack of distance and an excellent short game. But like all competitive golfers, the thrill for Tom is being in the hunt coming into the final holes: "People don't understand how wonderful that feeling is. To absolutely be scared to death that you are going to be able to perform. And then you do. You pull all the shots off. Sometimes to your own amazement. It's an incredible feeling. That being scared, that's the fun. That's good." Tom Kite joined the Senior Tour in 2000 and has won over $4.2 million.

50

Ben Crenshaw

1952–

I had a fifteenth club in my bag this week. It was Harvey Penick.

> —BEN CRENSHAW, who won the 1995 Masters after serving
> as a pallbearer for his mentor, Harvey Penick

Ben Crenshaw was born in Austin, Texas, in 1952. After he took up golf, he became a protégé of Harvey Penick's, the famous instructor at the Austin Country Club. Ben began to play golf at age six, and at age eighteen he tied for low amateur in the U.S. Open at Hazeltine, placing ahead of JACK NICKLAUS, ARNOLD PALMER, and GARY PLAYER in that event. Ben enrolled at the University of Texas and won the NCAA Championship in 1971, 1972 (shared with teammate TOM KITE), and 1973. Crenshaw was a member of the 1972 World Cup team and the following year won both the match and medal phases of the highly regarded Western Amateur. By age twenty-one, Ben had twice been low amateur in the Masters.

There were great expectations for Crenshaw when he joined the Tour in 1973 after he won the medalist honors in the Tour qualifier by twelve strokes over runner-up Gil Morgan. He won his first event on Tour in the 1973 San Antonio-Texas Open, then followed with a second-place finish in the World Open.

A superb putter and a creative escape artist from difficult situations, Crenshaw became bedeviled by a long swing and excessive lateral movement that caused his tee shots to stray. Crenshaw went through a crisis of confidence in 1974 and 1975. After tinkering with his swing to no avail, he returned to his basic form at the urging of his father and Harvey Penick. He won seven tournaments during the 1970s but could not win in the majors. He finished one shot back in the 1975 U.S. Open at Medinah after a disastrous double bogey on the par-3 seventeenth in the final round. In 1976 he was second to RAYMOND FLOYD at the Masters, by eight shots, due to Floyd's record-tying round of 271. In 1978 he finished second to Jack Nicklaus in the British Open at St. Andrews. He was second again, tied with Nicklaus, in the 1979 British Open at Royal Lytham and St. Anne's, losing by three shots to SEVE BALLESTEROS after taking a double bogey at the seventy-first hole.

Crenshaw again had doubts about his game in the early eighties. When he missed the cut at the 1982 PGA Championship, he retreated to his swing doctor, Harvey Penick, who helped Crenshaw with his setup, rhythm, and balance. Crenshaw won the Byron Nelson Classic in 1983, then won his first major, the 1984 Masters. Crenshaw led the tournament after an opening round of 67, then followed with 72 and 70 to trail Tom Kite, his college teammate, by two. He took the lead after birdieing holes eight and nine in the final round. Gil Morgan, David Edwards, and TOM WATSON were among the challengers, but Crenshaw, with his magical putting stroke, holed a 70-foot birdie putt on the tenth. He would later say, "It was absolutely off the charts. After it went in, I began to think it might be my day." Ben bogeyed the eleventh, birdied twelve, parred thirteen, then made a critical lag putt from off the green after hitting a solid recovery shot from behind some trees on the 420-yard, par-4 fourteenth. He saved his par and finished with a total of 68 and a seventy-two-hole score of 277, two shots better than Tom Watson.

Crenshaw won the Masters again in 1995. This was a special Masters for Ben and Tom Kite in particular because Harvey Penick, their mentor and friend, had passed away before the tournament. They both served as pallbearers and arrived at Augusta with little sleep and less practice. Kite did not make the cut, but Ben shot rounds of 70-67-69 to tie Brian Henninger for the lead after fifty-four holes. The final round began with twelve players within three shots of each other. Harvey had given Ben some putting tips a few weeks before the tournament: "The best way to help your confidence was to hole a few putts." Ben's putter was working for him on the final round. He birdied the six and the ninth on the front side, then made critical putts on the twelfth, thirteenth, sixteenth, and seventeenth to shoot a final-round 68 and win by one shot over DAVIS LOVE III and two over GREG NORMAN. Ben's most crucial putt was a curling 12-foot birdie putt on the seventeenth that gave him the victory. He claimed, "It was the prettiest putt I ever hit." He also credited Harvey Penick: "I had a fifteenth club in my bag this week. It was Harvey Penick."

The 1995 Masters is the last tournament that Ben Crenshaw has won on the Tour. His $396,000 first-place prize was his biggest payday. Ben has won a total of nineteen Tour events, tying him with Tom Kite, DOUG FORD, and HUBERT GREEN for thirty-sixth place. He has been selected to four Ryder Cup teams (1981, 1983, 1987, 1995) and captained the 1999 Ryder Cup team. Ben's record in Ryder Cup play is 3-8-1. He played on the 1972 and 1978 World Cup team and was a 1988 World Cup team and individual winner. Interestingly, Ben's PGA Tour play-off record is 0-8, including the 1979 PGA Championship. According to his own estimate, he has squandered seven majors. Yet he has still managed to win over $7 million on the Tour.

Crenshaw has an abiding interest in golf history and has one of the best golf-book collections available. He is a member of the USGA Golf Museum Committee and was the winner of the BOBBY JONES Award, in recognition of distinguished sportsmanship in golf, in 1991. Ben is also a golf-course architect, as are many other players on the modern Tour. Some believe that the lack of a killer instinct and limited interest in disciplined practice prevented Crenshaw from reaching his full golf potential. He has a temper, but he just couldn't seem to channel that fire into the cold, concentrated fury that the upper echelons of golf's all-time greats seemed to possess. A highlight of Crenshaw's career was, as nonplaying captain, leading the U.S. Ryder Cup team to a come-from-behind 14½-13½ victory over the Europeans at Brookline in 1999.

Mark O'Meara

1957–

*I like to think that I know how to stay calm when I'm
nervous. I'm thrilled to win, but like I said at Augusta,
I don't think I'm a great player. I'm still a nice player.
A nice, consistent player.*

> —MARK O'MEARA, after winning the British Open,
> his second major, in 1998

Until 1998, Mark O'Meara was a solid journeyman PGA Tour veteran who had qualified for the Tour in 1980 after graduating from Long Beach State. He had made over $8 million on the Tour, winning fourteen tournaments, beginning with the Greater Milwaukee Open in 1984. Then he met Tiger Woods, the PGA Tour phenom who won the 1997 Masters with a record score of 270 and garnered Player of the Year honors. Woods, who lives in the same exclusive golf community in Orlando as does O'Meara, became a close friend of the PGA veteran and pushed his game to a new level. Tiger got the forty-one-year-old O'Meara into a fitness regime, and his strength and stamina improved. O'Meara explains: "The most noticeable difference has been how fresh I have felt during the last few holes of each round and how much energy I have had on Sundays."

Before 1998 the highest that O'Meara had ever finished in the Masters was tied for fourth in thirteen appearances. Mark started out the 1998 Masters in modest fashion, with rounds of 74-70, placing him five shots behind David Duval and Fred Couples. He then shot a 68 to bring himself into contention, two shots behind Couples, who led after three rounds with a score of 210. Also within five shots of the lead were Phil Mickelson and Paul Azinger, at 212; David Duval and Jim Furyk (213); Jose-Maria Olazabal, Scott Hoch, and Jay Haas (214); and Tiger Woods, Jack Nicklaus, Ernie Els, and Colin Montgomerie (215). True to form, any of more than a dozen players could win the Masters, and it would likely be decided on the last few holes.

O'Meara shot a final-round 67 to emerge from the pack, dramatically birdieing the last two holes to finish with a 9-under-par 279. This was the first time that a Masters winner had closed with two birdies for a one-shot margin since thirty-year-old Arnold Palmer did it in 1960. David Duval and Fred Couples finished tied for second, Jim Furyk was fourth, Paul Azinger was fifth, and Jack Nicklaus and David Toms were tied for sixth, four shots back. The fifty-eight-year-old, six-time champion Nicklaus finished with a crowd-pleasing round of 68. David Toms shot a 29 on the final nine to close with a 64. Tiger Woods, the defending champion, was tied for eighth place, six shots back, but, as the defending champion, had the honor of helping O'Meara on with his green jacket. O'Meara took only 105 putts in the tournament, fewer than anyone else. He had only one 3-putt green.

On the way to Royal Birkdale for the British Open, O'Meara, Tiger Woods, and Payne Stewart stopped in Ireland for some golf and fishing. There O'Meara got a preview of the nasty winds that would greet him in England. Mark had played in the Open twelve times, his best finishes third-place ties in 1985 at Royal St. George's and 1991 at Royal Birkdale. The weather the first two days at Royal Birkdale was benign, and scores plummeted on the 7,018-yard, par-70 layout. Tiger Woods and John Huston shot 65s the first day to tie for the lead, and after 36 holes, Brian Watts, an Oklahoman who played the Japanese Tour, moved in front with a 68-69=137 total. O'Meara was three shots behind with a total of 72-68=140. Woods and NICK PRICE were one shot off the pace.

Winds of up to forty miles per hour sent scores upward the third day. O'Meara started 3 over par on the first five holes, and on the sixth, a 480-yard uphill par-4, he hit his approach shot to the right of the green but could not find his ball in the deep rough. After a long search, it was discovered that a fan had picked up the ball. There was some debate as to whether O'Meara had taken too long looking for his ball. (Five minutes is the limit for searching.) When it was determined that he hadn't gone over the limit, he was allowed a drop. When he twice dropped unsuccessfully, he was allowed to place the ball, giving him a decent lie from which he salvaged a bogey. This seemed to revitalize O'Meara, and he proceeded to play the rest of the holes in 2 under par for a total of 212 for the tournament, tied with Jim Furyk and Jesper Parnevik, two shots behind Brian Watts. Woods was five shots back at 215, having shot 77 in the wind. The scoring average for the day was 77.492, and no one broke par.

The final round was filled with drama. Playing ahead of O'Meara, Woods chipped in for a birdie on the seventeenth, then rolled in a 25-footer on the finishing hole to shoot 66 and finish with 281, 1 over par for the tournament. Justin Rose, a seventeen-year-old amateur from England, chipped in on the final hole for a 69 and a tournament total of 282, tying him with Parnevik, Furyk, and Raymond Russell. O'Meara, in the final pairing with Watts, was up one shot going into the seventeenth, but Watts birdied to tie. Then, on the final hole, after bunkering his approach, Watts hit a marvelous sand shot from a downhill lie to get up and down for par. O'Meara also parred, forcing a four-hole medal-play play-off. O'Meara called Watts's shot "one of the greatest shots I've ever seen under pressure in my entire life."

The fourteenth play-off in British Open history began at the par-5 fifteenth. O'Meara made a 5-foot birdie putt, but Watts missed a 3-footer to go down a stroke. Watts missed a 16-foot birdie attempt on the next hole, saved par on seventeen with a 10-footer, but lost the play-off to O'Meara by two strokes. At age forty-one, Mark O'Meara became the oldest player to win two majors in one year.

O'Meara's personal best year, 1998, added some symmetry to his career. Born in Goldsboro, North Carolina, he won the U.S. Amateur in 1979, graduated from Long Beach State in California in 1980, and was named Tour Rookie of the Year in 1981. In 1998 he was named Player of the Year and won $1,786,699 in PGA Tour earnings alone. He has won over $12.7 million in PGA prize money in his career, placing him in the top twenty all-time. In addition to his sixteen PGA Tour wins, including five AT&T Pebble Beach victories, he has won eight other international and unofficial Tour events. O'Meara has played on five Ryder Cup teams (1985, 1989, 1991, 1997, 1999) with a record of 4-9-1; six Dunhill Cup teams (1985, 1986, 1987, 1996, 1997, 1998) with a record of 18-6-1; and two President's Cup teams (1996, 1998), with a record of 7-2. In order to win a major, O'Meara believes you need "Number one, timing; number two, patience; number three, driving the ball very well; number four, a lot of luck."

Willie Park Sr.

1833–1903

His style was generally held to be most graceful; his swing was easy, with a pause at the end of it, and his balls traveled well; but perhaps, if any point of his game is to be particularised, it should be his putting.

—H. S. C. EVERARD, commenting on Willie Park, winner of the first British Open in 1860

Before the dawn of organized tournament golf run by professional associations, pro golfers were gunslingers who laid down the gauntlet in challenge matches, often for high stakes. When Willie Park Sr. began plying his trade, there were only four great golf professionals in the golfing world, which was then largely confined to Scotland. That quartet included Park, OLD TOM MORRIS, Allan Robertson, and Jamie Dunn.

Willie, who first learned to play golf in Musselburgh with a makeshift wooden club called a shinty, later procured a real set of clubs and proceeded to defeat his fellow caddies in Musselburgh. It was not uncommon for these caddie matches to continue over several rounds into the late Scottish night.

Having conquered everyone at home, the twenty-one-year-old Willie issued a challenge in the *Scotsman,* a newspaper, in 1854, offering to play Allan Robertson, Willie Dunn, or Tom Morris. His challenge went unanswered, and when Willie went to St. Andrews for the autumn meeting in 1854, his three professional golf peers were not anxious to play him. Finally, Tom Morris agreed to play a match of two rounds (thirty-six holes) over St. Andrews, and Willie won by five holes. Later, Willie offered to play against Robertson and Morris's better ball, but Robertson again refused to play. Park, who played Dunn only once, developed a keen rivalry with Morris, prevailing in most of their early matches.

Dunn, having taken a position as professional at Blackheath in England and out of practice, was not at his best in his sole contest with Park. The match, played over Musselburgh, Prestwick, and St. Andrews, was won by twelve holes by Willie Park. Willie next met Tom Morris at North Berwick and won by ten holes. In 1856, Willie and Tom played over Musselburgh, Prestwick, North Berwick, and St. Andrews for 100 pounds per side. Willie won at Musselburgh and Prestwick, Tom at North Berwick and St. Andrews, but Park won overall by six holes. Willie later won a similar match by nine holes. They continued to duel in minor matches on a regular basis until Tom Morris won in a major contest in 1862 by seventeen holes. Another match was held at Musselburgh in 1871 when Willie was thirty-eight years of age and Old Tom was fifty. This contest ended when Tom, down two with six to play, walked off the course because he considered the partisan crowd of Park supporters too rowdy. They repeatedly injured the position of Tom Morris's ball. On appeal, the referee stopped play and directed that the stakes be withdrawn. In Morris's absence, Park played on alone, covering the final six holes in twenty-one strokes, much to the delight of the crowd. After Tom finished the following day with a score of 26 for the final six holes, Willie claimed victory. But he lost their final match, in 1882 at North Berwick, by four holes.

In the early days of golf, before St. Andrews gradually set the standard for eighteen holes as a championship round of golf, courses had varying numbers of holes. Park's home course, Musselburgh, had eight holes. He set the course record with rounds of 31-32. Willie was a long driver for his day, hitting the gutta-percha ball an average of approximately 180 yards off the tee. But he was better known as an excellent putter. A great shotmaker, Willie sometimes lost tournaments because he was inconsistent, took unnecessary risks, and had limited stamina.

The golden age of private challenge matches was somewhat eclipsed by the inauguration of the first formal championships in the mid-nineteenth century. The Prestwick club in Scotland initiated this effort by contacting other leading clubs—St. Andrews, Perth, Musselburgh, Blackheath, Carnoustie, North Berwick, and Leven—in April 1857, inviting four members from each club to play doubles matches and foursomes to determine a club champion. All of the invited agreed to meet that summer, and the Honourable Company, Edinburgh Burgess, Bruntsfield, Montrose, and Divleton Castle also agreed to compete. These thirteen clubs, out of the total of nineteen Scottish golf clubs extant at the time, agreed to send players to meet at St. Andrews in July 1857. The match included twenty-two competitors from eleven clubs. (The Honorable Company and Carnoustie were unable to organize a team.) Royal Blackheath won the prize, a silver claret jug. The contests were eighteen holes, and halved match players both advanced. This tournament eventually became the present-day British Amateur, now a singles match-play event, which formally dates itself from 1885.

The amateur club championship initiated by Prestwick, where Tom Morris served as professional and greenskeeper from 1851 to 1863, served as a model for the British Open, first held at Prestwick, a twelve-hole venue, in October 1860. Allan Robertson, previously recognized as the best professional golfer, died in 1859, prompting a demand for an organized event to determine the best player. A challenge belt of red moroccon leather and ornamented with massive silver plates was to be awarded to the winner, which would be determined in a three-round, thirty-six-hole stroke-play contest. The belt would become the property of any player winning three years in succession. Willie Park emerged the winner in the first British Open held in 1860, the longest continuous golf championship in the world. Only eight players competed and the order of finish was:

Willie Park (Musselburgh)	174
Tom Morris (Prestwick)	176
Andrew Strath (Prestwick)	180
Bob Andrew (Perth)	191
Daniel Brown (Blackheath)	192
Charlie Hunter (Prestwick St. Nicholas)	195
ALEX SMITH (Bruntsfield)	196
William Steel (Bruntsfield)	232

The field in the first Open was confined to professionals, but the event was open to amateurs and professionals thereafter. The Open was won only by Scots until 1890, when JOHN BALL of England became the first Englishman and the first amateur to win the Open.

Willie Park won the Open in 1863 with a score of 168, in 1866 (169), and in 1875 (166), all at Prestwick. The first Open at a site other than Prestwick was in 1873, when it was held at St. Andrews. Tom Morris Jr. won three Opens in a row (1868–70) and retired the belt. The tournament was not held in 1871, and it was decided that a silver claret jug, purchased for thirty pounds, would be held by the winner for a year, until the next championship was decided. The first cash award in the Open was given in 1864 when Tom Morris Sr. received six pounds for his victory. In 1998, MARK O'MEARA earned $493,500 for his win at Royal Birkdale.

Willie Park also designed golf courses along with his son, Willie Junior, and his brother Mungo. Among his creations are Western Gailes Golf Club in Scotland, Tramore Golf Club in Ireland, Portstewart Golf Club in Northern Ireland, and several others. Willie Park ranks in the pantheon of pioneering professionals who played up until the 1880s. He won four British Opens and finished second in four. Willie Park died in Musselburgh in 1903 at the age of seventy.

53

Alex Smith

1872–1930

Miss 'em quick.
—One of ALEX SMITH's
instructional tips

At the turn of the century in the United States, golf was advancing as a sport as leisure time became more common among the general public. Unlike in the British Isles, where the average Scottish citizen might play recreational golf the way an American child plays basketball or baseball, golf was ushered into the United States by the upper classes and has since tried to shed its image as a game of the wealthy. It was affluent enthusiasts like Cornelius Vanderbilt, John Jacob Astor, Oliver Belmont, and Theodore Havemeyer who first founded the Newport Golf Club in Rhode Island, one of the five founding clubs of the USGA in 1894. Another founding club, Shinnecock in Southampton, Long Island, New York, was founded by W. K. Vanderbilt and others, who caught the golf bug when Willie Dunn, a young Scottish professional, demonstrated it to them in Biarritz, France, where he was designing a new golf course in 1889. There are records of golf being played in North America as early as the seventeenth century in the settlement of New Netherlands, along the Hudson River, but it was not until the formation of the USGA that organized golf and nationally recognized, organized competitions developed in the United States. At the end of the nineteenth century there were approximately 250,000 golfers in the United States. There are over 25 million today.

There was not enough home-grown talent to accommodate the golf boom in the United States, so since this is a nation of immigrants, skilled golfers were imported to lay out golf courses, teach the game, and oversee golf-course operations. The days of professionals who made clubs and golf balls for a livelihood were on the wane, and sporting-goods entrepreneurs, like A. G. Spalding, developed, promoted, and distributed equipment through such outlets as on-site pro shops, sporting-goods stores, mail-order houses, and other channels of distribution.

Among the more noteworthy golf pioneers in the United States were the Dunns of Musselburgh, the Rosses of Dornoch, the Parks of Musselburgh, the Andersons of St. Andrews, and the Smiths of Carnoustie. Although four-time U.S. Open champion WILLIE ANDERSON was the best player and Willie Dunn Jr. and WILLIE PARK JR. exercised wide-ranging influence, none of these men could match Alex Smith's combined success as a player and a teacher.

Alex Smith was born in Carnoustie in 1872. His father was the greenskeeper at Carnoustie, among other places, and an occasional designer of golf courses. Only five of the ten Smith children survived infancy; all eventually became golf professionals in the United States.

Following a basic education, Alex Smith became an apprentice blacksmith and acquired the skills that led naturally to clubmaking. Golf did not come easily to him, but his game began to improve in the mid-1890s, and he served as professional at the Luton and St. Neots golf clubs. He returned to Carnoustie in 1897 as foreman of Bob Simpson's clubmaking shop. After several victories in local competitions, he left for the United States in 1898, with four professionals from St. Andrews, to join the staff of the Washington Park Golf Club in Chicago. Alex was said to be the first of an estimated "300 men of Carnoustie" who soon came to occupy positions as golf professionals throughout the world.

The practice of professionals at the time was to use tournaments as a means to attract lucrative exhibition matches and to gain better positions at country clubs that were sprouting up all over the United States. Smith won a number of times on the irregular professional tournament circuit. These wins included two Western Opens (1903, 1906), three California Opens, and at least two Florida State championships. Alex won his first U.S. Open in 1906 at the Owentsia Club in Lake Forest near Chicago. By then Alex had moved up, securing the professional's position at the Nassau Country Club in Glen Cove, Long Island. He shot 73-74-73-75=295, eight shots better than the Open record, to win by seven shots over his brother Willie. The top five finishers in that Open, the Smiths, Laurence Auchterlonie, James Maiden (BOBBY JONES's teacher), and Willie Anderson, were all natives of Scotland.

Alex won the Open again in 1910 at the Philadelphia Cricket Club in the first play-off in U.S. Open history. He had shot 73-73-79-73=298 to tie with his brother, MACDONALD SMITH, and JOHNNY McDERMOTT, an American-born professional who would become the first American to win the Open (1911). Alex, now playing out of Wykagyl in Westchester County, had missed a 3-foot putt that would have won the tournament in regulation. He shot a 71 in the eighteen-hole play-off to edge McDermott (75) and his brother (77). In addition to his two U.S. Open wins, he won the first Metropolitan Open (1905) and three others (1909, 1910, 1913). In effect, Smith pioneered the professional Tour when, in 1899, the Acheson, Topeka and Santa Fe Railroad sent Alex and his brother Willie to California to play a series of matches, the first organized professional "Tour" in the United States. One year later, HARRY VARDON and J. H. TAYLOR, the great British professionals, would travel thousands of miles giving exhibitions and promoting golf and the equipment they endorsed.

Alex Smith was one of golf's best teaching professionals. He taught many excellent golfers, including JERRY TRAVERS, who won four U.S.

Amateurs and a U.S. Open, and Glenna Collett, one of the greatest lady golfers, who won six U.S. Women's Amateurs. Travers began to take instruction from Smith when he was at the Nassau Country Club, and Collett took instruction from Smith when he later moved to Shennecossett in New London, Connecticut, after his stop at Wykagyl in New Rochelle, New York. Beginning in 1925, Smith split his professional duties between Shennecossett and the new Westchester Biltmore Country Club in Rye, New York, and spent his winters at the Miami Biltmore. Collett used to take lessons two days a week at Shennecossett, then followed Smith to Florida for more instruction in the winter. Smith also tutored WALTER HAGEN, the first great American professional, but considered BOBBY JONES, whom he observed at age thirteen, too temperamental to be a good golfer.

As a player, the 5-foot-10-inch, 170-pound Smith, with huge blacksmith's hands, was known for his power and his solid short game. His sunny disposition enabled him to deal with golf's frustrations. He once blithely said to a competitor during a terrible round they were both having at the 1905 British Open, "Never mind, we're getting a lot of practice." Alex wrote a successful instructional book, *Lessons of Golf,* in 1907. He died in a sanatorium in 1930 after a long illness. He was among the first twelve players inducted into the PGA Hall of Fame in 1940.

54

Denny
Shute

1904–1974

He was a brilliant shotmaker with a swing as sweet as a Viennese waltz, a golfer who preceded Julius Boros as the lazy, velvety stylist who did what everyone thought was easy to do but wasn't.

—HERB GRAFFIS, describing Denny Shute's style

Densmore Herman Shute, the son of an English golf professional, was born in Cleveland, Ohio, in 1904 and, after winning the West Virginia Amateur (1923, 1935), Ohio Amateur (1927), and other amateur titles, turned professional in 1928. The 1929 Ohio Open was his first of fifteen Tour wins that he would register during his career. Shute was selected to the Ryder Cup team in 1931, 1933, and 1937. In the 1931 Ryder Cup at Scioto in Columbus, Ohio, Shute teamed with Ryder Cup captain WALTER HAGEN to thump George Duncan and Arthur Havers in the foursomes. Shute then easily won his singles match, eight and six, over Bert Hodson. In 1933, Shute was paired with OLIN DUTRA but lost, three and two, to Abe Mitchell and Arthur Havers at Southport and Ainsdale in England. In his crucial singles match, Shute played Syd Easterbrook in the decisive final, and the contest was even at the eighteenth green. Shute did not know the status of other matches on the course, nor did he realize the importance of his putt. Both golfers had putts of over 30 feet. Easterbrook just missed his, but Shute ran his effort four feet past the hole. He missed coming back, and Easterbrook won the match, 1-up. The British gained a 6½–5½ win to regain possession of the cup they had lost at Scioto. Samuel Ryder, the contributor of the cup and the tournament's namesake, was in attendance at this event for the last time. He died in 1936. Ryder had originally stipulated that only homebred players would compete on Ryder Cup teams. Later, when he realized that golfers such as TOMMY ARMOUR, JIM BARNES, HARRY COOPER, and others who migrated to the United States were ineligible, he made his wishes known that the rules should be changed to accommodate them as well as other deserving golfers. For various reasons, the rule was never amended by the professional-golf ruling bodies on both sides of the Atlantic.

Shute was able to recover from his crushing Ryder Cup disappointment. He stayed in Britain to play in the Open and tied CRAIG WOOD after seventy-two holes with a total of 73-73-73-73=292, one stroke ahead of Easterbrook, GENE SARAZEN, and LEO DIEGEL. That Open is often remembered for Diegel's collapse on the final five holes, which he needed to play in 1 over par to win. Leo needed to two-putt the final hole but could not do it. Shute decisively defeated Wood in the play-off, 149–154 to win his first major championship.

Shute won his first PGA Championship at the Pinehurst Country Club in North Carolina in 1936. Excluding the defending champion, Johnny Revolta, a qualifying round was held for the sixty-three open slots in the tournament. Notable players, including Walter Hagen, BYRON NELSON, Leo Diegel, and Jim Turnesa, did not make the cut. Shute defeated Alex Gerlat, five and four; Al Zimmerman, three and two; Billy Burke, two and one; HORTON SMITH, three and two; and Bill Mehlhorn, 1-up, and met Jimmy Thomson in the final. Thomson outdrove Shute by as much as 60 yards, but Shute's approach shots and putting enabled him to earn a 1-up lead in the morning round. Shute won the match at the par-5 thirty-fifth hole with an eagle for a three and two victory.

As defending champion, Shute did not have to qualify for the 1937 PGA, which was held at the Pittsburgh Field Club in Pennsylvania. He again reached the final, defeating Joe Turnesa, two and one; Olin Dutra, three and two; Ed Dudley, three and two; Jimmy Hines, four and three; and Tony Manero, 1-up. In the thirty-six-hole final, his opponent was Harold "Jug" McSpaden, who later teamed with Byron Nelson as the successful "Gold Dust Twins" during the war years. McSpaden jumped out to a 3-up lead after the first five holes, but Shute's putter heated up, and he one-putted nine of the next thirteen holes to move ahead 3-up after the first eighteen. McSpaden came back and evened the match at the twenty-eighth; then two consecutive bogeys by Shute enabled McSpaden to take a 2-up lead. After halving the thirty-third, McSpaden lost the thirty-fourth after bunkering his tee shot. Shute squared the match on the thirty-fifth after McSpaden pulled his second shot under a tree, losing to Shute's bogey. On the final hole, Jug hit his approach to within four feet, and it looked as if the match were his. However, he missed his short putt, and the match stayed even. Given a new life, Shute capitalized on McSpaden's error, holing his 4-foot putt on the first extra hole after McSpaden couldn't convert his 10-footer.

One month later, Shute played in the Ryder Cup competition. The American team, led by its perennial captain, Walter Hagen, included RALPH GULDAHL, Tony Manero, Byron Nelson, HENRY PICARD, Johnny Revolta, Gene Sarazen, Horton Smith, SAM SNEAD, and Ed Dudley. The contest was held at Southport and Ainsdale in England, and the American team won for the first time on British soil, eight and four. Shute halved both his foursomes match and his singles.

One of the memorable tournaments that Denny Shute played in was one he didn't win. That was the 1939 U.S. Open when Shute finished tied at 284 with Byron Nelson and Craig Wood in regulation at the Spring Mill course at the Philadelphia Country Club. Wood and Nelson tied after the first eighteen in the play-off, and Shute was eliminated with a score of 76. Nelson then won the second eighteen-hole play-off, 70–73, to become the first winner of a thirty-six-hole U.S. Open overtime match. The longest Open play-off was between Billy Burke and George Von Elm in 1931 at Inverness in Toledo, Ohio. Both golfers tied in regulation after thirty-six play-off holes. Burke finally prevailed, 297–298, after thirty-six more play-off holes. The difference between the two golfers in 144 holes of competition was a single stroke.

Denny Shute did play in the Masters, but the closest he came to winning was in 1935, when he finished fifth, five shots behind Gene Sarazen (who won in an eighteen-hole play-off) and Craig Wood, who both finished with scores of 282 in regulation. Shute's last Tour win was in 1939, when he won the Glens Falls Open. By then the PGA and America were feeling the full weight of the Depression. There had been 2,022 golf clubs in the PGA in 1929, but by 1939 the number had dropped to 1,813, It would take until the end of World War II for membership to show noticeable increases again.

Shute was a quiet, somewhat colorless golfer, but effective. Walter Hagen rated him, along with JIMMY DEMARET and Billy Burke, among the best 1-iron players he ever saw. Shute played a limited Tour schedule and very little Tour golf after World War II. In addition to his three major championships, he was runner-up to Tom Creavy in the PGA in 1931 and second to Craig Wood in the 1941 U.S. Open. Denny Shute died in 1974. He is in the PGA Hall of Fame.

55

Leo Diegel

1899–1951

"Third-Round Diegel"

—DIEGEL's nickname

Leo Diegel and his contemporaries MACDONALD SMITH and HARRY COOPER would become known as players with great shotmaking capabilities who let several major championships get away. In Diegel's case, he was tagged with the nickname "Third-Round Diegel" for his lapses down the stretch. Nevertheless, Leo managed to win twenty-nine official Tour events, putting him in fifteenth place on the all-time list. His victories included four Canadian Opens (1924, 1925, 1928, 1929) and consecutive PGA Championships in 1928 and 1929.

Leo Diegel was born in Detroit in 1899 and won his first Tour event, the 1920 Pinehurst Fall Pro-Am Bestball when he was twenty-one years of age. A high-strung, likable man who tended to become too tightly wound as he approached the final round of major golf tournaments, Diegel was also noted for his highly unorthodox putting style—

his elbows bent and his forearms parallel to the ground. Bernard Darwin, in his essay "On Diegeling," described Diegel's putting style:

> You take a putter, not outrageously upright in the lie, with a reasonably long shaft. You hold it at the very top of the grip with the left hand well under. You stand square to the line of the putt, the feet spread rather wide apart. . . . You next crook the elbows, particularly the left elbow, till you feel that something will break if you crook them anymore. You drop the nose—not the club's but your own—lower and lower and lower, till the top of the putter shaft lightly touches the stomach. Then, with the wrists perfectly rigid, you take the club back a short way. You give the ball a little push, apparently with the right hand, and in it goes.

One of Diegel's earliest disappointments in a major came in 1920 at the U.S. Open at Inverness. This event is remembered for HARRY VARDON's inability to protect a lead during the final nine holes when an unexpected gale threw the fatigued fifty-year-old, six-time British Open Champion off his game. TED RAY shot 295 to win by a single stroke, but Diegel, who scored 77 in the final round, was in an excellent position to win, finishing in a tie for second with Vardon, JACK BURKE JR., and JOCK HUTCHISON. Diegel had needed par over the final five holes to win, but on the fourteenth a friend informed Diegel that Ted Ray, playing ahead of Leo, had bogeyed number seventeen. Diegel, who had been about to address his second shot on the par-4 fourteenth, became irritated and distracted, not wanting to think about his opponents. He double-bogeyed the hole, added bogeys on the fifteenth and sixteenth, and finished with a back nine total of 40 and a seventy-two-hole score of 296. Diegel finished in the top ten in the Open in 1922, 1923, 1925, 1929, 1931, and 1932 but would never get as close to winning as he did at Inverness.

Leo Diegel finished eighth or better in the eleven British Opens he entered. Diegel's only serious assault on the British Open title was in 1929 when he opened 71-69 at Muirfield to take the lead. This early success was too much for Leo, and he then shot 82-77=299 to finish third, seven shots behind the winner, WALTER HAGEN. In 1930 he finished tied for second, two shots behind BOBBY JONES, with a 74-73-71-75=293 at Hoylake. In 1933, Leo lost by a heartbreaking single stroke at St. Andrews when he shot rounds of 75-70-71 to tie for the lead going into the final round but finished with a 77. He came up one short of CRAIG WOOD and DENNY SHUTE, who won the play-off. Despite these disappointments, Diegel was named to the first Ryder Cup team in 1927 and acquitted himself well, splitting his foursomes and singles matches in the 9½–2½ U.S. victory at the Worcester Country Club in Massachusetts. He also was selected to the 1929 team, pairing with Al Espinosa to win, seven and five, over Aubrey Boomer and George Duncan in the foursomes, then decisively defeating Abe Mitchell, nine and eight, in singles in the American team's 7–5 loss at the Moortown Club in Leeds, England. Leo was also on the Ryder Cup teams in 1931 and 1933 but never won another Ryder Cup match. His overall record is 3-3-0.

Leo Diegel's first major championship win came in 1928 at the Five Farms Country Club in Baltimore when he broke Walter Hagen's consecutive string of four straight PGA Championships. Diegel reached the final by defeating Tony Manero, ten and eight; George Christ, six and four; Walter Hagen, two and one; and GENE SARAZEN, nine and eight. Hagen, the master of gamesmanship, had had Diegel's number up until this point. In 1925, Walter came back from being 5-down to Diegel at the end of eighteen holes to catch Leo at the thirty-sixth and won on the fourth extra hole of the PGA. In 1926, Diegel was 2-down to Hagen in the PGA final after eighteen holes; then Hagen pulled away to a five-and-three win. But in 1928 Diegel holed a 15-foot putt to close out Hagen on the thirty-fifth green of their semifinal match. Diegel easily beat Al Espinosa, six and five, in the final for his first major championship.

Diegel defended his title in 1929 at the Hillcrest Country Club in Los Angeles, defeating P. O. Hart, ten and nine; Herman Barron, ten and nine; and Gene Sarazen, three and two, before again facing Hagen in the semifinals. Diegel rose to the occasion, shooting 68 to Hagen's 71 in the morning round and closing out Hagen on the thirty-fourth hole, three and two. Hagen's defeats at the hands of Diegel was the beginning of the end for him in a tournament that he had previously dominated. Hagen was eliminated in the first round of each PGA Championship in which he competed in the 1930s. The total purse for the 1928 PGA was $10,400. In 1929, because the tournament was played in December, after the stock-market crash, it was reduced to $5,000. The total purse for the PGA Championship did not reach its 1928 level until 1939, when it was $10,600, an increase of just $200, indicating how difficult it was to make a living as a Tour player in those days.

In addition to his two majors, Leo Diegel won the Canadian Open four times (1924, 1925, 1928, 1929). Diegel won his final Tour event, the New England PGA, in 1934. He died in 1951. Diegel is a member of the PGA Hall of Fame.

56

Old Tom Morris

1821–1908

"I could cope wi' Allan mysel' but never wi' Tommy."
—OLD TOM MORRIS, on his inability
to defeat his son, Young Tom

Tom Morris, Sr., affectionately known as Old Tom, was one of the early pioneers of modern golf. He was born in 1821 in St. Andrews in the era of the featherie ball, won four British Opens (1861, 1862, 1864, 1867) during the gutta-percha ball era, and died in 1908 at St. Andrews when the rubber-cored ball was revolutionizing the game. Morris played in the British Open until he was seventy-five years of age (1896); in 1881 at Prestwick, at the age of sixty, he finished tied for fifth.

The son of a postman, Tom took up the game of golf when he was seven, playing cross-handed at first. He soon became apprenticed to the legendary professional Allan Robertson as a maker of clubs and balls. He served four years as an apprentice and five as a journeyman at the shop. Tom partnered with Robertson on the golf course in high-stakes, match-play contests against the best golfers of the time. One of the most noteworthy of those matches was played for 400 pounds (over 65 times the first British Open winner's cash prize of 6 pounds in the 1864 tournament) against Willie and James Dunn, from the famous golfing and equipment-making family of Musselburgh, in 1849. The Dunns were heavily favored to win the 108-hole match played at Musselburgh, St. Andrews, and North Berwick. The Dunns were four holes ahead with eight to play, but Robertson and Morris managed to square the match at the 106th hole. The decisive point came on the last whole when the Dunn team could not dislodge its ball, which had landed in a cart track behind a curbstone. They took a few swipes at the ball and then requested a spade. The tournament officials intervened, and they had to play the ball backwards and then toward the green. Robertson and Morris successfully defended the honor of St. Andrews.

Robertson, who is considered the first eminent professional golfer, got into a dispute with Tom Morris in the 1840s when the new gutta-percha ball became a threat to the hand-crafted featheries produced by Robertson and other professionals. This was no small matter, for Robertson's St. Andrews shop produced over twenty-four hundred featheries a year at a time when one skilled worker could perhaps turn out three balls a day. It was inevitable, Tom felt, that the less expensive and more durable gutties, which could be mass-produced, would become the sphere of choice and bring more players into the game. He set up his own shop in 1848 but continued his partnership with Robertson on the golf course. In 1851 he moved from St. Andrews and became the designer and custodian of the Prestwick links, a newly formed twelve-hole establishment. In those days the club professional was usually responsible for course maintenance; instruction; making, repairing, and selling equipment, such as balls and clubs; and representing the club in tournaments and other activities.

The British Open, established in 1860, is the oldest ongoing national championship in the world. As with the U.S. Open, which debuted thirty-five years later, the British Open served the purpose of determining a national champion on one golf course using standard rules. An original code of thirteen basic golf rules had been defined in 1754 at the Royal and Ancient Golf Club of St. Andrews, but over time, the Royal and Ancient and the USGA have become the governing bodies in the world of golf, and as we all know, the rules have gotten quite complicated. In 1860 life was simpler, though, and WILLIE PARK SR. won the first Open (which wasn't open because only eight professionals participated). Nevertheless, it served the purpose of deciding a national champion, because Allan Robertson, then the king of golf, had died in 1859.

The Open, then available to both amateurs and professionals, was won by Tom Morris over three rounds, totaling thirty-six holes, in 1861 (with a score of 163), 1862 (163), 1864 (167), and 1867 (170). Until 1872 the Open was always held at Prestwick; it then moved to St. Andrews and other rotation venues. At the time, the Open was the world championship of golf, and the British still consider it such. Tom Morris was one of the few golfers, if not the only one, with worldwide fame. He supplemented his tournament income by playing match-play challenges. Willie Park Sr., who won four Opens, was one of his arch-rivals. One of Morris's earliest big matches against Park was in 1853, a 100-pound, four-green (St. Andrews, Prestwick, North Berwick, Musselburgh), 144-hole contest. The match concluded at St. Andrews in the second eighteen-hole round (thirty-six holes were played at each course) when Tom Morris birdied the second and third holes with threes to close out the match, sixteen and fifteen. Over the course of their long rivalry, Old Tom had a slight edge on Willie. Their followers and backers could become overenthusiastic, as described in *The Badminton Library of Sports and Pastimes*, a golf volume edited by Horace G. Hutchinson: "The crowd, anxious for their favourite, the local man (Park in this case) to win, transgressed all rules of fair play, and repeatedly injured the position of Tom Morris's ball, to such an extent that the latter declined to continue the match, and, on appeal, the referee stopped play, and directed that stakes should be gone." Crowd control aside, many golf connoisseurs thought, and still do, that match, rather than medal, play is the purist form of golf.

Tom Morris returned to St. Andrews in 1865 to become "keeper of the greens." In 1867, Old Tom set up his own clubmaking shop; it employed three men. Though Tom prematurely lost his oldest son, the great champion YOUNG TOM MORRIS, his sons Jamie and George and nephew Jack became part of the Morris golf-professional and clubmaking tradition. With Morris as a brand name, the family clubs became noteworthy, along with those produced by Hugh Philp, the Forgan family, the McEwans, the Dunns, the Patricks, and the Parks. In particular, the equipment business of the Morrisses, Parks, and Dunns benefited from their on-course prowess, just as TOMMY ARMOUR, WALTER HAGEN, BEN HOGAN, JACK NICKLAUS, and others would benefit later.

Tom Morris became the old sage of golf and was often called on to make rules decisions and arbitrate disputes at other clubs as well as at St. Andrews. By 1858 there were twenty rules of golf in force at St. Andrews. The prestige and integrity that Allan Robertson, Tom Morris, and others brought to the game contributed to St. Andrews becoming the home of golf, its ultimate shrine. Old Tom also left his mark as a golf-course designer. Up until the early 1850s, the Old Course at St. Andrews links had been played nine holes out and nine holes in, with nine common greens. As play increased with the introduction of the gutta-percha ball, two holes were cut in each green to make a total of eighteen cups in 1857. As time went on, the course was widened and modified further by Tom Morris and his successors. During the last half of the nineteenth century, eighteen holes became the standard for a championship round. Old Tom was called upon to design the original twelve holes at Prestwick, the additional six added in 1883, as well as the first nine at Royal Dornoch, Muirfield, and Royal County Down.

In his day, Tom considered himself the equal or better of Allan Robertson but not his son Tom, who won four British Opens and retired the championship belt before passing away at the young age of twenty-five: "I could cope wi' Allan mysel' but never wi' Tommy," old Tom would say. Tom had a grand funeral when he died in 1908, at age eighty-seven, as described by Andrew Kirkaldy: "It was a sad day in St. Andrews. Schoolchildren got a holiday to see Old Tom pass to his everlasting rest in the Cathedral burial grounds beside his son, Young Tommy, and not far from the grave of the golfing cronie of his youth, Allan Robertson." Old Tom is a member of the World Golf Hall of Fame.

57

Jerry Travers

1887–1951

Travers was the greatest competitor I have ever known. I could always tell just from looking at a golfer whether he was winning or losing, but I never knew how Travers stood.

—ALEX SMITH, two-time U.S. Open champion and Travers's instructor

Jerome Travers came from a wealthy New York family and learned to play golf on their Oyster Bay, Long Island, estate. Travers then played for a few years at the Oyster Bay Country Club; when his family joined the Nassau Country Club, he became a protégé of Alex Smith's. He reinforced the image of golf amateur champions coming from the country club and university set. (The professional Tour tended to be populated by modestly educated, rough-edged graduates from the caddie shack.) Travers played when he felt like it, but when he did, he was serious about the game and was a great competitor. In addition to having money and the time to play golf, he had the advantage of a great rivalry, which brought out the best in his game. That rivalry was with the 1904 British Amateur and three-time U.S. Amateur champion, WALTER TRAVIS, a native Australian who emigrated to the United States and became an American citizen. Travis set the standard for American amateur golf at the turn of the century. Travers also had the advantage of having Alex Smith, a wise two-time U.S. Open champion, as his instructor.

While foreign-born golfers from the British Isles tended to dominate American professional golf during its formative years in the late-nineteenth and early-twentieth century, the amateur ranks tended to be dominated by the swells. Those who cared to compete in serious amateur golf needed the time and money to be able to indulge themselves. Travers played the young man to Travis's "Old Man," which was easy to do because Jerry was twenty-five years younger than Walter. The two first met in a match during the Nassau Invitational Tournament on Long Island, at Travers's home course. Only a few weeks earlier, Travis had returned home the winner of the British Amateur. Travers and Travis played similar games in that they were not long off the tee but they were accurate and had great short games. Travers, then seventeen years of age and the National Interscholastic Champion, had been under the tutelage of Alex Smith since he was fifteen. Jerry had overcome his tendency to overswing, hold his arms too stiff, and use too weak a right-hand grip. Travers, like WALTER HAGEN, was a match-play genius who was described by H. B. Martin, quoted in *Golf's Greatest: The Legendary World Golf Hall of Famers* by Ross Goodner, as follows: "His skill for playing shots was combined with a cast-iron nerve that had never been known to crack. If one club failed him at a critical moment, he had the faculty for picking out another and making it serve the purpose; and if one bad shot or bad break in the game came his way, he could forget it quicker than it happened. The shot in hand, the one to be made, was the only thing that occupied his mind at that instant."

Travers eliminated former U.S. Amateur champion Findley S. Douglas to advance to the final round against Travis at the Nassau Invitational. The match turned into a short-game contest with Travis matching Travers shot for shot. However, Travers was 2-down by the time they came to the thirteenth hole. But Jerry rallied to square the match at the seventeenth, and won when he drained a 12-footer on the third extra hole. The teenager had just beaten the highest-ranked amateur in the world. Travis, who always wanted to win as much as Travers did, graciously remarked after the match, "There is no aftermath of bitterness in such a defeat. It is a match I shall always recall with pleasure." Travers's star was on the rise, and Travis's, then forty-two years of age, was slowly beginning to wane.

Travers won four U.S. Amateurs (1907, 1908, 1912, 1913), five Metropolitan Amateurs (1906, 1907, 1911, 1912, 1913), and the 1915 U.S. Open. He had come a long way since he improvised three holes on his ample front lawn when he was a youngster. When the handicap system was first developed in the United States, initially Travers and FRANCIS OUIMET were among the few leading golfers of the day who were rated scratch players. But during Travers's career he had a habit of taking long vacations from high-caliber competitive golf. In 1907 the Travers family moved to New Jersey, and Jerry Travers started playing out of the Montclair Country Club. After winning the U.S. Amateur in 1908, he did not bother to defend his title. He did venture to Great Britain in 1909 to compete in the British Amateur. Travers was eliminated in the first round of that match-play event. After a two-year layoff from the U.S. Amateur, he lost to Englishman HAROLD HILTON in the third round of the 1911 tournament at Apawamis. Travers came back the following year to defeat CHICK EVANS in the final, seven and six, at the Chicago Golf Club. After being down one at the end of eighteen holes, Travers shot 34 on the next nine and closed Evans out early. Then, in 1913, Travers won his fourth Amateur after having to play in a sudden-death play-off with eleven other golfers to get through the qualifying round and into the tournament. He eliminated Francis Ouimet, the young U.S. Open champion, in the semifinals, then easily won the championship, five and four, over John G. Anderson at the Garden City Golf Club. The following year, Ouimet defeated Travers, six and five, in the championship round at the Ekwonok Country Club, a course designed by Walter Travis; it was the last time that Travers got close to winning a U.S. Amateur title.

Not known as a championship-level medal player, Jerry Travers entered the 1915 U.S. Open at Baltusrol and won it. The other members of America's amateur triumverate, Chick Evans and Francis Oiumet, had finished in the top five of the 1914 Open at Midlothian. And the year before, Ouimet had become a national hero by becoming, at age twenty, the first amateur to win the Open, against HARRY VARDON and TED RAY. Using only a driving iron off the tee on long holes, Travers proved that he could compete with the best amateurs and professionals when he shot 297 to win by a stroke over Tom McNamara of

Boston. Travers, then twenty-eight years of age and about to give up national-championship golf, elected not to defend his Open title the following year. With Travers out of the way, Chick Evans won both the Open and the Amateur that year.

But Travers did have one last great match against Walter Travis in the 1915 Metropolitan Amateur at Apawamis in Rye, just north of New York City. When he arrived at the tournament site, Travers wandered over to the scoreboard to see whom he would play in his first match and, upon seeing it was the Old Man, remarked, "It looks as though I'm going to play that old son of a bitch again." Unfortunately, Travis, then fifty-three years of age, was standing nearby, heard the remark, and got his competitive juices flowing. He defeated Travers, two and one.

At one point, Jerry Travers was a member of several clubs, including Pine Valley, and had a large estate in New Jersey and a luxury apartment in New York. He worked as a cotton broker on Wall Street and had a seat on the commodities exchange. But when the stock market crashed in 1929, Travers never recovered. He was forced to sell his seat on the cotton exchange in 1931. Then he tried a variety of business schemes, including equipment manufacturing and promoting a line of Spalding Red Dot golf balls. He turned professional, played exhibitions, and taught for a while. At one stage, Travers's financial situation was so grim that Grantland Rice had to help him auction off some of his belongings to raise cash. One of his golf clubs sold for six dollars. BOBBY JONES had eclipsed his record of four U.S. Amateur titles by winning his fifth in 1930. Travers died in 1951 at the age of sixty-four. Three years later, his medals from the Amateur and the Open were found in his safe-deposit box along with a note to a friend, the president of Pratt & Whitney, who gave him a job when he needed it, which read in part, "In appreciation of your many favors." Jerry Travers is in the World Golf Hall of Fame.

Chick Evans

1890–1979

I've a semi-final hoodoo, I'm afraid.
I can never do as you do, Jimmy Braid
I've a genius not to do it,
I excel at almost to it,
But I never can go through it, I'm afraid.
— CHICK EVANS, in 1912

Charles "Chick" Evans, one of America's greatest amateur golfers, learned the game as a caddie at the Edgewater Club outside Chicago in 1898. He once described his ball-finding techniques as follows:

> I remember finding a brand-new ball by a method that I have always claimed to have originated, but of course I may have deceived myself. I saw a player drive into the long grass ... but although he looked for a long time, neither he nor

his caddie could find it. When he left I concluded to try an experiment and went over and lay down where I thought the ball had fallen. Then I rolled over with thoroughness, accompanied, I must confess, by dizziness, all around the spot until some part of my body struck a round, hard object. This, of course, was the ball, which I immediately proceeded to dig out. The method made me rich in golf balls, but what was better, it gave me a reputation among both members and caddies of never losing a golf ball.

Evans, who was born in Indianapolis in 1890, caddied until the day before his sixteenth birthday, then quit so as not to jeopardize his status as an amateur. He qualified for the Western Amateur when he was sixteen and eventually joined FRANCIS OUIMET and JERRY TRAVERS as the best American amateurs of his day. However, his early career was a checkered one, and he suffered many disappointments as the big one, the U.S. Amateur, seemed to constantly elude him, largely because of his shaky putting. A voluble man, Evans needed approval, especially the warm reaction of his galleries, and some of his close defeats brought out a certain bitterness and resentment in him.

Francis Ouimet eclipsed Evans in the golf-history books by, at the age of twenty, winning the 1913 U.S. Open at the Country Club in a play-off against HARRY VARDON and TED RAY. At the time, Evans, who played in that tournament, was considered one of the best players, amateur or professional, from tee to green. When asked which was the most impressive amateur he had seen in America, Vardon voted for Evans, not Ouimet or Travers. Like BOBBY JONES later, Evans spent seven years in the golf wilderness before breaking through. By 1916 he had played in seven U.S. Amateurs without a win. He reached the semifinals in 1909, 1910, and 1911 but was defeated by less talented players. In 1912 he reached the finals but lost a three-hole lead and faded in the afternoon round to a seven and six loss to Jerry Travers. In 1913 he was eliminated in the semifinals, played poorly in 1914, and was eliminated in the first round in 1915. For good measure, playing the British Amateur in 1911 for the first time, Evans was eliminated in the first round. He was eliminated again early in the 1914 British Amateur.

However, Evans won the Western Open in 1910 and the Western Amateur for the third time in 1914. His putting seemed to be improving, but his putter did fail him in the 1914 U.S. Open at the Midlothian Club, near Chicago. Evans, a local favorite, shot a third-round 71 to bring him within four shots of the leader, WALTER HAGEN. After closing to within one stroke with nine holes to play, Evans missed a putt from within three feet on the eleventh, three-putted the twelfth, and just missed a 15-footer at number sixteen. Chick still managed to hole a 25-footer on the seventeenth to pull within two. Needing an eagle on the 277-yard, par-4 finishing hole, Evans drove to the edge of the green and just missed a 50-foot chip shot to lose by one.

Evans seemed to have reached an all-time low in 1915 when he was eliminated in the first round of the U.S. Amateur. Armed with seven hickory-shafted clubs, including a jigger (chipper with the loft of a 4-iron), a mashie, a spoon (similar to a 3-wood), a brassie (2-wood), a lofter (similar to a 6-iron), a niblick, and a putter, Evans entered the 1916 U.S. Open at the Minikahda Country Club in Minneapolis. Evans opened with a 32 on the front nine, finished with a 70, then posted a 69 the next day to lead the tournament. A critical birdie on the 525-yard, par-5 thirteenth helped Evans finish his final round with a 73 after scoring a 74 in the morning round of the final day. His total score of 286 edged JOCK HUTCHISON by two shots. Jock shot a tournament-low 68 on the final round to join Evans as the only golfers to shoot par or better. Evans's score was a U.S. Open record which stood for twenty years, until Tony Manero shot 282 in the 1936 Open at Baltusrol. Evans's achievement is all the more notable because he won using seven clubs in an era when many players routinely carried twenty clubs or more. Like all clubs of his time, his set was not a matched set. He had used mainly irons forged by Tom Stewart of St. Andrews. He modified the clubs himself in an attempt to get the feel of a matched set. Evans's clubs cost a total of $20.75.

Like Francis Ouimet before him and Bobby Jones and Johnny Goodman after him, Chick Evans had to win the U.S. Open before he could win the U.S. Amateur. Ten weeks after his win at Minikahda, Evans teed it up at the Amateur at the Merion Cricket Club near Philadelphia. Evans easily reached the finals to play fellow Chicagoan, Bob Gardner, a former pole-vaulter at Yale, who barely eliminated fourteen-year-old Bobby Jones in the semifinals. Gardner, who had won the Amateur in 1909 and 1915, could not keep up the pace because Evans was putting well. Chick won the match, four and three. Chick Evans and Bobby Jones are the only Americans to have won the U.S. Open and the U.S. Amateur in the same year.

The closest Chick Evans came to winning the U.S. Open again was in 1920, when he finished sixth, behind the winner, Ted Ray. He won the Amateur again in 1920 and finished second in 1922 and 1927, losing to Bobby Jones, eight and seven. Evans played on the first Walker

Cup team in 1922. He also was a Walker Cupper in 1924 and 1928. Over his career Evans won a total of six Western Amateurs (1909, 1912, 1914, 1915, 1920, 1923), the French Amateur Open (1911), and the North and South Amateur (1911). Evans played in fifty consecutive U.S. Amateurs, his last in 1962. In 1931, with proceeds from instructional phonograph records that he had made, Evans set up the Evans Scholars Foundation, a scholarship fund for caddies, which has given scores of caddies a chance to improve their education. Chick Evans is in the World Golf Hall of Fame.

59

Francis Ouimet

1893–1967

Thank you, mother. I'll be home soon.

> —FRANCIS OIUMET to his mother, who
> congratulated him and wanted him to
> be home for dinner, after his historic
> 1913 U.S. Open win

Francis Ouimet was born in Brookline, Massachusetts, in 1893. As a child, he used to walk through the grounds of the Country Club, across from his home on Clyde Street. He watched the golfers and collected golf balls, then practiced on a few makeshift holes his older brother, a caddie, had built in the open fields behind the house. Beginning at age eleven, Francis caddied at the Country Club and saw WALTER TRAVIS, JERRY TRAVERS, WILLIE ANDERSON, ALEX SMITH, and others play there. At age sixteen Ouimet was good enough to win the Boston Interscholastic Championship, but in 1910 he just missed qualifying for the U.S. Amateur, held at the Country Club. He missed again in 1911 and 1912 but qualified in 1913 after winning the Massachusetts Amateur. Francis won his first match at the U.S. Amateur at the Garden City Golf Club on Long Island, but then he was eliminated, 1-up, by Jerry Travers, who holed a 20-foot birdie putt on the final hole to win.

Ouimet returned to Brookline and his job as a salesman at the Wright & Ditson sporting goods company. He had used his vacation time on the Amateur but had previously signed up for the Open, scheduled at the Country Club. Ouimet's supervisor, seeing the qualifying round-pairings posted in the newspaper, allowed Ouimet to play. Francis finished one stroke behind the leading qualifier, HARRY VARDON, long considered one of the best professional golfers in the world. Only one native-born American, JOHN MCDERMOTT, who won it in 1911 and 1912, had won the U.S. Open since the first tournament was held in 1895. Harry Vardon and TED RAY were among the foreign-born golfers who had come to reclaim the crown from the locals.

Vardon and Ray, in the United States for golf exhibitions and an extended promotional tour, were the heavy favorites to win the Open. Vardon had already won five of his six British Opens and the 1900 U.S. Open, and Ray had won the British Open in 1912. Other quality golfers, including Jerry Travers, Johnny McDermott, JIM BARNES, MACDONALD SMITH, Mike Brady, Tommy McNamara, and a young WALTER HAGEN, were in the field. Ouimet, then twenty years old, was a modest, soft-spoken, candid young man, accompanied by his ten-year-old caddie, Eddie Lowery, who carried his ten clubs. Francis wasn't intimidated as he teed it up at Brookline. Initially there was not pressure on him. He was happy to be in the Open in his hometown, and he wanted to do his best. He didn't know that he was about to make golf history and give American golf a boost, just as amateurs BOBBY JONES and TIGER WOODS would in the future.

At the end of the third round, Oiumet was tied for the lead with Vardon and Ray at 225. In those days the leaders were not paired in the final round. Francis played behind Vardon and Ray in rainy conditions. He shot a 43 on the front nine, and it looked as if his chances were waning. Coming to the last six holes, he needed to shoot 2 under the rest of the way to tie. He birdied the thirteenth, a short par-4, by chipping in from the edge of the green. He parred the fourteenth, a 5, and now needed fourteen strokes or less on the last four holes. Ted Ray later described Ouimet's finish in *A History of Golf* by Robert Browning:

> The par of these four holes is 4-3-4-4, so that Ouimet had to get one (under the par figures one of them) and par figures for the other three if America was to remain in the picture. At the fifteenth it was difficult to pitch over the bunker and stay on the green, and Ouimet's shot was pushed out to the right, but he got his four by laying a chip shot dead. He did not get on the green at the short sixteenth either, but again he put his chip near enough and got his three.
>
> Still, that was two of his chances to beat the par figure gone, and he could hardly hope to do better than a 4 at the last, which was over 400 yards with the track of a race course and the bank beyond it to carry with the second shot. As a matter of fact when Ouimet came to this hole, he did not quite carry the bank. His ball stuck at the top of it, and he had to play another good chip and hole a seven-foot putt to get his four.
>
> When he came to the seventeenth, therefore, he knew that if he was to get his three anywhere it must be here, a three at the seventeenth at Brookline is a man-size job. The hole was 360 yards long and the approach had to be played on to a sloping green, with the hole cut so close to a bunker that it was impossible to pitch for the pin. Ouimet's ball finished twelve feet or so from the tin [cup], leaving him the most difficult kind of putt in the world, but with a down-slope and a side-slope to negotiate at the same time.
>
> Only perfect judgment of both time and strength would get the ball in the cup, but Ouimet stepped up to it without batting an eyelid. His putter swung smoothly and evenly, and the ball took the slope down in a gentle curve, and hit the very centre of the cup. I have never seen such a putt more confidently played. Coming at such a crisis, with so much depending on it, I count that that putt was one of the master-strokes of golf.

Ouimet (77-74-74-79), Ray (79-70-76-79), and Vardon (75-72-78-79) were tied at 304. Ouimet walked back to his parents' home, ate dinner, had a full night's sleep, got up on another rainy day, and won the play-off with a score of 72, five shots better than Vardon and six shots better than Ray. Ouimet later modestly recalled, "I was an amateur who played for fun. I looked on professionals as magicians who knew all the answers. This was to be a match between Vardon and Ray. I was there by mistake."

Francis entered the British Amateur at Sandwich the following year. He used an interlocking grip, unusual for the time, and a "soldier" putting stance, his both heels together, his elbows sticking out, allowing him to swing like a pendulum. This putting style was considered American at the time, but Ouimet claimed to have copied it from Willie Anderson, the Scottish-born four-time U.S. Open champion. Ouimet, not familiar with British seaside courses like Sandwich, lost in the second round. He won the French Amateur and the U.S. Amateur in 1914 and won the U.S. Amateur again in 1931. By then he was a successful stockbroker, and he continued to promote amateur golf.

Ouimet was a major figure in Walker Cup play, participating in that event as a captain or player for twenty-seven years, since its inception in 1922. He raised funds and established a scholarship program for caddies. In 1951 the Royal and Ancient Golf Club of St. Andrews initiated Francis Ouimet, in a formal red tailcoat, as honorary captain of the club, the first American so honored.

There were an estimated 350,000 golfers in the United States in 1913 when Francis Ouimet transformed American golf. Ten years later, there were 2 million, and American golfers became the best in the world. Al Laney, a noted sportswriter from Pensacola, Florida, who, as a teenager in 1913, learned of Ouimet's feat, recounted the impact that Francis's win had on golf in America: "In 1913, golf was generally regarded as the exclusive pastime of the wealthy, the aged and the British born. Now young men everywhere, I among them, began to think about playing the new game. Ouimet's victory popularized the game, took the curse off it, so to speak, and put it on page one."

Francis Desales Ouimet died in 1967. He was elected to the World Golf Hall of Fame in 1974.

60

Johnny Farrell

1901–1988

The expert knows what to do about his hook. The weekend golfer sometimes does not even realize that his timing is at fault and can be corrected without the use of drugs or yoga.

—An instructional tip from JOHNNY FARRELL

Johnny Farrell was born on April 1, 1901 in White Plains, New York, where he became fascinated with golf at an early age. While serving as a caddie in the Westchester area, he decided to pursue golf as a career after watching the 1916 PGA Championship at Siwanoy. He became known for his well-groomed appearance, splendid attire, and excellent short game on the golf course.

Farrell won his first PGA-sanctioned event, the Garden City Open, in 1921. His best years came in the late 1920s, beginning with 1927, when he won eight consecutive tournaments, including the Metropolitan Open. The following year, he won the U.S. Open at Olympia Fields Country Club, outdueling BOBBY JONES in a thirty-six-hole playoff. Jones had a three stroke lead going into the final eighteen holes of regulation play, but Farrell, representing the Quaker Ridge Country Club in Scarsdale, New York, gained five shots on Jones to tie him with a total of 294. Roland Hancock, a twenty-one-year-old professional from Wilmington, North Carolina, needed two 5s on the final holes to win but finished with a pair of 6s to miss the play-off by one shot.

Farrell had had considerable experience in the U.S. Open, although he had not yet won it. He finished fifth in 1923 and tied for third in 1925 and 1926 and for seventh in 1927. In 1928 the U.S. Open play-off format, which had been eighteen holes the previous year when TOMMY ARMOUR defeated HARRY COOPER in overtime at Oakmont, was expanded to thirty-six holes. Farrell held the edge on Jones after the first eighteen, finishing with four consecutive birdies to hold a 70–73 lead.

Jones regained three strokes when Farrell three-putted the first two holes in the afternoon round. They then played even until the sixteenth, when Jones bogeyed to fall one behind. Farrell seemed about to pick up another stroke on seventeen after his approach rolled to within two feet of the cup. But Jones holed his 30-foot putt to match Farrell's birdie. The final hole was a 490-yard par 5, and Farrell was 50 yards short of the green after two shots. Bobby was on in two, and Farrell pitched to within eight feet. Jones two-putted for birdie, and Farrell made his birdie putt to win the U.S. Open by one stroke. This is the last time that Bobby Jones lost in a U.S. Open. He won a play-off against Al Espinosa in the 1929 Open, by twenty-three strokes at Winged Foot, and the 1930 Open at Interlachen, the third leg of his Grand Slam.

Johnny Farrell's best effort in the PGA Championship was second place in 1929, when he lost to LEO DIEGEL, six and four, at the Hillcrest

Country Club in Los Angeles. Diegel was 1-up going into the twenty-seventh when he hit his putt close to the hole to partially stymie Farrell. Farrell's 5-footer accidentally knocked Diegel's ball into the hole, giving him a 2-up lead. The same thing happened at the twenty-ninth. Farrell missed a 3-footer to go 4-down, a deficit from which he never recovered. Johnny reached the semifinals of the PGA Championship in 1926, losing to WALTER HAGEN, six and five, and in 1933, losing to GENE SARAZEN, five and four. He finished second in the 1929 British Open, losing six shots to Walter Hagen.

Farrell was appointed to the first Ryder Cup team in 1927 and again in 1929 and 1931. He teamed with Joe Turnesa in foursomes to defeat George Duncan and Archie Compston, eight and six, at the Worcester Country Club in 1927. He then defeated Arthur Boomer, five and four, in singles in the 9½–2½ American victory. In 1929 the British turned back the Americans, seven and five, at the Moorstown Golf Club in Leeds, England. Farrell and Turnesa halved their foursomes match, and Charles Whitcombe decisively defeated Farrell, eight and six, in singles. Farrell was paired with Gene Sarazen in the 1931 Ryder Cup foursomes, and they defeated Archie Compston and William Davies, eight and seven, at Scioto in Columbus, Ohio. Farrell lost his singles match, four and three, to William Davies, but the U.S. team won, nine and three.

Family responsibilities and the Great Depression caused Farrell to cut back on his tournament activities in the 1930s. He had five children, including three sons, who were excellent golfers. In 1934 he became the professional at Baltusrol and held that position until 1972. Johnny became a celebrated teacher whose pupils included Edward, the duke of Windsor, and other notables. Farrell moved well in any circle and made appearances on sports shows and in vaudeville, golf movies, and advertisements. He produced one of the first golf television shows. Johnny's last official PGA victory was in the 1936 New Jersey Open. Farrell is credited with twenty-two official PGA Tour wins, tying him for twenty-fifth place with RAYMOND FLOYD.

61

Henry Cotton

1907–1987

Golf is an individual game and will ever be so, whilst human beings vary in physique. The thoroughness with which American golfers have analyzed golf in an attempt to find "the secret" has further convinced me there is no secret. To watch a first-class field drive off must surely convince everyone that a golf ball can be hit in many ways.

—HENRY COTTON

Henry Cotton was born in Holmes Chapel, England, in 1907, and after attending Alleyn's school in Dulwich, he decided to make golf his career. He was the dominant European golfer of his time, and had it not been for World War II, he most likely would have had an important impact in the United States. He ended the ten-year reign of Americans in the British Open in 1934 when he shot 67-65-72-79=283 at Sand-wich to win by five strokes. At that time, Cotton, who was fluent in French, was the professional at the Waterloo Golf Club in Brussels. Cotton won the Open again, at Carnoustie in 1937, firing a 74-72-73-71=290 to win by two strokes. That field included the entire U.S. Ryder Cup team, most notably BYRON NELSON, who was fifth, six shots off the pace. Cotton's third Open win came at Muirfield in 1948: At the age of forty-one, he shot 71-66-75-72=284 to win by five shots. Cotton's second-round 66 was the new course record at Muirfield.

During Cotton's peak period he was a member of Britain's Ryder Cup team (1929, 1937) and was playing captain in 1947 and nonplaying captain in 1953. His Ryder Cup playing record is 2-4-0. He won three Belgian Opens (1930, 1934, 1938), three German Opens (1937, 1938, 1939), two French Opens (1946, 1947), two Czechoslovak Opens (1937, 1938), and the 1936 Italian Open. Henry was known as a student of the game. He was a prolific writer and an excellent teacher. Cotton wrote several books on golf, including *Thanks for the Game, A History of Golf Illustrated, Henry Cotton's Guide to Golf in the British Isles,* and instruc-tional books, such as *My Swing* and *Hints on Play With Steel Shafts.*

Cotton spent long hours disciplining his golf game and was nick-named "Concentration Henry" by WALTER HAGEN for his efforts. He not only was a student of the golf swing, he was also knowledgeable about the evolution of the golf swing as the ball changed from variable-sized gutty and then rubber core to standardized balls in the 1920s. He also under-stood how the change from large-gripped, individually manufactured wooden-shafted clubs to mass-produced, thinner-gripped, steel-shafted clubs, introduced in the 1930s, altered the mechanics of the swing.

Writer Brownlow Wilson in the book *The Methods of Golf's Mas-ters,* described Cotton's technique as follows:

> Cotton stands with his feet parallel and at right angles to the line of shot. This is natural to him, because a player should stand as he walks, in the most comfortable position, and Cotton walks slightly toed-in, Indian style. He places the ball for a drive, about two or three inches in from his left heel. He swings back slowly, with a very straight left arm. His head turns back slightly . . . until he seems to be looking at the ball over his left shoulder with his left eye at the top of his backswing. His right elbow is kept well into his side; the hallmark of a compact swing under absolute control. At the top of his backswing his wrists are cocked and his clubface is open. His hips have rotated through 45 degrees, while his shoulders have rotated the full ninety. His left heel is barely

off the ground, and the whole position is so perfectly poised that it gives the impression he could never hit a crooked shot.

Cotton starts down lazily, until you think he will never generate enough acceleration to hit a hard blow. However, once his hands are pressed down almost to the bottom of their arc, with the club in the horizontal position, his wrists begin to do their work and apply their whip. They sling the clubhead into the ball with amazing flicking motion, much faster than the eye can follow. He hits later than any other player I have ever watched, and hitting late is the real secret of the crack professional's supremacy over the ordinary amateur.

Cotton, unlike many of his contemporaries, strongly believed that the hands were the key to a good golf swing and that the growing emphasis on body action could be physically harmful, especially to the back. Henry admitted that his tendency to overmechanize and over-think his putting technique directly led to his mediocrity in that area.

Cotton did not see himself as someone who squeezed the life and spontaneity out of the game by emphasizing mechanics. He did see the standardization of the golf ball in the 1920s, which eliminated the need to select a particular ball for given course conditions, as contributing to the mass production of golf technique: "From this moment mechanical golf...was created, for all over the world golfers began to practice hard in order to learn all about this new standardized ball." Later, when hick-ory-shafted clubs gave way to steel-shafted implements, Cotton opines: "The day of learning to play all the shots was over—the steel shaft had made the game an easier game. Only one swing was necessary, and I had to find out soon as possible the swing which would suit me."

Cotton also became a golf-course architect and noted that as golf became an industry, courses had to accommodate more play. To increase speed of play for the duffer, courses were made more strategic and less punishing. Cotton trained as a designer under Sir Guy Campbell, then J. Hamilton Stutt before establishing his own business in the 1950s. All of his courses are located in Great Britain and on the Continent, includ-ing the Penina Golf Club in Portugal. Late in life, Cotton founded the Henry Cotton Golf Foundation, dedicated to constructing low-cost, simple golf designs with little rough, no bunkers, and minimal mainte-nance, to encourage beginners to take up the game and make it more affordable to all. Thomas Henry Cotton, a member of the World Golf Hall of Fame, died in London, England, in 1987 at the age of eighty.

62

Curtis Strange

1955–

It was kind of emotional last year. This year it's more a feeling of satisfaction, I guess, a feeling of accomplishment, because to win the Open two years in succession is really something. It's hard to describe the feeling.

> —CURTIS STRANGE, after winning the 1989 U.S. Open at Oak Hill

Curtis Strange, a native of Norfolk, Virginia, took up the game of golf at the age of seven, under the watchful eye of his father, who was the professional and owner of the local White Sands Country Club. When Curtis's dad died when he was fourteen, Chandler Harper, a three-time Virginia State Amateur champion and winner of the 1950 PGA Championship, became his teacher. Strange became an outstanding amateur, winning the 1973 Southern Amateur at age eighteen. In 1974, as a freshman at Wake Forest, he eagled the last hole to lead his college to the NCAA team championship and won the individual title for himself. He was the College Player of the Year, won the Western Amateur, and played on the winning U.S. World Amateur team.

With an eye on the PGA Tour, Strange, who was long off the tee, shortened his swing to make it more dependable. He continued to win as an amateur. In 1975 and 1976 he won back-to-back victories in both the North and South and the Virginia State Amateur. He played on the winning U.S. Walker Cup team at St. Andrews in 1975, winning twice in the foursomes, once in the singles, and halving another match. He left Wake Forest in his junior year and turned professional in 1976. After a few lean years, he won his first tournament, the 1979 Pensacola Open. He began to climb the money list and led the Tour in earnings in 1985 with $542,321. But 1988, when he won the first of his two consecutive U.S. Opens, the Independent Insurance Agent Open and the Memorial and the Nabisco Championships, would be his best year. He headed the money list ($1,147,644) for the second consecutive year and was named the PGA Player of the Year.

Strange won his first Open at the Country Club in Brookline, Massachusetts. He led the tournament through three rounds with a 70-67-69=206, but a bogey on the seventeenth in the final round enabled NICK FALDO to tie him at 278 at the end of regulation play. This necessitated the third Open play-off to be held at the Country Club, beginning with the famous three-way play-off among FRANCIS OUIMET, HARRY VARDON, and TED RAY in 1913, followed by another three-way battle among ARNOLD PALMER, JULIUS BOROS, and Jackie Cupit in 1963. Strange won the play-off against Faldo, 71–75, when the defending British Open champion bogeyed the last four holes.

The 1989 Open was played at the Oak Hill Country Club in Rochester, New York. The 6,902-yard, par-70 layout was flooded when heavy rains fell on Friday night, after the second round. Strange started out with a round of 71, then followed with an outstanding round of 64 to put him in the lead. Due to the soft fairways and difficult, wet rough, scores began to climb in the final rounds, but TOM KITE managed to score a 69 in the third round and took the lead with a total of 205. Kite led Strange, who shot a third-round 73, by three shots. Kite's final-round 78, punctuated by a disastrous triple-bogey 7 at the fifth, ended his chances for his first major. Strange outlasted everyone by firing a steady 70 on the final day to edge Chip Beck, Mark McCumber, and IAN WOOSNAM by one shot. Kite finished fifth, five shots back at 283.

Strange's 3-over-par 143 on the final thirty-six holes was among the highest final two rounds by a recent Open winner. Julius Boros won the 1963 play-off at the Country Club after shooting 148 in the last two rounds. Open winners JACK NICKLAUS shot 146 in 1972 at Pebble Beach, BEN HOGAN shot 146 at Merion in 1950, and Andy North shot 144 at Oakland Hills in 1985. Curtis Strange became the first golfer to win consecutive U.S. Opens since Ben Hogan did it in 1951. Other golfers to achieve this are WILLIE ANDERSON (1903–05), JOHN MCDERMOTT (1911–12), BOBBY JONES (1929–30), and RALPH GULDAHL (1937–38).

Many golf observers saw Curtis Strange as America's best hope to stave off the wave of quality international golfers eroding American golf supremacy that had begun after World War I. International players had won the British Open from 1984 through 1988 and three of the last six Masters. Players such as BERNHARD LANGER, SEVE BALLESTEROS, SANDY LYLE, Woosnam, and Faldo had led the Europeans to Ryder Cup victories in 1985 and 1987; by virtue of a tie, they would retain the cup at The Belfry in 1989. Strange alone could hardly turn back this onslaught. In 1988 he became the first professional to win $1 million on the Tour. To date the 1989 U.S. Open win was Curtis's last Tour victory, although he won the 1989 Palm Meadows cup and the 1993 Greg Norman Classic in Australia.

Strange played on the Ryder Cup team in 1983, 1985, 1987, and 1989, compiling a 6-9-2 record. He was selected again as captain's choice by his fellow Virginian and Wake Forest golf alum LANNY WADKINS for the 1995 Ryder Cup at Oak Hill, a course that Curtis knows well. Paired with BEN CRENSHAW, Curtis lost his alternate-shots match against Bernhard Langer and Per-Ulrik Johansson, 1-up. He and Jay Haas then lost to Nick Faldo and Colin Montgomerie. Curtis was matched against Nick Faldo, his U.S. Open play-off opponent, in singles, and this time it was Curtis who couldn't buy a par going down the stretch and lost, 1-up; the Americans went down, 14½–13½.

Curtis Strange has always been known as a fiery, determined competitor, and in 1990 he characterized himself thusly: "Curtis Strange is still pretty temperamental, still childish at times. When things aren't going my way, I get impatient and frustrated. And if I try to lay back and completely forget about things that frustrate me, I don't think I could play good golf. What drives me is my intensity." Strange was elected captain of the 2001 U.S. Ryder Cup Team, which lost 15½ to 12½ at the Belfry in 2002.

63

Jack Burke Jr.

1923–

It [the caddie yard at River Oaks in Houston] was a great place, we could put on boxing gloves or shoot dice. In the yard, you learned quite a bit about life. As they say, "It's hard in the yard."

—JACK BURKE JR.

Jack Burke Jr. was born in Fort Worth, Texas, in 1923. At age four, he was already playing golf. At twelve, he could break par, win wagers with grown men, and outdrive Babe Zaharias. He learned golf from his dad, who was head professional at the old River Oaks Country Club in Houston. Jack also caddied at River Oaks and sometimes played with legendary Olympian and all-round athlete Babe Zaharias, who was from Port Arthur, Texas. The Babe was Jack Burke Sr.'s student. "She was a player," Jack remembers. "She'd say, 'c'mon, Little Jackie, I'm gonna kick your butt out here,' which was just the way she talked. The day that I outhit Babe, I knew I was on my way." Jack turned professional in 1940, but his career was interrupted when he served in the marines in World War II.

He was stationed at Camp Pendleton in California, where he spent a lot of time with JIMMY DEMARET, another Texan, who used to baby-sit Jack as a child and was stationed in San Diego in the navy. Jack would later become a partner with Demaret in building and running the Champions Club in Houston. In 1941, Jack's father, who had won several professional tournaments in his day, won the PGA Seniors' Championship, but during the war, the respected River Oaks professional passed away.

In 1945, when he was discharged from the Marines, Burke returned to River Oaks to see his friends, including Oscar Collins, the River Oaks locker-room attendant, who referred him to D. B. McDaniel, a wealthy club member who literally gave Burke a blank check to cover his early Tour expenses. "Without Oscar, I'm history. I think about it all the time," Burke recalled in a 1995 interview with golf journalist Rhonda Glenn. Burke was not initially successful on the Tour. He dropped out in the late 1940s and was later helped by CRAIG WOOD, a friend of his father's who got him a job at the Hollywood Golf Club in Deal, New Jersey, and then at Winged Foot with Claude Harmon. He returned to the Tour in 1950 after becoming head professional of the Metropolis Club in White Plains, New York.

Jack's first tournament victory was in the Bing Crosby Pro-Am in 1950. After winning four tournaments in 1950, Jack became one of the leading players on the Tour during that decade. He had a relatively short career but managed to win seventeen titles, including the PGA Championship and the Masters. Another career highlight was the four consecutive tournaments that he won in 1952: the Texas Open, Houston Open, Baton Rouge Open, and St. Petersburg Open. Only BYRON NELSON, BEN HOGAN, and TIGER WOODS have equaled or bettered this feat.

Burke was an excellent putter and a good foul-weather player. In 1952 he made his first serious run at a major, the Masters. The winds were unusually high during that tournament, which caused scores to go up dramatically in the third round. SAM SNEAD, who was the leader after the first two rounds, had a 77. With a three-round total of 70-67-77=214, Snead still managed to hold a three-shot lead over Ben Hogan. But Hogan shot a 79, and Snead recorded a 72 to finish with a 286. Burke shot a final-round 69 to finish second, four shots off the pace. Burke played well in 1952, winning the Vardon Trophy for low scoring average (70.54).

It was Jack's turn to win the Masters in 1956. He shot 72-71-75=218 in the first three rounds, and it seemed unlikely that he would catch KEN VENTURI, who had shot 66-69-75=210. Venturi, still an amateur, had been invited to the tournament after he returned from a tour of military duty. His opening score of 66 was a record for an amateur, the result of hitting sixteen greens in regulation and one-putting eight greens. But Venturi's game began to unravel on the back nine of the final round. Burke was in the clubhouse with a score of 289 as Venturi ran off six bogeys on the final nine to fall short by a stroke. Venturi's final round of 80 enabled Burke to win his green jacket.

Jack won his second major in 1956, the PGA Championship, held at the Blue Hill Golf and Country Club in Canton, Massachusetts. It required seven match-play victories to win. Burke won eighteen-hole contests against Leon Pounders, two and one; Bill Collins, five and three; Fred Haas Jr., 1-up; and Chandler Harper, three and two. He then defeated Fred Hawkins, four and two, in the thirty-six-hole quarter final and Ed Furgol in a thrilling match in the thirty-six-hole semifinal. Burke was down five holes after the fourteenth but won the fifteenth, sixteenth, and eighteenth to close the gap to two at the lunch break. Burke and Furgol were all even going into the final hole, which they both birdied. Burke made a 12-foot birdie putt on the first extra hole to win the match and advance to the final against Ted Kroll, who had easily defeated William Johnson, ten and eight, in his semifinal match. In the final, Jack was down two holes after the morning round but shot 32 on the first nine of the afternoon round to build a 2-up lead. Burke closed out the match, three and two, at the thirty-fourth when Kroll bogeyed the hole. Burke was named PGA Player of the Year in 1956 for his fine season.

Jack Burke was a member of five consecutive Ryder Cup teams (1951–59) and posted a 7-1 record in singles and foursomes. His only loss came in singles, against Peter Mills, five and three, in the U.S. loss to Great Britain, 7½–4½, at the Lindrick Golf Club in England in 1957. His interest in the Champions Club in Texas and a hand injury reduced Burke's playing time on the Tour. He won his last tournament in 1963, the Lucky International, then dropped off the Tour.

Jack Burke's seventeen PGA Tour wins ties him for forty-first place all-time with Bobby Cruickshank, Harold McSpaden, and CURTIS STRANGE. At this writing he occupies his time managing the Champions Golf Club, which hosted the 1969 U.S. Open and the 1993 U.S. Amateur. Jack Burke was elected to the World Golf Hall of Fame in 2000.

64

Lanny Wadkins

1950–

*I've made some of my best shots when the heat's on,
and that's satisfying, but this was special because of the
situation. I'll never forget it.*

    —LANNY WADKINS, after his clutch birdie in the 1983
    Ryder Cup, guaranteeing the U.S. team a win

Jerry Lanston "Lanny" Wadkins, one of golf's fiercest competitors, gained success at an early age, winning the Richmond Junior Championship four times. His brother Bobby won it twice, giving the Wadkins family of Richmond, Virginia, six consecutive championship years. In 1966, at the age of sixteen, he shot 294 in the U.S. Amateur at Merion, nine shots behind the winner, Gary Cowan. Wadkins attended Wake Forest University on an Arnold Palmer Scholarship and played on the golf team. He captured the 1968 Southern Amateur and won the Eastern Amateur and played on the Walker Cup team the following year. In 1970, at age twenty, Lanny shot 299 in the U.S. Amateur at the Waverley Country Club in Portland, Oregon, to defeat TOM KITE by one shot. The U.S. Amateur had begun as a match-play event in 1895, was changed to medal play in 1965, and since 1973 has returned to a match-play format. Wadkins also won the U.S. Western and the Southern Amateur and played on the World Amateur Cup team in 1970.

Wadkins finished second in a Tour event, the Heritage Classic in 1970, and was named to the all-American golf team in 1970 and again in 1971. He was a member of the 1971 Walker Cup team, played number-one singles, and won in both his matches. His most important win in that event was a three-and-one victory over five-time British Amateur champion Michael Bonallack. Lanny turned professional in 1971 and played six Tour events, making the cut in each one. He won his first Tour event, the Sahara Invitational, in 1972 and placed fifteenth on the money list.

One of his best years was 1977. He won the PGA Championship at Pebble Beach in the first sudden-death play-off ever held in a major. Wadkins began that tournament with rounds of 69-71-72=212, six shots behind the leader, GENE LITTLER, who led the first three rounds with 67-69-70=206. In the final round, Wadkins was five shots behind after nine holes, but then Littler bogeyed five of the first six holes on the back nine. A Wadkins birdie on the par-5 final hole enabled him to finish with a 70 and a tournament total of 282 to tie Littler. Wadkins won on the third play-off hole to capture his only professional major. Wadkins's career play-off record is 3-3. Lanny also won the World Series of golf in 1977 and finished third on the money list.

Wadkins is noted for his attacking style and his quick pace of play. He is an excellent shotmaker and has the ability to imaginatively recover from a variety of trouble spots. Wadkins, after some roller coaster years (he was sixty-fourth on the money list in 1976, third in 1977, sixty-second in 1978, tenth in 1979, sixtieth in 1980, eighty-third in 1981, then seventh in 1982), became a more consistent golfer in the period 1982–92, winning fourteen of his twenty-one PGA career events. Lanny was named PGA Player of the Year in 1985. He has been named to the Ryder Cup team eight times (1977, 1979, 1983, 1985, 1987, 1989, 1991,

1993) and captained the U.S. team in its losing effort at Oak Hill in 1995. Now that many people are maniacal about Ryder Cup competition, especially since the Europeans started winning, Lanny took a lot of heat by selecting his pal CURTIS STRANGE as one of the two captains of that team rather than LEE JANZEN. Curtis lost two alternative-shot matches when paired with BEN CRENSHAW and Jay Haas, then lost the match-deciding singles contest to NICK FALDO while under a media microscope on the final afternoon. But six other Americans lost singles matches that afternoon. The real problem with that American team was its overall lack of Ryder Cup experience. (Ten players out of twelve are automatic selections based on a point system that is designed to favor the golfers currently playing well.) Five of its twelve players had never played a Ryder Cup match.

Wadkins himself built a strong record, and his excellent golf reputation became strongly associated with his Ryder Cup play and his competitive attitude. One of his bright, shining Ryder Cup moments came at the 1983 Ryder Cup contest at PGA National. Lanny was matched against the Spaniard José María Canizares, a hardened Ryder Cup veteran. Their match, it turned out, would decide the outcome of the Ryder Cup. Canizares was 1-up through fifteen, then protected his lead by parring the sixteenth after putting his ball into the water. He halved the hole with Wadkins, who missed a 12-foot birdie putt. Both players then parred the next hole, and Wadkins was informed that he needed to halve his match if the Americans were to win, 14½–13½, taking the Ryder Cup outright. Wadkins hit a good drive, a 3-wood over water, to within 75 yards of the green, then hit a wedge stiff to birdie the hole and halve the match. Wadkins would later say, "I've never been so nervous. When the pressure's on and you have to do things for yourself, you expect to do them; it's different when you have to do it for others."

Lanny's record is 20-11-3 in Ryder Cup play, one of the best all-time. His total number of matches played, thirty-four, is second only to BILLY CASPER on the U.S. side. Wadkins's twenty-one Tour victories place him tied for twenty-seventh on the all-time list, along with PHIL MICKELSON, CRAIG WOOD, and WILLIE MACFARLANE. Lanny was second three times in the PGA Championship (1982, 1984 [tie], 1987), tied for second in the U.S. Open (1986), and has two third-place ties in the Masters (1991, 1993). Lanny Wadkins has won more than $6 million on the Tour.

65

Hubert Green

1946–

The name of the game is to be the best at whatever you do.

—HUBERT GREEN

Hubert Myatt Green III, a doctor's son, grew up in his native Birmingham, Alabama, and took up golf at the age of five. He was an all-around athlete in high school but soon chose golf as his favorite sport. Short but accurate off the tee, Hubert developed a fine short game and learned how to score. He attended Florida State University and won the Southern Amateur, at the age of nineteen, in 1966. Green finished fourth in the 1968 U.S. Amateur at the Scioto Country Club in Columbus, Ohio. In 1969 he won the Southern Amateur again and was selected to the Walker Cup team but had to decline because he elected to turn professional.

In 1971, his first full year on the Tour, Green won the Houston Open and was named Rookie of the Year. During 1976 he won three straight tournaments—the Doral-Eastern Open, Greater Jacksonville Open, and the Sea Pines Heritage Classic. His three wins tied him with BEN CRENSHAW for most Tour wins. He earned $228,031, placing him fourth, behind the leader, JACK NICKLAUS, who earned $266,439. The following year, Hubert won the U.S. Open at Southern Hills in Tulsa, Oklahoma, where he shot rounds of 69-67-72 to hold a one-stroke lead over Andy Bean. The final round was rather harrowing because a clerk in the Oklahoma City office of the FBI had received a telephone call from a frantic woman claiming three men were on their way to Tulsa to kill Hubert Green. Uniformed policemen were dispatched to protect Green, who, although unaware of the threat, began to play shaky golf on the final nine. He bogeyed the ninth and tenth, and by the time Hubert finished the thirteenth, Lou Graham, who birdied the sixteenth, was only one shot behind Green. After playing the fourteenth, Green was informed of the death threat by tournament officials and was given the option to withdraw, ask for play to be suspended, or continue to play. Green joked that the threat was probably from an old girlfriend and opted to play on. Green then parred number fifteen, birdied the sixteenth, parred the seventeenth, and needed a bogey on the tough 458-yard, par-4 final hole to win the championship. Green left his approach shot short and in a bunker. Then he chunked his sand shot, leaving it twenty feet short. He left his next putt three and one half feet short, but he made his bogey effort to card a 70 and a total of 278. It was later concluded that the death threat was a hoax.

The following year, Green continued to play excellent golf. He missed a putt on the seventy-second hole at the Masters that would have put him in a play-off with GARY PLAYER, who won by one shot over Green, TOM WATSON, and Rod Funseth. Hubert won the Hawaiian Open and the Sea Pines Classic to finish ninth on the money list. He accumulated a total of eighteen Tour victories through 1984; then, in his last PGA Tour win, he captured the 1985 PGA Championship at the Cherry Hills Country Club, near Denver. Hubert dethroned defending champion LEE TREVINO by scoring rounds of 67-69-70-72=278 to win the $125,000 first prize, his biggest career paycheck. Trevino, who was hurt by a third-round 75, finished second, two shots off the pace. Green finished sixteenth on the money list that year but began to fade, finishing no higher than seventy-third thereafter. He completed his regular Tour career with $2,591,959. Hubert is tied with Ben Crenshaw, TOM KITE, and DOUG FORD for thirty-third place on the all-time PGA Tour win list. Green was a member of the 1977, 1979, and 1985 Ryder Cup teams. His Ryder Cup record is 4-3-0.

Green has a highly individual style. On the full swing he leans well over the ball, his hands very low. He picks the club up quickly to the outside, then brings it back inside, coming down. Though not a long hitter, he is a good shotmaker. When chipping, he positions the ball to the right of his right foot, hoods the club, and strikes the ball with great touch and accuracy. He has rekindled his competitive drive on the Senior Tour, which he joined in 1996. He has earned over $3.2 million on that circuit. Before he joined that Tour he said: "Until I get in the winner's circle, I will not be happy. There's only one place out there, and that's number one. A friend of mine back home [in Alabama], James Finch, races cars. His attitude is that second place is first loser. I'm taking that attitude. I'm not out there to survive." Through 2002, Hubert had won five times on the Senior Tour.

66

Bernhard Langer

1957–

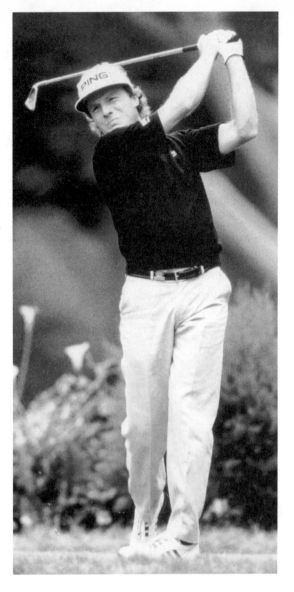

I was getting on for twenty-eight, had won many tournaments, but badly, badly I needed a major.

—BERNHARD LANGER, after winning his first Masters

Bernhard Langer, the son of a bricklayer, was born in Anhausen, in the former West Germany, in 1957. At the age of nine he took up the game of golf as a caddie at the Augsburg Country Club in Anhausen. In 1972, Bernhard went to work as an assistant professional to Heinz Fehring at the Munich Golf and Country Club. After finishing his apprenticeship there in 1976, he joined the European Tour.

Langer recorded his first victory in the 1979 World Under-25 Tournament, winning by seventeen strokes. In 1980 he became the first German to win a major European title, the Dunlop Masters. In 1981, Langer had fifteen top-ten finishes on the European Tour and became the first German to win the German Open. During his career he has won five German Opens (1981, 1982, 1985, 1986, 1993) and three German Masters (1989, 1991, 1997). From 1980 through 1995 he won at least one tournament for sixteen consecutive years. Langer has won the Order of Merit, awarded for most earnings in a season on the European Tour, twice (1981, 1984). During one period in the 1990s, Bernhard Langer played in seventy consecutive tournaments without missing a cut.

Beginning in 1984, the 5-foot-9-inch, 155-pound Langer started to play a selected number of PGA Tour events. He won the 1985 Masters his first full year on the Tour with rounds of 72-74-68-68=282 to win by two shots over SEVE BALLESTEROS, RAYMOND FLOYD, and CURTIS STRANGE. On the final nine, he had birdies on the fourteenth and fifteenth holes to overtake Curtis Strange, who bogeyed both those holes. Langer then clinched the $126,000 first prize by sinking a 15-foot birdie putt on the seventeenth hole to become the third continental European after ARNAUD MASSY (1907 British Open) and SEVE BALLESTEROS (British Open, 1979, 1984, 1988; Masters, 1980, 1983) to win a major tournament. From the period 1980–96, the Masters was won ten times by an international player. Langer won his second Masters in 1993, earning $306,000 for first place with a score of 68-70-69-70=277 to win by four shots over Chip Beck.

Langer has long been an excellent putter with an ability to make critical putts even though at different stages of his career he has had to battle the yips, a nervous affliction affecting hand control. To counter those problems, he adapted a putting style by which he extends the shaft of his putter up the inside of his left forearm. His right hand then grips both forearm and shaft. For his efforts, Langer has twice been rated the best putter on the European Tour. JACK NICKLAUS made this observation about Langer: "Germany's Bernhard Langer is a fine example of the difference between a 'wonderful putter' in a technical or aesthetic sense and a golfer with tremendous ability to get the ball in the hole under maximum pressure." Langer also led the European Tour in stroke average in 1981 (70.56) and 1984 (69.42).

In addition to his wins at the Masters and in many international golf tournaments, Langer has distinguished himself as a member of nine European Ryder Cup teams (1981–97) compiling a record of 16-12-5.

Bernhard Langer, along with other European stars, such as NICK FALDO, Seve Ballesteros, JOSE-MARIA OLAZABAL, and IAN WOOSNAM, made the Ryder Cup matches competitive after the former Great Britain and Ireland team was expanded to include continental Europe in 1979.

One of the most stunning wins for the Europeans was a fifteen-and-thirteen victory at Muirfield Village, Jack Nicklaus's course in Dublin, Ohio, in the 1987 Ryder Cup. The European team got off to a 6–2 lead the first day and increased its margin to $8^{1}/_{2}$–$3^{1}/_{2}$ the morning of the second day in the foursomes. Langer, teamed with SANDY LYLE, holed a critical bunker shot on the 441-yard, par-4 tenth in his morning foursomes match against LARRY NELSON and LANNY WADKINS. This helped his team to win, 1-up, despite birdies on the sixteenth and seventeenth by the Americans. Langer hit an 8-iron approach shot to within three feet on the final hole to ensure the victory. In the afternoon, Langer and Lyle again won, 1-up, in four-balls. Langer halved his singles match with Nelson the final day, and the Americans, despite a $7^{1}/_{2}$–$4^{1}/_{2}$ win in singles, could not overcome the deficit of $10^{1}/_{2}$–$5^{1}/_{2}$ the Europeans built in the first two days. The U.S. team had lost a Ryder Cup contest for the first time on American soil.

Langer will be remembered for a putt that he missed in Ryder Cup play. That was at Kiawah in the 1991 contest when, playing the final singles match against HALE IRWIN, Langer missed a 6-foot par putt on the final hole that would have given him a win in his match and the European team a tie, allowing them to retain the right to hold the cup that they had won at Muirfield and then retained by virtue of a tie at The Belfry in 1989. Langer's miss enabled the Americans to win by the slimmest of margins, $14^{1}/_{2}$–$13^{1}/_{2}$, in 1991. But Langer overcame that disappointment. He was a key figure in the European team win in the 1997 Ryder Cup match at the Valderrama Golf Club in Spain. He won three points for his team in singles and team play, including a critical two-and-one win over Brad Faxon in singles play on the final day which helped the Europeans to win, $14^{1}/_{2}$–$13^{1}/_{2}$.

Bernhard Langer has won over sixty golf tournaments worldwide, including over forty on the European Tour. He will be remembered for his Ryder Cup performances, his Masters wins, and as the greatest German golfer. He will also be remembered for the dignity with which he accepted his disappointment at Kiawah and the determination that enabled him to recover his form and continue to be a major force in international golf.

67

Jock Hutchison

1884–1977

That was something, Hutchison's victory in the Open.
For the first time since Arnaud Massy of France had won
at Hoylake in 1907, the cup had gone to a foreigner, and
this time the foreigner was from a distant country.

—HERBERT WARREN WIND, commenting on Jock Hutchison's
win in the 1921 British Open at St. Andrews

Jock Hutchison, along with JIM BARNES and WALTER HAGEN, was
among the best golfers in the United States prior to the reign of BOBBY
JONES. Born in St. Andrews, Scotland, in 1884, Hutchison emigrated to
the United States in the early 1900s and settled in the Pittsburgh area.
Hutchison entered the 1916 U.S. Open and finished second after firing
a final round 68 to close two shots behind amateur CHICK EVANS at
Minikahda. As a professional, Hutchison was able to collect the $500
first-prize money and a medal. He won important regional tournaments,

251

such as the Western Pennsylvania Open and the 1917 Patriotic Open, a wartime substitute for the U.S. Open, before breaking out in 1920, winning the Western Open and PGA Championship and finishing in a four-way tie for second place in the U.S. Open.

Although Hutchison was born in St. Andrews and started with a St. Andrews swing, his game was formed in the United States. He developed a three-piece swing. A nervous, fidgety player, Jock was nonetheless capable of streaks of great golf. During the World War I period, Hutchison, Hagen, "Long Jim" Barnes, Bobby Jones, and other great golfers raised their profile and money for Liberty Bonds, Red Cross, and War Relief. The 1916 U.S. Open was the last Open before America became involved in World War I. It was again held in 1919 at Brae Burn in West Newton, Massachusetts, and Walter Hagen won in a play-off against Mike Brady. Hutchison almost won the Open the following year at Inverness in Toledo, Ohio. There was a record-265 entries for that event, and after two days of qualifying rounds, seventy golfers teed off. Among the leading attractions were HARRY VARDON, then fifty, and TED RAY, forty-three, two of Britain's best golfers. Hutchison opened with a 69 to lead the tournament by one shot over young LEO DIEGEL. After thirty-six holes of play, Hutchison still held a one-shot lead with a total of 145. He shot a 74 in the next round to fall one shot behind Vardon and Diegel. Hutchison was still in the running on the final holes but missed a 3-foot putt on the fifteenth, dropping him into a four-way tie for second, one shot behind Ted Ray, who finished with a score of 295.

Hutchison was more fortunate the following week when he played in the PGA Championship at the Flossmoor Country Club in Glenview, Illinois. Jock got in as an alternate after failing to qualify. He reached the final against Douglas Edgar and went 1-up after Edgar missed a 3-footer on the sixteenth and an 18-inch putt on the seventeenth. Hutchison increased his lead to 3-up with five to play, but then Jock became erratic off the tee and Edgar came back to 1-down with three holes to play. A great recovery by Hutchison at the sixteenth and three putts by Edgar put Hutchison 2-up with two to play. Jock then lost the seventeenth after being stymied by Edgar, but Hutchison was able to close out the match on the final hole when both players halved with fives.

Edgar was an interesting opponent and an even more fascinating person. He was born in England in 1884 and developed into a fine golfer and a superb golf instructor. He gave TOMMY ARMOUR lessons and is considered the father of the modern-day golf swing. Harry Vardon lauded his game, saying, "This man will one day be the greatest of all." Edgar was obsessed with analyzing and refining the golf swing. A late bloomer in tournament golf, he won the French Open in 1914 and, after settling in the United States, became the professional at Druid Hills in Atlanta. He won the Canadian Open in 1919 and 1920. But he died mysteriously on August 8, 1921, the apparent victim of foul play. The case has never been solved. Before his death, Edgar wrote *The Gate to Golf*, explaining his teachings.

Hutchison's frantic style was to literally bound after each shot as he chattered and chuckled his way down the fairway. He used deeply scored clubs, later declared illegal, which imparted tremendous back-spin to the ball. Jock was known to have opinions about everything, and in a 1920 issue of the *American Golfer*, he gave this advice in an article called "How to Look at the Ball":

> Just remember that the head and neck are not fixed to any one place. That they have just as much right to freedom as the arms have. But in not moving the head on the back-swing, always let it come to the right as if you were looking at something back of the ball rather than to the left. You will find that most of the fine golf players adapt this system of looking at the ball. . . . Jerry Travers is a notable example in this respect. He makes it physically hard to look up, and by doing this he manages to keep his eye on the ball about as well as any man I know. . . . It will take some practice. But don't let anyone tell you that the head and neck should be held rigidly in one place without being moved through the course of a swing. There is no surer way to break up all rhythm in the swing and to destroy the freedom of the stroke, no matter what club you use.

Hutchison benefited from his Pittsburgh connections by imparting his wisdom to Andrew Carnegie, then one of the richest men in America. Few professional golfers of that era made a living just playing golf, as there was yet no Tour. Hutchison was lucky enough to be retained as a private tutor by Carnegie, a fellow Scotsman. In 1921, naturalized American citizen Jock Hutchison ventured to his homeland to play in the British Open at St. Andrews. Jock, whose father caddied for another golfer at the tournament, stayed with relatives and practiced on the course several times, mastering the nuances of the Old Course prior to the first tee-off.

Jock fired a 72 his first round, scoring a hole in one on the 135-yard eighth and just missing a double eagle on the 278-yard, par-4 ninth.

His rounds of 72-75-79-70=296 earned him a tie for first with twenty-two-year-old Roger Wethered, brother of the great lady champion Joyce Wethered. Wethered was the victim of a bizarre penalty during the regulation round that likely cost him the tournament. During his third round he accidentally kicked his ball at the fourteenth while backing up after walking ahead to study his run-up shot. It cost him a crucial penalty stroke. Hutchison prevailed in the thirty-six-hole play-off, 150–159, earning the first British Open win for an American. However, the locals did not recognize it as a real American win. It took Walter Hagen's win at Sandwich the following year to assert America's presence in the Open.

Hutchison's last good major tournament effort was his third-place finish in the 1923 U.S. Open. He played little tournament golf after 1928 until he won the inaugural Senior PGA Tournament, a fifty-four-hole event, then held at Augusta National, by eight shots in 1937. He won the Senior PGA again in 1947 after it was relocated to PGA National. Hutchison lost a championship play-off, to Al Watrous, in the 1951 Senior PGA when he was sixty-eight years old.

After World War II, Hutchison had moved to the Glen View Country Club, in the Chicago area. In his later years he became a fixture at the Masters when, beginning in 1963, he paired with Fred McLeod in the opening tee-off ceremonies. By the end of the 1960s, only a few survivors remained of the Scottish and English invasion of professionals that came to the United States at the turn of the century. Players such as Hutchison, ALEX SMITH, Alex Ross, Freddie McLeod, Tommy Armour, and others had taught Americans technique and tradition.

In addition to his wins in two modern majors, Hutchison won two Western Opens (1920, 1923) and a North and South Open (1921), major events of his day.

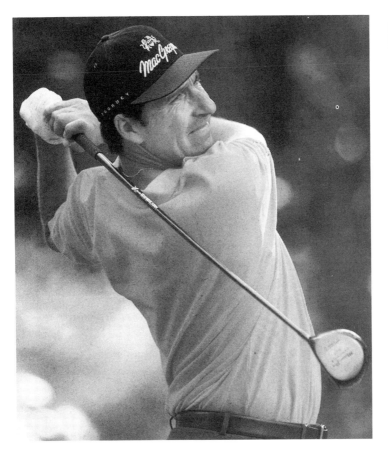

68

Jose-Maria Olazabal

1967–

You have all it takes to win. You are the best in the world.
—A note to Olazabal from two-time Masters winner SEVE
BALLESTEROS, before the final round of the 1994 Masters

Jose-Maria Olazabal, the greatest golfer Spain has produced other than
SEVE BALLESTEROS, is a native of Fuenterrabia, Spain, where he still
resides. He grew up in a home near the ninth green of the Royal San
Sebastian Golf Club and began to swing a golf club before he was two
years old. He had an outstanding amateur career, winning many titles,
including the Under-10 Spanish Championship when he was seven

years old and the British Amateur when he was eighteen. He is the only golfer ever to win Britain's Boys' Youths' and Amateur Championships.

Olazabal turned professional in 1985 and joined the European Tour in 1986 when he was nineteen years old. His first win was the Ebel European Masters in 1986. Jose-Maria finished second on the European money list and won three tournaments that year. He has won seventeen tournaments of the seventy-eight he has entered on the European Tour through 1998. He has also won four PGA Tour events: the World Series of Golf (1990), the International (1991), the Masters (1994), and the World Series of Golf (1994). He has won over $10 million worldwide, placing him among the top thirty-five on the all-time earnings list. Despite being hindered by back and foot problems, Olazabal has racked up an impressive record.

In addition to his appearances at selected PGA Tour events, especially the Masters, Olazabal is known for his contribution to the rise of the European Ryder Cup team. He has been especially impressive when paired with his countryman Seve Ballesteros in foursomes and four-balls. In 1987, Olazabal's first year in Ryder Cup competition, he and Seve made a major contribution to the European 15–13 upset win over the Americans at Muirfield Village in Dublin, Ohio. They defeated LARRY NELSON and PAYNE STEWART, 1-up, in foursomes and CURTIS STRANGE and TOM KITE, two and one, in four-balls the first day. The second day, they defeated BEN CRENSHAW and Payne Stewart, 1-up, in foursomes before losing a tight match in four-balls, two and one, to HAL SUTTON and Larry Mize. Through 1997, Olazabal and Ballesteros had only lost two matches in team play.

Before the 1993 Ryder Cup matches, former Ryder Cup competitor and journalist Peter Alliss, in an article in *Golf Digest* said of Olazabal: "[He] has formed a tremendous partnership in the past with Seve; it's been Ollie who has been the stronger half of that pairing. I'd say sixty percent." Olazabal has been on every European Ryder Cup team since 1987. In 1997, Olazabal, who could hardly walk in 1996 due to recurring foot problems, paired with Constantino Rocca in team play because Seve Ballesteros was nonplaying team captain of the Europeans in the Ryder Cup held at Valderrama in Sotogrande, Spain. Olazabal won two team matches with Rocca, halved a team match playing with Ignacio Garrido, lost a team match with Rocca, and lost a singles match to LEE JANZEN, 1-down, on the final day. The European team won, $14\frac{1}{2}$–$13\frac{1}{2}$, as America's big guns, 1997 major championship winners TIGER WOODS, Justin Leonard, and DAVIS LOVE III, combined for a 1-9-3 record.

Prior to the 1994 Masters, Olazabal was struggling in a slump beginning in 1993. He had not only not won a major tournament, he won no tournaments on the European or American Tours in 1993. His poor play began to take the enjoyment out of the game, and his frustration began to simmer. His manager, Sergio Gomez, summed it up: "Every time he played golf it was as if he was going to the slaughterhouse." Fortunately for Olazabal, John Jacobs, a respected instructor and player on the Senior Tour, was in Spain in February 1994 and gave Jose-Maria some lessons. He cured a reverse-pivot problem that Olazabal had and gave him some other pointers. Rejuvenated, Jose-Maria came to the United States in preparation for the Masters. He finished fourteenth in the Tournament Players Championship and second in the Freeport-McMoran Classic.

Olazabal shot a disappointing 74 in the first round of the Masters and angrily said to Gomez, "I am ashamed; I played safe, and it did not pay." He played more aggressively in the second round, shooting 67, two shots behind the leader, Larry Mize. He shot 69 the next day and was one shot behind the new leader, Tom Lehman. Lehman and Olazabal were paired on the final day, and Olazabal's ability to scramble and his deft putting would prove the difference. Jose-Maria tied for the tournament low with 110 putts, eight fewer than Lehman. After a series of brilliant recovery shots to save par, Olazabal was able to make a crucial putt when it counted, and Tom couldn't.

For example, on the 500-yard, par-5 fifteenth, Olazabal hit his 5-iron approach to within thirty feet of the pin. The shot barely made it over the pond fronting the green. Lehman was on the green in two, fifteen feet away, and was also putting for an eagle. Olazabal then ran a beautiful putt into the hole, putting all the pressure on Lehman. Tom barely missed his eagle putt but then also missed his short birdie effort and lost two crucial strokes on the hole. That proved to be the margin of victory. Olazabal went on to shoot a final-round 69 for a score of 279 to win by two over Lehman.

Prior to the final round, Seve Ballesteros, who won the Masters in 1980 and 1983, left a note for Jose-Maria to bolster his confidence. It read in part: "You have all it takes to win. You are the best in the world." In the years since Seve won his Masters, members of the European Ryder Cup team, including BERNHARD LANGER (1985, 1993), SANDY LYLE (1998), NICK FALDO (1989, 1990, 1996), and IAN WOOSNAM (1991) had won the Masters. Olazabal won his second green jacket at the Masters in 1999. Jose-Maria Olazabal has won twenty-eight golf tournaments worldwide.

69

Roberto de Vicenzo

1923–

I feel like many peoples are with me.
—ROBERTO DE VICENZO, before winning
the 1967 British Open

Roberto de Vicenzo was born in Buenos Aires in 1923. He developed his interest and skills in golf while serving as a caddie with his brothers, who all became golf professionals, at a local golf course in Buenos Aires. He turned professional at the age of eighteen, first played in North America in 1947, and made his first appearance in the British Open in 1948.

The British Open became the tournament by which Roberto de Vicenzo measured himself. In his first three championships he finished third twice and second once. But then he didn't place higher than third in the next fifteen tournaments. It seemed likely that Roberto would never realize his dream of becoming a British Open champion. By 1967, Roberto had won 130 tournaments and thirty national championships worldwide, but never a major tournament. At the age of forty-five and with strong competitors such as JACK NICKLAUS, GARY PLAYER, TONY JACKLIN, and others, the odds were against de Vicenzo in the Open. The 1953 Open was a reminder of his frustration in reaching his goal. After three rounds, Roberto, tied for the Open lead with BEN HOGAN at Carnoustie, broke down and wept under the strain in his hotel room, having concluded that his putter would fail him and that he would lose. Hogan shot 68 in the final round to win the only Open he ever played. De Vicenzo shot 73 to finish sixth, five shots behind Hogan.

De Vicenzo practiced for hours in preparation for the 1967 Open at Royal Liverpool in Hoylake. The bookmakers had him at 33–1 odds before the tournament. After the first round, Roberto trailed the leader, one Lionel Platts, who shot a 68. Jack Nicklaus, the U.S. Open champion and the defending British Open champion, had a 71; de Vicenzo, a 70. After two rounds Roberto trailed Devlin and Nicklaus by a shot with a total of 141. De Vicenzo then fired a tournament-low, course-record 67, as did Gary Player, to give him a total of 208 and a two-shot lead over Player, three over Nicklaus, and four over Clive Clark and Bruce Devlin.

The stage was set for a dramatic finish. The course itself, which played over 7,000 yards, is the second-oldest seaside golf course in England, after Westward Ho! Founded in 1869, Royal Liverpool (also called Hoylake) was responsible for starting the British Amateur, the oldest amateur championship, in 1885. The first international match between the English and Scots was held at Royal Liverpool here in 1902. In 1921 the first men's match between the United States and Britain was played here, inspiring George H. Walker to inaugurate the Walker Cup the following year. In 1930, BOBBY JONES won the British Open at Hoylake, the second leg of his Grand Slam.

The crux of the matter at Hoylake is the five finishing holes which consume over 2,300 yards and have a collective par of twenty-two strokes, an especially difficult test when the wind is severely blowing off the Irish Sea. Nicklaus, who was playing ahead of de Vicenzo, reduced Roberto's lead to two shots going into the back nine. De Vicenzo holed a putt for birdie on the 409-yard par-4 tenth to pick up a stroke, and Player faltered with a three-putt bogey. By the twelfth hole, Player had shot himself out of the tournament and eventually finished tied for third at 284. Meanwhile, Nicklaus birdied the 529-yard, par-5 sixteenth and the 395-yard, par-4 finishing hole. His round of 69 gave him a total of 280.

De Vicenzo, a long hitter, had to play the last three holes in par to win. He reached the sixteenth in two with an excellent spoon shot from the edge of the out-of-bounds line. He two-putted for a birdie and a two-shot lead. On each of the par-4 finishing holes, Roberto drove long and true, found the green with a 9-iron, and two-putted for par and a total of 278 to win his coveted British Open. Roberto de Vicenzo, at forty-four, was the oldest British Open winner of the twentieth century.

Despite his major accomplishment in the 1967 British Open, de Vicenzo is most remembered for what happened to him at the 1968 Masters. Roberto continued his fine shotmaking in the Masters, shooting a 69-73-70=212 to find himself among a group of eight golfers bunched within two strokes of the lead going into the final round. Gary Player led with a 210, Frank Beard, Bruce Devlin, RAYMOND FLOYD, Bob Goalby, and Don January were at 211, and LEE TREVINO and Roberto were at 212. De Vicenzo opened his final round with an eagle 2 and finished the front nine with a 5-under-par 31. Despite finishing with a bogey on the final hole, he scored what appeared to be a 65. This would have given him a total of 277. Bob Goalby, playing behind de Vicenzo, was also playing well. He birdied the thirteenth and the fourteenth, putting him two shots behind. A powerful man who could summon up a big tee shot, Goalby hit a 320-yard drive down the middle on the 520-yard, par-5 fifteenth. He then hit a perfect 3-iron to within eight feet and holed his putt to tie de Vicenzo. Goalby parred the next two holes; then, after driving poorly on the final hole, he hit an excellent recovery shot to the green, two-putting for par and an apparent tie.

As it turned out, de Vicenzo's playing partner, Tommy Aaron, who was scoring for Roberto, recorded a five for him at the seventeenth when he actually had a par 4. Roberto signed his scorecard without making the correction and thus had to take a final-round 66 and a total of 278, dropping him to second place. To de Vicenzo's credit, he took responsibility for his error and commended Goalby on his fine finish. USGA Rule 38, Paragraph 3, had penalized Roberto: "No alteration may be made on a card after the competitor has returned it to the Committee. If the competitor returns a score for any hole lower than actually played, he shall be disqualified. A score higher than actually played must stand as returned."

Roberto continued to play and win more tournaments. He won the 1973 Brazilian Open, the 1974 Panama Open, and the 1974 PGA Senior's Championship. Roberto de Vicenzo represented his country seventeen times in the World Cup, winning the team title with Antonio Cerda in 1953 and the individual title in 1969 and 1972. Roberto was elected to the World Golf Hall of Fame in 1989.

70

Doug Ford

1923–

My God, that's the best shot I ever made!

— DOUG FORD, after holing a bunker shot for a
birdie on the eighteenth hole of the final round
of the 1957 Masters

Doug Ford refined his shooting touch in pool rooms during his youth
in West Haven, Connecticut. He claimed that learning the touch and
feel of a pool cue and the angles on the felts later helped him develop
into an excellent putter. He turned professional in 1949, at the advanced
age of twenty-six. Doug won his first PGA Tour tournament, the Jacksonville Open, in 1952 and collected $2,000 in prize money. Ford then

became one of the most consistent players on the Tour, winning at least one tournament every year from 1952 through 1963, except 1956, when he had three second-place finishes and two third-place finishes. His nineteen PGA Tour victories put him thirty-third on the all-time list, tied with BEN CRENSHAW, HUBERT GREEN, and TOM KITE.

Ford had a controlled, dependable swing. His explanation of his swing mechanics: "This simplification occurred because modern equipment—tailored heads, steel shafts, firmer gripping, better distribution of weight, and torque—permits the development of more power with less effort. Yet the application of the power still is essential, but it must come with smoothness and precision."

Doug Ford won his first major, the 1955 PGA Championship, at the Meadowbrook Country Club in Northville, Michigan. A thirty-six-hole qualifying round to determine the match-play field was conducted the Wednesday and Thursday before the championship. Ford was the low qualifier with a 136. A score of 146 qualified for the main event, with eleven golfers who scored 147 having to play off for seven spots. CARY MIDDLECOFF reached the final by defeating JACK BURKE JR. in a nine-hour marathon match, 1-up, at the fortieth hole. Down two holes with two to play, Middlecoff birdied the last two holes to reach the play-off. Ford easily advanced to the final, four and three, over Shelly Mayfield on the strength of shooting 3 under through fifteen holes in the afternoon eighteen and 5 under for the thirty-three holes that they played.

The championship match was close for twenty-seven holes. Even though Ford shot a 5-under-par 66 in the morning round, Middlecoff led, 1-up, with a score of 67. Ford evened the match on the twenty-sixth hole with a birdie. Then he started to putt well and birdied the twenty-ninth, thirtieth, and thirty-second holes, closing out the match, four and three, with a par. Playing in his first PGA Championship, Ford was the fourth player to win both the medal for the qualifier and the match-play championship. Doug was named the PGA Player of the Year in 1955.

Ford's best year was 1957, when he won the Los Angeles Open, the Masters, and the Western Open. Only ARNOLD PALMER, with four, won more PGA tournaments than Ford that year. Ford, who had finished sixth in the 1956 Masters, five shots behind the winner, Jack Burke Jr., started off with ordinary rounds of 72 and 73 to put him five shots behind the leader, SAM SNEAD. One hundred and two golfers started, and for the first time, the field was cut for the final two rounds. Ford shot a third-round score of 72 for a fifty-four-hole total of 217, three shots behind Snead. On the final day, Ford pulled even with Snead on the 520-yard, par-5 fifteenth hole after birdieing the twelfth and fourteenth. After his drive, Ford hit a heroic 245-yard fairway wood over the pond fronting the green and birdied the hole. Doug was ahead by one shot going into the eighteenth hole but got himself into trouble when he hooked his approach into the left-front bunker. The ball was buried in the upslope of the bunker, and a bogey was a distinct possibility. He thrilled the gallery when he exploded his sand shot, which hit ten feet from the hole and rolled in for a birdie to give him a 66 and a total of 283, three shots better than Snead. Only four players equaled or bettered par that day: Ford, Snead, JIMMY DEMARET, and the amateur Harvie Ward.

The following year, Ford almost won another Masters when he reached the final hole needing a birdie for a score of 284 to tie Arnold Palmer. However, both he and Fred Hawkins missed makable birdie attempts, and they finished tied for second, one shot behind Arnie, who won his first Masters.

Doug Ford was named to four Ryder Cup teams (1955, 1957, 1959, 1961) and had an overall record of 4-4-1. He won the Canadian Open twice, in 1959 and 1963, his last PGA Tour victory. His total PGA earnings were $414,663, and his largest payday was $9,000, for winning the "500" Festival tournament in Indianapolis in 1960. In 1998, he broke Sam Snead's record by making his forty-fifth appearance in the Masters. Ford is a member of the PGA Hall of Fame.

Tommy Bolt

1919–

Usually, when I would throw a club toward water, I'd pick me a spot near the bank. I know how far I could throw every club in the bag. So when I threw toward water, I'd release it so that it would land near the bank on one side or the other. Then it would be easy for the caddie or some friendly spectator to retrieve it for me.

—TOMMY BOLT

Born in Haworth, Oklahoma, in 1919, Tommy Bolt was a disciple of BEN HOGAN's and one of the best shotmakers of his era. He also had a volatile temper and was known to throw clubs and tantrums on the golf course. He was an irascible but colorful sort, an old-school pro tutored in the hard knocks of playing the Tour. Among his nicknames were "Thunder Bolt" and "Terrible-Tempered Tommy."

Bolt developed his golf game as a youth by sneaking onto the Broadmore Country Club course in Shreveport, Louisiana. He liked to play three holes farthest from the clubhouse. Bolt's mother died when he was an infant, and his father, Walker Bolt, provided for the children by doing construction work. Tommy and his brother learned to play golf by caddying at the Lakeside Country Club, where Tommy took up the game at around age twelve. Bolt quit high school to pursue his golfing dreams, worked as a carpenter, built army air bases throughout Texas, and played as much golf as he could to escape the hammer, nails, and time clock. Tommy like to hustle money from golfers he called "mullets." "The first time I gave golf a serious thought was in Abilene. The cats fell out of the woodwork there. When I got time off from my job, I'd find them standing around with money jammed in all pockets. Cash without a home, boy!" When he played in amateur tournaments, he sold his prizes for cash in order to move on to the next competition.

After his Texas golf and construction odyssey, Bolt joined the Corps of Army Engineers and was fortuitously stationed in Rome, Italy, with Special Services. His assignment was as golf professional at one of Rome's elite golf clubs, which had been converted into an American officers' club by occupation forces. After his tour of duty, he returned to a construction job in Shreveport, where he joined his father. But the singing sirens of golf kept calling Tommy, so he played in local tournaments and improved his cash position by reeling in 'mullets. Encouraged and backed by friends, he took his first crack at the Tour in 1946 but finished in the top twenty-five only five times, hardly enough to make a living. Bolt dropped out to work construction in Houston until 1949, when he returned to the Tour, collecting $750 for a third-place finish in the Miami Open.

But things grew tougher for Bolt. Once he had to sell his golf clubs, the last thing a pro would want to do, to get to the next tournament on the Tour. He made a stop in Durham, North Carolina, in 1950 and worked at a driving range, where he served as professional. He later recalled: "I worked hard at those early lessons. I felt that with the lessons, and my pay, I would be able to save some. . . . I always said that this was the hardest work I have ever done in my life." Tommy returned to the Tour in 1951 and realized he was fully committed to succeed. "I had knowledge of what it was like not playing the Tour—driving nails and running a driving range. I knew the only life for me was the Tour. It caused me to protect my money and work harder than ever on golf."

Bolt finally worked his way onto the Tour for good in 1951. He played the last tournament of the year, the North and South Open, held at the No. 2 Course at Pinehurst in North Carolina. This was a course he knew well from his days in North Carolina. The field included all the U.S. Ryder Cup players, because that event was to be played at Pinehurst in early November of that year. Ben Hogan, SAM SNEAD, JIMMY DEMARET, and LLOYD MANGRUM were among the excellent Tour players on that team.

Bolt's win at Pinehurst was one of the biggest thrills of his life. At age thirty-three he had the first of his fifteen wins on the Tour. He won the 1952 Los Angeles Open, the first official tournament of the year, and placed in the top fifteen in earnings that year. Bolt was among the top-ten money winners in 1953, 1954, and 1955. And he was selected to the Ryder Cup team in 1955 and 1957; he recorded a 3-1-0 record.

Tommy won his first and only major when he captured the 1958 U.S. Open at the Southern Hills Country Club in his native state. He recalled: "I had the secret that week. I was happy. Happy all over. Nothing could have made me mad. I knew the minute I hit the first shot I was the complete master of my emotions. This is so important to a golfer, to a person. To everyone. It is important to be able to apply yourself totally to what you are trying to do. That week in Tulsa, I did it perfectly." The key to Bolt's four-shot win over GARY PLAYER was his consistency and his success on the twelfth hole, a 445-yard, par-4 dogleg left. Ben Hogan described this hole as "the greatest par-four twelfth hole in the United States." The tee-shot landing area is well protected by trees, rough, and a large bunker. The long approach is made difficult by a blind water hazard in front of the green and down its right side and by bunkers and trees to the back and along the left. Bolt was 3 under par on this hole during the tournament as he posted a score of 71-71-69-72=283. His run of six 3s in seven holes during his final round clinched the Open for Bolt.

Bolt was never one to hold back his opinions, and he had many. For one, he didn't believe the Masters was a true major. Nor did he believe the British Open was on the level of the U.S. Open or PGA Championship because of the relative weakness of the British Open and the Masters fields. He noted various ploys that pros would use to cheat in golf, including grounding a wood behind a ball in the rough, then switching to an iron after the surface behind the ball had been leveled. He also thought that ARNOLD PALMER was a very good golfer but was overrated compared to JACK NICKLAUS and Hogan. These and other opinions did not endear him to some people.

Bolt was his own man and knew the debilitating effect that playing golf could have on a professional or any other person who took the game seriously: "If you die a little many times, sooner or later you will die for good. That doesn't interest me." Throwing clubs was one way Tommy got back at the golf gods.

Tommy Bolt won his last PGA tournament, the Pensacola Open, in 1961. He won the PGA Seniors' Championship with a score of 70-70-71-67=278 in 1969. Sam Snead, who finished third to Tommy in the PGA Seniors', commented on Bolt's win: "You know it's real funny the way a guy is thirty-nine one year and beats you in the PGA Seniors' the next." Tommy Bolt was elected to the World Golf Hall of Fame in 2002.

72

Tom Weiskopf

1942–

*Never, ever, did I get mad. That is unusual. Never did I lose
my concentration or any determination to play the next shot.
I forgot the last shot all the time, and that is unusual, too.*
  —TOM WEISKOPF, after winning the 1995 U.S. Senior Open

As a lad in his native Ohio, Tom Weiskopf developed a swing that
might have come out of an instruction book. He took up the game when
he was fifteen and shot in the 70s a year later. Tom entered Ohio State
three years later than JACK NICKLAUS, played on the golf team, and won
the Western Amateur in 1963. He did not have the single-mindedness
that Nicklaus had, but he would win fifteen Tour events and a British
Open. His temper sometimes got in the way of his swing and kept him
from reaching his full potential. KEN VENTURI observed: "What makes
Tom's swing so beautiful to watch is that it is made by a tall man.
[Weiskopf is 6 feet 3 inches.] It is unusual to see such grace and even
flow of motion in a golfer of Tom's height. The aesthetics aside, Tom's

swing is also very sound fundamentally. That he hasn't won more with it is probably because of some temperamental problems that we won't go into here."

Tom turned professional in 1964 and joined the PGA Tour in 1965. He won his first tournament, the Andy Williams–San Diego Open in 1968. His best year was in 1973 when he won the Colonial National Invitation, the Kemper Open, the Canadian Open, and the IVB Philadelphia Classic. He finished third at the U.S. Open when JOHNNY MILLER closed with a record score of 63 to top the field at Oakmont. After his near miss at the U.S. Open, Weiskopf led the British Open after each round, the first golfer to do so since HENRY COTTON in 1934, and won the tournament with a score of 68-67-71-70 = 276 at Troon. Partnered with Weiskopf, Johnny Miller played the final two rounds and finished tied for second with a score of 279. Miller had taken the lead from Weiskopf by shooting a 32 to Tom's 37 on the front nine of the third round, but Weiskopf scored 34 on the back nine to Miller's 37 to take a one-shot lead into the final round. JACK NICKLAUS, whose final-round 65 could not offset a third-round 76, finished fourth at 280. Weiskopf also won the Piccadilly Matchplay Championship in 1973, defeating LEE TREVINO in the final, four and three.

In addition to his third-place finish in the 1973 U.S. Open, Tom tied for second in the 1976 Open at the Atlantic Athletic Club, losing by two strokes to Jerry Pate. His U.S. Open frustration continued in 1978 when he finished tied for fourth in the Open at Cherry Hills, three shots behind the winner, Andy North. Tom finished tied for fourth again at Inverness in 1979, four shots behind the winner, HALE IRWIN. This was Tom's last best finish in the U.S. Open. It seemed he would never win a USGA event. Weiskopf also fell short in the 1969 Masters, finishing tied for second, one shot behind George Archer. He finished tied for second again in 1972, three strokes behind Jack Nicklaus.

Tom did defeat Jack in a play-off to win his second Canadian Open in 1975. He was selected to the Ryder Cup team in 1973 and 1975, posting an excellent 7-2-1 record. He won over $2.2 million on the PGA Tour, but in 1984, at the age of forty-two, he left the Tour to become a full-time golf-course architect in partnership with Jay Moorish. Some of his courses, including the Troon North layouts in Arizona, are among the best in the world. Weiskopf's sixteen Tour victories place him forty-ninth on the all-time list, tied with RALPH GULDAHL and MARK O'MEARA.

Tom joined the Senior Tour in 1992 and finally got his USGA Championship when he won the 1995 U.S. Senior Open at Congressional, defeating his old nemesis, Jack Nicklaus, by four strokes.

73

Fuzzy Zoeller

1951–

*We've all got our ways of handling pressure. Being me is
my way.*

—FUZZY ZOELLER

Frank Urban "Fuzzy" Zoeller was born in New Albany, Indiana,
where he still resides on a two hundred-acre farm with his house at the
top of the hill. Fuzzy, who got his nickname from the initials to his first,
middle, and last names, grew up near the Valley View Country Club in
New Albany and started swinging a club at the age of three. He entered
his first tournament two years later, and after graduating from high
school, he went to Edison Junior College, where he won the Florida
State Junior College title in 1972, before transferring to the University
of Houston. In 1973 he won the Indiana State Amateur, turned professional, and in the fall of 1974, qualified for the Tour.

Fuzzy, a noted jokester on the Tour with a penchant for White Castle hamburgers and a sip of vodka, was noted for distance off the tee before he began to experience back problems in his later Tour years. He has a handsy swing that unfolds from a slightly hunchbacked stance and requires precise timing. Fuzzy made his first impact on the Tour in 1979 when he won the Wickes–Andy Williams San Diego Open and the Masters, the first time he had played at Augusta National. In the Masters, Fuzzy shot 70-71-69-70=280 to reach a three-way play-off with TOM WATSON and Ed Sneed. JACK NICKLAUS shot a final-round 69 but came up one stroke short of the leaders. Sneed had opening rounds of 68-67-69 to hold a five-shot lead going into the final round, but three bogeys after the fifteenth hole gave him a final round of 76. The sudden-death play-off, the first in Master's history, began at the tenth hole. All three golfers parred and advanced. Then, on the 455-yard, par-4 eleventh, called "Dogwood," Fuzzy birdied to become the first rookie to win the Masters since GENE SARAZEN the first time he competed in the tournament in 1935.

Because Fuzzy had never played Augusta, he retained Jariah Beard, a local caddie from Augusta's regular caddie corps. Beard, who had caddied for Doug Sanders, TOMMY BOLT, and Bob Toski in previous Masters, recalled the final hole:

> I read every putt and pulled every stick . . . I take that back. . . . He pulled the last stick on the play-off hole. We had one hundred thirty-six yards to the front of the green, and I wanted him to hit a nine-iron. He [Fuzzy] said to me, "I knock an eight-iron down better than anybody in the world." So I said, "Hit your shot!" The birdie putt was maybe ten feet uphill. It broke a little left. I told him to putt it that much [holds up and index finger and thumb an inch apart] right of the hole. It was tracking all the way. I looked away when it was about four feet from the hole, because I knew it was in. . . . Those were some magical times.

Fuzzy won $50,000 and got to name the meal at the Masters for the champions dinner. He wanted White Castle hamburgers, but when it was suggested to him that that might not be a good idea, the past Masters champions assembled were allowed to choose their own meal from the menu. It was a remark that Fuzzy made about Masters menu selection in 1997 after TIGER WOODS won the championship that would cause him grief and cost him over $2 million dollars in endorsements and other revenue. He jokingly suggested to a reporter, after other remarks, that Woods, of African-American, Asian, and Native American descent, should not select fried chicken "or collard greens or whatever they served." Zoeller's statement caused many people to label him a racist, and although many people came to his defense and he apologized to Woods, it harmed his reputation.

Fuzzy won his second major in 1984 at the U.S. Open at Winged Foot. The course was more playable, with less punishing rough, than it had been in 1974 when Hale Irwin won with a score of 287. In 1984, Irwin opened with a pair of 68s to hold first place at the end of thirty-six holes, one stroke ahead of Zoeller and two ahead of Greg Norman. Irwin shot a third-round 69 but then soared to a 79 to fall out of contention. It came down to a battle between Norman and Fuzzy. Norman, playing one group ahead of Zoeller, was trying to hold his game together as he scrambled for pars on the sixteenth and the seventeenth. His drive was well positioned on the eighteenth, but his 6-iron approach was a near shank to the grandstand area to the right of the green. Greg was given a drop, then flew his approach across the green to the collar some forty feet from the pin. The hole was in a similar placement to the 1929 Open in honor of Bobby Jones's final day 12-foot putt, which he somehow made, to get him into a play-off with Al Espinosa. Jones won the thirty-six-hole play-off by twenty-three shots, 141–164. Norman's putt was from the same angle, only much longer. Greg boldly rolled his shot up to the pin; it hit the flagstick and plopped in to save his par. Zoeller witnessed all these peregrinations from the fairway, thinking that Norman had made a birdie and his chances were nil. So he waved a white towel in surrender, much to the enjoyment of the gallery and Norman. But before he addressed his approach shot, Fuzzy learned that Norman had parred and all he needed was a par to tie. He made his par for a total of 276, scoring a 70 on the final round. Fuzzy was on his game in the play-off and easily won 67–75. Norman and Zoeller were the only golfers to break par over seventy-two holes. Curtis Strange finished in third place with a 281.

Zoeller, hampered by back problems, has won ten PGA Tour events. His last victory came in 1986, when he was thirty-four years old. He had back surgery after being hospitalized after the first round of the 1984 PGA Championship and has continued to struggle since then. Fuzzy's best money year was 1994; he won over $1 million, with five second-place finishes, including a play-off loss to Mark McCumber in the Tour Championship. Fuzzy has played on three Ryder Cup teams (1979, 1983, 1985) but had little success, posting a 1-8-1 record. Fuzzy Zoeller joined the Senior Tour in 2002.

Walter Travis

1862–1927

A reasonable number of fleas is good for a dog.

—WALTER TRAVIS, on being irritated by the British
at the 1904 British Amateur

Walter Travis was the exception to the rule that a golf champion had to begin playing the game early in life. Born in Malden, Victoria, Australia, in 1862 and educated at Trinity College, Travis emigrated to the United States at the age of twenty-three. Athletically inclined, Walter cycled and played tennis, not taking up golf until he was thirty-five. His friends at the Niantic Club in Flushing, New York, were thinking of starting a golf course, so while on a trip to England in 1896, Travis purchased some golf clubs and started to play at the Oakland golf course on Long Island. A meticulous man, Travis read the leading books on the subject of golf, including Horace Hutchinson's writing in *The Badminton Library* series and the writings of WILLIE PARK JR.

Slight of build, Travis knew he would have to develop a short game to succeed as a competitive golfer. He decided to begin with putting, adopting a pendulum stroke while holding his body still. He taught himself a reliable swing that produced limited length but great accuracy. Within a short time he was better than the players at his home club. He entered the U.S. Amateur at the Morris County Golf Club in Morristown, New Jersey, in 1898, his second year of golf, and reached the semifinals.

Travis was a rakish and imposing figure on the golf course. A study in quiet confidence and insouciance, in his early days he had a heavy, dark beard, wore a Rough Rider–type hat, and smoked a long black cigar. He did not engage in social banter but went about his business on the golf course, focusing on the main prize, the championship medal. He won his first significant championship in 1900, the U.S. Amateur at the Garden City Golf Club on Long Island, defeating Findlay S. Douglas, 2-up. Findlay was one of the best amateurs of the day, having won the Amateur in 1898. Travis also led the field of 120 in the qualifying round with a score of 166. Earlier that year, Travis won the New York Metropolitan Amateur Championship at the Nassau County Country Club.

He successfully defended his title the following year at the Atlantic City Golf Club in New Jersey, defeating Walter E. Egan, five and four, in the final. Travis won the qualifying medal with a score of 157. This was the first time that Travis used the new rubber core ball in competition, adding at least 20 yards to his shots off the tee. Travis won his third U.S. Amateur in 1903 after being eliminated in the semifinals of the 1902 amateur, 1-up, by Eben Byers. Travis got his revenge against Byers in 1903 by defeating him, five and four, in the final at the Nassau County Country Club. No qualifying round was held that year, but 128 players began the five-round elimination event, which took place over five days. Travis became the first player to win three U.S. Amateur championships. The event had come a long way since thirty-two golfers teed off in the first Amateur, won by Charles B. Macdonald, twelve and eleven, at the Newport Golf Club in Rhode Island. Only Travis, TIGER WOODS (1994, 1995, 1996), JERRY TRAVERS (1907, 1908, 1912, 1913), and BOBBY JONES (1924, 1925, 1927, 1928, 1930) have won three or more U.S. Amateurs. Travis's best finish in the U.S. Open was a tie for second in 1902 at Garden City, his home golf course. Travis tied with Stewart Gardner, six shots behind Laurence Auchterlonie.

While on holiday in Britain in 1901, Travis tested his game against the ranking Scottish and English players. They usually bested him in those informal matches, but he learned a considerable amount from the experience. By 1904, Travis was rated the best amateur player in the United States. He decided to enter the British Amateur, to be held at Sandwich, the windswept linksland course on the shores of the North Sea in England. Plotting his strategy, he arrived in Great Britain three weeks before the tournament and first went to St. Andrews to practice. He played poorly, then went to Sandwich one week before the Amateur to practice on the tournament course. Gradually he regained his game, except for his putting, which still gave him problems. After tinkering with his technique to no avail, he borrowed a friend's Schenectady putter, a center-shafted club with a mallet head not commonly in use at the time. Travis began to putt better with this club and decided to use it in the tournament.

Adding to Travis's difficulties was an ongoing battle of wills with the Englishmen in charge of the Royal St. George's Golf Club at Sandwich. Travis had felt that he was snubbed in not being able to obtain quarters in the buildings usually reserved for guests at Royal St. George's. The club did not accommodate him in arranging practice rounds with the British stars. Travis was assigned a cross-eyed caddie and was not allowed to switch to another. And he felt that some of the British amateur golfers from Oxford and Cambridge, who had entered the tournament and who had been entertained by Travis and his friends when their combined team had visited the United States the previous year, had excluded him from their social events. The British did not approve of some of Travis's behavior, causing a great deal of tension. Regardless of where the blame lay, Travis became more motivated to win, and the local crowds did not want to see a naturalized American win their national title.

All the matches in the British Amateur were eighteen holes except for the thirty-six-hole final. Travis putted well with his Schenectady and advanced to the quarterfinals, where he met HAROLD HILTON, winner of two British Amateurs (1900, 1901) and two British Opens (1892, 1897). Travis easily beat him, five and four. Next he met forty-six-year-old Horace Hutchinson, who had won the Amateur in 1886 and 1887 and was runner-up in 1885 and 1903. Hutchinson was past his prime and lost, four and three. Travis was playing excellent golf, and the British golf world feared that no one would stop him from winning the championship. In the final, the forty-two-year-old Travis was pitted against his opposite, thirty-eight-year-old Edward "Ted" Blackwell, a big hitter from St. Andrews who once drove a gutta-percha ball 365 yards. Though Blackwell outdrove Travis by big margins all day, Travis was deadly on his approaches and accurate with his Schenectady. He had a 4-up lead at the lunch break. Travis held steady in the afternoon round and closed out the match at the fifteenth, five and four. Travis's winning putt was met with the silence of stunned disbelief. Many blamed the Schenectady for Travis's success, but it was his steady all-around game that captured the championship. Nevertheless, the Schenectady-style, center-shafted putter was banned by the Royal and Ancient rules committee for almost half a century.

Travis returned to the United States and never went back to Great Britain. He won the Metropolitan Amateur in 1909 and again, at the age of fifty-three, in 1915. He also won the prestigious North and South Amateur in 1904, 1909, and 1912.

Walter Travis founded and edited the *American Golfer* and was the author of the instructional book *The Art of Putting*. He was an able golf-course architect who learned his trade as a consultant to John Duncan Dunn. He designed the Garden City Country Club on Long Island, the Westchester Country Club South and North Courses near New York City, the Ekwonok Country Club (with Dunn) in Manchester, Vermont, and various others. Travis died in Colorado at the age of sixty-five. He was inducted into the World Golf Hall of Fame in 1979.

75

Tony Jacklin

1944–

Although Tony did not sustain this pace [winning two majors in two years] for long, I believe it was his two major championship victories that stirred Europe from its long slumber.

—Jack Nicklaus

Tony Jacklin was born in Scunthorpe, Lincolnshire, in 1944. As a boy he sold newspapers outside the steelworks where his father drove a truck. His father loved the game of golf, but as Tony became more interested in it, he did not encourage him to make it a career. Tony, however, kept at it and played for the England Boys' team. He went to work as an assistant professional at the Potters Barn Golf Club in Middlesex when he was seventeen. In 1964 he played the winter Tour in South Africa and spent some time in the United States, playing in the Carling Open golf tournament in Pleasant Valley, Arkansas. In 1965, on his return home, he won the Assistants' title at the Hartsbourne Country Club in Hertfordshire. At the end of 1966 he represented England in the World Cup in Tokyo, and the following spring, he played in his first U.S. Masters and finished tied for sixteenth. He next won the 1967 Pringle, an important tournament in Great Britain, at Royal Lytham and St. Anne's. He finished fifth in the 1967 British Open at Hoylake.

At about this time, Jacklin retained Mark McCormack from IMG to manage his golf career. He promptly won the 1967 Dunlop Masters at Sandwich, highlighted by a hole in one and a 64 on the final round. Jacklin next decided to play the PGA Tour. He won the Jacksonville Open in 1968, showing other European and international players that it might be worthwhile to test their games in the States as GARY PLAYER and BOBBY LOCKE had done after World War II. The following year, he became the first British-born winner of the British Open since Max Faulkner won at Royal Portrush in 1951. Just as ARNOLD PALMER had increased the popularity of golf in the United States after the war, Jacklin's win in the 1969 Open at Royal Lytham made him a national hero and revived golf in a country that had been ravaged by World War II.

Tony shot rounds of 68-70-70-72=280 to defeat Bob Charles by two shots, ROBERTO DE VICENZO and PETER THOMSON by three, and Christy O'Connor Sr. by four. These were the only players to shoot under par. Tied for sixth were DAVIS LOVE III's father and Jack Nicklaus. In *Jack Nicklaus: My Story*, Nicklaus recalled the impact Jacklin had on European golf by honing his skills on the American tour:

> Although then only twenty-three, Tony realized that to beat the best you had to learn directly from the best, and the only way to do that was by competing regularly with and against them. . . . Following a win in the Jacksonville Open and a number of high placings in 1968, he had acquired by July of 1969 [the British Open date] not only the techniques but the confidence and assurance to beat anyone in the world. . . . Although Tony did not sustain this pace for long, I believe it was his two major championship victories that stirred European golf from its slumber.

Jacklin followed his success in the British Open with a win at the 1970 U.S. Open at Hazeltine National in Chaska, Minnesota. A 7,151-yard monster which played its full length because of heavy rains, Hazeltine was especially difficult because the greens were hard to see from the fairway due to the undulating terrain. The large greens also made it difficult to get a feel for pin position. PGA professional Dave Hill called the course "a cow pasture with flags," and the gallery mooed as Hill made his way along the fairways. Only 81 of the 150 qualifiers shot under 80 because of thirty-to-forty-mile-per-hour winds.

Jacklin, used to nasty playing conditions in his native land, adjusted well and opened 1-under, the only golfer to break par. After the second round, featuring milder weather, Jacklin shot 70 and led by two strokes over Dave Hill. Jacklin shot another 70 and led Hill by three after fifty-four holes. In the final round, Jacklin bogeyed the seventh and eighth, and it looked like the beginning of a collapse, but on the ninth he caught a break when his 25-foot putt, which was hit too firm, hit the back of the cup, hopped into the air, and plopped in the hole for a birdie rather than running several feet past. Tony closed out the competition when he shot a 34 on the back nine to finish with a 70 and a seven-shot win over Dave Hill, the only other player to shoot par or better. Jacklin became the second person, after LEE TREVINO in 1968, to shoot four subpar rounds in a U.S. Open. Jacklin had established himself as a world-class golfer. He was the first British-born double Open winner since TED RAY in 1920.

Jacklin placed fifth in the 1970 British Open at St. Andrews in 1970, then third, two shots behind Lee Trevino, at Royal Birkdale in 1972. Trevino had a solid chance to win at Birkdale. Paired with Jacklin and leading him by one going into the par-5 seventeenth, Trevino chipped in from off the green to save par when it seemed as if he would at least bogey. Jacklin, who was in front of the green in two and on in regulation with a shaky chip shot, took three putts to get down from within twenty feet, bogeyed the hole, and lost by two shots when Lee parred the last hole. Jack Nicklaus shot a final-round 66 to finish second.

Jacklin was awarded the Order of the British Empire for his golf contributions to the kingdom. He received appearance fees to play in tournaments in Europe and elsewhere, a common practice outside the United States, and won the 1972 Jacksonville Open and a variety of international events in the ensuing years. He joined the PGA Senior Tour in 1994 and has won over $1.4 million on that circuit.

Jacklin was very instrumental in the improvement of the European effort in Ryder Cup play. He played on seven consecutive Ryder Cup teams (1967–79), including the first team that involved continental European golfers in 1979. His overall playing record is 13-14-8. He was nonplaying captain in 1983, 1985, 1987, and 1989. He recorded an excellent 2-1-1 record at the helm, losing only the match in 1983, by one point, 13½–14½. Jacklin's determination and leadership have been major factors in the parity that now exists in Ryder Cup competition.

76

Fred Couples

1959–

I've never seen a ball stop there. My ball hit and almost plugged, just popped up and settled. I had a perfect lie. It wasn't a hard chip. After I made par, I really thought I could win.

—FRED COUPLES, describing his twelfth-hole adventure
at Amen Corner in the final round of the 1992 Masters

Frederick Steven Couples was introduced to golf in his native Seattle by his father, Tom, who worked in the Seattle Parks and Recreation Department. Tom Couples, who passed away in 1997 from leukemia, was originally named Coppola but changed the family name to Couples. The family lived in a modest home in a working-class neighborhood near a municipal golf course. Fred shagged range balls there in order to play for free. After attending the University of Houston and playing on its golf team, Fred turned professional and joined the PGA Tour after qualifying in the fall of 1980.

Couples has gotten a reputation for his long, flowing swing, which generates an average driving distance of just under 290 yards, and his relaxed, seemingly nonchalant manner under the strain of competition. He has always been a shy, reluctant superstar in waiting. He has won over $12 million on the Tour and in excess of $20 million in worldwide events, putting him among the top-ten money winners of all time.

Until he won the Masters in 1992, his determination and desire were questioned. He had his best run that year, winning three tournaments and posting two second-place finishes and three thirds, placing him first on the PGA money list with $1,344,188. He won the Vardon Trophy in both 1991 (69.59 average) and 1992 (69.38) and was named PGA Player of the Year in 1992. He has won fourteen Tour events and five international titles, including the Johnny Walker World Championship (1991, 1995), the World Cup individual title (1994), the Dubai Desert Classic (1995), and the Johnny Walker Classic (1995).

Nicknamed "Boom Boom" because of his distance off the tee, Couples also has an excellent all-around game. His 1992 Masters win showed that he could endure the crucible of pressure in a major, especially on the back nine on the final day, when the outcome is almost always decided. Couples was playing excellent golf coming into the 1992 Masters. He had won the 1991 Vardon Trophy, the Federal Express St. Jude Classic, and the B.C. Open that year. He had also played well in the Ryder Cup at Kiawah and had won the Johnny Walker World Championship. He continued his strong play in the early 1992 season by winning the Nissan Los Angeles Open and then the Nestlē Invitational at Bay Hill. As the Masters approached, he was the leading money winner on the Tour and sported a 69.04 scoring average. In his previous twenty-four tournaments, he had finished sixth or better nineteen times, including five wins. He also became the first American to reach the top of the Sony ranking, labeling him the number-one player in the world.

The wide fairways and lack of rough at Augusta are suited to Couples's power game. Heavy rains helped to slow the greens to a reasonable pace, causing scores to be low in the early stages of the tournament. Jeff Sluman and LANNY WADKINS tied for the first-round lead with 65s. Couples had a 69, then followed with a 67 the second day, putting him one shot off the lead held by Craig Parry and IAN WOOSNAM, the defending champion. Lightning and rain interrupted Saturday's round, suspending play for nearly three hours. Couples had to play four holes on Sunday to complete his Saturday round, finishing with a 69 and a three-round total of 205, one shot behind the leader, Craig Parry.

By the fifth hole in the final round, Couples and Parry were tied, and Parry began to falter as he lost his putting touch. RAYMOND FLOYD, who won the Masters in 1976 and lost in a Masters play-off to NICK FALDO in 1990, had pulled to within two shots of Couples. Fred birdied eight and nine, and by the time he reached the tee at the 155-yard, par-3 twelfth, "Golden Bell," he had a three-shot lead. The tee shot on Golden Bell requires anything from a 9-iron to a 5-iron, depending on the wind, which is usually swirling and not easy to gauge. The golf gods were with Freddie as his tee shot landed short, but somehow, no doubt because of the rain-soaked turf, hung on the nearly vertical bank which descends into the pond from in front of the green. Fred got up and down for his par, but Floyd birdied the fifteenth and reduced Fred's lead to two. Couples made a tricky 5-foot downhiller on seventeen and got home in 70 for a total of 275 and a two-shot win over Raymond, who, at age forty-nine, was trying to become the oldest golfer to win the Masters. In 1998, Freddie almost won another green jacket, losing by one shot to MARK O'MEARA, who birdied the final two holes.

In official Tour events, Couples took a bit of a nosedive after his career year in 1992. He won only three PGA events in the following five years, punctuated by a sixty-third-place earnings finish in 1995. However, Fred did win over $1.2 million in 1996, won one tournament, finished in the top ten nine times, and was sixth on the money list. Fred had a variety of personal and physical problems that contributed to his uneven play. He split up with his wife of eleven years in 1992, and a messy and expensive divorce ensued. His mother passed away in 1994, and then his father died of leukemia in 1997. In 1994, while on the Doral Golf Resort range, a disc low in his spinal column came apart, and he told his golf coach, "If I move in any direction, I'll scream." A degenerating disc had herniated. From that point on, Fred's performance largely depended on the condition of his back.

In 1998, Couples started to return to form, winning the Bob Hope Chrysler Classic and the Memorial Tournament and finishing ninth on the money list with $1,650,389. Fred has played on three President's Cup teams (1994, 1996, 1998) and has a solid 8-3-1 record. He has been named to five consecutive Ryder Cup teams (1989–97), but his performance has been spotty in that event. His best outing was at Kiawah in 1991, when he played a critical role in the American team's 14½–13½ win over the Europeans. He picked up a point with Raymond Floyd when they defeated BERNHARD LANGER and Mark James in foursomes, then won, five and three, over Nick Faldo and Ian Woosnam in fourballs the first day. Floyd and Couples lost to the Spanish Armada, SEVE BALLESTEROS and JOSE-MARIA OLAZABAL, in foursomes, three and two, but Couples and PAYNE STEWART saved half a point by tying the Spaniards in the afternoon four-balls on the second day. At this stage the match was all even, 8–8, and the outcome of the competition would be determined by the singles matches on day three. Couples won his match, three and two, over Sam Torrance, netting him 3½ points out of his team's total of 14½. Two years earlier, at The Belfry, Couples, who did not score a single point for his team, butchered a 9-iron in his singles match, which he lost, 1-up, to Christy O'Connor Jr. Raymond Floyd told Couples, "[That shot] is going to make you a better player, and one day you're going to tell me I'm right." At Kiawah, Fred Couples was a better player.

Fred Couples ranks fourth in all-time PGA tour earnings with over $13.3 million in prize money. He has fourteen tour wins and five victories in international events.

77

Craig Stadler

1953–

"The Walrus"
—STADLER'S nickname

Craig Stadler, the son of a pharmacist and a native of San Diego, took up the game of golf when he was five years old, and as he got more skilled, he started to play in peewee events. After his father introduced him to the game, he took his first golf lesson at age eight. Stadler played most of his junior golf at the LaJolla Country Club, where his father was a member. The variety of holes at LaJolla challenged Stadler to develop a wide array of shots which would help him during his professional career. As a teenager, Craig caddied at the nearby Wilshire Country Club and at age thirteen took lessons from John Hulbert, who had been an assistant pro under PAUL RUNYAN. He watched Tour events when the pros would swing through Southern California in the winter and, after watching ARNOLD PALMER, modeled his own golf behavior on Arnie's aggressive, go-for-it style. In 1971 he won the World Junior Championship, then, in 1973, he won the U.S. Amateur at Inverness in Toledo, Ohio, defeating the defending champion, Vinny Giles, in the semifinals and David Strawn in the final, six and five.

Stadler earned a golf scholarship and won eleven college tournaments while at the University of Southern California, making all-American in 1974 and 1975. Stan Woods, USC's head golf coach, helped Stadler become an excellent putter. Stadler remembers those years fondly: "College was terrific, the best time of my life. I guess it was during this stage that I got into some enthusiastic beer drinking, developed a gut, let my hair get out of control, and generally took on my semiunkempt, blue-collar image. I didn't study much, although I'm proud to say I eventually earned my degree." Stadler was selected to the 1975 Walker Cup team and won all three of his matches. He turned professional in 1975, missed the first half of 1976 because he failed to qualify for the Tour, but then qualified and played in nine events that year. He made five cuts and placed 190th on the money list with earnings of $2,702.

The portly 5-foot-10-inch, 210-pound Stadler, known as "the Walrus" because of his shape and his bushy mustache, gradually worked his way up the money list and finally won his first tournament, the Bob Hope Desert Classic, in 1980. He also won the Greater Greensboro Open that year, placing him eighth on the money list with $206,291. He won the Kemper Open in 1981 and placed in the top ten eight times and was eighth in Tour earnings again. Stadler's best year came in 1982 when he was first on the money list with $446,446 and won four tournaments: the Joe Garagiola Tucson Open, the Kemper Open, the World Series of Golf, and the Masters.

In the 1982 Masters, the Walrus opened with rounds of 75 and 69 and then finished his third round with three birdies for a 67 to go into the final day with a three-shot lead. Craig built his lead to five shots after eleven holes on Sunday but then bogeyed the twelfth, fourteenth, sixteenth, and eighteenth to stagger in with a 73 after he had shot a 33 on the front side. His total of 75-75-67-67=284 tied him with Dan Pohl, who shot a 67 in the fourth round. Jerry Pate and SEVE BALLESTEROS were tied at 285, one shot back.

The first play-off hole at the Masters is the 485-yard, par-4 tenth, which flows downhill and is cut through trees. Stadler made his par with a good drive, a 6-iron to the green, and two putts from forty feet. But Pohl, a journeyman from Mt. Pleasant, Michigan, could not. The Walrus had his green jacket. To date there have been eleven Masters decided by play-offs. Since the tournament began in 1934, they were won by GENE SARAZEN (1935), BYRON NELSON (1942), SAM SNEAD (1954), ARNOLD PALMER (1962), JACK NICKLAUS (1966), BILLY CASPER (1970), FUZZY ZOELLER (1979), Larry Mize (1987), NICK FALDO (1989, 1990), and the Walrus.

Craig Stadler is an excellent shotmaker with a fine touch around the greens. He has been named to two Ryder Cup teams, in 1983 and 1985. In 1983 he teamed with LANNY WADKINS to win, 1-up, over Ken Brown and Brian Waites in four-balls, then won his singles, three and two, over IAN WOOSNAM in the American team's 14½–13½ win at the PGA National in Florida. Wadkins and the Walrus lost a foursomes match, four and two, to Nick Faldo and BERNHARD LANGER. In 1985, at The Belfry in England, Stadler teamed with HAL SUTTON to defeat Howard Clark and Sam Torrance, three and two, in the foursomes and halved the four-ball with Langer and José María Canizares. The second day, Stadler and CURTIS STRANGE halved with Langer and SANDY LYLE in four-balls; then Stadler and Sutton lost, five and four, to Seve Ballesteros and Manuel Pinero in the foursomes. The Americans were down 9–7 going into the final day's singles matches, then lost 7½–4½ in those individual contests. Stadler won his match against Ian Woosnam, two and one, to round out a 4-2-2 record in Ryder Cup play.

Craig Stadler has won a total of twelve events and $9 million on the PGA Tour, placing him among the top-forty money winners in PGA history. He has won four international events and is in the top fifty in worldwide career earnings with over $10 million. One of Craig's more memorable moments was being disqualified for "improving his stance" by kneeling on a towel to get at his ball, which had rolled under a tree in the 1987 Shearson Lehman Brothers Andy Williams Open. In 1995, when the offending tree was diseased and ready for removal, the Walrus was invited back to cut it down with a chainsaw.

78

Ted Ray

1877–1943

Hit it bloody harder, mate.

—TED RAY's swing philosophy

Edward "Ted" Ray was born in 1877 in Crouville, Jersey, in the Channel Islands, where HARRY VARDON was born seven years earlier. Ray, in his career, thus had to contend with the Great Triumverate of Vardon, JAMES BRAID, and J. H. TAYLOR. Like BILLY CASPER, who in later years was a bit overshadowed by the modern triumvirate of ARNOLD PALMER,

GARY PLAYER, and JACK NICKLAUS, Ray was a notch below his contemporary golf gods.

Ray was raised within one mile of Vardon and followed him as a professional at Ganton in Yorkshire. He moved to Oxley in 1912, where he stayed for the rest of his life. A large man at 6 feet and over 200 pounds, Ray was a big hitter who tended to lurch into the ball, causing him to be susceptible to a wild shot at an inopportune time. He modified his game as time went on so that his body tended more to occupy the same space as his swing. Ray had a delicate touch on the greens, but it was his tee shots that Herbert Warren Wind described as "Brobdingagian" that are remembered.

BOBBY JONES, then eleven, saw Ray and Vardon play in an exhibition after the 1913 Open and recalled a recovery shot by Ray as one of the greatest he ever saw. Ray had hit a long, wild drive and was blocked from the green by a large, forty-foot-high tree. Ray needed 170 yards to reach the green with his mashie niblick, and Jones narrates: ". . . he hit the ball harder, I believe, than I have ever seen a ball hit since, knocking it as if it would drive to China. Up flew a divot the size of Ted's ample foot. Up also came the ball, buzzing like a partridge from the prodigious spin imparted by that tremendous wallop—almost straight up it got, cleared the tree by several yards, and sailed on at the height of an office building, to drop on the green not far from the hole."

Ray, who played in a suit with a hat (not a cap) on his head and usually a pipe in his mouth, first made his mark by finishing second to James Braid in the British Professional Matchplay Tournament (then called the News of the World Tournament) at Sunningdale in 1903. He also finished second in 1911, again to Braid, and in 1912 to Harry Vardon. Ray's combination of power, the ability to recover, a rhythmic swing, and touch around the green finally enabled him to win the British Open in 1912. He shot 71-73-76-75=295, only the second score below 300 ever recorded at Muirfield, to win by four shots over Vardon. A key adjustment Ray had made in his game was to use a niblick from 150 yards into the pin. The following year, he slipped back behind the Triumverate, finishing second to Taylor by a decisive eight strokes in the 1913 Open at Hoylake.

Ray ventured overseas with Vardon in 1913 to play a series of exhibitions and to compete in the U.S. Open. Sponsored by Lord Northcliffe, owner of the *Times* (London), Ray and Vardon won every challenge match they played before the Open. Vardon and Ray lost in the famous three-way play-off with twenty-year-old FRANCIS OUIMET, the defending Massachusetts State Amateur Champion, who tied Vardon and Ray under soggy conditions with a seventy-two-hole total of 304 at the Country Club in Brookline, where Ouimet had once served as a caddie. Vardon had led the qualifying round the first day with a score of 151, and Ray led the second day with a score of 148. Ouimet was a decided underdog as he won the draw and teed off first in the play-off. He calmly placed his ball on a sand tee, heeded the advice of his ten-year-old caddie, a friend by the name of Eddie Lowery, hit his ball true, and went on to win the tournament with a score of 72, five shots better than Vardon and six better than Ray. Just as Englishman JOHN BALL had signaled the end of Scottish golf supremacy by winning the British Open at Prestwick in 1890, Ouimet showed that homebred Americans could compete with the best in the world.

Vardon and Ray finished their exhibition tour, impressing at least one young future champion, Bobby Jones, lost only one match, then returned to England. World War I led to the discontinuance of the British Open and the British Amateur for five years, from 1915 to 1919, when Ray was at the peak of his powers. Ray finished third in the first postwar British Open, then played in the 1920 U.S. Open at Inverness in Toledo, Ohio. Vardon, then fifty, again joined him for exhibition matches and the Open. Going into the final round of the Open, Vardon led JOCK HUTCHISON and LEO DIEGEL by one shot and Ray by two. Ray played the front side in 35 on the final day, sinking putts of 35, 25, 40, and 15 feet on the first four holes, then came in with a 40 and a total of 75 to score a seventy-two-hole-total of 295, one better than Vardon, who was caught in a storm on the final seven holes and struggled in with a 78. Tied with Vardon for second were Jack Burke Sr., Leo Diegel, and Jock Hutchison. Eighteen-year-old amateur Bobby Jones finished tied for eighth. CHICK EVANS was the low amateur with a 298. Ray's first-prize money was $500. At age forty-three and four months, Ted Ray was the oldest man to win the U.S. Open until RAYMOND FLOYD won at age forty-three and nine months at Shinnecock Hills in 1986.

Ray's victory led to "The Pledge of Inverness," by which the Americans vowed to make the logistically difficult and expensive trip overseas to win the British Open. WALTER HAGEN succeeded in reaching this goal at Sandwich in 1922. Americans won twelve consecutive British Opens until 1934, when HENRY COTTON broke the streak.

Ray, after finishing as joint runner-up in the 1925 Open, retired to his home in Oxley, played billiards, and engaged in an occasional round of golf. He died in 1943.

79

Ken Venturi

1931–

For you to become the 1964 U.S. Open Champion would be one of the greatest things that can happen to our country this year. Should you win, the effect would be both a blessing and a tonic to so many people who desperately need encouragement and a reason for hope.

> —From a letter to KEN VENTURI before he won the 1964 U.S. Open

Ken Venturi, the son of a golf professional and manager of the pro shop at Harding Municipal Golf Course in San Francisco, began playing golf in the Bay Area when he was twelve, shooting 172 on his first round. He became an excellent amateur golfer, winning the San Francisco Interscholastic crown and finishing second in the USGA Junior in 1948. The following year, he won the San Francisco City Championship and later was a two-time California Amateur champion. Ken starred in the 1952 America's Cup matches and won both his singles and four-ball matches in the 1953 Walker Cup.

In addition to his father, an early influence on Venturi was BYRON NELSON, who completely remodeled his swing and continued to coach him during his career. Venturi met Nelson through Ed Lowery, a successful San Francisco car dealer who was a member of the USGA executive committee. Lowery, who caddied for FRANCIS OUIMET in his 1913 U.S. Open win, hired Venturi and sponsored his golf career. Venturi's style was to set up at address with his hands fairly low. He took his club back in an upright arc made up of three segments, which resulted in the hands being in perfect position at the top of his backswing. An excellent bunker player and an imaginative shotmaker, Venturi tailored his iron shots to fit the flow of the terrain, the wind and weather, and the position of the pin. Many observers thought that Venturi was a better iron player than the superb Byron Nelson and that he would succeed Hogan as golf's next dominant player.

Ken showed his potential as an amateur in the 1956 Masters. He was invited to play based on his 1953 Walker Cup performance. The twenty-four-year-old Venturi had just finished a stint in the U.S. Army, where he attained the rank of corporal while stationed in Germany. Ken made his presence felt at Augusta with an amateur-record 69 in his first round and a second-round 69 to prove it was no fluke. After shooting a 75 the third day, Venturi led the Masters by four strokes. Normally, Nelson, the unofficial club host, would play the final round with the leader, but because Byron was Venturi's mentor, this seemed inappropriate to him. So Venturi played with SAM SNEAD the final day.

The wind was gusting up to fifty miles per hour on Sunday, and the greens became hard and dry, causing scores to climb. JIMMY DEMARET, a three-time Masters winner, shot 81; Lionel Hebert, 83; JULIUS BOROS, 80; and Ken Venturi, 80, to lose by one shot to JACK BURKE JR. Ken needed a 40 on the final nine to win but bogeyed six holes coming in. Later explaining the Snead pairing, Venturi said: "Do you know the reason I was paired with Sam? I asked to play with him. They wouldn't let me play with Byron, which I thought was a fair decision, as we were so close. So they gave me a choice. I had played with Demaret and Hogan in earlier rounds, and I wanted to play the last round with another one of the greats."

Venturi broke down in tears when he reached the clubhouse after his final round in 1956. The Masters became his Great White Whale, the tournament that always got away. Two years later, after Ken had turned pro, he was again in contention at Augusta going into the final round. He was paired with ARNOLD PALMER, who was tied for the lead with Sam Snead after three rounds. Snead faded out of the picture, but Venturi cut Palmer's lead to one stroke coming into the twelfth, the infamous 155-yard, par-3 Golden Bell, fronted by Rae's Creek at Amen Corner. LLOYD MANGRUM once called the hole "the meanest little hole in the world." Venturi bounced his tee shot off the bank, and it rolled onto the green, but Palmer plugged his ball in the same bank. The local official ruled that Palmer would have to play the ball because tournament officials had decided earlier that only balls plugged in the green or fairway could be lifted. Palmer understood that the USGA's "wet weather" rule was in effect and that he could lift anywhere the ball was plugged. Because of television schedules and other considerations, Palmer and the on-site official agreed that he would play his ball and a provisional from the same spot and get a final ruling later. Palmer scored a double-bogey 5 with his plugged ball and a par with his lifted ball. Venturi, whose playing rhythm could not have been helped by the distraction and delay of the rules debate, parred out. Venturi and Palmer were left in limbo as to who had the lead. At the fourteenth tee, after Venturi and Palmer birdied thirteen, BOBBY JONES and Cliff Roberts arrived to make a final rules decision. Venturi claimed that Palmer's ball landed on the bank, popped in the air, and landed in another depression. There was no way to prove this. Palmer was allowed his lift and his par. He still led the Masters by one. Venturi three-putted the next three greens and finished tied for fourth. Palmer won his first Masters by one shot.

Venturi's last best chance to win the Masters was in 1960. Again he was in contention after three rounds, just one stroke behind his nemesis, Arnold Palmer, who by then was a national-television golf hero with a huge army of fans. Venturi, playing ahead of Palmer, was in the clubhouse with a total of 283, having finished with a solid round of 70. In order to win, Palmer needed to birdie the last two holes, the 400-yard, par-4 "Nandina" and the 420-yard, par-4 "Holly." After hitting his approach to within thirty-five feet on the seventeenth, Arnie drained his putt. Palmer then hit a 300-yard drive down the center on the eighteenth, hit his approach to within six feet, and holed his right-to-left putt for his second Masters victory. This is how legends are made.

By 1964, Venturi had won ten PGA tournaments, but he had not won anything since the 1960 Milwaukee Open. Ken suffered from back problems due to a minor car accident in which he was a passenger, and his controlled swing seemed to have left him as he tried to attain more length in order to keep up with the big hitters, like Palmer and JACK NICKLAUS, who were dominating the Tour. With his chronic back pain, Venturi's swing became more restricted. He finished in the top five in fifty-four tournaments through 1962; then, in 1963, Ken seemed to hit rock bottom. He was not invited to the 1964 Masters and had to lobby for sponsor exemptions to play in Tour events. His golf began to improve before the 1964 U.S. Open, as did his spirits, largely due to the guidance of Father Francis Murray, a parish priest and occasional golf partner from Burlingame, near Venturi's home in Hillsborough, California. Murray had sent Venturi a letter of encouragement which inspired him after his first rounds of 72-70 at Congressional.

Venturi's victory in the 1964 U.S. Open is a profile in golf courage that will be forever remembered as long as the game is documented. He was not even considered a contender going into the tournament, held at Congressional, a 7,053-yard test of endurance in Bethesda, Maryland. A summer heat wave withered the rough on the golf course, making it less formidable than most modern Open venues, but the length of the course and the 100-degree heat and high humidity turned the Open into a kind of Dante's golf inferno. After thirty-six holes, Venturi was six shots behind Tommy Jacobs, who shot 64 in the second round. Venturi then carded a 66, despite bogeys on the last two holes, to pull within two shots of Jacobs.

In those days the Open was decided over thirty-six holes of golf on the final day. After his third round, Venturi was dehydrated and suffering from heat exhaustion. He had tea, lemon, and salt tablets for lunch, and after a rest of fifty minutes between rounds, he returned to the first tee under the vigil of Dr. John Everett, who followed him during his final long march. It seemed that the winner of the 1964 U.S. Open would be the golfer left standing.

Venturi would later recall his walk to the first tee on his final round: "I don't remember how I got to the first tee, don't remember where I had come from. I teed up and went off pretty much in a trance. That might have been the highest stakes a man has ever placed on one round. I don't mean just my life. I mean my golfing life. If I gave up then, it would have been the end. I had no other place to go. . . ." Perhaps Venturi also remembered some words from his father after he threatened to quit at an early stage of his career: "Son, that's quite all right. But you know something? That's the only thing in this world I know that doesn't take talent. Anybody can do that."

Venturi made the mistake of being overconfident, thinking he needed a 72 to win the 1956 Masters. He usually played a course hole by hole, and he adopted that strategy in the 1964 Open. Playing with RAYMOND FLOYD, Venturi tied Jacobs at the sixth hole. The Open had become a two-man contest. Venturi finished the front nine in 35, two shots ahead of Jacobs. At this stage the temperature was over 100 degrees. Venturi, through sheer force of will, built up a four-shot lead after birdieing the 448-yard, par-4 thirteenth. Ken finished his round with a par, an eighteen-hole total of 70 and a seventy-two-hole score of 278, for a four-shot win over Jacobs. Venturi was the only golfer to equal or better par at Congressional for seventy-two holes. After sinking his final putt, Venturi exclaimed, "My God, I've won the U.S. Open." In the scorer's tent, Venturi was afraid to sign his card because he couldn't reconstruct his round. Joe Dey, USGA executive director, who followed Venturi's round, reassured him: "Sign it, Ken, it's right."

Venturi was the PGA Player of the Year in 1964 and a member of the Ryder Cup team in 1965. His record in Ryder Cup play is 1-3-0. A circulation problem which reduced the feel in Venturi's hands brought his career to a premature close. He won his last PGA tournament, the Lucky International Open, in 1966, and though he played sporadically, he never won after that. His final win was a sweet one because it was held at Harding Park Municipal, managed by his dad. Cheered on by hometown fans, Ken won by one shot over Frank Beard and two over Arnie.

Perhaps Venturi's biggest victory has been in the world of broadcasting. He has become an excellent television golf analyst. One reason why he took up golf was to play a sport where he could be alone; he wanted to be alone because he had a stammer and it was a huge embarrassment to him. He overcame that and other demons on and off the course. Venturi also remembers another bit of advice his father gave him after he bragged to his old man about his performance after winning the Northern California Amateur: "Son, if you're as good as you say you are, you can tell anybody, but when you get really good, they'll tell you."

Venturi captained the victorious U.S. team in the 2000 President's Cup.

80

Davis Love III

1964–

*Your golf shots showed me that there will be more wins,
that you would hit those shots under pressure, that you
like being in the hunt. Some don't. You belong there. My
hat is off to you. For your courage—and your composure.*

> —DAVIS LOVE JR. in a letter to his son, Davis Love III,
> after he won his first PGA Tour event,
> the MCI Heritage Classic, in 1987

Davis Love III, the son of noted golf instructor Davis Love Jr.,
seemed destined to be a professional golfer from the day he was born in
Charlotte, North Carolina, in 1964. His dad, who once finished sixth in
the British Open, was the head professional at the Charlotte Country
Club, then moved the family to Atlanta when he became head pro at

the new Atlanta Country Club. In 1978, he took a job at the Cloisters on St. Simons Island, off the coast of Georgia, where he taught at the resort and for *Golf Digest* schools around the country. Davis's father brought him to the practice range at the Atlanta Country Club, and Davis III developed a love for the game. As a teenager he traveled with his dad to the *Golf Digest* schools and saw other great teachers, including PAUL RUNYAN, Bob Toski, Peter Kostis, Jack Lumpkin, and Jim Flick. Davis went to his first PGA Championship as a ten-year-old in 1974. His dad played in the tournament, as did his friends LEE TREVINO, ARNOLD PALMER, JACK NICKLAUS, and GARY PLAYER. Man, this is the life, young Davis thought.

By age twelve Davis could break 80, and at age thirteen, when the family moved to St. Simon's Island, with the help of his father he became serious about the game. When Davis announced that he wanted to give up other sports to concentrate on golf, his father asked, "How hard are you willing to practice?" And then he said, "I'll help you reach your goals. But you have got to listen to me." Davis played on his high school golf team and as a senior shot in the 60s in his last eight competitive rounds. In 1981 he won the Georgia State Junior Championship, and in 1982, Davis entered the University of North Carolina at Chapel Hill, where he was a three-time all-American on the golf team. He loved basketball and was an usher at the North Carolina basketball games. He gave Michael Jordan his first set of golf clubs. Davis won the North and South Amateur at nearby Pinehurst in 1984 and played on the Walker Cup team in the matches at Pine Valley in New Jersey in 1985. He then entered the Tour qualifying school and finished sixth out of a field of 825 golfers and earned his card and $3,325.

Davis joined the Tour with full family support. His brother Mark caddied for him in the PGA qualifying-school tournament. His father coached him, and his mother, Penta, an avid golfer, was behind him, as was his new wife, Robin. Davis gradually weaned himself away from his father and got golf tips from others. But Davis Love Jr. was still young Davis's main man. Just before Davis won his first Tour victory, the MCI Heritage Classic at Hilton Head in 1987, his dad worked on knockdown shots with him. Davis had a final round of 67 to win by one shot. His caddie was Herman Mitchell, who was also a looper for Lee Trevino. A few months later, in 1988, Davis Love Jr. died in a plane crash. It was the most traumatic event in the life of Davis Love III.

Love finished seventy-fifth on the money list in 1988, forty-fourth in 1989, then bottomed out in early 1990. Finally, he asked for some help with his game. He got it from Butch Harmon, who began to work with him. Gradually, golf and life became a bit more fun, and Love got back into the tournament hunt. He won the International in 1990, his second MCI Heritage Classic in 1991, four tournaments in 1992 (finishing second on the money list with $1,191,630), two wins in 1993, and a win at the Freeport-McMoran Classic in 1995. Davis narrowly missed winning the Masters in 1995 when he fired a 66 on the final round but came up one shot short of the winner, BEN CRENSHAW. Davis tied for fourth in the 1995 PGA Championship and won his fourth consecutive World Cup team title with FRED COUPLES. He played on the Ryder Cup team for the second time. In 1996, Davis won the Buick Invitational in San Diego and just missed winning the U.S. Open, bogeying the final two holes to finish in a tie for second with Tom Lehman, one shot behind Steve Jones. Davis seemed on the verge of something big.

Love won a major for himself, his dad, and his other supporters at Winged Foot in 1997. After shooting rounds of 66-71-66, Love was tied for the lead with Justin Leonard, fresh from his British Open win at Troon the previous month. Love's 66 the final day was too much for everyone. He shot a Winged Foot record score of 269 for seventy-two holes to win by five shots over Leonard. A rainbow was visible in the distance as Davis Love III holed his final putt. At the victory ceremony Davis acknowledged his father and the importance of the moment: "It's a great feeling to be called the PGA champion. And it's a great thing to have won on this course. . . . My dad was a proud member of the PGA of America, and so am I."

Davis Love has won fourteen PGA Tour events and a total of over $20 million in career earnings, placing him third on the all-time list behind TIGER WOODS and PHIL MICKELSON. He is 8-9-4 in five Ryder Cup appearances (1993, 1995, 1997, 1999, 2002), and 12-5-2 in four Presidents Cup events (1994, 1996, 1998, 2000).

81

Corey Pavin

1959–

I don't believe that just hitting it far makes you a better golfer. I suppose I get a little bit of pleasure out of beating players who hit it farther.

—COREY PAVIN

Corey Pavin, the son of a shoe-store owner in Oxnard, California, grew up playing the Los Posas golf course in nearby Camarillo. Los Posas is a short, 6,300-yard track with numerous doglegs that required the 5-foot-9 inch, 150-pound Pavin to shape his shots according to the terrain and the situation. Over time he became a superb shotmaker, especially off the tee and around the green. Pavin attended UCLA, was a member of the 1981 Walker Cup team, and then turned professional in 1982 and joined the Tour in 1983. He was named PGA Rookie of the Year in 1984.

Corey won tournaments each of his first five years on the Tour and to date has won fourteen PGA Tour events and ten international tournaments. He has played in a series of international tournaments each year and has many friends on the international circuit dating back to when he won three events in 1983: the German Open, the South African PGA Championship, and the Calberson Classic in Europe.

Pavin's best money year was 1991; he won the Bob Hope Chrysler Classic and the Bell South Atlanta Classic and earned $979,430 to win the Arnold Palmer Award for most Tour prize money. He also won PGA Player of the Year honors. But Pavin's most prestigious win was the 1995 U.S. Open at Shinnecock Hills, the site of the hundredth-anniversary celebration of the founding of the USGA.

Shinnecock is one of the five founding-member clubs of the USGA, the first in the United States to have an eighteen-hole course and a substantial clubhouse. Similar to a seaside links course, Shinnecock has prevailing winds off the Atlantic to its southwest, sandy and rolling terrain, thick, reedlike grasses, and undulating fairways that require accuracy off the tee and versatile shotmaking capabilities. The shorter par-4s are made more challenging because virtually all of them play into the wind.

There was little to indicate that Pavin would be successful in this Open. Beginning in 1981, he failed to qualify three times and missed the thirty-six-hole cut in six other tries. In the Open at Shinnecock in 1986, Pavin shot 159 and missed the cut by nine strokes. In the 1995 Open, Pavin, grouped with DAVIS LOVE III and VIJAY SINGH in the first round, started out with two bogeys, then returned to even par when he holed a 100-yard wedge and eagled the 535-yard, par-5 fifth. He bogeyed four holes and birdied two the balance of his round, giving him a 2-over-par 73, tying him for forty-sixth. Pavin had hit seven fairways and seven greens in regulation.

The wind then shifted overnight, and during the second round it was coming from the southwest, almost the opposite direction from Thursday. This led to new club-selection decisions and in some ways made Shinnecock play like a different course. Pavin made the necessary adjustments, shot a 69, and moved up to eleventh place, seven shots behind the leader, GREG NORMAN. At this juncture all the amateurs, including TIGER WOODS, who retired with a wrist injury when 8 over par on the fifth hole of the second round, had been eliminated from the tournament. And noted professionals, including former Open champions JACK NICKLAUS, ERNIE ELS, and HALE IRWIN, missed the cut.

During the third round the wind kicked up at midday, causing the greens to become firm and less yielding. High shots were likely to stray into the high, untended natural duneland rough. TOM KITE shot 82, NICK FALDO 79, and Jumbo Ozaki 80 as scores started to soar. Norman shot a 74 and fell into a tie with Tom Lehman, who carded a 67. Pavin's 71 put him three shots behind the leaders. Among the contenders were Bob Tway and PHIL MICKELSON, one shot behind, and NICK PRICE, Scott Verplank, Steve Stricker, IAN WOOSNAM, and Pavin, bunched at three back.

On the final day, Pavin finished the front nine 2 over par. At that point, Lehman, Norman, and Bob Tway were tied for the lead. Corey picked up a stroke on the 472-yard, par-4 twelfth by taking advantage of a tailwind, enabling him to reach the green in regulation with a drive and an 8-iron. He holed a putt to go 1 under on the day. On the 158-yard, par-3 eleventh, Lehman bogeyed after he missed the green with his tee shot, but Norman, who had also missed the green, managed to get up and down to save par. At the twelfth, Norman bogeyed, and Lehman birdied, putting Tway, Lehman, Norman, and Pavin in a tie for the lead at 1 over.

Pavin gained the lead for the first time when he hit a wedge to within twelve feet at the fifteenth and holed another birdie putt. Then, on the sixteenth, Pavin's courage and shotmaking ability came to the fore. Playing into a brisk wind on the 544-yard par-5, he elected to hit a low 8-iron on his approach shot rather than risk a windswept wedge. His shot landed within twelve feet, but he missed his birdie effort and parred. Norman birdied the fifteenth to pull within one shot, but he bogeyed the seventeenth to fall two shots back of Pavin. Lehman's double bogey at the par-3 seventeenth all but eliminated his chances. Pavin then made a critical 6-foot putt to preserve his two-shot lead going into the final hole, a 450-yard par-4. He hit a solid drive down the right side, then beautifully shaped the most memorable shot of the Open, a 230-yard 4-wood onto the green. Pavin two-putted for his par for a final-round 68 and an even par-280 for the tournament. Norman, who finished with a 73, was second, two shots behind. Lehman was third, three shots back after shooting a 74. At the end, twelve golfers had finished within five shots of the lead. Pavin won $350,000, the traditional gold medal, and the championship cup for the ensuing year. Because Corey had won his first major, Greg Norman, who has never won an Open, took it upon himself to "welcome Pavin to the club."

Pavin's tenacity on the course has earned him the nickname "Bulldog." He has been selected to the Ryder Cup three times (1991, 1993, 1995) and has posted an 8-5 record, including a 4-1 performance in the U.S. team's disappointing 14½–13½ loss to Europe at Oak Hill in 1995. Pavin has played on two President's Cup teams (1994, 1996) and is 3-5-2 in that competition. Pavin's wife, Sharon, has been a positive influence on his life and he feels that his conversion from Judaism to Christianity in 1991 has helped him balance his competitive golf career with family and other interests: "If I played good golf, I was a good person. Bad golf and I wasn't such a good person. But that's just not the way it works. . . . I've grown up and matured to the point where I feel it's great to play good golf, and I want to play as best I can. But now if I don't do well, it doesn't mean I'm not a good person. It's how you behave and raise your kids and treat your wife that are important in life."

Corey Pavin has fourteen career PGA Tour wins and twelve international victories. He has won over $10 million on the PGA Tour, thirtieth all-time.

82

Sandy Lyle

1958–

*I could tell from the feel of the club it was a good shot.
I did the right thing for a change.*

—SANDY LYLE after hitting a 7-iron shot from a fairway
bunker to within ten feet on the seventy-second
hole to win the 1988 Masters

Alexander Walter Barr Lyle, a native of Shrewsbury, Scotland, started
to play golf as a child and by the time he was ten years old could break
80. He developed into a superb amateur and played on the 1977 British
Walker Cup team. Lyle turned professional in 1977 and won the Niger-
ian Open in 1978. Since then he has logged over twenty wins in inter-

national competition and has won over $2 million on the U.S. Tour. Sandy's first U.S. Tour victory was the 1986 Greater Greensboro Open. The following year, he won the Tournament Players Championship. In 1988, Lyle had his best year on the PGA Tour, winning three events and $726,934 in prize money, seventh on the earnings list.

He became the first Briton to win the Masters when he captured that title in 1988 with a score of 71-67-72-71=281. During the first round of the tournament, winds caused scores to average over seventy-six strokes, making Lyle's opening round of 71 all the more commendable. Lyle held the lead after thirty-six holes with a total of 138 and had a two-shot lead, with a total of 210, after fifty-four holes. When Sandy came to the par-4 eleventh hole during the final round, he had a three-shot lead but bogeyed. Then he double-bogeyed the short par-3 twelfth after he put his tee shot into the pond in front of the green. Lyle gathered his wits and got a birdie on the sixteenth and came to the final tee all even with Mark Calcavecchia. GARY PLAYER, who won the Masters in 1978, describes number eighteen as follows: "Eighteen is a strong finishing hole, an uphill dogleg right with two bunkers at the left elbow. The green slopes noticeably from back to front, although it has been slightly leveled from the old days." He hit his tee shot into a fairway bunker to the left. The pin was placed on the lower-front portion of the green, tucked behind a yawning bunker. Lyle selected a 7-iron and looked toward the green, which was at a level approximately seventy-five feet above where he stood, about 150 yards away. Lyle hit a beautiful shot to within ten feet of the pin. He holed his putt to win the Masters by a shot. The Scottish dish haggis appeared at the Champions dinner for the first time in the history of the Masters.

Sandy Lyle has played on five Ryder Cup teams (1979, 1981, 1983, 1985, 1987) and has a career record of 7-9-2. His best event seems to be the team matches; his best partner, BERNHARD LANGER. Sandy and Bernhard teamed up to win crucial points in the foursomes and four-balls in the Europeans' 1987 win over the United States at Muirfield in Dublin, Ohio. Lyle, at 6 feet and 187 pounds, is a big hitter, capable of hitting a 1-iron 270 yards. He honed his game on the European Tour with one of his best years, 1985, when he won the British Open and the Benson and Hedges International Open.

In the 1985 British Open at Royal St. George's in Sandwich, Kent, England, Lyle started off with a strong 68, then followed with rounds of 71 and 73 to trail DAVID GRAHAM and Bernhard Langer by three shots. Royal St. George's at Sandwich, a seaside links with rolling fairways and yawning dune-side bunkers, has a rich tournament history. In 1904,

WALTER TRAVIS became the first foreign player to win the British Amateur here. In 1922, WALTER HAGEN won the British Open here, and in 1930 Sandwich was the first English venue for a Walker Cup contest. HENRY COTTON won the British Open at Sandwich in 1935; BOBBY LOCKE, in 1949.

The critical point in the 1985 Open came at the notorious 508-yard, par-5 fourteenth, the "Suez Canal" hole, named for the wide brook that crosses the fairway just beyond the 300-yard mark. The fairway sweeps inland from the English Channel and the mouth of Pegwell Bay. The tee is set in a corner of the course, close to the old clubhouse of the neighboring Prince's Golf Club, where GENE SARAZEN won the 1932 British Open. The boundary to the right is out-of-bounds all the way to the green, and a string of four bunkers guards the approach to the green on the left side. When Lyle approached the tee, the wind was blowing out to sea. Lyle, trying to keep the ball to the left and away from trouble, hit it too far left and into the deep dune grass. He then hit a wedge recovery short of the Suez Canal and 200 yards from the green. Lyle next drilled a 2-iron that bore through the wind to the back of the green, forty-five feet from the flag. He drained his long putt for an improbable birdie. Sandy birdied the next hole to take the lead.

Despite a stabbed chip and a weak finish at the final hole, Lyle recorded a 70 and a total of 282, then held on to win the Open by one shot over PAYNE STEWART and two shots over Graham and Langer, who shot 75s on the final eighteen.

83

Ian
Woosnam

1958–

*I just wanted it to be over with; I just wanted to know
the result.*

—IAN WOOSNAM, describing the pressure with
six holes to go in the 1991 Masters

Ian Woosnam was born in Oswestry, Wales, and took up sports at an
early age, beginning with boxing when he was five. Ian started to play
golf when he was seven and, encouraged by his father, who was a dairy
farmer, became a good amateur player. One of Woosnam's toughest
local opponents was SANDY LYLE, later a Masters and British Open
champion, who lived twenty miles away. Sandy regularly beat Woosnam
when they were growing up, but Woosnam finally beat Lyle in the 1987
Suntory World Matchplay Championship.

Woosnam grew to be a powerful and stocky 5-foot-4½-inch golfer with a smooth swing and an aggressive style. His tendency was to play against the field with a vengeance, not against "Old Man Par." Ian's father converted from dairy farming to cereal farming because it was less time consuming, allowing him to spend more time helping his son play golf. Though not yet a scratch player, the determined Woosnam turned pro at age eighteen and lived in a converted cow shed at the nearby Hill Valley Golf Club, where he worked as a greenskeeper and practiced his game.

While trying to break in as a regular player on the European circuit, Woosnam played local golf courses that made different demands on his game. The Hill Valley course, for example, was an American-style layout with soft, holding greens, many well guarded by water hazards and bunkers, and where a player had to learn how to play an airborne game. The Llanymynech course was more of a traditional linksland-style bump-and-run course where Woosnam could work on his ground game. In his early European Tour years he traveled from tournament to tournament in a van, ate baked beans, and slept in his golf rain clothes if the weather was cold. The first few years he earned less than $5,000 per year as he tried to figure out his game. There was no college coach, no swing doctor, no minitour, and no sports psychologist. This was blue-collar retrogolf where players worked out their own problems, digging it out of the ground. In 1981, when Woosnam started playing on the African Safari Tour, his game started to come together.

Woosnam's first significant win was the 1979 News of the World Under-23 Match-Play Championship. His first European Tour win was the 1982 Swiss Open. He steadily advanced in the Tour rankings with earning money and winning tournaments his main goal. He played on his first Ryder Cup team in 1983 and has played on every European Ryder Cup team since. In 1987 and 1990 he won the European Order of Merit for most earnings on that Tour. Through 1998, Woosnam had won twenty-eight of the eighty-five European Tour tournaments he entered and had accumulated over $13 million in worldwide earnings, placing him among the top-fifteen money winners in golf history.

In 1991, Woosnam, who seldom plays tournaments on the PGA Tour partly because of appearance fees that he can garner at European Tour events, decided to set his sights on winning a major. He entered the Masters, a tournament his old rival Sandy Lyle had won in 1987 and where he tied for thirtieth in 1990. He traveled to the United States early and won the USF&G Classic in New Orleans the week before the Masters. At Augusta, Woosie opened with a score of 72, five behind three other golfers, who held the early lead. He then shot a 66 to trail Tom Watson, the leader at the halfway mark, by two. Ian then fired a 67 to take the lead going into the final round. He was paired with Jose-Maria Olazabal, who was three shots behind, and Tom Watson, who trailed by one, on the final day. As is often the case at Augusta, the outcome of the Masters was determined at the final hole. All three players arrived at the eighteenth tee tied for the lead. Watson pushed his tee shot into the trees on the right and took a double bogey to finish tied for third. Olazabal hit his drive into the bunker guarding the left side of the dogleg right and bogeyed. Woosie hit his 280-yard tee shot over the bunker to the left, then hit a solid approach to the green and two-putted for par. Woosnam had become the first Welshman and the shortest player (slightly shorter than the 5-foot-5-inch Gene Sarazen) to win the Masters. Woosnam finished with a score of 72-66-67-72=277. Looking like Mutt and Jeff, 6-foot-3 inch Nick Faldo, the previous year's champion, helped Woosie on with his size-40-short jacket.

Woosnam had won his major and earned increased attention from the media and his supporters. He moved his family from his hometown to Jersey in the Channel Islands, where Harry Vardon was born long ago, to find some privacy. As of yet, he has not won another major, but he continues to be a solid member of the experienced European Ryder Cup team. One of his best performances was in 1993 at The Belfry when he won in foursomes, with Bernhard Langer, seven and five, over Payne Stewart and Fred Couples; and then with Peter Baker, 1-up, over Corey Pavin and Jim Gallagher Jr. the first day. On the second day, Woosnam and Langer defeated Paul Azinger and Fred Couples, two and one; and in the afternoon, Woosnam and Baker defeated Azinger and Couples, six and five. Woosie halved his singles match with Couples on the final day. Woosnam contributed 4½ points, but his team lost, 15–13. In his most recent outing, in 1997, Woosnam had a 1-1 record in the European Ryder Cup 14½–13½ victory at Valderrama.

84

David Graham

1946–

If you quit school and become a golf pro, I will never talk to you again.

> —DAVID GRAHAM's father when Graham, at age fourteen, declared that he wanted to be a professional golfer

Davidd Graham, a native of Windsor, New South Wales, Australia, grew up independent, resolute, and determined. He went against his father's wishes to pursue his dream of being a professional golfer. After their disagreement, David did not see his father again until 1970, when the latter showed up at the U.S. Open at Hazeltine that year. By then it was too late to reconcile.

He left school on his fourteenth birthday in 1960 to pursue his dreams of playing golf. He lived with his mother and began his career working in a pro shop in a Melbourne club, but he was dismissed for allegedly addressing a member by his first name. At eighteen he became head pro at a club in Tasmania, the island state off the southern coast of Australia. But in three years he accumulated debts of $6,000. Determined to pay back his creditors, he took a job with an Australian club manufacturer, and for eighteen months he lived on baked beans and fish and chips and paid off his debts. He also became an expert on golf equipment. This streak of Dickensian self-discipline and determination would serve him well during his golf career.

Graham started as a left-handed golfer but was converted to the right side by George Naismith, the man who gave him his first job. In the late 1960s he joined the tournament circuit in Australia and the Far East. He gradually built a reliable, repeating swing that looked awkward but was effective. He stood erect to the ball, his back straight, and took the club back at a slow, steady pace and in an upright plane, then came through with a controlled stroke. In the 1970s he won a variety of international events, including the French Open (1970), the Thailand Open (1971), the Caracas Open (1971), the Australian Open (1977), and others. He teamed with fellow Australian Bruce Devlin to win the 1970 World Cup.

Graham qualified for the PGA Tour in 1971 and won his first PGA Tour event, the Cleveland Open, in 1972. He won his first major in 1979 when he won the PGA Championship at Oakland Hills in Birmingham, Michigan. Graham shot opening rounds of 69-68-70=207, four shots behind Rex Caldwell. David then fired a final-round 65, despite a double bogey on the final hole, to tie BEN CRENSHAW with a seventy-second-hole total of 272, the second-lowest PGA Championship score since a medal-play format was adopted in 1958. A lack of communication with his caddie possibly cost David $100,000 in that tournament. Graham had been making his own decisions during the tournament until the seventy-second hole, when he had a two-shot lead. He drove his tee shot into the right rough and needed to know the yardage from that awkward angle. When he asked his caddie for the distance, he replied, "You haven't asked me one question all the way around. I don't know. Figure it out yourself." A magazine was offering a $50,000 bonus to any golfer who shot the course record and $50,000 for breaking the tournament record. A par would have given Graham both records. But unsure of the proper club selection, he hit a 6-iron over the green, chili-dipped his wedge recovery shot, chipped onto the green, and missed his putt for a double bogey. Graham scrambled to halve the first two play-off holes, requiring only one putt on each green, then birdied the next hole to win the $60,000 first prize.

Graham won his next major, the U.S. Open, at Merion, the 6,544-yard par-70 shotmakers course in Ardmore, Pennsylvania. It was here that LEE TREVINO defeated JACK NICKLAUS in a play-off in 1971 and where BEN HOGAN hit his classic 1-iron approach on the final hole that enabled him to tie and then win in a play-off against LLOYD MANGRUM and George Fazio in the 1950 Open. Graham shot rounds of 68-68-70 to position himself three shots behind the leader, George Burns, who had a score of 203 through fifty-four holes. Graham, who was paired with Burns in the final round, picked up two strokes on the leader with birdies on the first two holes. He evened the match at the tenth, and they were still even going into the last five holes, one of the great finishing stretches in golf.

On the 424-yard, par-4 fourteenth, Graham birdied with a driver down the center, a 7-iron to within ten feet, and a putt to take the lead for the first time. On the dogleg par-4 fifteenth, he hit a 1-iron, then an 8-iron, to within eight feet and recorded another birdie to go up two. On the 430-yard, par-4 Quarry hole, Graham hit a 3-wood to the center of the fairway, carried the old tree-filled, worked-out quarry with a 5-iron to the flat crown of the green, then two-putted for par but picked up another stroke from Burns, who bogeyed. On the 224-yard, par-3 seventeenth Graham hit a 2-iron which rolled to the rear collar of the green. Burns chipped in for a birdie from the rough to the left of the green, and Graham lost a stroke when he parred. The 458-yard, par-4 finishing hole is likely the most difficult on the course, but Graham continued his superb play, hitting the fairway with his tee shot, landing a 4-iron approach to within eighteen feet and barely missing his putt for a Hoganesque round of 67 and a total of 273, just one stroke over the Open record set by Nicklaus at Baltusrol the previous year. Burns finished three strokes back, tied with Bill Rogers for second.

David Graham, who had become the first Australian to win the U.S. Open, played one of the finest rounds of golf ever in the final eighteen holes of a major championship. He missed only one fairway off the tee and made every green in regulation except three, where his approaches were just off the edge. He received a call from Ben Hogan, who said, "Congratulations. That's one of the best rounds of golf I have ever seen."

Graham's last PGA Tour win was the Houston Coca-Cola Open in 1983. In 1994 he captained the first President's Cup international team, but after the 1996 President's Cup, he was ousted through a secret vote by the players, and PETER THOMSON, another Australian golfing legend, replaced him. Graham, who is stubborn, blunt, and sometimes dogmatic, felt he had been betrayed and publicly humiliated by the incident. The Dallas-based Graham, whose two sons are American citizens, was asked in a *Golf Digest* magazine interview prior to the 1998 matches which team he would be rooting for, and he emphatically replied, "The Americans."

The International team stunned the Americans with a 20$\frac{1}{2}$–11$\frac{1}{2}$ victory at Royal Melbourne in Australia. But David Graham did not watch the matches. He has other pursuits, including a new career on the PGA Senior Tour, where he has won five tournaments and over $5.8 million. He has a golf-course design business whose projects include the highly regarded Grayhawk Golf Club in Scottsdale, Arizona. Graham is considered an expert on golf equipment and has collaborated with Guy Yocum on the golf book *Mental Toughness Training for Golf.*

85

Dave Stockton

1941–

"The King of Corporate Outings"
—STOCKTON's nickname

Dave Stockton grew up in Southern California and was an all-round athlete until he cracked six vertebrae in his back while surfing at the age of fifteen. After that, Dave, the son of a golf professional, concentrated on golf. He enrolled at the University of Southern California, captained the golf team, and was an all-American. He graduated with a degree in business management in 1964 and joined the PGA Tour. He soon became noted for his accuracy off the tee, his skill with a putter, and his ability to score.

In 1967, Stockton won the first of his eleven Tour victories when he finished first in the Colonial National Invitation. He was among the top sixty on the money list from 1967 through 1978 and won over $1.2 million in his PGA career. Dave won his first major, the 1970 PGA Championship, at Southern Hills in Tulsa, Oklahoma. Stockton shot opening rounds of 70-70-66=206 to lead the tournament after three rounds. He almost lost the championship at the thirteenth hole when he put his approach shot into a pond in front of the green. Stockton then hit a great recovery shot with a wedge to within inches of the hole to save bogey. Dave finished with a round of 73 and a total of 279 to win by two strokes over Bob Murphy and ARNOLD PALMER. This was the third time that Palmer finished second in the only major that he never won.

Stockton's second major victory came at the 1976 PGA Championship at the Congressional Country Club in Bethesda, Maryland. Dave had opening rounds of 70-72-69=211 to trail the leader, Charles Coody, by four shots. The final round of the tournament was postponed by rain for the first time in PGA Championship history. The seventy-three finalists teed it up on Monday, August 16, to determine who would be the champion. Stockton shot a steady final round of 70 to outlast the field, whose top fifteen finishers included such notables as RAYMOND FLOYD, JACK NICKLAUS, BEN CRENSHAW, Arnold Palmer, GARY PLAYER, TOM KITE, DAVID GRAHAM, and TOM WATSON. Stockton made a 13-foot putt on the final hole to win by one shot over Floyd and Don January, who tied at 282. Coody's final round of 77 dropped him into a tie for eighth. This was Stockton's last PGA Tour win.

Stockton was selected to the Ryder Cup team in 1971 and 1977. In 1971 he was paired with Jack Nicklaus, and they lost their first-day foursomes match, three and two, to Brian Huggett and TONY JACKLIN at the Old Warson Country Club in St. Louis. Dave halved his singles match with Bernard Gallacher the morning of the final day, then defeated Peter Townsend, 1-up, that afternoon. The U.S. team won, 18½–13½, over the British team. In 1977, at Royal Lytham and St. Anne's, Stockton and Jerry McGee defeated Neil Coles and Peter Dawson, 1-up, in foursomes the first day. On day two, Dave teamed with Dave Hill in four-balls to defeat Tony Jacklin and Eamonn Dury, five and three. The U.S. team defeated the Great Britain and Ireland team, 12½–7½. Stockton's overall record in Ryder Cup play is 3-1-1. He was nonplaying captain of the U.S. Ryder Cup team that won, 14½–13½, over the European team at the Ocean Course in Kiawah, South Carolina in 1991. Stockton also played on the 1970 and 1976 World Cup teams.

When Dave Stockton was firmly established on the PGA Tour, he made an art out of mixing golf-outing business appearances with his regular tournament schedule. During the 1980s he averaged more than ninety outings a year, earning him the title "King of the Golf Outings." Dave was the runner-up in the 1975 Masters and the 1978 U.S. Open, narrowly missing a chance to add to his list of majors. He joined the Senior Tour in 1991 and has won over $11 million and fourteen tournaments on that circuit, placing him ninth on the all-time Senior Tour earnings list. He was the Player of the Year in 1993 and led the Tour in earnings in 1993 and 1994. Among his wins are the 1996 Senior Open and two Ford Senior PGA Championships (1992, 1994). Stockton, who is a descendant of Richard Stockton, who signed the Declaration of Independence for New Jersey, has two sons, Dave Jr. and Ronnie, who have played in PGA events. Stockton owns a bison ranch in northern California and has been very active in PGA and Senior PGA committees.

86

Bob Charles

1936–

As you can see, Bob Charles has the temperament needed in his unnerving profession. It is rooted in his deep confidence that he can play golf as well as anyone in the world.

—HERBERT WARREN WIND after Charles won
the 1963 British Open

Bob Charles is the first New Zealander and the first left-hander to win the British Open. The slender 6-foot-1-inch professional has long been noted for the beautiful rhythm to his swing and his deadly short game, which compensates for a lack of distance off the tee. Born in Carlerton, New Zealand, Charles won the New Zealand Open in 1954 at the age of eighteen, the youngest person to win that championship.

After playing with distinction in the first two Eisenhower Trophy tournaments (1958, 1960), Bob left his job as a bank teller in Christchurch and turned professional. He won the New Zealand Professional in 1961, the Swiss Open in 1962, and in 1963 the Houston Classic and the British Open at Royal Lytham and St. Anne's.

In the 1963 British Open, Charles led by two shots over Phil Rodgers after recording rounds of 68-72-66=206. One shot back was PETER THOMSON, and in contention at 208 was the ever-dangerous JACK NICKLAUS, who had won the Masters and would win the PGA Championship that year. Royal Lytham has five par-4 finishing holes measuring 448, 456, 354, 428, and 379 yards, respectively. It was on this stretch of holes that the tournament was decided. Nicklaus, playing ahead of Rodgers and Charles, opened a two-shot lead when he birdied the fourteenth. He bogeyed the next hole but birdied the sixteenth, then, over-clubbing with a 2-iron on his approach to the seventeenth, hit through the green into the rough, chipped poorly, and putted for a bogey. Because the leader boards were not current and were barely visible, Nicklaus did not know exactly where he stood in the tournament. He assumed that he still had a safe lead. Unbeknownst to Jack, Charles and Rodgers had birdied the sixteenth to pull even. Nicklaus had no cushion. Attempting to fade his shot on the final hole, Nicklaus hit it dead straight into a bunker on the left, pitched out of the steep pot bunker sideways, then bogeyed for a tournament total of 71-67-70-70=278. Charles and Rodgers both parred in to finish at 277. Peter Thomson shot 78 to place fifth with a total of 285, and Kel Nagle was fourth with a 283. This was one of the few times that a mental error possibly cost Jack Nicklaus a tournament.

Bob Charles is rated one of the best putters since BOBBY LOCKE. His putting was critical to his play-off victory in the Open. Charles takes his wrists out of his stroke by using his arm and club exactly like a pendulum. The movement of the clubhead originates from the shoulders, although Charles feels that a point at the center of the back of his neck is the pivotal spot. He has used the same center-shafted putter throughout his career and has constantly practiced basically the same technique.

The Open play-off was the last to be played under a thirty-six-hole format. Rodgers, a native of San Diego and an ex-marine, had won the Los Angeles Open and two other Tour events after turning professional in 1961. He was noted for his considerable knowledge about the mechanics of the golf swing and his hot temper. PAUL RUNYAN once observed of Rodgers's volatile nature: "He is one of the few players who can make his anger work for him." Charles demoralized Rodgers by one-putting eleven holes in the morning round. He won the Open by eight shots, 140–148, as he patiently worked his way around the course. The closest he would come to winning an Open again was in 1969 when he finished second to TONY JACKLIN by two shots at Royal Lytham.

Charles won five PGA Tour events during his career, his last the Greater Greensboro Open in 1974. He won several international events, including four New Zealand Opens (1954, 1966, 1970, 1973), three New Zealand PGAs (1961, 1979, 1980), two Swiss Opens (1962, 1974), the 1968 Canadian Open, the 1969 Piccalilli, the 1972 Dunlop Masters, the 1973 Scandinavian Open, the 1973 South African Open, and others. He joined the PGA Senior Tour in 1986 and has thrived, registering twenty-three Senior Tour wins and more than $9 million in prize money. His best Senior Tour years were 1988 and 1989, when he won both the Byron Nelson scoring award and the Arnold Palmer earnings title. Charles is in the top fifteen all-time in worldwide earnings from tournaments on all PGA Tours with over $9 million. He is still one of the best putters on the Senior Tour and one of the most accurate off the tee.

87

Lee Janzen

1964–

The kid is a good closer, and it stems from confidence. And he relies on the swing he's worked on. He's worked like hell, and he knows what he is doing with the ball and the club. That means a lot. That's what makes guys who can finish.

—LEE TREVINO's assessment of Lee Janzen,
a two-time U.S. Open winner

Lee Janzen learned to play golf at the Imperial Lakes Golf Course in Lakeland, Florida, after his family moved from his native Minnesota. He worked at the driving range at Lakeland to cover his golf expenses and won his first golf tournament at age fifteen. He liked to wager on his game with his golfing buddies because he liked the action and knew that the competition, with money on the line, sharpened his game. In the tradition of Lee Trevino, RAYMOND FLOYD, and other money players, Lee would play with a group of sixteen or more players on weekends, engaging in Nassau, automatic 2-down presses and other exotic forms of bets. Janzen recalls: "If I wasn't playing too well and I came to the ninth and eighteenth holes, I knew there was only one way to get out, and that was to make a birdie. I lost a few times, but not many. Once I learned to never lose focus, no matter how I was playing, I would usually birdie the ninth and eighteenth and turn things around."

Janzen attended Florida Southern College, where he played on the golf team. He birdied five of the last nine holes to win the 1986 NCAA Division II Championship. Known for a hot temper, Lee turned professional in 1986. A few years later, in a qualifying round, he broke three golf clubs—a wedge, a sand wedge, and a 9-iron—on the eighth hole. He later related: "Then I really was motivated to qualify because I needed to get my clubs reshafted." To become more goal-directed and focused, he used motivational tapes, such as those by Tony Robbins. To bring more focus to his life, he married Beverly, an older single parent who has added stability and responsibility to his life.

Lee joined the PGA Tour in 1989 and won his first tournament, the Northern Telecom, in 1992. He finished ninth on the money list, earning $795,299 that year. He won the Phoenix Open in 1993, then burst on the national scene with a win in the U.S. Open at Baltusrol. Janzen wasted no time at the Open; he started with two 67s to equal the thirty-six-hole tournament record set by JACK NICKLAUS in 1980 and T. C. Chen in 1985. He then added a 69 to equal the fifty-four-hole record set by George Burns in 1981 and T. C. Chen in 1985. Janzen was paired with PAYNE STEWART, who was one shot behind with a 70-66-68=204, in the final round. Stewart was still down one after they played the front nine. On the tenth, a 454-yard par-4, Janzen seemed to be in trouble when he pushed his drive to the right into tangled rough. Lee's line to the green was blocked by a pair of huge oak trees, so he opted to go over them with a 5-iron. Instead, hitting the ball lower than he planned, he somehow got the ball through the branches and onto the green and saved his par. Stewart evened the score at the twelfth when Janzen three-putted, but Lee got back a stroke on the fourteenth when he birdied. Then Janzen hit the highlight-film shot of the tournament when he holed a wedge shot for a birdie from the rough at the edge of the green on the sixteenth, giving him a two-shot advantage, which he held until the end. Janzen's record-tying score of 67-67-69-69=272 was only the second time in ninety U.S. Opens that a golfer had broken 70 on each round. Lee Trevino was the first one to do it, at Oak Hill in 1968. Janzen's score equaled the tournament record set by Jack Nicklaus, who shot 63-71-70-68=272, also on the Lower Course at Baltusrol, in 1980.

Janzen won the 1994 Buick Classic, then placed third on the PGA Tour money list in 1995 when he won the Players Championship, Kemper Open, and Sprint International. Inexplicably, Lee Janzen was not chosen as a member of the 1995 Ryder Cup team even though he was third in earnings. This no doubt motivated Lee, who, after a slight earnings dip in 1996 and 1997, won the 1998 U.S. Open at Olympic in another great finish against Payne Stewart. Janzen was selected to the 1997 Ryder Cup team. He and Scott Hoch defeated Constantino Rocca and JOSE-MARIA OLAZABAL, 1-up, in foursomes; Janzen and Jim Furyk then lost a tough foursomes match, two and one, to Colin Montgomerie and BERNHARD LANGER. But on the final day Janzen defeated José María Olazabal, 1-up, in his singles match in a 13½–14½ disappointing team defeat at Valderrama in Spain. Lee was selected to the President's Cup team in 1998 and posted a 1-1-2 record in a U.S. loss, 11½–20½, to the International squad at Royal Melbourne in Australia.

Payne Stewart, who had won nine PGA Tour events, including the 1982 PGA Championship and the 1991 U.S. Open, led the 1998 U.S. Open at Olympic in San Francisco by four shots with opening rounds of 66-71-70=207. Stewart and Tom Lehman were paired as the last to tee off on the final day. It was the fourth year in a row that Lehman had gone into the final round the leader or in second place. Janzen, in the third-from-last pairing, was five shots back with scores of 73-66-73=212. Lee got off to a shaky start with two bogeys but then began to play great golf on a course that is much less forgiving than Baltusrol. Janzen had said, "I come to the U.S. Open expecting nothing to be fair. Hit it in the rough, you can't hit it out. Put it above the hole, you can't two-putt. Hit it in the bunker, you don't have a shot. . . . It's a test of wills, to find out who overcomes adversity best and who has the most patience. . . ." From the third hole forward, Lee made four birdies and no bogeys to finish with a 68 and an even-par total of 280, the only golfer to equal par. Stewart could only hit six fairways and nine greens in the final round as he shot a 74 to lose by one nerve-racking stroke.

Stewart had made a 15-foot birdie putt at the fourteenth to get back to par and tie for the lead, but he was done in on the 609-yard, par-5 sixteenth, which he bogeyed after failing to get up and down from a green-side bunker. Payne missed a downhill 20-footer by two inches on the final hole and blew a chance to tie. Stewart joined Bert Yancy (1968), T. C. Chen (1985), and Gil Morgan (1992), golfers who, in recent years, held the lead in the Open in each of the first three rounds and lost. A disappointed but gracious Stewart said, "Give Lee Janzen all the credit in the world. There's nobody in the golf tournament that shot par except Lee Janzen. So he deserves to be the champion."

By the end of 2002, Janzen had won eight PGA Tour events and over $10 million.

88

Olin Dutra

1901–1983

What we all need is a cool head among hazards like Olin Dutra's. Dutra once had to pass seventeen golfers in the homestretch to win the National Open, and he did it.

—SAM SNEAD, commenting on Olin Dutra

Olin Dutra, a descendant of early Spanish settlers in the Americas, was born in Monterey, California, in 1901 and in his early years became a dedicated golfer. From the time he was fourteen, he rose at four o'clock in the morning and practiced before going to work. After eight years of this regimen, he gave up his job in the hardware business and became a professional golfer. He later took a job at the Brentwood Country Club in Los Angeles and was noted for the long hours he spent instructing golf.

A large, burly man standing 6 feet 3 inches and weighing 230 pounds, Dutra won the Southern California Professional Tournament in 1928, 1929, 1930, 1932, and 1933. His first major national tournament win came in 1932 when he won the PGA Championship at the Keller Golf Club in St. Paul, Minnesota. Dutra shot the lowest qualifying score, 140, and then defeated George Smith, Reggie Myles, Herman Barron, and Ed Dudley to reach the finals. Olin then defeated Frank Walsh, four and three, in that thirty-six-hole contest. Over the course of his matches, Dutra played 19-under par.

Dutra was selected to the Ryder Cup team in 1933 and 1935. In 1933, teamed with DENNY SHUTE, he lost his foursomes match to Abe Mitchell and Arthur Havers, three and two, then was defeated in singles, nine and eight, by Mitchell. The British won that contest, 6½–5½, at the Southport and Ainsdale Golf Club in England. In 1935, Dutra and Ky Laffoon lost their foursomes, 1-up, to the Whitcombe brothers. Dutra then won his singles, four and two, against Alf Padgham as the Americans prevailed, nine and three, at the Ridgewood Country Club in New Jersey.

Dutra won his second major title, the 1934 U.S. Open, at the Merion Cricket Club in Ardmore, Pennsylvania. He fell eight shots off the pace after shooting 76-74=150 for the first two rounds. Even though Olin was suffering severe stomach pains before he teed off the second day, he elected to play and shot 71 in the morning round to bring him back to three shots behind the leader, GENE SARAZEN. During the final round that afternoon, Dutra shot 72 to finish with a total of 293, thirteen strokes over par. Sarazen could not hold his lead, firing a final round 76 to lose by one to Dutra. Bobby Cruickshank, the leader after thirty-six holes, finished tied for third with Wiffy Cox and HARRY COOPER at 295.

Dutra almost won another major in 1935 when he finished third in the Masters. Playing in a field of sixty-three, Dutra opened with a solid round of 70, placing him one shot behind CRAIG WOOD. After two more rounds of 70, Dutra was one shot behind Wood, who was still in the lead. On the final day, the weather was damp and cold, and scores were rising. Dutra finished with a 74 and a total of 284 to finish two shots behind Wood and Sarazen. Sarazen came back to tie Wood, holing his famous double-eagle 2 on the par-5 fifteenth and then parring in the rest of the way. Sarazen defeated Wood in a thirty-six-hole play-off.

Olin Dutra won his last Tour-sanctioned event, the California Open, in 1940. He is credited with winning ten PGA Tour events. Dutra should receive minor credit for assisting Babe Didrikson Zaharias with her golfing career. During the 1932 Olympics in Los Angeles, where Babe medaled in track and field, she played a round of golf at the Brentwood Country Club at the urging of Grantland Rice, one of the leading sportswriters of the day and a founding member of Augusta National. She borrowed Dutra's clubs and showed the sportswriters assembled, including Rice and Damon Runyon, that she had an aptitude for the game.

Dutra continued to be active as a teaching professional and a member of various PGA committees after he left the PGA tournament circuit.

89

Hal Sutton

1958–

*Today's young players aren't in awe of anybody. They come
out here ready to compete and ready to win. I was young
and naïve, and when I had some success, it probably led to
a false sense of security.*

> —HAL SUTTON, in a *Golf Digest* interview

Hal Sutton, the son of an affluent oil executive, was born in Shreveport, Louisiana. He took up the game of golf at a young age but did
not have his first formal instruction until Harvey Penick gave him some
lessons when he was a teenager. Hal attended Centenary College in
Shreveport, won the U.S. Amateur in 1980, joined the PGA Tour in
1981, and earned Rookie of the Year in 1982.

Sutton had his best year in 1983, when he won the PGA Championship, his only major, and the Tour Championship. Hal won the PGA championship at Riviera by one stroke over his idol, JACK NICKLAUS. Sutton fired opening rounds of 65 and 66, then closed with rounds of 72 and 71 to finish with a score of 274. Nicklaus mounted a challenge on the final day by shooting a 66, but he could not quite win his sixth PGA championship. Sutton's strong 1983 season earned him Player of the Year.

After this early success, Sutton's career went into a tailspin. He lost his feel for his golf swing, after taking advice from a variety of swing doctors. He won only occasionally until the early 1990s. Floyd Morgan, his college coach, contacted him and helped him with his game. About the same time, in 1996, Sutton met his wife, Ashley, who has been a steadying influence. Sutton described his earlier golf woes to a *Golf Digest* interviewer: "My downswing was too steep, and I hit a lot of shots fat. When I tried to make it more shallow, I would drag the hosel and shank one every now and then, and had too many things going on in my head. It got to a point where I would listen to anybody who might have something to say."

Hal Sutton made the 1999 Ryder Cup team after a twelve-year hiatus. (He played on the losing 1985 and 1987 teams.) He helped rally the American team at The Country Club by winning his singles match, which helped the team win 14½–13½. Sutton credited team captain BEN CRENSHAW with creating the sense of family that enabled the United States squad to pull together and win on the final day. Sutton also felt that the Europeans made a strategic mistake by having less-experienced players, such as Sandelin, Coltart, and Van de Velde, start at the top of their final-day singles lineup.

Sutton has recorded fourteen PGA Tour victories, including the Memorial (1986), the Canadian Open (2000) and two Players Championships (1983, 2000), in addition to his PGA Championship. He ranks tenth in all-time earnings with $14,205,947 through 2002.

90

David Duval

1971–

When you have to kinda—you have to do it. I mean there's no way around it. You have to do it.

—DAVID DUVAL, after winning the 2001 British Open

David Duval learned the game of golf from his father, Bob Duval, a teaching professional in Jacksonville, Florida, and later a player on the Senior Tour (now the Champions tour). David won the U.S. Junior Championship and attended Georgia Tech, where he was a four-time All-American on the golf team. After college, Duval played on the satel-

lite tour, winning the Nike Tour Championship in 1995. In eight years
on the Tour, he has won over $16 million, placing him sixth on the all-
time PGA Tour earnings list. Duval has won thirteen tour events,
including the Tour Championship (1997), Players Championship (1999),
and the 2001 British Open championship. During the period
1997–2002, Duval was the only other player besides Tiger Woods who
won the Arnold Palmer Award for most earnings in a season on the
PGA Tour. He won the Byron Nelson Award with a 69.3 scoring average in 1998. Duval's $2,591,031 in 1997 earned him that title.

Duval came into his own as a global champion when he won the
British Open at Royal Lytham & St. Annes in 2001. David had been in
contention the previous year at St. Andrews but carded a disastrous
eight on the seventy-first hole of the Open Championship to take himself out of contention. Observers began to wonder whether Duval had
the right stuff to win a major. Duval, nursing a bad back, had doubts
himself. "You know, some people have written that I've had an *arm* in
the green jacket in the past—it hasn't worked out. They didn't write in
a mean way—I was just so close." Duval had tied for third in the 2000
Masters and second in 2001. Many skeptics felt that he might not win a
major.

But Duval rose to the occasion despite nagging back problems.
The British Open, golf's oldest major, dating back to 1860, is a test of
versatility, patience and skill. The tournament rotates among a variety of
challenging venues, including St. Andrews, Royal Birkdale, Royal Troon,
Muirfield, Royal St. Georges, Carnoustie, and Royal Lytham & St.
Annes. Conditions such as wind and rain can be major factors at these
venues. Duval entered the final round in a four-way tie for first place.
This was the highest number of golfers to tie for first after three rounds
of a major in twenty-three years. Duval shot a final round of 67 to
defeat Niclas Fasth of Sweden by three shots. Among the other contenders who fell by the wayside were Ian Woosnam, Bernhard
Langer, and Ernie Els, all at 278. Woosnam had to take a two-shot
penalty at the beginning of the final round because his caddie inadvertently left an extra driver in his bag.

Duval started the final round with solid putting, sinking an 18-foot
birdie putt on No. 3, then birdied the next two par 5s to take a three-
shot lead. In 2000, Duval had played in the final twosome with Tiger
Woods at St. Andrews, so he had a good feel for the excitement and
pressing crowds at the conclusion of a British Open. As Duval noted, "I
think as much as anything, I was just lucky to play my way into the last
group (in 2000)—to experience the crowd on 18 the final day of the

Open Championship. Some of that helped, I believe. I knew what it was going to feel like, and I did not worry about it. I just went out and played."

David Duval's Ryder Cup (1999, 2002) record is 2-3-2, and his Presidents Cup (1996, 1998, 2000) record is 7-6-1. David Duval's future impact on golf will likely be determined by his health. He suffered a bad back in 2000 and had to take several weeks off after the British Open. In 2002, he was diagnosed with positional vertigo, an inner-ear problem that results in brief, violent bouts of dizziness with any turn of the head; these are accompanied by queasiness that can last for hours. At this writing, David Duval's last victory was in the Dunlop Phoenix in Japan at the end of 2001.

91

Arnaud Massy

1877–1958

Massy's success was a story of remarkable application and strength of character, for at the turn of the century when he started to learn, it was extremely rare for a Frenchman to play golf.

—From *The Encyclopedia of Golf,*
published by Viking Press in 1973

Arnaud Massy is France's greatest male golfer, having won the French Open four times (1906, 1907, 1911, 1925), the British Open (1907), the Belgian Open (1910), and three Spanish Opens (1912, 1927, 1928). He finished second in the French Open three times and was runner-up in the British Open once.

Golf was slow to take hold in France when it was introduced by Scottish regiments after Wellington's victory at Orthez in 1814. The Scots, who were billeted at Pau, played a crude form of golf on the plain of Billere. The first golf club in France was the Pau Golf Club, a

330

nine-hole layout established in 1856. Pau was the first of many continental resorts in which golf was introduced to attract British tourists.

Arnaud Massy was born in Biarritz, Basson-Pyrenees, in 1877 and started to learn golf at a time when it was very rare for a Frenchman to play the game. He became skilled at the game and set his sights on the British Open, then the ultimate test of golf. Massy obtained backing from local supporters for a trip to North Berwick in Scotland in 1902. Though a left-handed golfer when he started his voyage, he converted to right-handed clubs during his practice sessions in Scotland. Massy entered the British Open at Royal Liverpool in Hoylake that year and shot rounds of 77-81-78-84=320 to finish a presentable tenth, tied with Andrew Kirkaldy, thirteen shots behind the winner, Sandy Herd. In that field were the great golfers of the day: HARRY VARDON, JAMES BRAID, HAROLD HILTON, J. H. TAYLOR, TED RAY, JOHN BALL, WILLIE PARK JR., and others. He returned in 1905 and played in the Open at St. Andrews and shot 81-80-82-82=325 to finish tied for fifth, seven strokes behind the winner, James Braid of Scotland. The following year, at Muirfield, he shot 76-80-76-78=310 to finish sixth, ten shots behind Braid.

Massy clearly had the game to compete at the highest levels of golf at the time, as was evidenced by his win at Hoylake in 1907. Arnaud won the two-round qualifier (thirty-six holes) and then fired a 76-81-78-77=312 to edge J. H. Taylor by two shots. Massy played at his best in the wind, and it was blustery when he became the first Frenchman, the first continental European, and the first golfer other than a Scot or an Englishman to win the Open.

Because of Massy's victory, the British challenged the French entering the French Open Championship at LaBoulie. Massy had won the first French Open in 1906 and won again in 1907, with countryman Jean Gassiat second and James Braid third. The British caught up with the French in 1908 when Taylor won the French Open. He won again in 1909, and Braid won in 1910. The growth of the French Open contributed to golf's popularity in that country.

Massy had excellent hand-eye coordination. He was fun for the gallery to follow because he carried himself like a Grenadier, his chest thrust out, and played with élan. His club gave a "pigtail" flourish at the top of his backswing, and he was masterful with his pitch shots. After the Open, Arnaud returned to France and became the professional at Chantaco. He died in 1958.

92

Bob Ferguson

1848–1915

In determination and resolute courage he was second to none; his style was most powerful, and it is difficult to say whether he appeared to most advantage in the long game, the quarter game, or on the green.

—Golf journalist H. S. C. EVERARD,
describing Bob Ferguson's game

Bob Ferguson is one of four golfers to win three consecutive British Opens (1880–82). The others are YOUNG TOM MORRIS (1868–70, 1872), JAMIE ANDERSON (1877–79), and PETER THOMSON (1954–56). Born in Musselburgh in 1848, Ferguson started to caddie at the age of eight on the Musselburgh links. The custom then was that every caddie was brought up in a trade independent of golf; the two most popular caddie trades at the time were weaving and shoemaking. Those with special aptitude for play passed their mornings in the town at work and came down to the links at about ten or eleven o'clock, caddied for a few hours, then returned to work.

Ferguson came closer than any other golfer to equaling Young Tom's record of four straight British Opens. He succeeded Jamie Anderson, his fellow Musselburgh native, by winning the 1880 championship at Musselburgh by five strokes over Peter Paxton and with a thirty-six-hole score of 162. The following year, at Prestwick, with a total of 170, he won by three shots over Jamie Anderson. In 1882, at St. Andrews, with a score of 171, he bettered runner-up Willie Fernie by three shots. But the following year, Fernie, then the professional at Dumfries, got his revenge at Musselburgh. He tied Ferguson in regulation with a score of 159 after closing his final round with three consecutive 3s. He also had a score of 10 on one hole. This required the second play-off in British Open history. Bob Martin won the first one, in 1876, over David Strath, at St. Andrews. In the thirty-six-hole play-off, the two golfers came to the final hole with Ferguson one stroke ahead. He scored a par-4 on that short finishing hole, but Fernie drove the green and sank a long putt for an eagle to win by one. This was Fernie's only Open win, though he finished second five times.

Among the top golfers of the era, beginning with the British Open in 1860 and ending in 1885, OLD TOM MORRIS, Young Tom Morris, WILLIE PARK JR., WILLIE PARK SR., Jamie Anderson, Bob Ferguson, Bob Martin, Willie Fernie, and Andrew Strath, Scotsman all, were the finest of the day. Top amateurs, such as W. H. M. Dougall, L. M. Balfour, and others, were not quite in their league. Ferguson was often backed in challenge matches by Sir Charles Tennant, who put up money in 1868 and 1869 when Ferguson defeated Old Tom Morris six times in matches at Musselburgh and Luffness. Anderson and Ferguson had four big matches at St. Andrews, Aberdeen, North Berwick, and Musselburgh. Each player won two matches. Young Tom Morris had the slight edge over Bob Ferguson in head-to-head contests, but Tom died in 1875, before Bob had reached his peak. Ferguson proved to be an excellent medal- as well as match-play competitor, as his three Open titles indicate.

Ferguson played his entire competitive career with the same eight clubs made for him by Douglas McEwan after Bob won a tournament at Leith when he was eighteen years old. Ferguson was extremely skilled with a cleek and iron, as evidenced by his win over Young Tom

Morris in a cleeks- (a driving cleek similar in loft to a 4-wood) only match at Prestwick. Ferguson was noted for his accuracy but according to Robert Browning, author of the classic A *History of Golf,* his disposition might have been the deciding factor: "The greatest factor in his success was undoubtedly the Scot's 'dourness' of character that made him rise superior to every ill turn of fortune and every disadvantage of conditions. When the wind was high or the turf slow, Bob Ferguson would be doing well as ever, while less tenacious rivals were going to bits." Ferguson was credited with using the putter from off the green at a time when purists advocated the use of a lofted club. Facetious caddies sometimes then referred to the putter as "the Musselburgh iron."

H. G. Hutchinson, the noted golf journalist and two-time British Amateur champion, commented on Ferguson's swing style in his essay "On Styles-Various Styles" in the Badminton Series book, *Golf:* "Greatly admired is the swing and style of Bob Ferguson . . . so square and solid he looks, his very stance expressive of the dogged resolution of his play, yet with great loose free-working shoulders swinging as true as if the backbone were a pivot! And that forward dig of his with the iron, which used to lay the balls up on the plateau-pitched holes of North Berwick as if by magic!"

Bob Ferguson won his three Opens with an average score of 167.67 (just under eighty-four strokes per eighteen) and against an average of forty opponents in the field. His scores were fully five strokes per round more than Young Tom Morris, but Tom played against an average of twelve other golfers in each of his four Open victories. And he played only at Prestwick, where he learned to play as a child when his father was the professional and greenskeeper there. The Open rotation did not begin until 1873, when the Open was first rotated among Musselburgh, Prestwick, and St. Andrews. Ferguson won his three Opens once on each of those courses.

93

Jamie Anderson

1842–1912

*I always play to get into the hole as soon as I am in reach
of it with my club.*

—JAMIE ANDERSON

Born in St. Andrews in 1842, Jamie Anderson was the first golfer
after YOUNG TOM MORRIS to win the British Open in three consecutive
years. The son of "Old Daw" Anderson, a St. Andrews caddie, Jamie
began to golf at the age of ten and was often compared to the great
champion WILLIE PARK SR. A percentage player with a strong sense of
strategy, Anderson was not as long off the tee as Park but was extremely
accurate with his approach shots. Anderson was a decisive player and
took very little time over the ball. He practiced his short game, espe-

cially his putting, often with his young son in tow at the practice putting green. He was seldom known to come up short with his putts, following the maxim "The hole will not come to you."

Anderson won his first British Open at Musselburgh in 1877, shooting a 160 to defeat Robert Pringle by two shots. At Prestwick the following year, he needed seventeen strokes on the last four holes to tie J. O. F. Morris, who was in with a 161. "I can dae't," Anderson lamented when he realized the task at hand. He hit a weak drive short of a bunker on the ninth hole (Prestwick was a twelve-hole course), a par-5, then hit a brassie and holed a full iron shot for an eagle. He parred the next hole with a 4 and then holed his tee shot on the eleventh, a short par-3. His tee shot, an iron, was a bit long but pitched on a mound at the far edge of the green, hesitated a moment, and then trickled down back into the hole. He parred the final hole, a par-5. Anderson's scores of 3-4-1-5=13 enabled him to win his second straight Open. His hole in one on the second-last hole was the second in British Open history. Young Tom Morris recorded the first Open hole in one at Prestwick in 1868. Bob Kirk came in after Anderson with a score of 159, making Anderson's margin of victory two shots. Kirk had almost tied Anderson with his approach shot, which rimmed the cup. In disgust he missed his easy tap-in. The fourteen-year-old amateur JOHN BALL, from England, finished tied for fourth with a score of 165. Jamie won his third consecutive Open at St. Andrews in 1879, establishing a St. Andrews British Open record—a thirty-six-hole score of 84-85=169. This St. Andrews course record was not surpassed until 1891, when Hugh Kirkaldy shot a 83-83=166 to win the Open. In 1897 the Open became a seventy-two-hole contest.

Jamie Anderson and Young Tom Morris attempted to pair up in challenge matches, but there were few takers, even though they often offered favorable odds to the opposition. Davie Strath and Bob Kirk once accepted the challenge but, up two holes with three to play, lost by one at the final hole. The medal scores were 80–81 in favor of Anderson's team. Journalist H. S. C. Everard commented on Anderson's disciplined approach to the game in his essay "Some Celebrated Golfers": "He was the very embodiment of machine-like accuracy, and when properly in his game, and in the real swing of the thing, as it were, conquered his opponents by tiring them out. No matter if they went away with a flourish of trumpets, they generally came back to him: one half-missed shot at rare intervals, was his opportunity, always profited by."

Anderson was noted as an excellent clubmaker in St. Andrews, Ardeer, and Perth. He died in St. Andrews in 1912.

94

Willie Park Jr.

1864–1925

A man who can putt is a match for anyone.
—WILLIE PARK JR.

Willie Park Jr., born in Musselburgh in 1864, the son of WILLIE PARK SR., the winner of the first British Open in 1860, ably carried on the Park family golf tradition. At the age of sixteen he was appointed assistant greenskeeper and professional under his uncle Mungo at the Tynesdale Club, an inland nine-hole course. He later became head greenskeeper and professional when his uncle Mungo returned to Alinmouth in 1892. Four years later, he returned to Musselburgh and joined his father's club- and ball-making business. His first notable tournament win was a victory against professionals at Alinmouth in 1881. His first important match-play contest was in 1885; he lost to Willie Campbell, a leading professional of that era. The same year, he lost a play-off to Willie Fernie, failing to defend his title at Alinmouth.

After testing his skill in match-play and medal contests around Scotland, Park won the 1887 British Open, in his sixth attempt, by one stroke, with a score of 161 over two-time Open winner Bob Martin at St. Andrews. Park had previously played in the Open. He tied for eighteenth at St. Andrews in 1882, placed eighth in 1883 at Musselburgh, and tied for fourth in 1884 at Prestwick, fourth in 1885 at St. Andrews, and fourth again in 1886 at Musselburgh. After placing tied for eleventh at St. Andrews the following year, he won in a play-off at Musselburgh in 1889. Park and Andrew Kirkaldy tied with scores of 155 in regulation. They played a thirty-six-hole play-off the following day, and Park won by five strokes, 158–163.

Park was a good all-round player, but he was most noted for his putting skill. His father taught him the importance of practice, not a common ritual in nineteenth-century golf. The senior Park had honed his skills on the four "baker's" holes, a square putting area near the finishing green at Musselburgh. The area was named the baker's holes because a local baker used to sell pies to golfers when they congregated there. Young Willie was known to spend as much as twelve hours a day practicing on that green.

Park believed that the putting stroke should be played with the action of a pendulum, only the hands and wrists being used in the swing and the club head moving in a short but wide arc struck from a center somewhere between the feet. In fact, Park did not teach a straight-line putting technique, and it took the Americans, in the form of WALTER TRAVIS, WALTER HAGEN, BOBBY JONES, and others to advance the method.

Park's club- and ball-making business flourished to the point where he had over thirty employees. He also published *The Game of Golf* in 1896, the first book written by a golf professional. The book begins with a discussion of clubs and clubmaking, contending that light clubs produce faster clubhead speed and greater distance. As a clubmaker, he was credited with introducing new clubs, such as "the lofter" (a lofted club used chiefly for approach shots); the "patent cleek" (a narrow-bladed iron that could be used for long fairway, bunker, and other shots, including putting), and the first "bulger" (a convex-faced driver that attempted to minimize the likelihood of heel and toe shots). The rest of Park's book covers the fundamentals of the game, shot techniques, hints on handicapping, managing competitions, and other aspects of the game. It was an early attempt to define basic golf principles in writing so they could be handed down from one generation to the next.

Park became a golf-course architect and designed Western Gailes in Scotland with his father; the Sunningdale Old Course in England; the Waterford Golf Club in Ireland; and many others in the British Isles and Europe. He traveled twice to the United States before the turn of the century, a six-month stay in 1895 and a shorter visit in 1896. He promoted golf, played exhibitions, and designed a few courses. He later returned to the United States in 1916 and designed the Grove Park Inn course in North Carolina, Olympia Field (North) in Illinois, the Ottawa Hunt and Golf Club in Ontario, Canada, the Penn State University Blue course, and others. Park established architectural offices in New York and Toronto, spending the rest of his life in North America. His second book, *The Art of Putting,* was published in 1920.

Willie last played in the British Open in 1905, when he finished tied for thirteenth. His last best finish was in 1898; he finished second, one shot behind HARRY VARDON, at Prestwick. When Park wasn't tending his various golf-business activities, he engaged in many challenge matches, as was the common practice of his day. Often he initiated the challenge himself in order to control the stakes and the venues where the contests took place. He was usually accompanied by his colorful caddie, John "Fiery" Carey, who had carried for Young Tom Morris and other notables. An article in England's *Golf* magazine described "Fiery" at work: "It is a perfect study to watch him performing his duties for Willie Park when that player is engaged in an important contest. Quiet, watchful and ever at his master's elbow with the right club, and never getting in the way, he never offers advice until it is asked for, and never betrays, even by movement of a muscle of his face, the slightest emotion of the varying fortunes of the game."

Willie Park Jr. won many challenge matches, but his most famous was a loss to Harry Vardon in their challenge match of thirty-six holes each on the "green" of North Berwick in Scotland and Ganton, Vardon's home course in England. Park issued this challenge after Vardon had beaten him in the Open. Vardon led by two holes after they played eighteen at North Berwick and then closed out the match, winning at Ganton, which required more carry off the tee than Willie could handle.

Willie Park Jr. was one of golf's pioneer international entrepreneurs. He leveraged his tournament success into further successes in equipment making, instruction, publishing, and golf-course design. He died in Edinburgh, Scotland, in 1925 at the age of sixty-one.

95

Dow Finsterwald

1929–

I never rooted against another player, but I never rooted for them, either. Dow Finsterwald was a helluva player and a friend. And I wanted him to do well. But when he was playing against me, I wanted me to do better.

—ARNOLD PALMER, commenting on his rivalry and friendship with Dow Finsterwald

Dow Finsterwald, a native of Athens, Ohio, was an excellent amateur as a young man. He received his B.A. degree from Ohio University and, after shooting a 61 as an amateur in the 1950 St. Louis Open, turned professional in 1951 and joined the PGA Tour in 1952. Finsterwald, noted as a cautious but intelligent strategist on the golf course, kept the ball in play and tried to hit the center of the green on his longer approaches. He gradually built up a track record on the Tour, winning his first tournament, the Fort Wayne Open, in 1955 and the British

Columbia Open Invitational the same year. He won the Carling Open in 1956 and the Tucson Open in 1957. Dow almost won the PGA Championship at the Miami Valley Golf Club in Dayton, Ohio, that year, losing to Lionel Hebert in the thirty-six-hole match-play final, three and one. Finsterwald won six match-play contests, including a three-and-one victory over SAM SNEAD, to reach the championship match. This was the last time the PGA Championship was decided in match play.

The following year, the PGA was played at the Llanerich Country Club in Havertown, Pennsylvania. The new championship format was four rounds of medal play over four days. Finsterwald opened with a 3-under-par 67 on the 6,710-yard layout to lead the tournament. After thirty-six holes, Jay Hebert shared the lead with Finsterwald with a score of 139. Sam Snead was the leader after fifty-four holes with a total of 207, two shots ahead of Finsterwald. Dow then shot a final-round 67 to defeat the sixty-three other golfers who had advanced. Finsterwald had a 67-72-70-67=276 to edge BILLY CASPER by two shots and Sam Snead by four. Finsterwald collected $5,500 in first prize money. The gallery had paid $95,000 in admissions fees, and any player in the final round who finished below fortieth place was paid $100 for his troubles. In contrast, TIGER WOODS, the winner of the 2000 PGA Championship, received $900,000; the last-place golfer, $5,300. Finsterwald won the Vardon Trophy in 1957 with a 70.30 scoring average and was named to the Ryder Cup team. Dow was named Player of the Year in 1958.

Finsterwald won five more tournaments up until the 1962 Masters, where he shot himself into a play-off with Arnold Palmer, one of his best friends on the Tour, and GARY PLAYER. Along with Arnold, Dow Finsterwald was one of superagent Mark McCormack's earliest clients when McCormack's company was called National Sports Management. During regulation play at the Masters, Finsterwald and Player had finished with seventy-two-hole scores of 280. Dow had shot 74-68-65-73; Gary, rounds of 67-71-71-71. Arnie, still out on the course, needed birdies on two of the last three holes to tie. Palmer hit his 5-iron tee shot to within forty-five feet of the pin on the 170-yard par-3 sixteenth and then rolled in his second shot to get his birdie. He then hit his approach shot on the par-4 seventeenth to within ten feet and birdied that hole to tie for the lead. Arnie got his par on the eighteenth, and an eighteen-hole play-off commenced the following day. Finsterwald shot 40 on the front nine of the play-off and was never in contention, finishing with a score of 77. Player led by three at the turn, but Arnie charged and won, 68–71.

Finsterwald was named to four Ryder Cup teams (1957, 1959,

1961, 1963). In 1957, he teamed with DOUG FORD to defeat Peter Alliss and Bernard Hunt, two and one, in foursomes; then Finsterwald lost his singles, seven and six, to Christy O'Connor Sr. as the British team won, 8½–3½ at the Lindrick Golf Club in Yorkshire, England. In 1959, Finsterwald and JULIUS BOROS won their foursomes match, 2-up, against Dai Rees and Ken Bousfield; then Finsterwald beat Rees, 1-up, in singles as the Americans won, 8½–3½, at the El Dorado Country Club in Palm Desert, California. In 1961, Ryder Cup play was expanded to twenty-four points, with sixteen singles matches and eight foursomes. Finsterwald and playing captain Jerry Barber defeated Tom Haliburton and Neil Coles, 1-up, in the foursomes at Royal Lytham and St. Anne's in England. Dow defeated Christy O'Connor Sr., two and one, in morning singles, then lost in the afternoon to Neil Coles, 1-up. The Americans won that contest, 14½–9½. Finsterwald played in his final Ryder Cup at the East Lake Country Club in Atlanta. Four-ball matches were added to the venue, and the United States, led by playing captain Arnold Palmer, easily won, 23–9. Finsterwald teamed with Palmer to win two four-ball matches, teamed with GENE LITTLER to win 1½ points in foursomes, and split his two singles matches. Finsterwald's 9-3-1 record gives him one of the best winning percentages in Ryder Cup play.

Finsterwald joined the Senior Tour on a limited basis and with modest success beginning in 1981. He has been active in the PGA as a member of its Tournament Committee (1957–59) and vice president (1976–78). He has long been a Director of Golf at the Broadmoor in Colorado Springs.

96

Tony Lema

1934–1966

I feel that I have been visiting an old grandmother. She's crotchety and eccentric but also elegant, and anyone who doesn't fall in love with her has no imagination.

—TONY LEMA, characterizing the Old Course
after winning the 1964 British Open at St. Andrews

Anthony David Lema, the son of a Portuguese immigrant, was raised near the docks in his native Oakland, California. His father died when he was three, and his mother raised her three sons and a daughter as best she could. Tony didn't especially like school, but he loved golf. He began to caddie at age twelve at the Lake Chabot municipal course and refined his game on the local courses in the Bay Area. In his book

Golfer's Gold, written with Gwilym Brown in 1963, Lema relates that golf might have kept him out of jail: "I was very hard to handle in high school, ran with a rough crowd, and though we got in trouble quite a bit we were lucky enough to stay out of the local lockup. . . . Thank goodness for golf." He often skipped school to play golf, and after high school, with no plans, he joined the marines. Lema served as an observer in the Artillery Corps in Korea and, when he returned to the states, played in some military golf tournaments before he was mustered out. Then, at the suggestion of an old golfing buddy, he applied for a position at the San Francisco Golf Club and became the assistant professional in 1955 when he was twenty-one years old. As Lema describes it: "Working there proved to be quite an experience. I learned how to dress [conservatively], how to behave in polite society [relaxed, but attentive good manners], and how to play golf with professional flair."

Lema qualified for the 1956 U.S. Open at Oak Hill in Rochester and made the cut, finished well down the list with a score of 308 (CARY MIDDLECOFF won with a 281), and earned $200 for his efforts. He intermittently played in various tournaments and finally joined the Tour in 1958 but had limited success until 1962, when he won three tournaments. His second win came at the Orange County Open in Southern California, where, when Lema led after three rounds, he announced to the press that he was buying champagne if he won. He did, and the nickname "Champagne Tony Lema" became his.

Lema won one tournament in 1963 and finished a strong second in the Masters with rounds of 74-69-74-70=287. JACK NICKLAUS had to par the last two holes to win, which he did, by one stroke. Tony won $14,000 and decided to marry his fiancé, Betty Cline, an airline stewardess he had met in 1961. Lema had his best year in 1964 when he won four tournaments—the Crosby National Pro-Am in January and the Thunderbird Classic, the Buick Open, and the Cleveland Open on consecutive weeks in June—before going to the British Open at St. Andrews in early July.

Lema had played golf in Britain before, but he had never played the Old Course at St. Andrews. He had come over on an overnight flight from the United States with his manager, Fred Corcoran, one of golf's first agents and a pioneer promoter of the PGA and LPGA Tours. Corcoran tried to explain the nuances of the Old Course to Lema, who said, "I don't build golf courses; I play 'em."

Lema played only ten practice holes at St. Andrews before the tournament. Luckily, he was assigned Tip Anderson, the caddie who shepherded ARNOLD PALMER to his Open wins in 1961 and 1962. Arnie had withdrawn from the Open in 1964, so Anderson was available. Lema charmed the Scots. Picking up a coin that he found near the first tee on the first day, he exclaimed: "Look at this; I'm already the leading money winner in the British Open." Lema fired rounds of 73-68-68-70=279 to win by five shots over Jack Nicklaus. At his caddie's suggestion, a key part of Lema's strategy was to bump and run his shots onto the huge greens at the Old Course. Tony used a black-painted putter given to him as a present by TOMMY ARMOUR, the "Silver Scot," who had won the three majors of his day: the U.S. Open, British Open, and PGA Championship.

Lema's caddie, Tip Anderson, gave him high praise: "He's a great player. His swing is about as sweet as SAM SNEAD's. When you compare his game to Mr. Palmer's, there's very little difference. But he is more relaxed. When something goes wrong, like the six he took at the fifth hole Friday, he forgets it immediately." A critical point in the tournament came on the final day, when each golfer played thirty-six-hole rounds. Lema teed off four and one-half hours after Nicklaus, and they walked past each other while Lema was playing the sixth and Jack the fourteenth in the third round. At that point Jack was 5 under for his round and Lema 3 over for the first five holes. Recognizing the challenge, Lema birdied the seventh, ninth, tenth, fourteenth, fifteenth, and eighteenth holes for a 68 to answer Jack's 66. Lema then shot 70 on the final round to Jack's 68 to win by five. The deficit caused by Nicklaus's first rounds of 76-74 was too much for him to overcome.

As was the tradition when Lema won, champagne was served to the press and others. He had had a champagne party after thirty-six holes because he was the leader. He had won the Open for the first time he entered the tournament, his first time on the Old Course, and the first time he had used the British small ball.

Lema had another good year in 1965, placing second in earnings with $101,817. He won the Buick and Cleveland Opens and tied for fifth in the British Open at Royal Birkdale. He played on the Ryder Cup team that year and was instrumental in the American win at Birkdale. On the first day, paired with JULIUS BOROS in foursomes, they defeated Lionel Platt and Peter Butler, 1-up, in the morning, then Jimmy Martin and Jimmy Hitchcock, five and four, in the afternoon. The second day, Boros and Lema lost in four-balls to Neil Coles and Bernard Hunt, 1-down, but in the afternoon, Lema, partnered with KEN VENTURI, defeated Coles and Hunt, 1-up. On the third day, Lema won both his singles matches, 1-up, over Butler in the morning, and six and four over Christy O'Connor in the afternoon. The U.S. Team won, 19½–12½, and Tony contributed five points. His overall Ryder Cup record, including his 1963 performance, was 8-1-2.

In 1966, Lema's last year, he won the Oklahoma City Open to bring his total number of victories, in addition to his British Open win, to thirteen in eleven years on the Tour. Lema played his final round at the 1966 PGA Championship in Akron, Ohio. The next day, he traveled to Chicago with his wife for an exhibition date. Lema's charter flight crashed and burned on June 26 on the seventh hole of the Sportsmen's Club in Lansing, Illinois. Tony, then thirty-two years old, his wife, Betty, and both pilots were killed in the blaze.

97

Phil Mickelson

1970–

I don't care if I ever win a major. I am not going to play this game without enjoyment, without the fun that I have right now.

—PHIL MICKELSON, interviewed by Jaime Diaz,
Golf Digest, November 2002

Phil Mickelson had twenty-one PGA Tour victories through the 2002 season. At the age of thirty-two, this placed him tied for twenty-seventh in all-time wins along with WILLIE MACFARLANE, LANNY WADKINS, and CRAIG WOOD. Phil ranks second on the all-time PGA Tour money list with $22,149,969, second only to TIGER WOODS, and over $12 million more than DAVIS LOVE III, in third place.

Mickelson was born in San Diego, and started swinging a golf club when he was a year old. A left-handed golfer, the best since BOB CHARLES, he started playing full rounds of golf at age four. Mickelson won several San Diego golf titles as a junior player before attending Arizona State University, where he won the NCAA singles championship three times. He also won the U.S. Amateur (1990) and the PGA Tour's Northern Telecom Open while still a collegian. Phil joined the PGA Tour in 1992. He won two tournaments in his first two professional seasons: the Buick Invitational of California and the International (1993). Phil's best year thus far was 1997, when he won four events: the Bellsouth Classic, the Buick Invitational, the MasterCard Colonial, and the Tour Championship.

A long hitter off the tee, Mickelson averages over 285 yards on his drives. He also has an effective, if inconsistent, short game. Mickelson has all the tools to win major tournaments on tour, but many observers feel that he needs to tighten up his game and take fewer risks. Mickelson himself believes that his game is too inconsistent to stand up under the pressure of major tournaments in particular. Rick Smith, a noted golf instructor who has worked with Mickelson, claims that Phil will make the necessary changes: "People don't understand, it isn't easy playing with the changes Phil has made. . . . People think he is always 'Mr. Aggressive,' but he throttles back a lot and has hit a lot of 2-irons and 3-woods and cut drives off the tee, like he did at Bethpage [during the 2002 U.S. Open], where he was swinging well. His technique just has to keep getting better." Dave Peltz, a short-game expert and instructor of Mickelson, notes: "As far as skill, Phil is the best I have seen. But he thinks of the short game as a way to save himself from disaster more than as a way to create scoring opportunities."

Thus far, Mickelson has not won a major event, though he has come close on various occasions. For example, he finished second to PAYNE STEWART in the 1999 U.S. Open in Pinehurst, when Stewart made a clutch putt on the final hole. Phil finished second to Tiger Woods in the 2002 Open at Bethpage Black. He has twice finished third in the Masters (2001, 2002) and finished second in the 2001 PGA Championship.

Phil has played on four Ryder Cup teams (1995, 1997, 1999, 2002) and has compiled an 8-5-3 record. Mickelson has a 6-7-5 record in four President's Cup events (1994, 1996, 1998, 2000). With all of his talent and his record of success on the PGA Tour, it is only a matter of time before Phil Mickelson starts winning majors.

98

Johnny McDermott

1892–1971

We hope our foreign visitors had a good time; but we don't think they did, and they sure won't win the National Open.

—JOHNNY McDERMOTT to the foreign competitors
at the 1913 Shawnee-on-Delaware tournament
in Pennsylvania, before the U.S. Open

John J. McDermott, the son of a mailman, developed an interest in golf and began to caddie at Aronimink, within walking distance of his Philadelphia home, at the age of nine. At age eighteen, the 130-pound McDermott began to make an impact on the golf world when he finished second in the Metropolitan Open, won the Philadelphia Open, and was runner-up in the U.S. Open at the Philadelphia Cricket Club, all in 1910. McDermott had dropped out of Philadelphia High School to become a professional golfer, working first at the Merchantville Field Club, then, on the basis of his tournament performance in 1910, at the Atlantic City Country Club in New Jersey. Quiet and mannerly, he didn't drink or smoke, and he rarely missed Sunday mass. He was a driven perfectionist who began to practice at the break of dawn and played until dark after a long day at the pro shop. He was especially skilled with a mashie, practicing by hitting shots at a tarpaulin spread on the ground 150 yards away. He gradually reduced the size of the target to a few feet in diameter.

McDermott had a long, loose, flowing swing like the old St. Andrews swing of the featherie-ball era. He used long-shafted clubs, and his swing had more body turn than the old style and a flatter plane. Occasionally, unwelcome hooks could wreak havoc on his game. He had finished forty-eighth in the 1909 U.S. Open, his first, but managed to fight his way to a three-way tie for first in the 1910 Open at the Philadelphia Cricket Club. The brothers ALEX SMITH and MACDONALD SMITH, of Carnoustie, Scotland, were McDermott's opponents in the play-off after they had finished at 298 in regulation play. Alex Smith won the Open by shooting a 71 in the play-off, four better than McDermott and six better than Mac Smith.

The following year, McDermott, then only nineteen, again tied for first in the Open, held at the Chicago Golf Club. Johnny shot rounds of 81-72-75-79=307 to tie Mike Brady, a highly regarded American professional from Massachusetts who carried only six clubs in his bag, and George Simpson, a professional from Wheaton, Illinois. The opening hole in the play-off provided an inauspicious beginning for McDermott. He had switched from using his normal Rawlings Black Circle ball to a ball called the Colonel because a manufacturer's rep offered him $300 to do so. He hit his first two tee shots out of bounds. Johnny managed to card a 6 on that first hole, benefiting from the current rule that out of bounds meant only loss of distance, and recovered at the end of nine to lead Brady by four shots and Simpson by five. His final score of 80 was somehow enough to win the tournament because Brady shot an 82; Simpson, an 85. McDermott was, and still is, the youngest player to win a U.S. Open and the first American born golfer to win that national title.

The 1912 Open was held at the Country Club of Buffalo and had 131 entries, the first time the tournament drew more than a hundred participants. The U.S. Amateur, by comparison, had eighty-six entries that year, the first time it had fewer participants than the Open. The Buffalo Country Club measured 6,326 yards, the longest venue to date for the Open. Par was set at 74. Some critics thought McDermott's win in the 1911 Open was a fluke. He was determined to prove them wrong. He opened with rounds of 74-75=149 to put him two shots behind the leaders, Mike Brady and Alex Smith. After firing a 74 in the third round, he was four shots behind the leader, Mike Brady. In the final round, McDermott shot a 71 to finish with a score of 294 to win the Open. Brady ruined his chances with a final-round 79 and tied for third with Alex Smith, at 299. Tom McNamara, a twenty-year-old who had been runner-up in the 1909 Open, finished second. McNamara had shot a second-round 69 to become the first golfer to break 70 in a round at the U.S. Open and closed with a 69 and a total of 296 to finish second. McDermott's score was the second-lowest seventy-two-hole score in U.S. Open history. His score was achieved on a more difficult course than the Englewood Golf Club, where George Sargent won the 1909 Open with a score of 290.

In 1912, McDermott, Brady, and McNamara sailed to Britain for the British Open at Muirfield. McDermott alienated some of the locals with his cocky attitude but was soon put in his place when he shot a 96 and did not qualify. In June 1913, McDermott returned to play the British Open at Hoylake. He adopted a shorter, more controlled swing, and his driving accuracy improved under difficult weather conditions. This time he qualified and shot a seventy-two-hole score of 315 to finish a respectable fifth, far behind J. H. TAYLOR, who won with a score of 304.

McDermott's fortunes took a bad turn when he returned to the United States. He lost money in stock-market transactions and developed other personal problems. He managed to win a tournament at Shawnee-on-Delaware on the first course designed by A. W. Tillinghast, who later designed Winged Foot and other great golf courses. TED RAY and HARRY VARDON, touring the United States and scheduled to play in the U.S. Open at the Country Club, were among the competitors. In a short speech afterward, McDermott made some injudicious remarks: "We hope our foreign visitors had a good time; but we don't think they did, and they sure won't win the National Open." The young McDermott later apologized to Ray and Vardon when it was pointed out that his remarks were ungracious. Criticism from the press, fellow golfers, and the USGA added to McDermott's growing depression. He played in September in the 1913 U.S. Open, won in dramatic fashion by twenty-year-old amateur FRANCIS OUIMET in a play-off against Vardon and Ray. McDermott finished eighth, four shots behind the leaders.

Determined to win the British Open, McDermott set sail again for Britain and the Open at Prestwick the following year. But he was late for his qualifying start after missing a transportation connection. The tournament officials offered to let him tee off for the qualifier, but Johnny refused, saying it would be unfair to the other players. He booked passage home on the *Kaiser Wilhelm II*, which, due to heavy fog, collided with another boat in the English Channel. McDermott was escorted to a lifeboat and returned to England, and the *Kaiser Wilhelm* sank. McDermott finally returned to the United States and finished ninth in the U.S. Open at Midlothian, ten shots behind the winner, WALTER HAGEN.

But something was seriously wrong with Johnny McDermott. He blacked out in his pro shop at the Atlantic City Country Club. Then he returned to his parents' home in Philadelphia, his golfing career over at age twenty-three. He had had a nervous breakdown, was diagnosed as a chronic schizophrenic, and would be in and out of treatment centers for the rest of his life. Johnny McDermott, after playing nine holes of golf at Valley Forge, died quietly in his sleep at age seventy-nine in 1971.

99

Willie MacFarlane

1890–1961

There is only one way to play the game. You might as well praise me for not robbing a bank.

—BOBBY JONES, when he called a penalty shot on himself
in the U.S. Open, won by Willie MacFarlane in 1925

Willie MacFarlane was born in Aberdeen, Scotland, in 1890 and was another one of the many Scottish golf professionals who came to North America at the turn of the century to become professionals at the growing number of golf clubs in the region. Noted for his smooth swing and his ability with middle and short irons, MacFarlane is credited with twenty-one PGA victories, tying him with PHIL MICKELSON, LANNY WADKINS, and CRAIG WOOD for twenty-seventh place on the all-time list.

353

MacFarlane's most significant win was the 1925 U.S. Open at the Worcester Country Club in Massachusetts. Willie, then the professional at the Oak Ridge Club in Tuckahoe, New York, shot rounds of 74-67-72-78=291 to tie amateur phenom Bobby Jones at the end of regulation. One shot behind were FRANCIS OUIMET and JOHNNY FARRELL. Two shots back were WALTER HAGEN and GENE SARAZEN. All of these players, along with Mike Brady and LEO DIEGEL, had a chance to win on the final nine holes.

MacFarlane, who was tall and slim and wore rimless glasses, looked a bit like a schoolmaster out on the golf course. He was not a regular member of the loosely formed touring circuit but preferred to spend his time as a teaching professional. A smart player, Willie preferred to play for fun rather than blood. MacFarlane was very skilled. He once hurt his wrist playing on hard ground at the Baltimore Country Club early in his career. He discovered that he could shoot in the high 70s to low 80s playing one-handed. He was a streaky player. In a series of rounds in the metropolitan New York area, Willie shot a 64 at Quaker Ridge, 64 at Hudson River, 66 and 67 in one day at Dunwoodie, and 64 at his home club.

The U.S. Open was one of the few tournaments MacFarlane enjoyed playing. But in 1925, at the Worcester Country Club, he was competitive enough to shoot a new U.S. Open single-round record of 67 on his second round, and he was calm enough when he approached the seventy-second tee needing a par-4 to tie Jones in regulation. The eighteenth hole at Worcester played 335 yards and had a severely forward sloping, raised green protected by deep bunkers. MacFarlane's approach settled at the top side of the green, leaving a steep 40-foot downhill putt. He hit a good lag putt to within a foot of the hole, but it settled in a ball mark. Having to play it as it was, MacFarlane used a midiron instead of his putter and coaxed it into the hole. Jones would have won the tournament outright, but he called a penalty on himself and penalized himself a stroke when a blade of grass that his grounded iron touched at his address slightly moved the ball. The tournament officials tried to talk him out of penalizing himself, but he insisted. When praised for his behavior later, he was insulted and remarked: "There is only one way to play the game. You might as well praise me for not robbing a bank."

In the eighteen-hole play-off the next day, MacFarlane went out in 37, and Jones in 38, on the first nine. At the fourteenth, still holding his one-shot lead, MacFarlane had reached the green in two and likely would make his 8-foot putt for birdie. Jones was in the rough, twenty yards from the pin. He stunned MacFarlane when he chipped in for a birdie. The shaken MacFarlane missed his putt, and the match was all even. At the eighteenth, MacFarlane missed a six-foot putt for birdie, and Jones made a 5-footer for par to tie at 75. As a result, the play-off was extended another eighteen holes.

Jones shot a 35 going out to build a four-shot lead that seemed insurmountable. But MacFarlane gamely came back with a 33 on the final nine to win, 72–73. Jones, who was trying to win his second U.S. Open, took a double bogey on the par-4 fifteenth, costing him the tournament.

100

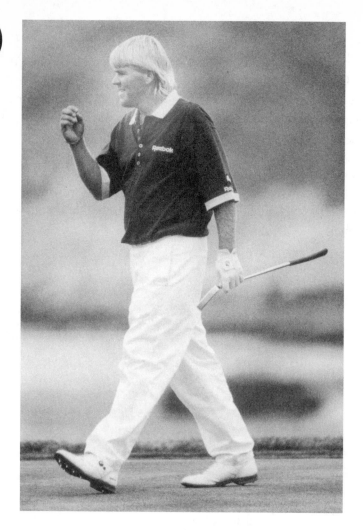

John Daly

1966–

Grip it and rip it.

—JOHN DALY, on taking the
club below parallel

John Daly, like JOHNNY McDERMOTT, hasn't won that many tournaments and hasn't really played that long, just ten years on the Tour at
this writing. But he has made a major impact, just as Johnny did, and he
has had his personal problems, although they're of a different variety

than the chronic schizophrenia that ended McDermott's career all too soon. Daly is rather like a Babe Ruth figure, a bit rough around the edges, totally unpretentious, and with a golf swing that's bigger than life. A stocky 5-foot-11-inch 220-pounder, Daley has an awesome backswing that goes well beyond parallel. He hits the ball over 300 yards off the tee with ease, but he also has a delicate finesse game around the greens. He first realized he had talent when he started to win tournaments in high school. He had taken up golf when he was four, was playing in scrambles when he was five, and was reading golf tips in the newspaper at an early age so he could teach himself the latest techniques. When he was eight, he had his first beer. And when he was fourteen, he moved up to Jack Daniels, which he would sometimes carry in his bag during junior golf tournaments. He's been trying to manage his alcohol problem and himself ever since.

Even though John was a championship-level golfer in high school in Arkansas, he did not receive many college offers. The coach at Texas told him: "Son, you will never play college golf with that swing." Daly ignored that advice and attended the University of Arkansas, where he played on the golf team, though he and the coach didn't see eye to eye all that much. He left the university his junior year and played in state tournaments, on the South African Tour, and on the Nike Tour. He almost died after a drinking binge in 1990 but recovered and continues to live on the edge. He played in a few Tour events, but then he received a break in 1991 when, as ninth alternate, he was called on short notice to play in the PGA Championship at Crooked Stick. John drove all night and arrived at the tournament just in time to tee off. He had never played Crooked Stick, nor had he had time for a practice round. Daly had an opening-round 69, then added rounds of 67-69-71 to win by three shots over Bruce Lietzke. Daly won $574,783 that year and placed seventeenth on the money list. He placed in the top twenty-five in eleven of the thirty-three events he played. With his new fame and the power of his golf swing, Daly drew thousands of fans when he played and attracted millions of dollars in endorsement deals. He won the 1992 B.C. Open, the 1994 Bell South Classic, and his second major, the 1995 British Open at St. Andrews.

Daly demonstrated his awesome length at St. Andrews, reaching the green on the 316-yard twelfth hole with a long 1-iron and arriving at the 567-yard fourteenth with a driver and a 6-iron. After three rounds, 67-71-73=211, Daly was four strokes off the lead. John finished with a 71 and a 6-under-par total of 282. Only Constantino Rocca, a former caddie and plastics factory worker from Bergamo, Italy, had a chance to catch him. Rocca needed a birdie on the 348-yard, par-4 finishing hole to tie Daly. He hit his drive to the landing area before the Valley of Sin, a deep swale in front of the green. Rather than bump and run the ball up to the hole, Rocca elected to chip, but he chili-dipped it, and it ended up fifty feet from the hole. Daly thought he had won the British Open, as did any other sane person who was watching. But Rocca, looking totally crestfallen at first, gathered himself and hit a wonderful putt into the hole. He fell to the ground and acknowledged the golf gods. Daly now was the one who had to collect himself. The Open had its first four-hole, medal-play play-off format in 1989 when Mark Calcavecchia beat GREG NORMAN and Wayne Grady at Troon. In 1995 several players, including COREY PAVIN, Brad Faxon, and Mark Brooks, went over to encourage Daly and to give him some advice. Faxon reminded him that it was a four-hole, cumulative-stroke-play play-off. Brooks let Daly use his yardage book when John's caddie couldn't find his.

The play-off was played on the first, second, seventeenth, and eighteenth holes to determine the championship. Rocca three-putted the first hole, and Daly birdied the second and easily won, 15–19. John would later say that when Rocca chunked his approach on eighteen, he thought he had won the tournament. He went from high, to low, to mad: "It was a good mad, a real competitive feeling. Every shot I hit in the play-off was just solid, hard. I was really focused on what I was doing. I didn't have any doubts about anything."

Daly has been through two marriages, has been in and out of rehab, and has lost some endorsement deals and a considerable amount of money due to his behavior. He has a variety of other problems, some of them with players on the Tour who don't think he's good for the game. John is on the cusp. He's number 100. He could go either way.

THE TOP 41 WOMEN GOLFERS

THE TOP FORTY-ONE
WOMEN GOLFERS

Women have long been golfers, going back before the time of Mary, Queen of Scots, who teed it up in the sixteenth century. In the 1800s, outstanding amateur women golfers such as Britain's Lady Margaret Scott and America's Beatrix Hoyt dominated national competition. This select list honors the best forty women of all time, including all sixteen members of the LPGA Hall of Fame and twenty-four other outstanding female golfers.

1. MICKEY WRIGHT, a native of San Diego, California, won the 1952 U.S. Girls Junior and the 1954 World Amateur. She turned professional in 1955 and won eighty-two LPGA (Ladies' Professional Golf Association) tournaments in her career, which began in 1956, after she attended Stanford University. Mickey won thirteen majors including four U.S. Women's Opens (1958, 1959, 1961, and 1964), four LPGA

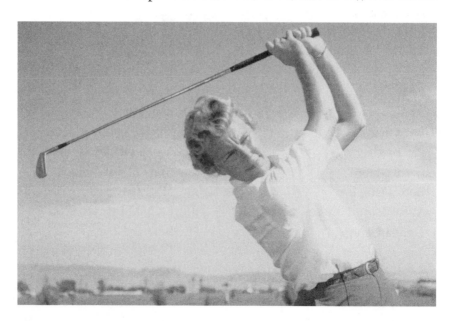

Championships (1958, 1960, 1961, 1963), two Titleholders (1961, 1962), and three Western Opens (1962, 1963, 1966). LPGA Hall of Famer Betsy Rawls described Wright: "She set a standard of shotmaking that will probably never be equaled. Mickey's swing was flawless as a golf swing can be—smooth, efficient, powerful, rhythmical, and beautiful." A member of the World Golf Hall of Fame, Wright was the leading money winner four times (1961–64) and the Vare Trophy winner five consecutive times (1960–64). Mickey won thirteen tournaments in 1963, an LPGA record, including four in a row. She also won four consecutive scheduled LPGA events in 1962. Only Kathy Whitworth (who won four in a row in 1969) and Nancy Lopez (who won five consecutive events that she entered in 1978) have equaled or bettered this mark. Mickey's biggest money year was 1963, when she earned a total of $31,269. From 1956 through 1969, Mickey won at least one tournament per year. Only Kathy Whitworth (seventeen) and Betsy Rawls (fifteen) have bettered this mark of fourteen consecutive years in the winners circle. Mickey won seventy-nine of her eighty-two victories in a ten-year span, from 1959 to 1968, a stunning average of 7.9 wins per year. Wright was inducted into the LPGA Hall of Fame in 1964. In her book *Play Golf the Wright Way*, Mickey explained the fascination that golf had for her: "Something happened to me when I swung a golf club. I felt free and graceful like somebody. I still do. Golf to me is not only a way of life, it's a creative outlet, a constant, never-ending challenge; frustrating but never dull; infuriating, but satisfying." She stopped playing regularly on the Tour in 1969, at the age of thirty-four, because of foot problems, adverse reactions to sunlight, and an aversion to flying.

2. KATHY WHITWORTH has won more LPGA golf tournaments (88) than anyone. The 5-foot-9-inch Texan was the leading money winner seven times (1965, 1966, 1967, 1968, 1971, 1972, 1973) and Player of the Year seven times (1966, 1967, 1968, 1969, 1971, 1972, 1973) and was the seven-time winner of the Vare Trophy (1965, 1966, 1967, 1969, 1970, 1971, 1972). She won six major championships, including three LPGA Championships (1967, 1971, 1975) and two Titleholders Championships (1965, 1966), and she was the last winner of the Women's Western Open in 1967. Whitworth led or tied for the lead in LPGA in tournaments and won seven times (1965, 1966, 1967, 1968 [tied], 1971, 1972 [tied], 1973). During those seven years she won a total of fifty-two tournaments. Her best earnings year was 1983, when she won $191,492. In 1981 she became the first golfer to reach $1 million in career winnings on the Tour. Kathy holds the LPGA career record with eleven holes in one. She was captain of the U.S. team in the inaugural Solheim Cup in 1990 and again in 1992. Before joining the Tour in 1958, Whitworth attended Odessa (Texas) College. She was awarded the first Powell Award in 1986, given to an LPGA member who, in the opinion of her playing peers, by her behavior and deeds best exemplifies the spirit, ideals, and values of the LPGA. She was inducted into the LPGA Hall of Fame in 1975.

3. PATTY BERG was an all-around athlete in her native Minneapolis, Minnesota. She learned to play golf at the age of thirteen; three years later she won the 1934 Minneapolis City Championship. This was the first of twenty-eight amateur championships that she won in a seven-year period. Her amateur wins included three Titleholders (1937–39), the 1938 U.S. Amateur, the 1938 Western Amateur, two Trans-Mississippi Championships (1938, 1939), the 1938 Western Derby, and five consecutive Helen Lee Doherty Championships (1936–40). Patty was a member of the U.S. Curtis Cup team in 1936 and 1938. She turned professional in 1940, and the first six of her fifty-seven recognized LPGA victories came before the formation of the Women's Professional Golf Association (WPGA) in 1946. After serving as a lieutenant in the Marine Corps during World War II (1942–45), she led the WPGA Tour, the predecessor of the LPGA, with three victories in both 1948 and 1949. She was a founding member of the LPGA and was its first president, from 1949 to 1952. Berg was the leading money winner on the LPGA Tour in 1954, 1955, and 1957. Her best earnings year was 1955, when she won $16,492. Patty was the first winner of the Vare Trophy, named for the six-time U.S. Amateur winner Glenna Collett Vare and donated by LPGA founding member Betty Jameson. Berg won the inaugural Vare Trophy in 1953 with an average of seventy-five strokes and again in 1954 and 1956. Berg won a record fifteen LPGA major championships: seven Titleholders, three as an amateur (1937, 1938, 1939), including the first Titleholders in 1937, and four as a professional (1948, 1952, 1955, 1957); seven Western Opens (1941, 1943, 1951, 1954, 1955, 1957, 1958); and the inaugural U.S. Women's Open in 1946. Berg won the only U.S. Women's Open to be played in a match-play format, five and four, over Betty Jameson. Berg was named the Associated Press Athlete of the Year in 1938, 1943, and 1955. She was among the four original inductees into the LPGA Hall of Fame in 1951 and, along with Babe Zaharias, was among the first inductees into the World Golf Hall of Fame in 1974. Berg is a member of numerous other halls of fame and has received many awards for her outstanding athletic achievements, her courage, her humanitarianism, and her dedication to the game. Berg, one of the first female golfers to become a spokesperson for a sporting-goods company, has represented Wilson Sporting Goods since 1940.

4. JoAnne Gunderson Carner, at 5 feet 7 inches, was known as "the Great Gundy" in her amateur days when she won the 1956 U.S. Girls' Junior, five U.S. Amateur titles (1957, 1960, 1962, 1966, 1968) and competed on four Curtis Cup teams. On the LPGA Tour, which she joined in 1970 at the age of thirty, she became known as "Big Mama." A member of the World Golf Hall of Fame, she won forty-three LPGA Tour events in a span of sixteen years (1970–85), including two U.S. Women's Opens (1971, 1976). She is the only woman to have won the U.S. Girls' Junior, the U.S. Women's Amateur, and the U.S. Women's Open. Carner led the LPGA in earnings in 1974, 1982, and 1983. In 1981 she became the second player to win $1 million in career earnings on the LPGA Tour. She has won over $3 million on the Tour, placing her among the top-twenty-five money winners of all time. Carner is the last amateur to win an LPGA event, the 1969 Burdine's Invitational in Miami, Florida, and the oldest to win an LPGA event, the 1985 Safeco, at the age of forty-six years, five months, and nine days. Carner also is only one of three players to defeat four other golfers in a sudden-death play-off. She outplayed Donna Caponi, Jan Stephenson, Nancy Lopez, and Chako Higuchi in the 1979 Women's Kemper Open. JoAnne was inducted into the LPGA Hall of Fame in 1982 after winning her thirty-fifth LPGA title at the Chevrolet World Championship of Women's Golf. Her forty-three LPGA wins ties her for seventh on the all-time list.

5. Louise Suggs is a founder and charter member of the LPGA. She learned golf from her father, a former baseball player with the New York Yankees, at the age of ten. Her father owned a golf course in Lithia Springs, Georgia, an ideal place for Louise to learn. She wanted to go to college, but her family could not afford it, having lost much of their money during the Depression. After graduating from high school, Louise worked for Gulf Oil as a service representative. Before turning professional in 1948, she won several amateur events, including the Georgia State Amateur Championship (1940, 1941), the Southern Amateur Championship (1941, 1947), the North/South Championship (1942, 1946, 1948), the Titleholders (1946), the U.S. Women's Amateur (1947), and the British Amateur (1948). Suggs also played on the 1948 Curtis

Cup team. After turning professional, she won the 1949 U.S. Women's Open by a record fourteen strokes at Prince George's Country Club in Landover, Maryland, her first of fifty-eight LPGA Tournament wins. She won eight major championships, including two U.S. Women's Opens (1949, 1952), the LPGA Championship (1957), three Titleholders (1954, 1956, 1959), and two Western Opens (1949, 1953). She was the leading money winner in 1953, when she led the LPGA with eight wins, earning $19,816, and in 1960, when she won $16,892. Suggs won the Vare Trophy in 1957. She was inducted into the LPGA Hall of Fame in 1951, along with Patty Berg, Betty Jameson, and Babe Zaharias. Her fifty LPGA tournament wins is fifth in the history of the Tour. Suggs was president of the LPGA from 1955 to 1957. In 1966 she was the first woman inducted into the Georgia Athletic Hall of Fame. She was inducted into the World Golf Hall of Fame in 1979.

6. JOYCE WETHERED, born in England in 1901, was considered the supreme lady golfer of her era. She captured five consecutive English Ladies' Championships (1920–24) during which she won thirty-three consecutive matches, four British Ladies' (1922, 1924, 1925, 1929), the French Ladies' Open (1921), and eight Worplesdon Foursomes (1922, 1923, 1927, 1928, 1931, 1932, 1933, 1936). Wethered was known for her great rivalries with Cecil Leitch, whom, as a nineteen-year-old, she first defeated in the 1920 English Ladies,' and Glenna Collett Vare, whom she defeated in the 1925 English Ladies' and again in 1929. Wethered was noted for her classic golf swing, which generated power with effortless grace, and her amazing concentration on the golf course. Joyce was the playing captain of the first Britain and Ireland Curtis Cup team in 1932. Bobby Jones made these comments about Wethered's abilities after he had occasion to play golf with her on the Old Course at St. Andrews in 1930: "She did not miss one shot. She did not even half-miss one shot, and when she finished, I could not help saying that I never played with anyone, man or woman, amateur or professional, who made me feel so utterly outclassed. I have no hesitancy in saying she is the best golfer I have ever seen." Wethered is a member of the World Golf Hall of Fame.

7. MILDRED "BABE" DIDRIKSON ZAHARIAS, born in Port Arthur, Texas, in 1914, was perhaps the greatest female athlete ever. She excelled at baseball, tennis, basketball, rollerskating, diving, bowling, track and field, and other sports. She won two gold medals in track and field in the 1932 Olympics in Los Angeles and then began concentrating on

golf in 1935 at the suggestion of sportswriter Grantland Rice. In 1946 and 1947 she won seventeen amateur tournaments in a row, including the 1946 U.S. Women's Amateur and the 1947 British Amateur. Her British Amateur win was the first by an American since the championship was inaugurated in 1893. The Babe turned professional in 1947 and became a founder and charter member of the LPGA. She won 41 of the 128 LPGA tournaments in which she played during her brief eight-year career. One of the four original inductees into the LPGA Hall of Fame in 1951, Zaharias led the LPGA in earnings for four consecutive years, from 1948 to 1951. She won ten major championships, including three U.S. Women's Opens (1948, 1950, 1954), three Titleholders Championships (1947, 1950, 1952), and four Western Opens (1940, 1944, 1945, 1950). In 1954 she won the Vare Trophy for low scoring average on the Tour. The Babe was named the Woman Athlete of the Year by the Associated Press in 1931, 1945, 1946, 1947, 1950, and 1954. She had cancer operations in 1953 and 1956 and succumbed to the disease in 1956, at the age of forty-five. In 1957 Zaharias became the first lady golfer to win the Bob Jones Award. The award is presented by the USGA to a person who, by a single act or over the years, emulates Jones's sportsmanship, respect for the game and its rules, generosity of spirit, sense of fair play, self-control, and perhaps even sacrifice.

8. GLENNA COLLETT VARE, a member of the World Golf Hall of Fame, was the greatest U.S. Women's Amateur champion of all time. The New Haven, Connecticut, native was a pupil of Alex Smith, the noted U.S. Open champion and teaching professional from Carnoustie. Vare won the Amateur a record six times (1922, 1925, 1928, 1929, 1930, 1935). She also won two Canadian Ladies' Opens (1923 and 1924), the French

Ladies' Open (1925), and played on four Curtis Cup teams (1932, 1936, 1938, 1948). She was runner-up in two British Ladies', losing in the final to Joyce Wethered at the Old Course at St. Andrews in 1929, then to nineteen-year-old Diana Fishwick at Formby in 1930. In her book *Ladies in the Rough*, written in 1928, Glenna Collett recalled how Alex Smith helped shape her game: "He taught me a sound philosophy as well as a better way of handling the mashie and the putter. He strengthened my driving to such a degree that when I was eighteen, five-feet-six-inches tall, and weighed a hundred and twenty-eight pounds, I drove a ball a measured distance of three hundred and seven yards—thirty-six yards longer than the longest drive Babe Ruth ever belted and, at that time, the longest drive ever hit by a woman."

9. NANCY LOPEZ was born in Torrance, California, in 1957 and, encouraged by her father, started to play golf at the age of eight. Nancy won the New Mexico Women's Amateur at the age of twelve and two U.S. Junior Girls' Championships (1972, 1974). In 1976 she played on the Curtis Cup and World Amateur teams and was an all-American at Tulsa University before turning professional. Nancy won a record-five tournaments in a row in 1978 and has totaled forty-eight LPGA wins, including three LPGA Championships (1978, 1985, 1989). Lopez was named Player of the Year in 1978, 1979, 1985, and 1988, and has won the Vare Trophy three times (1978, 1979, 1985). Lopez has won over $5 million on the LPGA Tour, thirteenth on the all-time list. She was inducted into the LPGA Hall of Fame in 1987 and the World Golf Hall of Fame in 1989.

10. BETSY RAWLS, a Phi Beta Kappa graduate in math and physics from the University of Texas, won fifty-five LPGA Tour events, beginning with the 1951 U.S. Women's Open and concluding with the GAC Classic in 1972. The Spartanburg, South Carolina, native won eight major championships, including four U.S. Women's Opens (1951, 1953, 1957, 1960), two LPGA Championships (1959, 1969), and two Western Opens (1952, 1959). Rawls won at least one event every year from 1951 to 1966 and led the Tour in victories in 1952, 1957, and 1959. Rawls led the LPGA in earnings in 1952 with $14,505 and 1959 with $26,774. She won the Vare Trophy for low scoring average in 1959, when she won a personal-best ten tournaments. Betsy Rawls was inducted into the LPGA Hall of Fame in 1960. Her fifty-five victories place her fourth on the all-time list behind Kathy Whitworth, Mickey Wright, and Patty Berg. Rawls served as LPGA tournament director for six years after she retired from the Tour in 1976. An expert on the rules of golf, Rawls was the first woman to serve on the Rules Committee for the men's U.S. Open.

11. JULI SIMPSON INKSTER, a native of Santa Cruz, California, became the fifth person to win three consecutive U.S. Women's Amateur titles (1980–82), joining Beatrix Hoyt (1896–98), Alexa Stirling (1916, 1919, 1920), Glenna Collett (1928–30), and Virginia Van Wie (1932–34). She was also a four-time all-American at San Jose State University before joining the LPGA Tour in late 1983. Inkster won the 1984 LPGA Rookie of the Year award and became the first rookie to win two majors, the Nabisco–Dinah Shore and the du Maurier Classic. She won her third major, the Nabisco–Dinah Shore, in 1989. Inkster has lost two play-offs in majors, to Dottie Pepper in the 1991 Nabisco and to Patti Sheehan in the 1991 U.S. Women's Open. Inkster earned her way into the LPGA Hall of Fame and the World Golf Hall of Fame by winning five tournaments in 1999, including the U.S. Women's Open and the LPGA Championship. She is only the second woman in LPGA history, after Pat Bradley in 1986, to complete the modern-day LPGA Grand Slam.

Inkster won her sixth major, the McDonald's LPGA Championship, in 2000, and her seventh, the U.S. Open, in 2002. She has won a total of twenty-eight LPGA Tour events, tied with Karrie Webb for eighteenth on the all-time list. Juli has won over $7.7 million on the LPGA Tour, third behind Annika Sorenstam and Karrie Webb. She was a member of the 1992, 1998, and 2000 U.S. Solheim Cup teams.

12. ANNIKA SORENSTAM was born in Stockholm, Sweden, in 1970. She took up golf at the age of twelve, was a member of the Swedish National team from 1987 to 1992, the NCAA Champion and College Player of the Year in 1991 when she led the University of Arizona golf team, and the World Amateur Champion in 1992. Prior to joining the LPGA Tour, Sorenstam competed on the Women Professional Golfers' European Tour where she was named 1993 Rookie of the Year. Sorenstam joined the LPGA Tour in 1994, won the Rookie of the Year award, and she has won forty-two events—tying for seventh all-time—through 2002, including the U.S. Women's Open (1995, 1996) and the Nabisco Championship (2001, 2002). She has been named Rolex Player of the Year five times and has also won the Vare Trophy for lowest scoring average five times. Annika had her best year in 2002, when she won a record-tying eleven events. She set the single-season earnings record with $2,863,904. Her 2002 scoring average (68.7) is an LPGA record. She set or tied thirty LPGA records in 2002. Sorenstam is the all-time LPGA career money winner with over $11 million in earnings. Sorenstam has accumulated enough points to enter the LPGA Hall of Fame.

13. KARRIE WEBB, in her first five years on the LPGA Tour, recorded twenty-two victories and won over $6 million. In 1995, Webb's first year on the tour, she was named Rookie of the Year. The following year she became the first player to win $1 million on the LPGA Tour in a single season. In 1997, she won the Vare Trophy for lowest scoring average. She won it again in 1999, with an average of 69.43, an LPGA record, and again in 2000. The native of Queensland, Australia, won six times in 1999 and was named the Rolex Player of the Year. The following year, she again won six events and earned a record $1,876,853 and the Rolex Player of the Year honor. Karrie has won six majors, including the du Maurier (1999), the Nabisco (2000), the U.S. Women's Open (2000, 2001), the McDonald's LPGA Championship (2001), and the Weetabix British Open (2002), which has replaced the du Maurier as a major. During the 2000 season, Webb, then twenty-five years of age, became eligible, based on points earned, to qualify for the LPGA Hall of Fame. She will be eligible for induction in 2005. Karrie Webb has won over $8.8 million on the LPGA Tour, second only to Annika Sorenstam. She has been named Rolex Player of the Year twice (1999, 2000). She has twenty-eight LPGA victories.

14. PATTY SHEEHAN was born in Middlebury, Vermont, in 1956, and had a fine Amateur career, with four consecutive wins in the Nevada State Amateur (1975–78) and two in the California Amateur (1978, 1979). As a Curtis Cup team member in 1980, she won all four of her matches. She attended the University of Nevada and San Jose State University, where she won the 1980 AIAW National Championship before joining the LPGA Tour, where she earned Rookie of the Year honors in 1981. She has won thirty-five LPGA events, including six majors: three LPGA Championships (1983, 1984, 1993), two U.S. Women's Opens (1992, 1994), and the 1996 Nabisco–Dinah Shore. Sheehan was named Player of the Year in 1983 and was the Vare Trophy winner in 1984. Patty is among the top-fifteen LPGA career money winners, having earned over $5.5 million on the Tour. She has been selected to the U.S. Solheim Cup team four times (1990, 1992, 1994, 1996). A member of the World Golf Hall of Fame, Patty was inducted into the LPGA Hall of Fame in 1993.

15. SANDRA HAYNIE was born in Fort Worth, Texas, in 1943, and started to play golf at age eleven. She won the Texas State Publinx in 1957 and 1958, and the Texas Amateur in 1958 and 1959. She won the Trans-Mississippi in 1960, then joined the LPGA Tour the following year. Haynie won forty-two LPGA events, including four majors: two LPGA Championships (1965 and 1974), the U.S. Women's Open (1974), and the Peter Jackson Classic (now the du Maurier Classic) in 1992. From 1965 through 1974, Haynie was never worse than ninth on the money list. In 1974 she became the only player (other than Mickey Wright) to win the LPGA Championship and the U.S. Women's Open the same year. Sandra won the Player of the Year award in 1970. She was inducted into the LPGA Hall of Fame in 1977, and is a member of the World Golf Hall of Fame. Haynie's forty-two wins put her tied for eighth place on the all-time LPGA list with Annika Sorenstam.

16. BETSY KING, born in Reading, Pennsylvania, in 1955, was a member of the 1976 National Collegiate Championship team at Furman University. She joined the LPGA Tour in 1977 after graduating with a B.A. degree in physical education. Her thirty-one LPGA victories include six majors: three Nabisco–Dinah Shores (1987, 1990, 1997), two U.S. Women's Opens (1989, 1990), and the 1992 LPGA Championship. Although King did not win her first Tour event until seven years after she joined the circuit, she won twenty tournaments in a span of six years (1984–89). King won Player of the Year honors in 1984, 1989, and 1993, and she won the Vare Trophy in 1987 and 1993. King is the all-time leading money winner on the LPGA Tour with over $6.8 million in earnings. King has won thirty-four tournaments and over $7.5 million on the LPGA tour. She was inducted into the LPGA Hall of Fame in 1995 and is a member of the World Golf Hall of Fame.

17. PAT BRADLEY, a native of Westford, Massachusetts, joined the LPGA Tour in 1974 and has accumulated thirty-one victories and over $5.6 million in earnings. Her major wins include the 1981 Peter Jackson Classic, the 1983 U.S. Women's Open, two du Maurier Classics (1985, 1986), the 1986 Nabisco–Dinah Shore, and the 1986 LPGA Championship. Bradley and Julie Inkster are the only LPGA golfers to have won all the modern majors. Bradley won Player of the Year in 1986 and 1991 and the Vare Trophy, also in 1986 and 1991. She was the leading money winner with $492,021 in 1986 and $763,118 in 1991. She was selected to the U.S. Solheim Cup team in 1990, 1992, and 1996. In 1988, Pat contracted Graves disease and in 1991 won the Golf Writers of America's Ben Hogan Award for her comeback from that disease. Bradley's three major victories in 1986 makes her one of three LPGA players, with Babe Zaharias (1950) and Mickey Wright (1961), to win three majors in one year. Pat was inducted into the LPGA Hall of Fame in 1991. Before becoming a professional golfer, Bradley won the New Hampshire Amateur (1967 and 1969), two New England Amateurs (1972, 1973), and was an all-American at Florida International in 1970. Bradley graduated from Florida International University with a B.S. in physical education in 1974.

18. CAROL MANN was born in Buffalo, New York, in 1941. She began playing golf at the age of nine, won the Western Junior and Chicago Junior in 1958, and won the Chicago Women's Amateur in 1960. After attending the University of North Carolina in Greensboro, the 6-foot-3-inch Mann joined the LPGA Tour in 1960 and won thirty-eight tournaments, including the 1964 Western Open and the 1964 U.S. Women's Open. Mann was so elated with her Western Open win that she held a champagne party: "I threw a champagne party for the press to be like Tony Lema. I won $1,200, the champagne cost me $120, and I had blisters from popping every cork myself." One of Mann's best years was 1968, when she won ten tournaments and the Vare Trophy with a record scoring average of 72.04 that stood until Nancy Lopez broke it in 1978. She won the money title in 1969, earning $49,152, when she had eight tournament victories. Carol's thirty-eight career wins is tenth on the all-time LPGA list. She was inducted into the LPGA Hall of Fame in 1977. Mann is a former president of the LPGA (1973–76) and has remained active in its administration. She owns and operates her own golf consulting and services company.

19. BETH DANIEL took up the game of golf at age eight, was a quarter finalist in the U.S. Junior Girls' Championship at age thirteen, and won the U.S. Women's Amateur in 1975 and 1976. The Charleston, South Carolina, native was a member of the U.S. Curtis Cup team in 1976 and 1978 and the World Cup team in 1978. She graduated from Furman University with a degree in education and turned professional in 1978, earning LPGA Rookie of the Year in 1979. Daniel has won thirty-two LPGA events, including one major, the 1990 LPGA Championship. She was named Player of the Year after winning four tournaments in 1980, and won the Vare Trophy in 1989 with a record 70.38 scoring average. In 1990, she set a new single-season earnings record with $863,578 and won both the Vare Trophy and Player of the Year honors. In 1994, she won the Player of the Year award for the third time. Daniel, a member of the World Golf Hall of Fame, was elected to the LPGA Hall of Fame in 1999 under a new point system. Under the old system, Daniel would have needed another major to qualify with fewer than thirty-five career victories. Up until this time, only twenty-one LPGA players had gained entrance to the Hall of Fame since 1950, making it the most difficult sports hall of fame to reach. Daniel has won over $7.5 million on the Tour, second all time.

20. AMY ALCOTT, a native of Kansas City, Missouri, won her first national title, the U.S. Girls' Junior Amateur, in 1973. She turned professional in 1975 and won the Orange Blossom Classic, her third tournament, at age nineteen. She has won a total of twenty-nine LPGA Tournaments, including five majors: the Peter Jackson Classic (1979), the U.S. Women's Open (1980), and three Nabisco–Dinah Shores (1983, 1988, 1991). In an interview with journalist Liz Kahn, Alcott recalled the impact of winning the U.S. Women's Open: "After that, when people announced me as U.S. Open Champion on the first tee, my drive would automatically go ten yards further. No one can ever take it away. . . . That one achievement is worth a lifetime of working for it." A member of the World Golf Hall of Fame, Alcott was elected to the LPGA Hall of Fame under a revised point program, which makes it less difficult to enter the hall. Under the old system, Alcott would have qualified with thirty LPGA wins, including at least two major victories. She has won over $3.4 million on the LPGA Tour, placing her twenty-second in all-time earnings. She is active in youth and sports charity work. She has created an endowment for the UCLA Children's Hospital and its Neonatal Intensive Care Unit.

21. DONNA CAPONI, a native of Detroit, Michigan, won her first significant golf title, the 1956 Junior Los Angeles Open, at the age of eleven. She turned professional in 1965 after graduating from high school and won her first LPGA Tour event, the U.S. Women's Open, in 1969, winning by one shot by scoring a birdie on the final hole. She became the second woman, after Mickey Wright, to win consecutive Opens when she won in 1970 at the Muskogee Country Club in Oklahoma. Caproni won two more majors, both LPGA Championships (1979, 1981), and a total of twenty-four LPGA Tour events, nineteenth all-time. Caponi's best money year was 1980, when she won five tournaments and $220,619, ranking second on the Tour. Caponi is now a golf commentator on various broadcast networks.

22. JUDY RANKIN, a petite 5-foot-3-inch dynamo from St. Louis, Missouri, was taught golf by her father. By the time she was eight years old she had won four St. Louis PeeWee titles. At fourteen she was the youngest ever to win the Missouri State Women's Amateur Championship, and at age fifteen, she was the low amateur in the 1960 U.S. Women's Open. She joined the LPGA Tour at the age of seventeen and won the first of her twenty-six Tour events, the Corpus Christi Open, in 1968. She candidly said: "In spite of the fact that there wasn't much money out there in 1962, it was the reason I turned professional. I care a great deal about the game, but I was not out there for the love of it." Rankin won seven tournaments and led the LPGA in earnings in 1976, setting a single-season money record with $150,734. She won the LPGA Player of the Year Award and the Vare Trophy, which she also had won in 1973. In 1973, Rankin won five tournaments, the Player of the Year award, and her third Vare Trophy. She was elected president of the LPGA in 1976 and has been active in its various organizational activities. She was also the leading money winner in 1977 with twenty-five top-ten finishes, still an LPGA record, netting her $122,890. Judy retired from the Tour in 1983 due to back problems. She captained the victorious 1996 and 1998 U.S. Solheim Cup teams. Rankin is now one of the most respected television golf commentators. She was inducted into the World Golf Hall of Fame in 2000.

23. JANE BLALOCK, a native of Portsmouth, New Hampshire, developed an early interest in golf, caddying and baby-sitting to buy her first set of clubs. She once said: "I spent a lot of time alone playing golf and developed a sense of a relationship between myself, the golf ball, and the golf club. We were a team." Blalock had a notable amateur career, winning the 1963 New Hampshire Junior Championship and the 1963 New England Junior. She won four consecutive New Hampshire State titles (1965–68), the 1965 Florida Intercollegiate, and the 1968 New England Amateur. After attending Rollins College, she joined the LPGA Tour in 1969. She won the Rookie of the Year award in 1969 and began a streak of 299 tournaments without missing a cut. She finished among the top ten on the LPGA money list from 1971 to 1980 and was the first to record four consecutive $100,000 seasons (1977–80). During her career, Blalock won twenty-six official LPGA events, placing her nineteenth all-time. Blalock currently manages her own sports consulting firm in Boston and is a golf commentator.

24. MARLENE BAUER HAGGE, born in Eureka, South Dakota, in 1934, is a charter member and founder of the LPGA. A dominant player on the amateur circuit in California in the late 1940s, Hagge became the youngest athlete, at age fifteen, ever to be named Associated Press Athlete of the Year after she won the first U.S. Girls' Junior in 1949, defeating Barbara Bruning, 2-up, at the Philadelphia Country Club. Hagge recalled her younger years: "There were not any junior golf programs when I was growing up, and girls were generally not very athletic at the time, so I played my golf with men or with older boys on golf teams." She joined the LPGA Tour at the age of sixteen and won her first event, the Sarasota Open, in 1952 and her last tournament, the Burdine's Invitational, in 1972. Hagge was the leading money winner in 1956, with eight wins and $20,235 in earnings. She won twenty-five LPGA tournaments, including the 1956 LPGA Championship, placing her eighteenth on the all-time LPGA victory list. Hagge is still the youngest person to have played on the LPGA Tour and the youngest, at age eighteen, to win an LPGA tournament. She now lives in Palm Springs, California, and provides golf-consulting services to a variety of clients.

25. CATHERINE LACOSTE is the daughter of Rene LaCoste, France's famous tennis champion and sports clothing pioneer, and Mlle. Thion de la Chaume, winner of the British Ladies' Golf Championship in 1927. In 1967 she became the first foreigner, the first amateur, and at age twenty-two, the youngest player to win the U.S. Women's Open. An excellent long-iron player and a great competitor, LaCoste won four French Ladies' Opens (1967, 1969, 1970, 1972), two French Ladies' Closes (1968, 1969), the 1969 British Ladies', and the 1969 U.S. Women's Amateur. LaCoste played in the Women's World Amateur Team Championship for the Espirito Santo Trophy from 1964 until 1970, when she retired to raise a family. In 1968 she won the individual World Team Championship title and in 1964 contributed to the French team victory by one stroke over the United States.

26. LAURA DAVIES took up golf at age ten and won several amateur titles before turning professional. Among these are the 1983 English Intermediate Championship, the 1984 Welsh Open Stroke Play Championship, and two South Eastern Championships (1983, 1984). The native of Coventry, England, was a member of the 1984 Great Britain and Ireland Curtis Cup team before she joined the European professional circuit, established in 1979, where she won the Women Professional Golfers' European Tour Order of Merit in 1985, 1986, and 1996. Davies won her first of twenty LPGA victories in 1987, when she won the 1987 U.S. Women's Open in a play-off with JoAnne Carner and Ayako Okamoto. Her other major championship victories include two LPGA Championships (1994, 1996) and the 1996 du Maurier Classic. A big hitter who averages over 255 yards off the tee, the 5-foot-10-inch Davies has won over forty worldwide titles and is ranked ninth in LPGA career earnings with over $6 million. In 1988 she was awarded the MBE (Member of the Order of the British Empire), presented at Buckingham Palace by the Queen of England. Davies holds the LPGA record for most times winning the same tournament in consecutive years, the Standard Register Ping (1994–97). In 1996 she was named LPGA Player of the Year, the first British lady golfer to be so honored. Laura has been a member of six European Solheim Cup teams (1990, 1992, 1994, 1996, 1998, 2000, 2002). She is the all-time leader in Solheim Cup points.

27. SE RI PAK was born in Daejeon, Korea, in 1977. She began playing golf at the age of fourteen and won thirty tournaments in Korea before she became a professional in 1996. She joined the LPGA in 1997 and, in her first full season in 1998, won two majors: the McDonald's LPGA Championship and the U.S. Women's Open. Pak was named Rolex Rookie of the Year in recognition of her four LPGA tournament wins. During the 2001 season, Pak won five LPGA events, including another major, the Weetabix Women's British Open. In 2002, she won her fourth major, the McDonald's LPGA championship. Se Ri had a total of eighteen LPGA Tour wins and $5,724,762 in career earnings, eleventh all-time.

28. MEG MALLON was born in Natick, Massachusetts, in 1963. After attending Ohio State University she joined the LPGA Tour in 1987. Since then, she has won fourteen events and over $6.4 million, placing her seventh on the all-time earnings list. Mallon's best year was 1991, when she won two majors, the Mazda LPGA Championship and the U.S. Women's Open. Mallon has played on six U.S. Solheim Cup teams (1992, 1994, 1996, 1998, 2000, 2002). In 1999, she was awarded the William and Mousie Powell Award, given annually by the LPGA to a member who, in the opinion of her playing peers, by her behavior and deeds best exemplifies the spirit, ideals, and values of the LPGA. She won her third major, the du Maurier Classic, in 2000.

29. DOTTIE PEPPER was born in Saratoga Springs, New York, in 1965. She won the New York State Junior Amateur and the New York State

Amateur in 1981, and the Junior Amateur again in 1983. Pepper attended Furman University, where she played on the golf team and was twice named Female Athlete of the Year. After graduating with a degree in physical education in 1987, Pepper joined the LPGA Tour and was named Rookie of the Year in 1988. She has won seventeen LPGA events, including the Nabisco–Dinah Shore twice (1992, 1997). She won both the Rolex Player of the Year Award and the Vare Trophy in 1992. Pepper has won over $6.6 million on the Tour, sixth all-time. Pepper was a member of the U.S. Solheim Cup Team in 1990, 1992, 1994, 1996, 1998, and 2000.

30. MARILYNN SMITH's favorite sport as a child was baseball: "I thought golf was a sissy sport, since I ran a boy's baseball team, where I was pitcher, coach, and manager." But her father introduced her to the game of golf at the Wichita Country Club when she was eleven. A long hitter, the native of Topeka, Kansas, became an excellent amateur golfer and won three consecutive Kansas State Amateurs (1946–48) and the 1949 NCAA title while attending the University of Kansas. She left college to represent Spalding equipment and became a charter member and founder of the LPGA in 1950. Smith won a total of twenty-one tournaments, including two majors, the 1963 and 1964 Titleholders. Her biggest golfing thrill was defeating Mickey Wright in a play-off to win her first Titleholders in 1963. She served as LPGA president from 1958 to 1960 and has been an energetic ambassador for women's golf. Smith received the 1979 Patty Berg Award for distinguished service to golf, the first golfer to be so honored. She currently teaches golf, plays in charity events, and conducts golf tours worldwide.

31. SANDRA PALMER started playing golf at the age of thirteen in Bangor, Maine, where she was a caddie. As an amateur she won the West Texas Women's Amateur Championship four times and was state champion in 1963. She was runner-up in the 1961 National Collegiate Championship while a student at North Texas State. Palmer joined the LPGA Tour in 1964, then won at least two events per season the next seven years. Sandra has nineteen PGA victories, including two majors, the 1972 Titleholders and the 1975 U.S. Women's Open. In 1986 she became the thirteenth woman to win $1 million in career earnings on the LPGA Tour when she won the Mayflower Classic, her last Tour victory. Palmer is a Class A member of the LPGA Teaching and Club Professional Division. She is also an active teaching professional.

32. HOLLIS STACY, one in a family of ten children, is one of two women to win three consecutive U.S. Junior Girls' Championships (1969–71), and by winning the 1969 event at the age of fifteen years and four months, she is the youngest ever to win it. A native of Savannah, Georgia, Hollis modeled her fluid swing after Julius Boros: "Basically, I just swing the club. When I was young, I went to the Masters at Augusta, where I got autographs and watched Julius Boros. He was my idol. I would imitate his swing and copy his tempo, and he remained one of my favorites." Stacy won the 1970 North/South Amateur, was on the 1972 Curtis Cup team, and after attending Rollins College, joined the LPGA Tour in 1974. She has won eighteen Tour events, including four majors: three U.S. Women's Opens (1977, 1978, 1984) and the Peter Jackson Classic in 1983. Only four others have won the U.S. Women's Open three times: Mickey Wright (four), Betsy Rawls (four), Babe Zaharias (three), and Susie Berning (three). Stacy won her last Tour event, the Crestar–Farm Fresh Classic, in 1991. An excellent match-play player, she has won six of the seven play-offs she has been in as a professional. Hollis designed the Blackhawk Golf Course in Austin, Texas. She is a golf coach at the University of Southern California.

33. CHARLOTTE CECILIA "CECIL" PITCAIRN LEITCH was born in Silloth, Cumberland, England, in 1891, and became one of the leading women players in the world beginning just before World War I. Noted for her outstanding power off the tee and her iron play, Leitch won twelve national titles, including two English Ladies' (1914, 1919), five French Ladies' Opens (1912, 1914, 1920, 1921, 1924), four British Ladies' (1914, 1920, 1921, 1926), and the 1921 Canadian Ladies' Open. Her epic battles against Joyce Wethered raised the level of play in women's golf and increased the popularity of the ladies' game. Enid Wilson, an excellent British golfer and pioneer journalist, characterized Leitch:

> Miss Leitch was a natural leader who took command of the game of golf on the first tee as instinctively as she drew breath. Her swing was not pretty to watch; it was incredibly flat compared with modern teaching. She used the palm grip with her right hand very much under the shaft. . . . She revealed to her sex that there were distinct possibilities of their being able to reproduce the artistry of the irons, which had hitherto been the prerogative of the best men golfers.

34. DOROTHY CAMPBELL HURD HOWE was born in North Berwick, Scotland, in 1883, and became the first British-born player to win the U.S. Women's Amateur Championship, the British Ladies', and the Canadian Ladies' in the same year. Dorothy won a total of eleven national titles, including three Scottish Ladies' (1905, 1906, 1908), two British Ladies' (1909, 1911), three U.S. Women's Amateurs (1909, 1910, 1924), and three Canadian Ladies' Opens (1910, 1911, 1912). Howe played a significant role in women's golf history when she was a participant in the British Ladies' Amateur at the Royal and Ancient Golf Club of St. Andrews in 1908, the first national women's championship held at that venue. Howe lost in the final, 1-up, to Maude Titterton, but won the following year and again in 1911. One of Howe's specialties was a 5-iron run-up shot from several yards off the green. It is estimated that she won over seven hundred tournaments in her long career. She is a member of the World Golf Hall of Fame.

35. PAM BARTON was born in London in 1917 and died in a plane crash in 1943 in Kent, while serving in the Women's Auxiliary Air Force in World War II. She played on the British Curtis Cup Team in 1934 and 1936 and won the French Ladies' Open in 1934. In 1936, at the age of nineteen, she won both the U.S. Women's Open and the British Ladies' Open. By winning both these events, she became the first British golfer since Dorothy Campbell (Mrs. D. C. Hurd Howe) in 1909, to hold both titles. Of medium height but powerfully built, Barton was long off the tee and brought verve and enthusiasm to the game. Her promise as a youngster was recognized when she was allowed to play the men's course at the Royal Mid-Surrey Club at a time when women were usually confined to their own courses.

36. JAN STEPHENSON, a native of Sydney, Australia, had an outstanding career, winning five consecutive New South Wales (NSW) Schoolgirl Championships (1964–68), four New South Wales Juniors (1969–1972), three Australian Junior Championships (1967, 1968, 1971), and two New South Wales Amateurs (1971, 1972). After turning professional in 1973, she won the Australian Open and three other events. A strong influence on her career was her late father, Frank, who encouraged her and caddied for her at many of her tournaments. Stephenson joined the LPGA Tour in 1974 and won Rookie of the Year honors. She has won three modern majors: the 1981 Peter Jackson, the 1982 LPGA Championship, and the 1984 U.S. Women's Open. Her best money year was 1987, when she won $227,303. Her career earnings total over $3 million, twenty-eighth on the all-time LPGA list. She has won sixteen LPGA events and seven others, including two Australian Opens (1973, 1977). An attractive woman, Stephenson was the pinup girl of the LPGA in the 1970s. In a *Playboy* magazine interview, when asked whether golfers are good lovers, she theorized: "Maybe it's because they have a good touch. In golf you have to be good in all areas; you have to be powerful, strong, have stamina, and be able to control yourself. Plus you have to have unbelievable touch. All those things are important in making love, especially discipline and patience." Stephenson has been active as a golf-course designer and in numerous charitable activities.

37. AYAKO OKAMOTO, a native of Hiroshima, Japan, did not take up golf until she was twenty-three years old. Prior to that she was one of the top women's softball pitchers in Japan and a national hero. Ayako turned professional at the age of twenty-six and won twenty Japanese LPGA events between 1975 and 1981. She qualified for the LPGA Tour on her first attempt and has won a total of seventeen LPGA tournaments, beginning with the Arizona Copper Classic and concluding with the 1992 McDonald's Championship. Okamoto, who lives in Tokyo, has always played a restricted LPGA Tour schedule but has won over $2.7 million on the circuit. In 1987 she won four tournaments, led the money list with $466,034, and became the first non-American to win the LPGA Player of the Year Award. Okamoto has won over forty-five tournaments on the international circuit.

38. ANNE QUAST SANDER is one of the best American amateur lady golfers in history. Born in Everett, Washington, in 1937, she achieved a notable record in the U.S. Women's Amateur, beginning with her win in 1958 while a senior at Stanford University. She shot 4 under par on the last seven holes to defeat Barbara Romack, three and two, in her final match. Anne also won the Amateur in 1961, with a stunning fourteen-and-thirteen win in the final, and again in 1963. She finished second in the Amateur in 1965, 1968, and 1974. Sander has won two Western Women's Amateurs (1956, 1961) and has been on eight Curtis Cup teams (1958, 1960, 1962, 1966, 1968, 1974, 1984, 1990). She played on the winning U.S. Women's World Amateur teams in 1966 and 1968, and she won the British Ladies' Amateur in 1980. Sander has won four U.S. Senior Women's Amateurs (1987, 1989, 1990, 1993).

39. MARLENE STREIT, born in Cereal, Alberta, Canada, in 1934, is the greatest Canadian lady golfer of all time. Standing only five feet tall but with a reliable, consistent, compact swing, Streit won her first significant event when she captured the 1951 Ontario Junior Championship, then won the Ontario Ladies', the Canadian Ladies' Close, and the Canadian Ladies' Championship the same year. She attended Rollins College in Florida and went on to win the Canadian Ladies' Close nine times (1951, 1952, 1953, 1954, 1955, 1956, 1957, 1963, 1968), ten Canadian Ladies' Opens (1951, 1954, 1955, 1956, 1958, 1959, 1963, 1968, 1969, 1972, 1973), the 1953 British Ladies', the 1956 U.S. Women's NCAA, the 1956 U.S. Women's Amateur, and the 1963 Australian Ladies'. Streit was voted Canadian Woman Athlete of the Year five times and was twice selected Canada's Athlete of the Year.

40. LADY MARGARET SCOTT was the dominant lady golfer at the end of the nineteenth century. She won the first three British Ladies' Championships by match-play scores of nine and seven, eight and seven, six and four, and seven and five at the Royal Lytham and St. Anne's ladies' course in 1893. She won the British Ladies' at Littlestone in Kent in 1894, and captured her third straight at Royal Portrush in Ireland the following year. Scott held course records at Bath (70) and at Royal Lytham. She had also won men's tournaments, including one at the Cheltenham Club in the 1890s. Scott used the old St. Andrews swing, winding up in a twisted fashion with elbows bent on the backswing, the club shaft close to her neck. Lady Margaret retired from national British golf competition after her third British Ladies' win and gave up the membership to the three clubs to which she belonged—Cotswold Hills, Cheltenham, and Westward Ho! She married and became Lady Margaret Hamilton-Russell. She won three consecutive Swiss Ladies' Championships under that name.

41. BEATRIX HOYT, of the Shinnecock Hills Club on Long Island, was one of the outstanding early American women golfers. She won her first U.S. Amateur in 1896 at the age of sixteen, defeating Mrs. Arthur Turnure, two and one, at the Morris County Golf Club in New Jersey. The following year, she defeated Nellie Sargent, five and four, in the final at the Essex Country Club in Manchester, Massachusetts. Hoyt won her third consecutive Amateur in 1898, defeating Maude Wetmore, five and three, at the Ardsley Club in Ardsley-on-Hudson in New York. Altogether, Hoyt won the medal for best qualifying round in the Amateur five years in succession, beginning in 1896. After winning the qualifying medal with an eighteen-hole score of 94 at Shinnecock Hills in the 1900 Amateur, Hoyt lost to sixteen-year-old Margaret Curtis, one of the contributors of the Curtis Cup, on the second extra hole (the twentieth) in the semifinals. Hoyt retired from national competitive golf at the ripe young age of twenty!

We wish to acknowledge the courtesy of the providers of photographs appearing in *The Golf 100*:

Jamie Anderson   *Cowie Collection/St. Andrews University Library Photographic Collection*
Willie Anderson   *R. W. Miller Golf Library*
Tommy Armour   *USGA*
John Ball   *USGA*
Seve Ballesteros   *USGA*
Jim Barnes   *USGA*
Tommy Bolt   © *Bettman/Corbis*
Julius Boros   *Tufts Archive*
James Braid   *Tufts Archive*
Jack Burke Jr.   *Tufts Archive*
Billy Casper   *USGA*
Bob Charles   *USGA*
Harry Cooper   *USGA*
Henry Cotton   *USGA*
Fred Couples   © *John Mummert/USGA*
Ben Crenshaw   © *Reuters NewMedia Inc./Corbis*
John Daley   *USGA*
Jimmy Demeret   *USGA*
Roberto de Vicenzo   *USGA*
Leo Diegel   *USGA*
Olin Dutra   *Rotofotos/USGA*
David Duval   © *AFP/Corbis*
Ernie Els   © *John Mummert/USGA*
Chick Evans   *USGA*
Nick Faldo   © *John Mummert/USGA*
Johnny Farrell   © *Bettmann/Corbis*
Bob Ferguson   *Cowie Collection/St. Andrews University Library Photographic Collection*
Dow Finsterwald   *USGA*
Raymond Floyd   *USGA*
Doug Ford   *USGA*
David Graham   *USGA*
Hubert Green   *USGA*
Ralph Guldahl   *Tufts Archive*

Walter Hagen   *Ralph G. Miller Golf Library*
Harold Hilton   *USGA*
Ben Hogan   *Ralph W. Miller Golf Library*
Jock Hutchison   *USGA*
Hale Irwin   *USGA*
Tony Jacklin   *USGA*
Lee Janzen   © *John Mummert/USGA*
Bobby Jones   *USGA*
Tom Kite   © *Robert Walker/USGA*
Bernhard Langer   © *John Mummert/USGA*
Tony Lema   *Ralph W. Miller Golf Library*
Lawson Little   *Tufts Archive*
Gene Littler   *USGA*
Bobby Locke   *USGA*
Davis Love   © *J. D. Cuban/USGA*
Sandy Lyle   *USGA*
Johnny McDermott   *USGA*
Willie MacFarlane   *USGA*
Lloyd Mangrum   © *Bettmann/Corbis*
Arnaud Massey   *USGA*
Phil Mickelson   © *Duomo/Corbis*
Gary Middlecoff   *USGA*
Johnny Miller   *USGA*
Tom Morris   *USGA*
Tom Morris Sr and Tom Morris Jr.   *USGA*
Byron Nelson   *Ralph W. Miller Golf Library*
Larry Nelson   *Ralph W. Miller Golf Library*
Jack Nicklaus   *Ralph W. Miller Golf Library/Lester Nehamkin*
Greg Norman   © *John Mummert/USGA*
Mark O'Meara   *USGA*
Jose-Maria Olazabal   © *AFP/Corbis*
Francis Ouimet   *USGA*

Arnold Palmer   *Ralph W. Miller Golf Library*
Willie Park Jr.   *USGA*
Willie Park Sr.   *USGA*
Corey Pavin   © *Robert Walker/USGA*
Henry Picard   *USGA*
Gary Player   *USGA*
Nick Price   *USGA*
Ted Ray   *USGA*
Paul Runyon   *USGA*
Gene Sarazen   *USG*
Denny Shute   *USGA*
Vijay Singh   © *Reuters NewMedia Inc./Corbis*
Alex Smith   *USGA*
Horton Smith   *USGA*
Macdonald Smith   *USGA*
Sam Snead   *Tufts Archive*
Craig Stadler   *USGA*
Payne Stewart   *USGA*
Dave Stockton   © *Robert Walker/USGA*
Curtis Strange   *USGA*
Hal Sutton   © *AFP/Corbis*
J. H. Taylor   *USGA/Wide World*
Peter Thomson   © *Bettmann/Corbis*
Jerry D. Travers   *USGA*
Walter Travis   *Ralph W. Miller Golf Library*
Lee Trevino   © *Tony Roberts/Corbis*
Harry Vardon   *USGA*
Ken Venturi   *USGA/UPI*
Lanny Wadkins   *USGA*
Tom Watson   *USGA*
Tom Weiskopf   *USGA*
Craig Wood   *USGA*
Tiger Woods   © *J. D. Cuban/USGA*
Ian Woosnam   *USGA*
Mickey Wright   *Ralph W. Miller Golf Library*
Babe Zaharias   *USGA*
Fuzzy Zoeller   © *Reuters NewMedia Inc./Corbis*

INDEX